KU-685-535

San Francisco

THE ROUGH GUIDE

T12448
SAINT BENEDICT SCHOOL
DUFFIELD ROAD
DERBY DE22 1JD

Written and researched by
Deborah Bosley and Jamie Jensen

With additional contributions by
Bruce P Gerstman and Julie Soller

THE ROUGH GUIDES

Contents

List of Maps

MAP SYMBOLS

Interstate	Lighthouse
Highway	Mountains
Cable car route	Mountain peak
Ferry route	Transport stop
River	Tourist office
Chapter division boundary	Building
Airport	Church
Accommodation (regional maps)	Cemetery
Church	Park
Historical house	National park
Point of interest	

Introduction

The Bay Area is so beautiful, I hesitate to preach about heaven while I'm here

Billy Graham

America's favourite city sits at the edge of the Western world, a location that lends even greater romance to its legend. Pastoral, cosmopolitan and surprisingly small, **San Francisco** is a ravishing city, conforming to every cliché the tourist board can throw at it and acting as a magnet for nearly three million visitors a year. Famous for its liberal attitudes, radical politics and eccentricity, it occupies a special place in the hearts of Americans and is considered the last bastion of civilization on the lunatic fringe that is California. For all its nostalgic, even provincial feel, San Francisco is an affluent, world-class city – its visitors alone pour nearly $2 billion into its coffers every year, and as the financial centre of the West Coast, its business community thrives.

San Franciscans enjoy a rarefied kind of mutual appreciation, priding themselves on being the cultured counterparts to their cousins in LA. This narcissism is often rooted in the sheer physical aspect of the place. The city is indisputably beautiful, a unique confection of switchback hills, wooden Victorian houses, open green spaces and the shimmering bay that surrounds. With a moody weather pattern that has San Francisco alternately drenched in sunshine or bathed in swirling fogs, the romance factor is high. Turning a corner, climbing a hill and stumbling across an unexpected vista literally takes your breath away. An easy city to negotiate, one of the few US centres where you do not need a car, it also has an excellent public transport system that will whisk you round its appealing, diverse neighbourhoods. And yet, San Francisco's problems are real: drug use and violent crimes are a fact of life; as the gay capital of the world it is has a massive AIDS crisis on its hands; and the level of homelessness is a disgrace. This is America on the brink of the twenty-first century, with all the attendant economic and social woes.

Climate and When To Go

The city of **San Francisco** emphatically does not belong to the California of monotonous blue skies and slothful warmth. Flanked

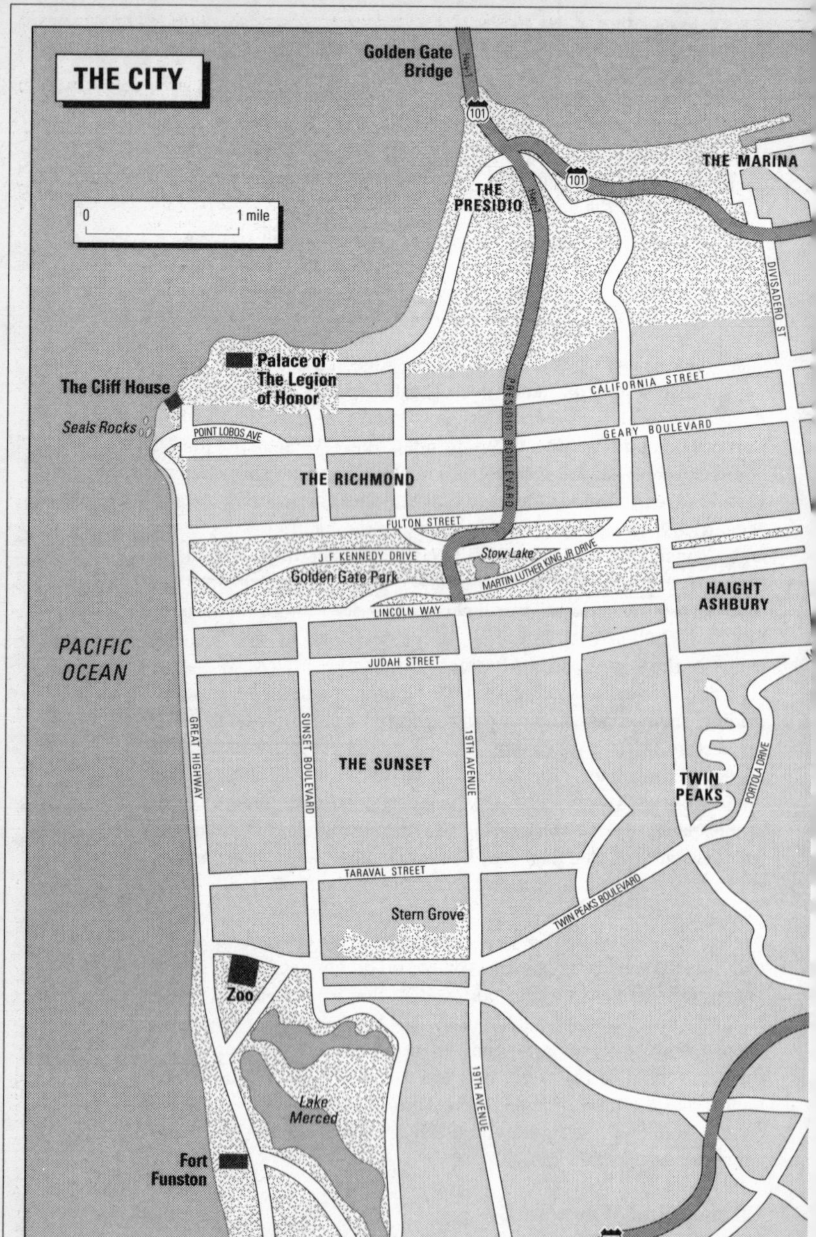
THE CITY
0
1 mile
Golden Gate
Bridge
101
101
THE MARINA
THE
PRESIDIO
DIVISADERO ST
Palace of
The Legion
of Honor
The Cliff House
Seals Rocks
CALIFORNIA STREET
GEARY BOULEVARD
POINT LOBOS AVE
PRESIDIO BOULEVARD
THE RICHMOND
FULTON STREET
J F KENNEDY DRIVE
Stow Lake
MARTIN LUTHER KING JR DRIVE
Golden Gate Park
HAIGHT
ASHBURY
LINCOLN WAY
PACIFIC
OCEAN
JUDAH STREET
GREAT HIGHWAY
SUNSET BOULEVARD
THE SUNSET
19TH AVENUE
TWIN
PEAKS
PORTOLA DRIVE
TARAVAL STREET
TWIN PEAKS BOULEVARD
Stern Grove
Zoo
Lake
Merced
19TH AVENUE
Fort
Funston
280

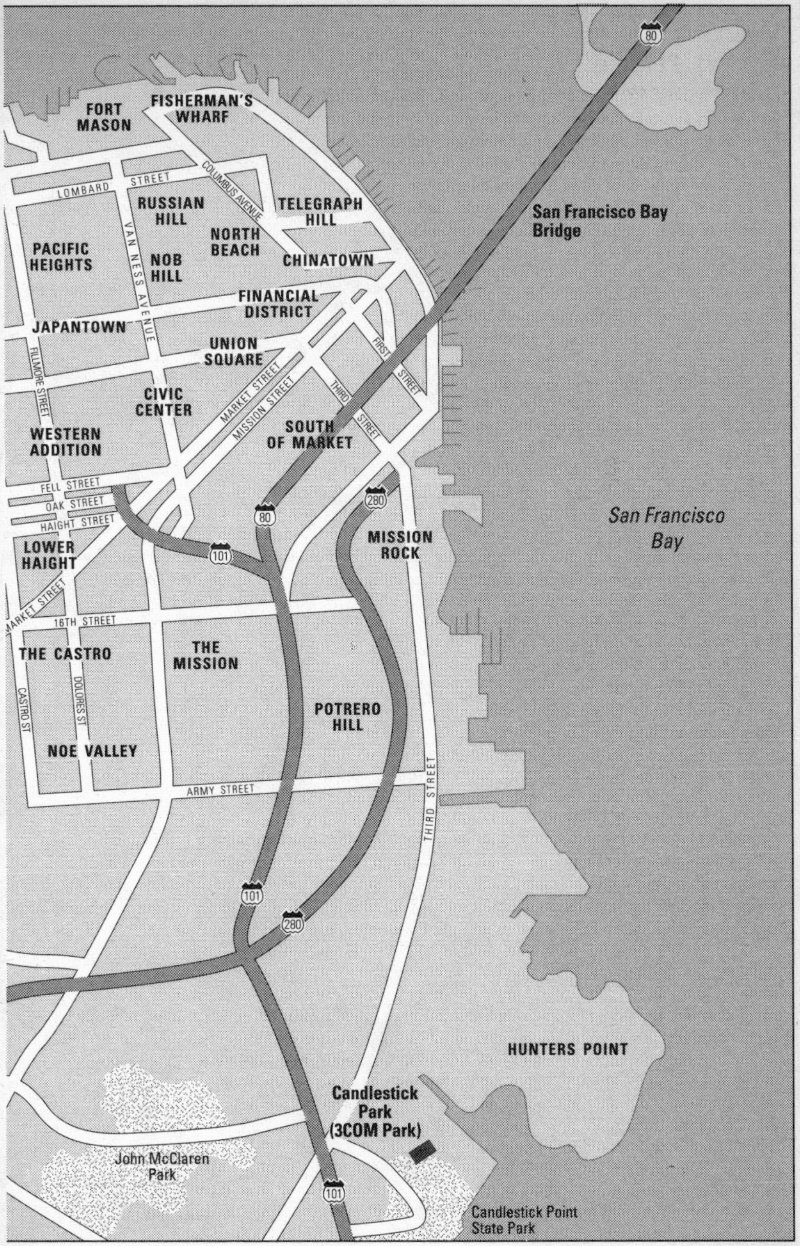

80
FORT MASON
FISHERMAN'S WHARF
LOMBARD STREET
COLUMBUS AVENUE
RUSSIAN HILL
TELEGRAPH HILL
San Francisco Bay Bridge
NORTH BEACH
VAN NESS AVENUE
PACIFIC HEIGHTS
NOB HILL
CHINATOWN
FINANCIAL DISTRICT
JAPANTOWN
UNION SQUARE
FIRST STREET
FILLMORE STREET
MARKET STREET
MISSION STREET
THIRD STREET
CIVIC CENTER
SOUTH OF MARKET
WESTERN ADDITION
FELL STREET
OAK STREET
HAIGHT STREET
280
80
San Francisco Bay
MISSION ROCK
101
LOWER HAIGHT
MARKET STREET
16TH STREET
THE CASTRO
THE MISSION
CASTRO ST
DOLORES ST
POTRERO HILL
NOE VALLEY
ARMY STREET
THIRD STREET
101
280
HUNTERS POINT
Candlestick Park (3COM Park)
John McClaren Park
101
Candlestick Point State Park

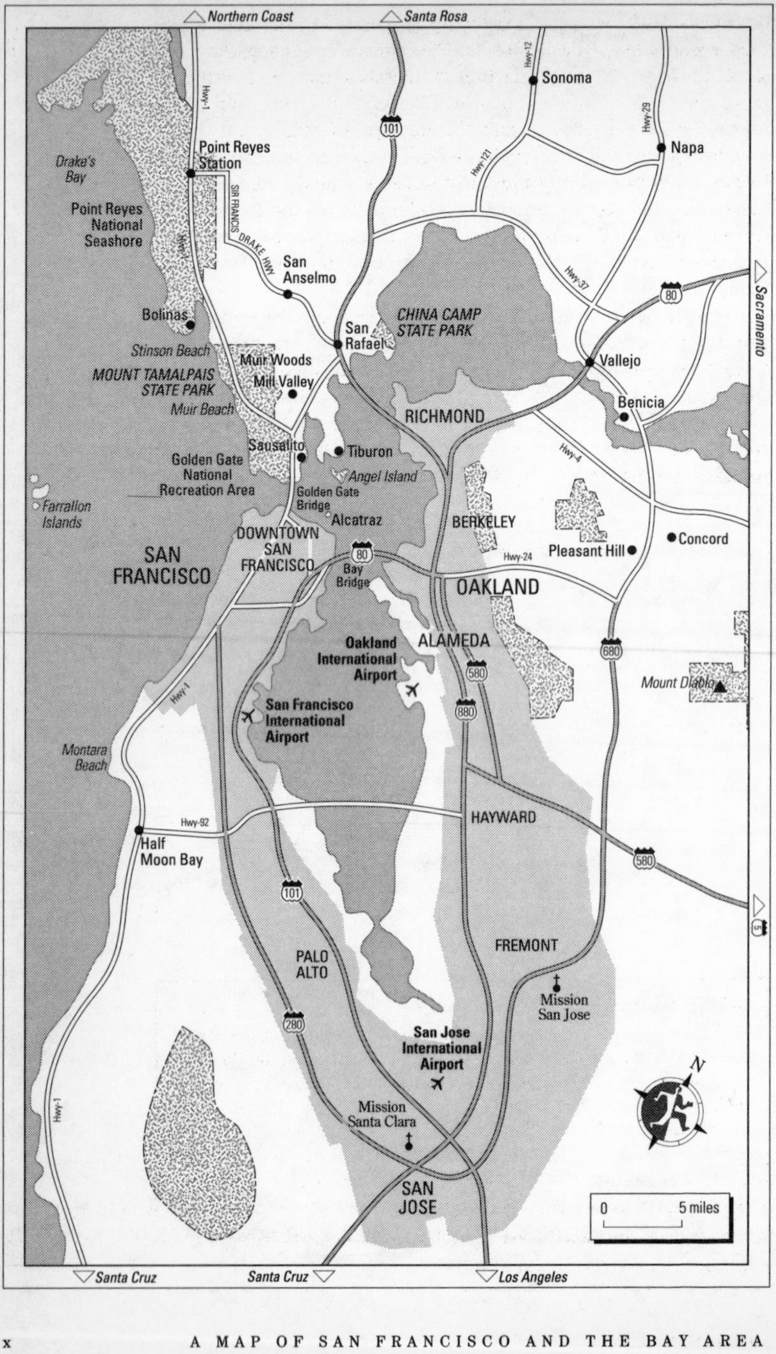
Northern Coast
Santa Rosa
Sonoma
Napa
Point Reyes Station
Drake's Bay
Point Reyes National Seashore
Sir Francis Drake Hwy
San Anselmo
Bolinas
San Rafael
China Camp State Park
Stinson Beach
Muir Woods
Mount Tamalpais State Park
Mill Valley
Muir Beach
Vallejo
Benicia
Richmond
Sausalito
Tiburon
Golden Gate National Recreation Area
Angel Island
Golden Gate Bridge
Farallon Islands
Alcatraz
Berkeley
Pleasant Hill
Concord
Downtown San Francisco
San Francisco
Bay Bridge
Oakland
Alameda
Oakland International Airport
San Francisco International Airport
Mount Diablo
Montara Beach
Half Moon Bay
Hayward
Palo Alto
Fremont
Mission San Jose
San Jose International Airport
Mission Santa Clara
San Jose
Sacramento
Santa Cruz
Santa Cruz
Los Angeles
Hwy-1
Hwy-12
Hwy-29
Hwy-121
Hwy-37
Hwy-4
Hwy-24
Hwy-92
101
80
580
880
680
280
5
N
0
5 miles

on three sides by water, it is regularly invigorated by the fresh winds that sweep across the peninsula. The climate is among the most stable in the world, with a daytime temperature that rarely ventures more than 5°F either side of a median 60°F but can drop much lower. Summer does offer some sunny days, of course, but it also sees heavy fogs roll in through the Golden Gate to smother the city in gloom. **Winters** bring most of the city's rainfall, sometimes in quite torrential storms. Almost everywhere else in the **Bay Area** is warmer than San Francisco, especially in the summer when the **East Bay** cities bask in sunshine, and the **Wine Country** and other inland valleys are baking hot.

As for **when to go**, if you want to avoid the crowds, it makes sense not to come in the summer, although even then most of the tourist congestion is confined to a few of the most popular parts of the city, and is rarely too off-putting. The nicest times to visit are late May and June, when the hills are greenest and covered with wild flowers, or in October, when you can be fairly sure of good weather and space in the hotels and restaurants.

Average Temperature (°F) and Rainfall (inches)

	Jan	Feb	Mar	April	May	June	July	Aug	Sept	Oct	Nov	Dec
Max °F	55	59	61	62	63	66	65	65	69	68	63	57
Min °F	45	47	48	49	51	52	53	53	55	54	51	47
Rainfall	4.7	3.8	3.1	1.5	0.7	0.1	0	0	0.3	1.0	2.5	4.4

Help Us Update

We've gone to a lot of effort to ensure that this edition of the *Rough Guide to San Francisco* is completely up-to-date and accurate. However, things do change – if you feel that there's something we've missed, or that you'd like to see included, please write and let us know. We'll credit all contributions, and send a copy of the new book (or any other *Rough Guide*, if you prefer) for the best letters. Please mark letters "Rough Guide San Francisco Update", and send to:

The Rough Guides, 1 Mercer Street, London WC2H 9QJ, or

The Rough Guides, 375 Hudson Street, 9th Floor, New York NY 10014.

Email: sanfrancisco@roughtravl.co.uk

Part 1

The Basics

Getting there from Britain and Europe

> One word of **warning**: it's not a good idea to buy a **one-way** ticket to the States. Not only are they rarely good value compared to a round-trip ticket, but US immigration officials usually take them as a sign that you aren't planning to go home, and may refuse you entry.

Though flying to San Francisco from Europe is pretty straightforward, choosing the best route can be more complicated than you might think, with prices fluctuating wildly according to how and when you go. Some airlines have non-stop services from Britain, but the majority of options are so-called "direct" flights, which can land several times, waiting an hour or so at each stop – a flight is called direct as long as it keeps the same *flight number* throughout its journey. The first place the plane lands is your point of entry into the US, which means you'll have to collect your bags and go through customs and immigration formalities there, even if you're continuing on to San Francisco on the same plane. This can be a real pain after a ten-hour journey, so it's worth finding out before you book a ticket.

All international flights use the main **San Francisco International Airport** (SFO); for transportation details from there into the city, as well as from the two other Bay Area airports, see p.10.

Fares, routes and agents

Although you can fly to the US from any of the regional airports, the few **non-stop flights** from

Flights from Britain

The following carriers operate **non-stop** or **one-stop flights** between London and San Francisco (all from Heathrow unless stated otherwise):

American Airlines daily via Dallas.

British Airways daily non-stop.

Continental daily from Gatwick via Denver, Houston or Newark.

Delta three times daily: one non-stop from Heathrow, one via LA from Heathrow and one via Cincinnati from Gatwick.

Northwest two flights daily via Minneapolis from Gatwick.

TWA daily via St Louis from Gatwick.

United daily non-stop. Two flights daily in high season.

Virgin Atlantic daily non-stop.

Airlines

American Airlines	☎0181/572 5555	**Northwest**	☎01293/561000
British Airways	☎0181/897 4000	**TWA**	☎0171/439 0707
Continental	☎0800/776464	**United**	☎0181/990 9900
Delta	☎0800/414767	**Virgin Atlantic**	☎01293/747747

Toll-free phone numbers for airlines **in the United States** are listed on p.10.

Britain to San Francisco are from London. Most of the direct flights offered are via Los Angeles, though many fly via other US cities such as Minneapolis, Denver or Chicago. The non-stop **flight time** is around eleven hours from London to San Francisco; add an hour at least for each intervening stop on direct flights, twice that if you have to change planes. Following winds ensure that return flights are usually an hour or so shorter than outward journeys. Because of the time difference between Britain and the West Coast (eight hours almost all year), flights usually leave Britain mid-morning, while flights back from the US tend to arrive in Britain early in the morning.

Generally, the most expensive time to travel is **high season**, roughly between June and August and around Christmas. May and September are slightly less pricey, and the rest of the year is considered **low season** and cheaper still. Keep an eye out for slack season bargains and, additionally, make sure to check the exact dates of the seasons with your operator or airline; you might be able to make major savings by shifting your departure date by a week – or even a day. **Weekend rates** for all return flights tend to be around £30 more expensive than those in the week.

Britain remains one of the best places in Europe to obtain flight bargains, though **fares** vary widely according to season, availability and the current level of inter-airline competition. The comments that follow can only act as a general guide, so be sure to **shop around** carefully for the best offers by checking the travel ads in the weekend papers, on the holiday pages of ITV's *Teletext* and, in London, scouring *Time Out* and the *Evening Standard*. Giveaway magazines aimed at young travellers, like *TNT*, are also, useful resources.

Stand-by deals (open-dated tickets which you pay for and then decide later when you want to fly – if there's room on the plane) are few and far between, and don't give great savings: in general you're better off with an **APEX** ticket. The conditions on these are pretty standard whoever you fly with – seats must be purchased seven days or more in advance, and you must stay for at least one Saturday night; tickets are normally valid for up to six months. Some airlines also do less expensive **Super-APEX** tickets, which fall into two categories: the first are approximately £150 cheaper than an ordinary APEX but must be bought 21 days in advance and require a minimum stay of seven days and a maximum stay of one month; the second are around £100 less than an APEX, must be purchased fourteen days in advance and entail a minimum stay of a week and a maximum stay of two months – such tickets are usually non-refundable or -changeable. **"Open-jaw"** tickets can be a good idea, allowing you to fly into San Francisco,(for example) and back from LA for little or no extra charge; fares are calculated by halving the return fares to each destination and adding the two figures together. This makes a convenient option for those who want a fly-drive holiday (see below).

For an overview of the various offers, and unofficially discounted tickets, go straight to an **agent** specializing in low-cost flights (we've listed some below). Especially if you're under 26 or a student, they may be able to knock up to thirty percent off the regular APEX fares when there are no special airline deals.

The same agents also offer cut-price seats on **charter flights**. These are particularly good value if you're travelling from a British city other than London, although they tend to be limited to the summer season, be restricted to so-called "holiday destinations", and have fixed departure and return dates. Brochures are available in most high-street travel agents, or contact the specialists direct.

Sample Air Fares from Britain

The prices given below (in £ sterling) are a general indication of the (minimum) transatlantic air fares currently obtainable from specialist companies; remember to add £25–35 airport tax to these figures. Each airline decides the exact dates of its seasons. Prices given apply to departures from London and Manchester.

LOW		SHOULDER		HIGH	
Nov 1–Dec 14, Dec 25–March 28 April 11–30		March 29–April 10, May 1–June 30 Sept 1–Oct 31		July 1–Aug 31, Dec 15–24	
one-way	return	one-way	return	one-way	return
195	289	195	332	235	475

Low-Cost Flight Agents in Britain

Bridge The World 1–3 Ferdinand St London NW1 8ES ☎0171/916 0990	**Globeair Travel** 93 Piccadilly London W1V 9HB ☎0171/493 4343
Campus Travel 52 Grosvenor Gardens London SW1W 0AG ☎0171/730 2101 *Also many other branches around the country.*	**STA Travel** 86 Old Brompton Rd London SW7 3LQ ☎0171/937 9962 *Offices nationwide.*
Council Travel 28a Poland St London W1V 3DB ☎0171/437 7767	**Travel Cuts** 295a Regent St London W1R 7YA ☎0171/637 3161
Destination Group 41–45 Goswell Rd London EC1 7EH ☎0171/253 2000	**Trailfinders** 42–50 Earls Court Rd London W8 6FT ☎0171/938 3366

Finally, if you've got a bit more time, or want to see a bit more of the USA, it's often possible to stop over in **another city** – New York especially – and fly on from there for little more than the cost of a direct flight to California. Also, with increased competition on the **London–Los Angeles** route, thanks to *Virgin Atlantic* among others, and price wars between US carriers, the cost of a connecting flight from LA to San Francisco has been brought down to as low as £40.

Courier flights

It's still possible, if not as common as it used to be, for those on a very tight budget to travel as **couriers**. Courier firms such as *Bridges Worldwide* (☎0181/759 5040) offer opportunities to travel at discounted rates (as low as £200 return to the West Coast) in return for delivering a package. There'll be someone to check you in and to meet you at your destination, which minimizes any red-tape hassle. However, you'll have to travel light, with only a cabin bag, and accept tight restrictions on travel dates. For other phone numbers, check the *Yellow Pages*, as these businesses come and go.

Packages

Packages – fly-drive, flight/accommodation deals and guided tours (or a combination of all three) – can work out cheaper than arranging the same trip yourself, especially for a short-term stay. The obvious drawbacks are the loss of flexibility and the fact that most schemes use hotels in the mid-range bracket, but there is a wide variety of options available.

High-street travel agents have plenty of brochures and information about the various combinations.

Fly-drive

Fly-drive deals, which give cut-rate (sometimes free) car rental when buying a transatlantic ticket, always work out cheaper than renting on the spot, and give especially great value if you intend to do a lot of driving. However, if you're planning to stay pretty much within San Francisco itself, having a car is a bonus but not strictly necessary. You'll probably have to pay more for the flight than if you booked it through a discount agent, but competition between airlines (especially *Northwest* and *TWA*) and tour operators means it's well worth phoning to check on current promotions.

Northwest Flydrive offers excellent deals for not much more than an ordinary APEX fare; for example, a return flight to San Francisco and a week's car rental costs around £350 per person in low season. Several of the other companies listed (see box overleaf) offer similar, and sometimes cheaper, packages. Watch out for hidden extras, such as local taxes, and "drop-off" charges, which can be as much as a week's rental, and Collision Damage Waiver insurance (see p.33). Remember, too, that while you can drive in the States with a British licence, there can be problems renting vehicles if you're under 25. For complete car-rental details, see "Getting Around the City" (p.30).

Flight and Accommodation Deals

There's really no end of combined **flight and accommodation deals** to San Francisco and, although you can often do things cheaper independently, you won't be able to do the *same* things cheaper – in fact, the equivalent room booked separately will normally be a lot more expensive – and you can leave the organizational hassles to someone else. Drawbacks include the loss of flexibility and the fact that you'll probably have to stay in hotels in the mid-range to expensive bracket, even though less expensive accommodation is almost always available.

A handful of tour operators (see below) offer quite deluxe packages. Of these, *Virgin Holidays* are about the least expensive: for example, seven nights in San Francisco plus return flight costs around £629–849 per person. Discount agents can set up more basic packages for just over £500 each. Pre-booked accommodation schemes, under which you buy vouchers for use in a specific group of hotels, are not normally good value.

Touring and adventure packages

If you want to combine your stay in San Francisco with trips out into the rest of California, particularly the state's extensive wilderness areas, there are a number of tour operators (see below) you might want to contact. Specialist **touring and adventure packages** include transportation, accommodation, food

Specialist Holiday Operators

Airtours
Wavell House, Helmshore
Rossendale, Lancs BB4 4NB ☎01706/240033

American Express
Phone enquiries only ☎0171/828 7411

AmeriCan Adventures
45 High St, Tunbridge Wells
Kent TN1 1XL ☎01892/511894

Bon Voyage
18 Bellevue Rd, Southampton
Hants SO1 2AY ☎01703/330332

British Airways Holidays
Astral Towers, Bettsway
London Rd, Crawley
West Sussex RH10 2XA ☎01293/722727

Contiki Travel
Wells House, 15 Elmfield Rd
Bromley, Kent BR1 1LS ☎0181/290 6422

Destination USA
41–45 Goswell Rd
London EC1V 7EH ☎0171/253 2000

Explore Worldwide
1 Frederick St, Aldershot
Hants GU11 1LQ ☎01252/319448

First Choice
First Choice House
London Road, Crawley
West Sussex RH10 2HB ☎01293/560777

Greyhound International
Sussex House, London Rd
East Grinstead
West Sussex RH19 1LD ☎01342/317317

Key to America
1–3 Station Rd, Ashford
Middlesex TW15 2UW ☎01784/248777

North America Travel Service
7 Albion St, Leeds LS1 5ER ☎0113/246 1466
Also branches in Nottingham, Manchester and Barnsley.

Northwest Flydrive
PO Box 45, Bexhill-on-Sea
East Sussex TN40 1PY ☎01424/224400

Premier Holidays
Westbrook, Milton Rd
Cambridge CB4 1YQ ☎01223/516516

Top Deck
131 Earls Court Rd
London SW5 9RH ☎0171/370 4555

Trans Atlantic Vacations
3a Gatwick Metro Centre
Balcombe Rd
Horley, Surrey RH6 9GA ☎01293/774441

TrekAmerica
4 Waterperry Court
Middleton Rd
Banbury, Oxon OX16 8Q6 ☎01869/338777

Unijet
"Sandrocks", Rocky Lane
Haywards Heath
West Sussex RH16 4RH ☎01444/459191

Virgin Holidays
The Galleria
Station Rd, Crawley
West Sussex RH10 1WW ☎01293/617181

and a guide. Some of the more adventurous carry small groups around on minibuses and use a combination of budget hotels and camping (equipment, except a sleeping bag, is provided). Most also have a food kitty of maybe £25 per week, with many meals cooked and eaten communally, although there's plenty of time to leave the group and do your own thing, as does the more unconventional *Green Tortoise* (see p.13). If you're interested in **back-country hiking** to balance out a week in the city, the San Francisco-based *Sierra Club* (730 Polk St, SF, CA 94110 ☎776-2211) offers a range of tours that take you into parts of the state that most people never see. Again, see the box for addresses.

Flights from Ireland

Both *Delta* and *Aer Lingus* fly to California **direct from Ireland**. The cheapest flights **from Ireland** – if you're under 26 or a student – are available from *USIT*. Student-only return fares to **San Francisco** range from IR£389 to IR£569. Ordinary APEX fares are only marginally higher.

USIT can be contacted at Aston Quay, O'Connell Bridge, Dublin 2 (☎01/677 8117), while *Aer Lingus* is at 40 O'Connell St, Dublin 1 (☎01/844 4777), and *Delta Airlines* is at 24 Merrion Square, Dublin 2 (☎01/676 8080; or 1800/768080).

Flights from Europe

It is generally far cheaper to fly non-stop to San Francisco from London than any other European city. However, for the best deals to New York from Brussels and Paris, contact **Nouvelles Frontières**, 87 boulevard de Grenelle, 75015 Paris (☎1/41.41.58.58), and 2 boulevard M Lemonnier, 1000 Brussels (☎2/547 4444). The London branch is at 2/3 Woodstock St, W1R 1HE (☎0171/629 7772).

Other options are the cut-price charter flights occasionally offered from major European cities; ask at your nearest travel agent for details. In Germany, look for discount **youth fare deals** which *United* offers (to those under 26 booking 72 hours or less in advance) from Frankfurt, its continental hub.

Getting there from Australasia

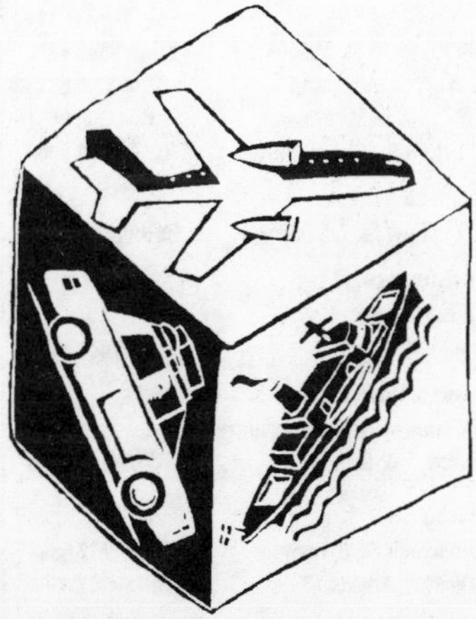

Other than charter deals, seasonal bargains and all-in packages which may be on offer from high-street travel agents, the cheapest flights from Australasia to the US are available from the specialists listed overleaf.

From Australia and New Zealand, Los Angeles and San Francisco are the main points of entry to the US. With any of the American carriers, you can continue on to **New York** for around US$170 on top of the fare to the West Coast. Most flights stop off in Honolulu, Hawaii;

> The **low** season for flights to the US from Australia and New Zealand is Feb–March and Oct 16–Nov 30; the **shoulder** season is Jan 16–31, April–May and July 1–Oct 15; the **high** season is Dec 1–Jan 15.

you can usually stay over for as long as you like for no extra charge. Various **coupon deals** which are valid in continental US are available with your main ticket, allowing you to fly to destinations across the States. A minimum purchase of three coupons usually applies, for example *American Airlines*' **Coupon Pass** costs $US319 for the first three, and between $50 and $100 for subsequent tickets (maximum of ten in total).

From **Australia**, there are direct flights to **San Francisco** with *United Airlines* daily from Sydney (low season AU$1752/high season AU$3007), *Air New Zealand* five times a week from Sydney (AU$1750/3005), and *Qantas* daily from Cairns, Brisbane, Sydney and Melbourne (AU$1878/3005), Darwin (AU$2360/2751) and Perth (AU$2618/3200).

From **New Zealand**, the best direct deals are out of **Auckland** (add about NZ$100 for Christchurch and Wellington departures) to Los Angeles with *Air New Zealand* (daily, NZ$1869/2819), *MAS* and *Qantas* (both fly several times weekly, NZ$1860/2805), or *United Airlines* to **San Francisco** (daily NZ$1869/2809).

Round-the-world deals from Australasia, such as *Cathay Pacific/United Airlines*' "Globetrotter" and *Air New Zealand/KLM/*

Airlines and Agents in Australasia

Air New Zealand
5 Elizabeth St, Sydney ☎02/9223 4666
Quay St, Auckland ☎09/357 3000

Anywhere Travel
345 Anzac Parade, Kingsford
Sydney ☎02/663 0411

Brisbane Discount Travel
360 Queen St, Brisbane ☎07/3229 9211

British Airways
64 Castlereagh St, Sydney ☎02/9258 3300
154 Queen St, Auckland ☎09/356 8690

Budget Travel
69 Fort St, Auckland ☎09/309 4313

Discount Travel Specialists
Shop 53
Forrest Chase, Perth ☎09/221 1400; ☎08/9221 1400 from Sept 1997

Flight Centres
Circular Quay, Sydney ☎02/9241 2422
Bourke St, Melbourne ☎03/9650 2899
205–225 Queen St, Auckland ☎09/309 6171
152 Hereford St, Christchurch ☎03/379 7145
50–52 Willis St, Wellington ☎04/472 8101

KLM
5 Elizabeth St, Sydney ☎02/9231 6333 or 1-800/505747

MAS Malaysian Airlines
16 Spring St, Sydney ☎02/364 3500; local-call rate 13 2627
Floor 12, Swanson Centre
12–26 Swanson St, Auckland ☎09/373 2741

Northwest
309 Kent St, Level 13, Sydney ☎02/290 4455

Passport Travel
320b Glenferrie Rd, Malvern
Melbourne ☎03/9824 7183

Qantas
Chifley Square, cnr Hunter and
Phillip streets, Sydney ☎02/957 0111
Qantas House, 154 Queen St
Auckland ☎09/357 8900

Singapore Airlines
17–19 Bridge St, Sydney ☎02/9236 0144
West Plaza Building, cnr Customs
and Albert streets, Auckland ☎09/379 3209

STA Travel
732 Harris St, Ultimo, Sydney ☎02/9212 1255 or 1-800/637 444
256 Flinders St, Melbourne ☎03/9347 4711
10 High St, Auckland ☎09/366 6673
233 Cuba St, Wellington ☎04/385 0561
221 High St, Christchurch ☎03/379 9098

Topdeck Travel
45 Grenfell St, Adelaide ☎08/8232 7222

Trailfinders
Hides Corner
Shield St, Cairns ☎07/041 1199

Tymtro Travel
Wallaceway Shopping Centre
Chatswood, Sydney ☎02/413 1219

United
10 Barrack St, Sydney ☎02/237 8888
7 City Rd, Auckland ☎09/307 9500

Northwest's "World Navigator" packages, both of which offer six stopovers worldwide and limited backtracking, start at AU$2349/2899 NZ$2999/3449. The most US-oriented package, only available in Australia, is *Singapore/TWA*'s "Easyworld", which allows unlimited stopovers worldwide with a maximum of eight within the US (flat rate AU$3023).

Specialist Agents and Operators

Adventure Specialists
69 Liverpool St, Sydney ☎02/9261 2927

Adventure World
73 Walker St, Sydney ☎02/956 7766
8 Victoria Ave, Perth ☎09/9221 2300
101 Great South Rd, Auckland ☎09/524 5118

American Travel Centre
2nd Floor, 262 Adelaide St, Brisbane ☎07/3221 4788

CreativeTours
Grafton St, Woollahra, Sydney ☎02/386 2111

Exodus Expeditions
81a Glebe Point Rd, Sydney ☎1-800/800 724

Insight
39–41 Chandos St, St Leonards, NSW ☎02/437 4660

Peregrine
258 Lonsdale St, Melbourne ☎03/663 8611
407 Great South Rd, Penrose, Auckland ☎09/525-3074

Sydney International Travel Centre
75 King St, Sydney ☎02/9299 8000

Triangle Vacations
181 Brunswick St, Fortitude Valley, Brisbane ☎07/3216 0855
Gay-oriented tours and accommodation packages.

Wiltrans/Maupintour
189 Kent St, Sydney ☎02/255 0899

Getting There from North America

Getting to San Francisco from anywhere else in North America is never a problem; the Bay Area is well serviced by air, rail and road networks. All the main airlines operate daily scheduled flights into San Francisco from across the country, and there are daily flights from Toronto and Vancouver as well. Flying remains the best, but most expensive, way to travel; taking a train comes a slow second. Travelling by bus is the least expensive method, but again is slow, and much less comfortable than either train or plane.

By air

Besides the main **San Francisco International Airport** (SFO), two other airports, both in the Bay Area, may be useful – particularly **Oakland**

Airlines in the USA and Canada

Aer Lingus	☎1-800/223-6537 or 212/557-1110
Aero California	☎1-800/237-6225
Aeromexico	☎1-800/237-6639
Air Canada	☎1-800/776-3000; for local toll-free number in Canada call directory enquiries
Air France	☎1-800/237-2747; in Canada 1-800/667-2747
America West	☎1-800/2FLYAWA
American Airlines	☎1-800/433-7300
British Airways	☎1-800/247-9297; in Canada 1-800/668-1059
Canadian	☎1-800/426-7000; in Canada 1-800/665-1177
Continental	☎1-800/525-0280
Delta Airlines	☎1-800/221-1212; for local toll-free number in Canada, call directory enquiries
Iberia	☎1-800/772-4642; in Canada 1-800/423- 7421
Icelandair	☎1-800/223-5500
KLM	☎1-800/374-7747; in Canada 1-800/361-5073
Lufthansa	☎1-800/645-3880; in Canada 1-800/563-5954
Mesa	☎1-800/933-6372
Northwest	☎1-800/225-2525
SAS	☎1-800/221-2350
Southwest	☎1-800/435-9792
Tower Air	☎1-800/221-2500
Trans World Airlines	☎1-800/221-2000
United Airlines	☎1-800/241-6522
US Air	☎1-800/428-4322
Virgin Atlantic	☎1-800/862-8621

Note that not all the above airlines fly domestic routes within the US. The **Canadian directory enquiries** number is ☎1-800/555-1212.

International (OAK), across the bay but easily accessible. The third Bay Area airport, **San Jose Municipal** (SJO), forty miles south, is a bit out of the way but has good connections with the western US, LA especially.

As airlines tend to match each other's prices, there's generally little difference in the quoted fares. Barring another fare war, round-trip prices start at around $350 from New York, slightly less from Midwest cities, slightly more from Toronto and Montréal. What makes more difference than your choice of carrier are the conditions governing the ticket – whether it is fully refundable or not, the time and day and, most importantly, the **time of year** you travel. Least expensive of all is a non-summer-season midweek flight, booked and paid for at least three weeks in advance. While it's good to call the airlines directly to get a sense of their official fares, it also worth checking with a reputable **travel agent** (such as the ones listed below) to find out about any **special deals** or student/youth fares that may be available.

In addition to the big-name scheduled airlines, a few lesser-known carriers run no-frills flights, which can prove to be very good value, especially if you're only planning to buy a **one-way** ticket to San Francisco. *Tower Air*, the New

Discount Agents in the USA and Canada

For travel agents **in San Francisco**, see p.47.

Council Travel Offices in the USA

Head office

205 E 42nd St
New York, NY 10017 ☎212/661-1450

Other main offices at

3300 M St NW, 2nd Floor
Washington, DC 20007 ☎202/337-6464

1153 N Dearborn St
Chicago, IL 60610 ☎312/951-0585

729 Boylston St, Suite 201
Boston, MA 02116 ☎617/266-1926

2000 Guadalupe St, Suite 6
Austin, TX 78705 ☎512/472-4931

1314 NE 43rd St, Suite 210
Seattle, WA 98105 ☎206/632-2448

STA Travel Offices in the USA

Nationwide information ☎1-800/777-0112

Main offices at

10 Downing St
New York, NY 10014 ☎212/627-3111

7202 Melrose Ave
Los Angeles, CA 90046 ☎213/934-8722

297 Newbury St
Boston, MA 02115 ☎617/266-6014

4929 S Dearborn St
Chicago, IL 60605 ☎312/786-9050

4341 University Way NE
Seattle, WA 98105. ☎206/633-5000

3730 Walnut St
Philadelphia, PA 19104 ☎215/382-2928

Travel CUTS Offices in Canada

Head office

187 College St
Toronto, ON M5T 1P7 ☎416/979-2406

Other main offices at

MacEwan Hall Student Centre
University of Calgary
Calgary, AB T2N 1N4 ☎403/282-7687

12304 Jasper Ave
Edmonton, AB T5N 3K5 ☎403/488-8487

1613 rue St Denis
Montréal, PQ H2X 3K3 ☎514/843-8511

1 Stewart St
Ottawa, ON K1N 6H7 ☎613/238-8222

2383 Ch Ste Foy,
Suite 103
Ste Foy, Quebec,
PQ G1V 1T1 ☎418/654-0224

Place Riel Campus Centre
University of Saskatchewan
Saskatoon,
SA S7N 0W0 ☎306/975-3722

501–602 W Hastings
Vancouver, BC V6B 1P2 ☎604/681-9136

University Centre,
University of Manitoba
Winnipeg, MA R3T 2N2 ☎204/269-9530

York-based charter operator, has five flights a week from New York to Los Angeles for $162; an onward flight (usually on *Southwest* or *United*) to San Francisco adds another $59 or so. *Southwest* flies from a host of Midwestern and Western cities at rock-bottom prices; eight-daily flights leave Salt Lake City for Oakland (it doesn't go directly to San Francisco) from between $49 and $109; its lowest fare out of Seattle to Oakland is $39, while LA to Oakland can go as low as $19.

Travellers intending to fly from **Canada** are likely to find that, with less competition on these routes (*Canadian* flies to SF only from Vancouver; other routes are monopolized by *Air Canada*), fares are somewhat higher than they are for flights wholly within the US. You may well find that it's worth the effort to get to a US city first, and fly on to San Francisco from there.

By train

If you have a bit more money and hanker after a few more creature comforts (all the trains have private cabins and dining cars) or simply have the time and inclination to take in some of the rest of the US on your way to San Francisco, then an *Amtrak* **train** may be just the ticket for you. There's only one long-distance train per day from the north or east, and only a few from the south, but all three routes are among the most scenic on the entire *Amtrak* system.

The most spectacular train journey to San Francisco, the *California Zephyr*, runs all the way from Chicago but comes into its own during the ride through the Rockies west of Denver. After climbing alongside raging rivers through gorgeous mountain **scenery**, the route drops

> Note that *Amtrak* trains arrive in Emeryville and Oakland across the Bay; they do not enter San Francisco itself, but a free shuttle service is provided to the Ferry Building on the Embarcadero in San Francisco. See pp.31, 143 and 163.

down the west flank of the Rockies and races across the Utah and Nevada deserts by night, stopping at Salt Lake City and Reno. The next day the train climbs up and over the mighty Sierra Nevada, following the route of the first transcontinental railroad on its way into Oakland, where you change to a bus for the ride into San Francisco.

A shorter but equally memorable route is the *Coast Starlight*, winding along the coast north from Los Angeles. The most incredible section is between Santa Barbara and San Luis Obispo, a 100-mile coastline ride during which it's not unusual to see seals, dolphins or even whales in the waters offshore. (The other LA–SF *Amtrak* routes head inland, by bus to Bakersfield then by rail north through the dull San Joaquin Valley. Avoid these if at all possible.)

The final route to San Francisco, also called the *Coast Starlight*, is the southbound leg of the above journey. Starting out in Seattle, it runs south along the Puget Sound and across the Columbia River to Portland, past the mountains and forests of the Pacific Northwest. Unfortunately, it passes through the prettiest stretch, around Mt Shasta, by night, but it's still a lovely ride.

One-way cross-country fares are around $250, though Americans travelling round-trip can

Amtrak Rail Passes

Foreign travellers have a choice of four **rail passes** that include the Bay Area; the **Coastal Pass** permits unlimited train travel on the East and West Coasts, but not between the two.

	15-day (June–Aug)	**15-day**(Sept–May)	**30-day** (June–Aug)	**30-day** (Sept–May)
Far West	$205	$185	$265	$235
West	$265	$215	$330	$290
Coastal	–	–	$230	$205
National	$355	$245	$440	$350

On production of a passport issued outside the US or Canada, the passes can be bought at *Amtrak* stations in the US. In the **UK**, buy them from *Destination Marketing*, 2 Cinnamon Row, York Place, London SW11 3TW (☎0171/978 5212); in **Ireland**, contact *Eurotrain* (☎01/741777); in **Australia**, *Walshes World* (☎02/232-7499); and in **New Zealand**, *Atlantic & Pacific* (☎09/302-9720).

For all information on ***Amtrak* fares and schedules**, and to make reservations, use the toll-free number

☎ **1-800/USA-RAIL**

Do not call individual stations.

take advantage of "**All-Aboard America**" fares, which are zone-based and allow three stopovers in between your origin and eventual return. This enables you to visit one or more additional cities without paying any extra. Travel within the West (from Denver to the Pacific) costs $198 between September and May or $228 June to August; within the West and Midwest (west of Chicago) costs $258/318; and for the entire USA the cost is $318/378. While *Amtrak*'s basic fares are quite good value, if you want to travel in a bit more comfort the cost rises quickly. While *Amtrak*'s basic fares are quite good value, if you want to travel in a bit more comfort the cost rises quickly. **Sleeping compartments**, which include small toilets and showers, start at around $100 per night for one or two people, but can climb as high as $400 depending on class of compartment, number of nights, season, etc, but all including three meals a day. **Foreign** travellers can take advantage of the rail passes detailed in the box opposite.

By bus

Bus travel is the most tedious and time-consuming way to get to San Francisco, and, for all the discomfort, won't really save you much, if any, money. *Greyhound* (☎1-800/231-2222) is the sole long-distance operator; its fares average around 10¢ a mile – which adds up to around $300 coast-to-coast. A one-way APEX ticket from New York to San Francisco, bought 21 days in advance, costs $89 ($178 round trip) purchased on the day of travel it's $199 ($199 round trip).

The only reason to go *Greyhound* is if you're planning to visit a number of other places en route; *Greyhound*'s **Ameripass** is good for unlimited travel within a certain time, and costs $250 for 7 days, $350 for 15 days and $450 for 30 days. Valid from the day of purchase, it doesn't make sense to buy them in advance. **Foreign visitors** can buy Ameripasses before leaving home: in the UK, they cost £65 (4-day), £80 (5-day), £105 (7-day), £145 (15-day), £195 (30-day) or £325 (60-day). *Greyhound*'s office is at Sussex House, London Road, East Grinstead, West Sussex RH19 1LD (☎01342/317317). Extensions can be bought in the US for the dollar equivalent of £12 a day.

By car

Driving your own car gives the greatest freedom and flexibility, but if you don't have one (or don't trust the one you do have), one option worth considering is a **driveaway**. Companies operate in most major cities, and are paid to find drivers to take a customer's car from one place to another. The company will normally pay for your insurance and your first tank of gas; after that, you'll be expected to drive along the most direct route and to average 400 miles a day. Companies are keen to use foreign travellers (German tourists are ideal, it seems), but if you can convince them you are a safe bet, they'll take something like a $350 deposit, which you get back after delivering the car in good condition. Availability varies greatly, but usually there are as many cars leaving San Francisco as there are arriving. *Auto Driveaway*, 330 Townsend St (☎415/777-3740), is the main San Francisco

Green Tortoise

One alternative to Long-Distance Bus Hell is the slightly more cheerful ***Green Tortoise***, whose buses, furnished with foam cushions, bunks, coolers and sound systems, ply the major cities of the West Coast, running between Los Angeles, San Francisco and Seattle. In summer, they also cross the country to New York and Boston, transcontinental trips which amount to mini-tours of the nation, taking around a dozen days (at a current cost of around $279/379, not including contributions to the food fund), and allowing plenty of stops for hiking, river-rafting and hot springs. Other *Green Tortoise* trips include excursions to the major national parks (in 16 days for $499), and north to Alaska, and winter trips to Central America and Mexico. *Green Tortoise* has year-round excursions to Yosemite.

Main office:
494 Broadway, San Francisco CA 94133 ☎956-7500 or ☎1-800/227-4766

company using drivers; look under "Automobile Transporters and Driveaways" in the Yellow Pages for your local branch office.

Though it's not really necessary if you're planning to stay in San Francisco itself, **renting a car** is the usual story of phoning your local branch of one of the majors (*Avis, Hertz, Budget, Thrifty*, etc – listed on p.33), of which *Thrifty* tends to be the cheapest. Most companies have offices at destination airports, and addresses and phone numbers are comprehensively documented in the Yellow Pages.

Also worth considering are **fly-drive deals**, which give cut-rate (and sometimes free) car rental when buying an air ticket. They usually work out cheaper than renting on the spot and are especially good value if you intend to do a lot of driving.

Package tours

Many operators run all-inclusive **packages** which combine plane tickets and hotel accommodation with (for example) sightseeing, wining and dining, or excursions to tourist sites. Even if the "package" aspect doesn't thrill you to pieces, these deals can still be more convenient and sometimes even work out to be more economical than arranging the same thing yourself, providing you don't mind losing a little flexibility. With such a vast range of packages available, it's impossible to give an overview – major travel agents will have brochures detailing what's on offer.

Travellers with disabilities

Travellers with mobility problems or other physical disabilities are likely to find San Francisco – as with the US in general – to be much more in tune with their needs than any other country in the world. Steep hills aside, the Bay Area is generally considered to be one of the most barrier-free cities around, catering well to physically challenged travellers. All public buildings must be wheelchair-accessible and have suitable toilets, most city street corners have dropped kerbs, and most city buses are able to kneel to make access easier and are built with space and hand grips for wheelchair users. Most hotels and restaurants (certainly any built in the last ten years or so) have excellent wheelchair access.

Getting to and around San Francisco

Most **airlines**, transatlantic and within the US, do whatever they can to ease your journey, and will usually let attendants of more seriously disabled people accompany them at no extra charge. The Americans with Disabilities Act of 1990 obliged all air carriers to make the majority of their services accessible to travellers with disabilities within five to nine years.

Almost every ***Amtrak* train** includes one or more coaches with accommodation for disabled passengers. Guide dogs travel free, and *Amtrak* will provide wheelchair assistance at its train stations, adapted seating on board and a fifteen percent discount on the regular fare, all provided 24 hours' notice is given. Passengers with hearing impairment can get information on ☎1-800/523-6590.

Travelling by ***Greyhound*** and ***Amtrak Thruway* buses**, however, is not to be recommended. Buses are not equipped with lifts for wheelchairs, though staff will assist with boarding (intercity carriers are required by law to do this), and the "Helping Hand" scheme offers two-for-the-price-of-one tickets to passengers unable to travel alone (carry a doctor's certificate).

The major **car-rental** firms can, given sufficient notice, provide vehicles with hand controls (though these are usually only available on the more expensive models, and you'll need to reserve well in advance). The *American Automobile Association* (see p.23) produces the *Handicapped Driver's Mobility Guide* for **drivers with disabilities** (available from *Quantum-*

Precision Inc, 225 Broadway, Suite 3404, New York, NY 10007). There are no longer differences in state **parking regulations for disabled motorists**; the Department of Transportation has decreed that all state licences issued to disabled persons must carry a three-inch-square international access symbol, and each state must provide placards bearing this symbol, to be hung from the rear-view mirror – the placards are blue for permanent disabilities, red for temporary (maximum of six months). More information can be obtained from your state motor vehicle office.

As in other parts of the world, the rise of the **self-service gas station** is unwelcome for many disabled drivers. The state of California has addressed this by changing its laws so that most service stations are required to provide full service to disabled drivers at self-service prices.

Information

The California Office of Tourism's free 200-page *California Travel Planning Guide* lists "handicap facilities" at accommodations and attractions (though perhaps a bold capital **H** would have been easier to pick out than mentions in the text – and some attractions which do have facilities for disabled visitors are not listed as accessible). The *San Francisco Lodging Guide* (free from the San Francisco CVB, PO Box 6977, San Francisco, CA 94101) lists many "wheelchair-accessible" properties – hotels, motels, apartments, B&Bs, hostels, RV parks – in the city and surrounding counties; as always, travellers should call to confirm details.

San Francisco's **Mayor's Council on Disabilities**, PO Box 1595, San Francisco, CA (☎252-3112), puts out an annual guide for disabled visitors. The **Center for Independent Living**, 2539 Telegraph Ave in Berkeley (☎841-4776), has long been one of the most effective disabled people's organizations in the world; it has a variety of counselling services and is generally a useful resource.

Accommodation

The big motel and hotel chains are often the safest bet for accessible **accommodation**; there are plenty of excellent local alternatives, of course, but with a chain at least you'll know what to expect. At the higher end of the scale *Embassy Suites* (☎1-800/362-2779 voice; 1-800/458-4708 TDD) have been working to implement new standards of access which meet and exceed ADA requirements, involving both new construction and the retrofitting of all 100 existing hotels, and providing special training to all employees. Although the President of **Hyatt International Corporation** (☎1-800/233-1234) summed up the hotel industry's initial reaction to the ADA as "the end of the world as we know it", *Hyatt* has also committed itself to extensive redesign to improve accessibility.

National Organizations

Mobility International USA, PO Box 10767, Eugene, OR 97440 (voice and TDD ☎503/343-1284). Answers transportation queries and operates an exchange programme for disabled people.

Society for the Advancement of Travel for the Handicapped (SATH), 345 Fifth Ave, #610, New York, NY 10016 (☎212/447-7284). A non-profit travel-industry grouping which includes travel agents, tour operators, hotel and airline management, and people with disabilities. It will pass on any enquiry to the appropriate member; allow plenty of time for a response.

Travel Information Service, Moss Rehabilitation Hospital, 1200 W Tabor Rd, Philadelphia, PA 19141 (☎215/456-9600).

Travelin' Talk, PO Box 3534, Clarksville, TN 37043-3534 (☎615/552-6670). The brainchild of Rick Crowder, energetic Disabled American of the Year 1991, this is a network to assist travellers with disabilities, on the principle that the most reliable information and advice comes from another disabled person. Extensive listings of services for travellers with disabilities are disseminated in a quarterly newsletter (also available in large print, or on cassette).

Twin Peaks Press, Box 129, Vancouver, WA 98666 (☎206/694-2462 or 1-800/637-2256). Publisher of the *Directory of Travel Agencies for the Disabled* ($19.95), listing more than 370 agencies worldwide; *Travel for the Disabled* ($14.95); the *Directory of Accessible Van Rentals* and *Wheelchair Vagabond* ($9.95), loaded with personal tips.

Entry requirements for foreign visitors

Visas

Under the **Visa Waiver Scheme,** designed to speed up lengthy immigration procedures, British citizens and citizens of Andorra, Austria, Belgium, Brunei, Denmark, Finland, France, Germany, Iceland, Ireland, Italy, Japan, Liechtenstein, Luxembourg, Monaco, the Netherlands, New Zealand, Norway, San Marino, Spain, Sweden and Switzerland visiting the United States for a period of less than ninety days only need a **full passport** (UK citizens should note that a British Visitor's Passport is *not* acceptable) and a **visa waiver form**. The latter will be provided either by your travel agency, or by the airline during check-in or on the plane, and must be presented to immigration on arrival. The same form covers entry across the land borders with Canada and Mexico as well as by air. However, those eligible for the scheme must apply for a visa if they intend to work, study or stay in the country for more than ninety days.

Prospective visitors from Australia and all other parts of the world not mentioned above require a valid passport and a **non-immigrant visitor's visa**. How you'll obtain a visa depends on what country you're in and your status on application, so telephone the nearest Embassy or Consulate listed opposite.

In **Britain**, only British or EU citizens, and those from other countries eligible for the visa waiver scheme, can apply by post – fill in the application form available at most travel agents and send it with a full passport and a stamped SAE to the nearest US Embassy or Consulate. Expect a wait of one to three weeks before your passport is returned. All others must apply in person, making an appointment in advance. Visa application fees in Britain are currently £13.75.

In **Australasia** application forms are available through travel agents; you need to include your passport and one signed passport photo, and either post it (include SAE) or personally lodge it at the American Consulate in Sydney or Auckland (see p.17) or Non-Immigrant Visas, Private Bag 92022, Auckland 1. Processing takes ten working days for postal applications, two for personal applications; there is no application fee. In Sydney, the **USA Tourist Service**, 75 King St (☎02/299-1222), can advise on visa issues.

Whatever your nationality, visas are not issued to convicted felons and anybody who owns up to being a communist, fascist or drug-dealer.

Canadian Visitors

Canadian citizens are in a particularly privileged position when it comes to crossing the border into the US. Though it is possible to enter the States without your passport, you should really have it with you on any trip that brings you as far as San Francisco. Only if you plan to stay for more than ninety days do you need a visa.

Bear in mind that if you cross into the States in your car, trunks and passenger compartments are subject to spot searches by US Customs personnel, though this sort of surveillance is likely to decrease as remaining tariff barriers fall over the next few years. Remember, too, that Canadians are legally barred from seeking gainful employment in the US.

Immigration control

The standard immigration regulations apply to all visitors, whether or not they are using the Visa Waiver Scheme.

During the flight, you'll be handed an **immigration form** (and a customs declaration: see below), which must be given up at immigration control once you land. The form requires details of where you are staying on your first night (if you don't know, write "touring") and the date you intend to **leave** the US. You should be able to prove that you have enough money to support yourself while in the US – $300–400 a week is usually considered sufficient – as anyone revealing the slightest intention of working while in the country is likely to be refused admission. You may also experience difficulties if you admit to being HIV positive or having AIDS or TB. Part of the immigration form will be attached to your passport, where it must stay until you leave, when an immigration or airline official will detach it.

Customs

Customs officers will relieve you of your customs declaration and check whether you're carrying any fresh foods. You'll also be asked if you've visited a farm in the last month: if you have, you may well have your shoes taken away for

US Embassy and Consulates in Canada

Embassy
100 Wellington St, Ottawa
ON K1P 5T1 ☎613/238-5335

Consulates
Suite 1050, 615 Macleod Trail
Calgary, AB T29 4T8 ☎403/266-8962

Suite 910, Cogswell Tower
Scotia Square
Halifax, NS B3J 3K2 ☎902/429-2480

Complex Desjardins
South Tower
Montréal, PQ H5B 191 ☎514/281-1468

2 Place Terrace Dufferin
Québec City, PQ 91R 4T9 ☎418/692-2095

360 University Ave
Toronto, ON M59 184 ☎416/595-1700

1095 W Pender St
Vancouver, BC V6E 2M6 ☎604/685-4311

US Embassies and Consulates Elsewhere

UK
24 Grosvenor Square
London W1A 1AE ☎0171/499 9000; visa hotline ☎0891/200290

3 Regent Terrace
Edinburgh EH7 5BW ☎0131/556 8315

Queens House, 14 Queen St
Belfast BT1 6EQ ☎01232/328239

Australia
Moonhah Place
Canberra ACT 2600 ☎62/270 5000

39 Castlereagh St
Sydney ☎1800/805 924

Denmark
Dag Hammerskjöld Allé 24
2100 Copenhagen ☎31/42 31 44

Ireland
42 Elgin Rd, Ballsbridge
Dublin ☎01/687122

Netherlands
Museumplein 19
1071 DJ Amsterdam ☎020/575 5309

New Zealand
29 Fitzherbert Terrace
Thorndon
Wellington ☎4/722068
cnr Shortland and O'Connell streets
Auckland ☎09/303 2724

Norway
Drammensveien 18
0244 Oslo ☎22 44 85 50

South Africa
11th Floor, Kine Centre
Commissioner and Kruis streets
PO Box 2155, Johannesburg ☎11/331 1681

Sweden
Strandvägan 101
Stockholm ☎08/783 5300

inspection. The **duty-free allowance** if you're over 17 is 200 cigarettes and 50 cigars (*not* Cuban) and, if you're over 21, a litre of spirits. As well as foods and anything agricultural, it's prohibited to carry into the country any articles from North Korea, Iran, Iraq, Libya, Serbia, Montenegro or Cuba, obscene publications, lottery tickets, chocolate liqueurs or pre-Columbian artefacts. Anyone caught carrying drugs into the country will not only face prosecution but be entered in the records as an undesirable and probably denied entry for all time.

Extensions and leaving

The date stamped on your passport is the latest you're legally allowed to stay. Leaving a few days later may not matter, especially if you're heading home, but more than a week or so can result in a protracted, rather unpleasant, interrogation from officials which may cause you to miss your flight. Overstaying may also cause you to be turned away next time you try to enter the US.

The only official way to get an **extension** is to go through the **US Immigration and Naturalization Service** (INS), whose San Francisco office is at Room 200, 630 Sansome St (Mon–Fri 8am–4pm; ☎705-4411). They will automatically assume that you're working illegally and it's up to you to convince them otherwise. Do this by providing evidence of ample finances and, if you can, bring along an upstanding American citizen to vouch for you. You'll also have to explain why you didn't plan for the extra time initially.

Staying on

While San Francisco may be a great place to live, it's becoming increasingly difficult for foreigners to find **work** in the Bay Area.

Anyone planning an extended legal stay should apply for a **special working visa** at any US embassy at least six months *before* setting off for the States. There are a whole range of visas, depending on your skills and length of stay, but unless you've got relatives (parents or children over 21), or a prospective employer to sponsor you, your chances at best are slim. For details on finding long-term **accommodation**, see p.45.

Work and study

Illegal work, once quite easy to find, has become much more difficult to obtain in recent years, since the government introduced fines of up to $10,000 for businesses caught employing a foreigner without a **social security number** (which effectively proves you're part of the legal workforce). Understandably, most are now reluctant to employ travellers.

Any work you do find will be of the casual washing-up/baby-sitting and farm-hand variety – traditionally low-paid cash work. Even restaurants can be reluctant to employ foreign waiters because of the visibility of the work. And remember San Francisco is a small town with an economy to match – this is not the Los Angeles of work for anybody who wants it and success for those who can stick it.

Making up a fictitious social security number, or borrowing one from somebody else, is of course completely illegal, as are **marriages of convenience**; usually inconvenient for all concerned and with a lower success rate than is claimed.

Foreign students have a slightly better chance of a prolonged stay in San Francisco, especially if those who can arrange some sort of "year abroad" through their university at home. Otherwise you can apply directly to a Bay Area university: if they'll have you (and you can afford the painfully expensive fees charged to overseas students), it can be a great way to get to know the city, and maybe even learn something useful. The US grants more or less unlimited visas to those enrolled in full-time further education.

Another possibility for students is to get onto an Exchange Visitor Program, for which participants are given a J-1 visa that entitles them to accept paid summer employment and apply for a social security number. However, most of these visas are issued for jobs in American **summer camps**, which aren't everybody's idea of a good time: they fly you over, and after a summer's work you end up with around $500 and a month to blow it in. If you live in Britain and are interested, contact *BUNAC* (16 Bowling Green Lane, London EC1; ☎0171/251 3472) or *Camp America* (37 Queens' Gate, London SW7; ☎0171/589 3223).

Insurance and health

Travel Insurance Companies in the UK

Columbus Travel Insurance, 17 Devonshire Square, London EC2M 4SQ (☎0171/375 0011).

Endsleigh Insurance, 97–107 Southampton Row, London WC1B 4AG (☎0171/436 4451).

Frizzell Insurance, Frizzell House, County Gates, Bournemouth, Dorset BH1 2NF (☎01202/292 333).

Insurance

Though not compulsory, **travel insurance** is *essential* for **foreign travellers**. The US has no national health system and you can lose an arm and a leg (so to speak) having even minor medical treatment. Bank and credit cards (particularly *American Express*) often have certain levels of medical or other insurance included, especially if you use them to pay for your trip.

If you plan to participate in water sports, or do some hiking or skiing, you'll probably have to pay an extra premium; check carefully that any insurance policy you are considering will cover you in case of an accident. Note also that very few insurers will arrange on-the-spot payments in the event of a major expense or loss; you will usually be reimbursed only after going home. In all cases of loss or theft of goods, you will have to contact the local police to have a report made out so that your insurer can process the claim.

British cover

Most **travel agents** and tour operators will offer you insurance when you book your flight or holiday, and some will insist you take it. These policies are usually reasonable value; though, as ever, you should check the small print. If you want to compare prices, check out any insurance broker, or bank, though the cheapest is generally *Endsleigh*, which charges around £41 for three weeks to cover life, limb and luggage (with a 25 percent reduction if you choose to forgo luggage insurance or if you are a student). Its forms are available from most youth/student travel offices (though its policies are open to all), or direct from the address above. If you are planning to do a lot of travelling, *Columbus Travel Insurance* has an annual multi-trip policy which offers twelve months' cover for £125.

Travel Insurance Companies in North America

Access America, PO Box 90310, Richmond, VA 23230 (☎1-800/284-8300).

Carefree Travel Insurance, PO Box 310, 120 Mineola Blvd, Mineola, NY 11501 (☎1-800/323-3149).

International Student Insurance Service (ISIS), sold by *STA Travel*, which has several branches in the US (head office is 48 E 11th St, New York, NY 10003; ☎1-800/777-0112).

Travel Assistance International, 1133 15th St NW, Suite 400, Washington, DC 20005 (☎1-800/821-2828).

Travel Guard, 1145 Clark St, Stevens Point, WI 54481 (☎1-800/826-1300).

Travel Insurance Services, 2930 Camino Diablo, Suite 300, Walnut Creek, CA 94596 (☎1-800/937-1387).

On all policies, read the small print to ensure the cover includes a sensible amount for medical expenses – this should be at least £1,000,000, which will cover the cost of an air ambulance to fly you home in the event of serious injury or hospitalization.

Australasian cover

In **Australia**, *CIC Insurance*, offered by *Cover-More Insurance Services* (Level 9, 32 Walker St, North Sydney; ☎02/202-8000; branches in Victoria and Queensland), has some of the widest cover available which can be arranged through most travel agents. It costs around AU$190 for 32 days. Other major operators include *UTAG* (347 Kent St, Sydney; ☎1800/809 462), *AFTA* (144 Pacific Hwy, North Sydney; ☎02/956 4800) and *Ready Plan* (141–147 Walker St, Dandenong, Victoria; ☎1800/337462; and 10th Floor, 63 Albert St, Auckland, ☎09/379 3399).

In **New Zealand**, a good range of policies is offered by *STA* and *Flight Centres* (see p.8).

North American cover

American travellers should find that their **health insurance** covers any health charges or costs; if you don't have any you can get adequate coverage either from a travel agent's insurance plan or from specialist travel insurance companies such as *The Travelers*. If you are unable to use a phone, or if the practitioner requires immediate payment, save all the **forms** to support a claim for subsequent reimbursement. Remember also that time limits may apply when making claims after the fact, so promptness in contacting your insurer is highly advisable.

If you have anything **stolen** (including money), register the loss immediately at the nearest police station (main addresses are given on p.29, or look under "Police" in the Emergency listings at the front of the phone book). They will issue you with a reference number to pass onto your insurance company – an accepted alternative to the full statement insurers usually require. Not surprisingly, however, few if any American health insurance plans cover against **theft** while travelling, though most **renter's or homeowner's insurance** policies will cover you for up to $500 while on the road.

After exhausting the possibilities above, you might want to contact a specialist **travel insurance** company; your travel agent can usually recommend one. Policies are comprehensive (accidents, illnesses, delayed or lost luggage, cancelled flights, etc), but maximum payouts tend to be meagre. Premiums vary, so shop around. The best deals are usually to be had through student/youth travel agencies – *ISIS* policies, for example. If you're planning to do any "dangerous sports" (skiing, mountaineering, etc), figure on a surcharge of 20–50 percent.

Most North American travel policies apply only to items lost, stolen or damaged while in the custody of an identifiable, responsible third party – hotel porter, airline, luggage consignment, etc. Even in these cases you will have to contact the local police within a certain time limit.

Health advice for foreign travellers

If you have a serious **accident** while in San Francisco, don't worry about being left to die on the sidewalk; emergency medical services will get to you quickly and charge you later. For emergencies or ambulances, dial ☎**911**, the nationwide emergency number (or whatever variant may be on the information plate of the pay phone).

Should you need to see a **doctor**, lists can be found in the Yellow Pages under "Clinics" or "Physicians and Surgeons". A basic consultation fee is $50–75, payable in advance. Medications

Hospital Emergency Rooms Open at all Times

San Francisco General Hospital
1001 Potrero Ave near 22nd St
the Mission ☎206-8111

Highland Hospital
1411 E 31st St, Oakland ☎510/437-4261

University of California Medical Center
Parnassas Ave at Third
Sunset District ☎476-1037

Mount Zion Hospital
1600 Divisadero St at Post
Western Addition ☎885-7520

Pacific Medical Center
2333 Buchanan St at Washington St
near LaFayette Park
Pacific Heights ☎923-3333

For advice on personal safety, and how to cope with emergency situations – including phone numbers to report lost cheques or credit cards, see p.29.

aren't cheap either – keep all your receipts for later claims on your insurance policy. For **dental care**, contact the *Dental Society Referral Service* (☎421-1435).

Many **minor ailments** can be remedied using the fabulous array of potions and lotions available in **drugstores**. Foreign visitors should bear in mind that many pills available over the counter at home need a prescription in the US – most codeine-based painkillers, for example – and that local brand names can be confusing; ask for advice at the **pharmacy** in any drugstore.

Travellers from Europe do not require **inoculations** to enter the US.

Information and maps

Advance information can be obtained by post from the **California Office of Tourism**, Suite 103, 1121 L St, Sacramento, CA 95814 (☎916/322-1396), though the best source of specific information on San Francisco is the **San Francisco Convention and Visitors Bureau**, Suite 900, 201 Third St, San Francisco, CA 94103 (☎974-6900), which publishes the handy eighty-page *San Francisco Book* and a very useful map, both of which they'll send to you for $2 including postage.

Tourist offices

Once in the Bay Area, there are a number of offices which dispense brochures and information to callers, though these can vary from indispensable to absolutely useless. Among the former is the main **San Francisco Visitor Information Center**, in Hallidie Plaza on the concourse of the Powell Street *BART/MUNI* station (Mon–Fri 9am–5.30pm, Sat 9am–3pm, Sun 10am–2pm; ☎391-2000). They have free maps of the city and the Bay Area, and can help with accommodation and travel information. The centre also makes a good bench mark for getting your bearings, as it's centrally located and at the hub of city transit systems.

All the various **Bay Area regions** also have at least one main source of information, usually some kind of visitors' bureau, and almost every town will have at least an office operated by the very business-oriented local **Chamber of Commerce**. Where useful we've listed them under the appropriate sections of the Bay Area chapters.

Maps

Most of the tourist offices we've mentioned can supply you with good **maps**, either for free or for a small charge, and, supplemented with our own, these should be enough for general sightseeing and touring. The best of the commercially available alternatives are the easy-to-read city plans published by *Rand-McNally* and *Gousha Publications* (£2.50 each), both of which have especially detailed sections on downtown, showing important buildings – very handy for keeping your bearings. They also do maps of Oakland and the East Bay, San Jose and the Peninsula, and Marin County. For the habitually lost, *Flashmaps* (£3.50) do a handbook on the city.

Map and Travel Book Suppliers

UK

Daunt Books, 83 Marylebone High St, London W1 ☎0171/224 2295.

John Smith and Sons, 57–61 St Vincent St, Glasgow G2 5TB ☎0141/221 7472.

National Map Centre, 22–24 Caxton St, London SW1 ☎0171/222 4945.

Stanfords, 12–14 Long Acre, London WC2 ☎0171/836 1321; 52 Grosvenor Gardens, London SW1W 0AG; 156 Regent St, London W1R 5TA.

Thomas Nelson & Sons Ltd, 51 York Place, Edinburgh EH1 3JD ☎0131/557 3011.

The Travel Bookshop, 13–15 Blenheim Crescent, London W11 2EE ☎0171/229 5260.

Maps by **mail or phone order** are available from *Stanfords* ☎0171/836 1321.

IRELAND

Easons Bookshop, 40 O'Connell St, Dublin 1 ☎01/873 3811.

Fred Hanna's Bookshop, 27–29 Nassau St, Dublin 2 ☎01/677 1255.

Hodges Figgis Bookshop, 56–58 Dawson St, Dublin 2 ☎01/677 4754.

Waterstone's, Queens Bldg, 8 Royal Ave, Belfast BT1 1DA ☎01232/247355.

UNITED STATES

The Complete Traveler Bookstore, 199 Madison Ave, New York, NY 10016 ☎212/685-9007; 3207 Fillmore St, San Francisco, CA 92123 ☎415/923-1511.

Forsyth Travel Library, 9154 W 57th St, Shawnee Mission, KS 66201 ☎1-800/367-7984.

Map Link Inc, 25 E Mason St, Santa Barbara, CA 93101 ☎805/965-4402.

Phileas Fogg's Books & Maps, #87 Stanford Shopping Center, Palo Alto, CA 94304 ☎1-800/233-FOGG in California; ☎1-800/533-FOGG elsewhere in US.

Rand McNally,* 444 N Michigan Ave, Chicago, IL 60611 (☎312/321-1751); 150 E 52nd St, New York, NY 10022 (☎212/758-7488); 595 Market St, San Francisco, CA 94105 ☎415/777-3131; 1201 Connecticut Ave NW, Washington, DC 20003 ☎202/223-6751.

The Savvy Traveller, 310 S Michigan Ave, Chicago, IL 60604 ☎312/913-9800.

Sierra Club Bookstore, 730 Polk St, San Francisco, CA 94109 ☎415/923-5500.

Travel Books and Language Centre, 4931 Cordell Ave, Bethesda, MD 20814 ☎1800/220-2665.

Traveler's Bookstore, 22 W 52nd St, New York, NY 10019 ☎212/664-0995.

Note: *Rand McNally* now has 24 stores across the US; call ☎1-800/333-0136 (ext 2111) for the location of your nearest store, or for **direct mail** maps.

CANADA

Open Air Books and Maps, 25 Toronto St, Toronto, ON M5R 2C1 ☎416/363-0719.

Ulysses Travel Bookshop, 4176 St-Denis, Montréal ☎514/289-0993.

World Wide Books and Maps, 714 Granville St, Vancouver, BC V6Z 1E4 ☎604/687-3320.

AUSTRALIA

The Map Shop, 16a Peel St, Adelaide, SA 5000 ☎08/8231-2033.

Bowyangs, 372 Little Bourke St, Melbourne, VIC 3000 ☎03/9670-4383.

Travel Bookshop, 20 Bridge St, Sydney, NSW 2000 ☎02/9241-3554.

Perth Map Centre, 891 Hay St, Perth, WA 6000 ☎09/322-733; ☎08/9322-5733 from Sep 1997.

NEW ZEALAND

Specialty Maps, 58 Albert St, Auckland ☎09/307-2217.

The *American Automobile Association* – Triple A – based at 1000 AAA Drive, Heathrow, FL 32746 (*AAA*; toll-free ☎1-800/222-4357), provides free maps and assistance to its members, and to British members of the *AA* and *RAC*; they also have an office in San Francisco (150 Van Ness Ave; ☎565-2012), near the Civic Center, and at other locations all over the Bay Area.

For something more detailed, say for **hiking** purposes, it's best to wait till you're in San Francisco. Ranger stations in parks and wilderness areas all sell good-quality local hiking maps for $1–2, and camping stores generally have a good selection. Most bookstores will have a range of local trail guides, the best of which we've listed under "Books" in *Contexts*.

Communications: phones and the mail

Because of the strong emphasis placed on business efficiency, and the fact that Americans in general demand excellent service, all forms of communication in the US *have* to be good – something that's especially true on the commercially important and comparatively far-flung West Coast.

Telephones

San Francisco **telephones** are run by *Pacific Telephone (Bell System)* – commonly abbreviated to *PacBell* – and linked to the nationwide *AT&T* network. Dial-phones are scarce: the vast majority are the push-button kind, emitting a different audio tone for each button pressed. Some numbers, particularly those of consumer services, employ letters as part of their "number", for example ☎992-*BART*, for information on the Bay Area Rapid Transit system. The letters are printed on the buttons. For help, call the **operator** (☎0).

The San Francisco **area code** – a three-figure number which must precede the seven-figure number if you're calling from another region – is ☎415. All San Francisco phone numbers are within this area code and, in general, we have omitted it from our listings; those numbers that are not – such as in Bay Area regions like the East Bay (☎510), the Wine Country (☎707) and San Jose (☎408) – are given with the relevant code. To phone one area code from another you have to dial a 1 before the code and number – for example ☎1-707/963-9611 for *Robert Mondavi Winery* in the Napa Valley.

Useful Numbers

Emergencies	☎911
Ask to be connected with the appropriate emergency service: fire, police or ambulance.	
Local directory information	☎411
Operator	☎0
Long-distance directory information	☎1-(Area Code)/555-1212
Directory enquiries for toll-free numbers	☎1-800/555-1212

International Telephone Calls

International calls can be dialled direct from private or (more expensively) public phones. You can get assistance from the **international operator (☎00)**, who may also interrupt every three minutes asking for more money, and call you back for any money still owed immediately after you hang up. The **lowest rates** for international calls to Europe are between 6pm and 7am, when a direct-dialled three-minute call will cost roughly $5.

In **Britain**, it's possible to obtain a free **BT Chargecard** (☎0800/800838), using which all calls from overseas can be charged to your quarterly domestic account. To use these cards in the US, or to make a **collect call** (to "reverse the charges"), contact the carrier: *AT&T* ☎1-800/445-5667; *MCI* ☎1-800/444-2162; or *Sprint* ☎1-800/800-0008.

British visitors who are going to be making a number of calls **to the US**, and who want to be able to call ☎1-800 numbers, otherwise inaccessible from outside the country, should take advantage of the **Swiftcall** telephone club. You need a touch-tone phone. Call your nearest office (see box; daily 8am–midnight); once you've paid, by credit card, for however many units you want, you are given a PIN. Any time you want to get an international line, simply dial ☎0171/488 0800, punch in your PIN, and then dial as you would were you in the US, putting a 1 before the area code, followed by the number. Calls to the USA – including ☎1-800 calls – cost about 16p per minute, a **saving** of over 50 percent.

SWIFTCALL NUMBERS

London ☎0171/488 2001 Manchester ☎0161/245 2001 Glasgow ☎0141/616 2001
Dublin ☎01/671 0457 Belfast ☎01232/314524

Australia's **Telstra Telecard** (application forms available from Telstra offices) and **New Zealand Telecom**'s **Calling Card** (contact ☎04/382-5818) can be used to make calls charged to a domestic account or credit card.

To call **to San Francisco** from the rest of the world (excluding Canada), the US country code is always ☎1. Thus from the UK you dial ☎00-1-415, followed by the seven-digit number.

To make international calls **from the US**, dial 011 followed by the country code (a complete listing of codes can be found in the front section of the Yellow Pages):

Australia 61 **Ireland** 353 **New Zealand** 64 **United Kingdom** 44

Public telephones invariably work and can be found everywhere – on street corners, in train and bus stations, hotel lobbies, bars, restaurants – and they take 25¢, 10¢ and 5¢ coins. The cost of a **local call** from a public phone (within the same area code) varies according to the actual distance being called (some area codes cover vast territories). The minimum is 20¢, usually 25¢, for the first few minutes, plus a further amount if you talk for a long time; the operator – or a synthesized voice – will come on the line and ask you for the money.

Non-local calls ("zone calls") are more expensive – to numbers within the same area code but sometimes requiring you to dial 1 before the seven-digit number. Pricier still are **long-distance calls** (to a different area code and always prefixed by a 1), for which you'll need plenty of change. Non-local calls and long-distance calls are far cheaper if made between 6pm and 8am, and calls from **private phones** are always much cheaper than those from public phones. Detailed rates are listed at the front of the **telephone directory** (the "White Pages", a copious source of information on many matters).

Making a telephone call from a **hotel room** is usually more expensive than from a payphone, though some budget hotels offer free local calls from rooms – ask when you check in. An increasing number of phones accept **credit cards**, while anyone who holds a credit card issued by an American bank can obtain an **AT&T charge card** (information on ☎1-800/874-4000 ext 359). Foreign visitors will have to make do with **phone cards** – in denominations of $5, $10 and $20 – bought from general stores, some hostels and relatively few *7-Elevens*. These provide you with a temporary account (just tap in the number printed on the card), and work out a lot cheaper than feeding coins into a payphone, especially if calling abroad.

Many government agencies, car rental firms, hotels and so on have **toll-free numbers**, which always have the prefix ☎1-800. From within the US, you can dial any number which starts with those digits free of charge. Phone numbers with the prefix ☎1-900 are pay-per-call lines, generally quite expensive and almost always involving either sports or phone sex.

Mail services

Post offices are usually open Monday to Friday from 9am until 5pm, and Saturday from 9am to 1pm, and there are blue **mail boxes** on many street corners. Ordinary **mail within the US** costs 32¢ for a letter weighing up to an ounce; the sender's address should be written on the envelope. **Air mail** between the West Coast and Europe generally takes about a week. Postcards, aerograms and letters weighting up to half an ounce (a single thin sheet) cost 60¢.

The last line of the address is made up of an abbreviation denoting the state (California is "CA") and a five-figure number – the **zip code** – denoting the local post office. (The additional four digits you will sometimes see appended to zip codes are helpful but not essential.) Letters which don't carry the zip code are liable to get lost or at least delayed.

Letters can be sent c/o **General Delivery** (what's known elsewhere as **poste restante**) to:

Your Name
General Delivery
San Francisco CA 94142
USA

Letters so addressed can be picked up at the post office at 101 Hyde St, in the Civic Center (Mon–Sat 10am–2pm; ☎441-8329), but will only be held for thirty days before being returned to sender, so make sure there's a return address on the envelope. If you're receiving mail at someone else's address, it should include "c/o" and the regular occupant's name; otherwise it, too, is likely to be returned.

Main SF and Bay Area Post Offices

220 Harrison St
San Francisco, CA 94101 ☎512-0397

Chinatown 867 Stockton St
San Francisco, CA 94108 ☎956-3566

North Beach 1640 Stockton St
San Francisco, CA 94133 ☎956-3581

Marina 2055 Fillmore St
San Francisco, CA 94123 ☎284-0755

Oakland Main 1675 Seventh St
Oakland, CA 94607 ☎510/874-8200

Berkeley Main 2000 Allston Way
Berkeley, CA 94704 ☎510/649-3174

Rules on sending **parcels** are very rigid: packages must be sealed according to the instructions given at the start of the Yellow Pages. To send anything out of the country, you'll need a green **customs declaration form**, available from a post office. **Postal rates** for sending a parcel weighing up to one pound are $9.75 to Europe, $11.20 to Australasia. Packages can be guaranteed for **overnight delivery** in the US by private companies. The most popular and omnipresent is *Federal Express* at 1150 Harrison St near the Civic Center (☎877-9000).

Telegrams and faxes

To send a **telegram** (sometimes called a *wire*), don't go to a post office but to a *Western Union* office (listed in the Yellow Pages). Credit card holders can dictate messages over the phone. **International telegrams** cost slightly less than the cheapest international phone call: one sent in the morning from the US should arrive at its overseas destination the following day. For domestic telegrams ask for a **mailgram**, which will be delivered to any address in the country the next morning.

Public **fax** machines, which may require your credit card to be "swiped" through an attached device, are found at photocopy centres, libraries and, occasionally, bookstores.

Costs, money and banks

To help with planning your San Francisco vacation, this book contains detailed price information for lodging and eating (see pp.207–246). Naturally, costs will increase slightly overall during the life of this edition, but the relative comparisons should remain valid.

Your biggest single expense is likely to be **accommodation**. Few hotel or motel rooms cost under $40 – it's more usual to pay between $50 and $80 for anything halfway decent. Although dorm beds in hostels costing around $12–15 do exist, they are a bit thin on the ground; besides which, San Francisco is not a city you want to do on the cheap – no point slumming in a ritzy city.

As for **food**, $15 a day is enough to get you an adequate life-support diet, but, again, the city is filled with wonderful restaurants and if you can manage $25 per day and upwards you should spend it and get the most out of this most cuisine-conscious of cities. Beyond this, everything hinges on how much sightseeing, taxi-taking, drinking and socializing you do – in San Francisco it's easy to get through a bank roll in a couple of days. The city seems to invite spending and having fun; above all, this is a place to come and **shop**.

Rates for travelling around using the *MUNI* system are very reasonable. If you're going to be in the city for at least a week or two, consider a one-month **Fast Pass** ($35) sold at all underground *MUNI* stations – the pass permits unlimited *BART* and *MUNI* use throughout San Francisco. See "Getting around the city" p.30. To make the most of the city, especially if there are two or more of you, renting a **car** can be a very good investment.

Sales Tax of 8.5 percent is added to virtually everything you buy in stores, but it isn't part of the marked price. Watch out for surprises at the checkout.

Money: A Note for Foreign Travellers

Even when the exchange rate is at its least advantageous, most foreign visitors find virtually everything – accommodation, food, gas, clothes and more – to be better value in the US than it is at home. However, if you're used to travelling in the less expensive countries of Europe, let alone in the rest of the world, you shouldn't expect to scrape by on the same minuscule budget once you're in the US.

Regular upheaval in the money markets causes the relative value of the **US dollar** against the currencies of the rest of the world to vary considerably. Generally speaking, one **pound sterling** will buy $1.40–1.80; one **Canadian dollar** is worth between 70¢ and $1; one **Australian dollar** is between 67¢ and 88¢; and one **New Zealand dollar** is worth 55–72¢.

Bills and Coins

US currency comes in **bills** worth $1, $5, $10, $20, $50 and $100, plus various larger (and rarer) denominations. Confusingly, all are the same size and same green colour, making it necessary to check each bill carefully. The dollar is made up of 100 cents in **coins** of 1¢ (known as a **penny**), 5¢ (a **nickel**), 10¢ (a **dime**) and 25¢ (a **quarter**). Very occasionally you might come across **JFK half-dollars** (50¢), **Susan B. Anthony dollar coins**, or a **two-dollar bill**. Change (quarters are the most useful) is needed for buses, vending machines and telephones, so always carry plenty.

Traveller's cheques

US dollar traveller's cheques are the best way to carry money, for both American and foreign visitors; they offer the great security of knowing that lost or stolen cheques will be replaced. You should have no problem using the better-known cheques, such as *American Express* and *Visa*, in shops, restaurants and gas stations (don't be put off by "no checks" signs, which only refer to personal cheques). Be sure to have plenty of the $10 and $20 denominations for everyday transactions.

Banks in San Francisco are generally open from 10am until 3.30pm or 4pm Monday to Thursday, and 10am to 6pm on Friday. Most major banks change dollar traveller's cheques for their face value (not that there's much point doing this – and some charge for the privilege, so ask before you do), and **change foreign traveller's cheques and currency**. Exchange bureaux, always found at airports, tend to charge less commission: *Thomas Cook* or *American Express* are the biggest names. Rarely, if ever, do hotels change foreign currency. **Emergency phone numbers** to call if your cheques and/or credit cards are stolen are on p.29. To find the nearest bank that sells a particular brand of traveller's cheque, or to buy cheques by phone, call the following numbers: *American Express* (☎1-800/673-3782), *Citicorp* (☎1-800/645-6556), *Mastercard International/Thomas Cook* (☎1-800/223-7373), *Visa* (☎1-800/227-6811).

Plastic money and cash machines

If you don't already have a **credit card**, you should think seriously about getting one before you set off. For many services, it's simply taken for granted that you'll be paying with plastic. When renting a car (or even a bike) or checking into a hotel you may be asked to show a credit card to establish your creditworthiness – even if you intend to settle the bill in cash. ***Visa***, ***Mastercard/Access***, ***Diners Club***, ***Discover*** and ***American Express*** are the most widely accepted.

With *Mastercard* or *Visa* it is also possible to **withdraw cash** at any bank displaying relevant stickers, or from appropriate automatic teller machines (**ATMs**). *Diners Club* cards can be used to cash personal cheques at *Citibank* branches. *American Express* cards can only get cash, or buy traveller's cheques at *American Express* offices (check the Yellow Pages) or from the traveller's cheque dispensers at most major airports. Most **Canadian** credit cards issued by hometown banks will be honoured in the US.

> Each of the two main ATM networks operates a **toll-free** line to let customers know the location of their nearest machine; **Plus System** ☎1-800/THE-PLUS and **Cirrus** is ☎1-800/4CI-RRUS

ATM cards held by visitors from other states, and overseas cash-dispensing cards linked to international networks such as *Cirrus* and *Plus*, may well work in some Californian machines. Check with your bank before you leave home. Not only is this method of financing safer, but, at around only a dollar per transaction, it's economical as well.

Most major credit cards issued by **foreign banks** are accepted in the US. Overseas visitors should also bear in mind that fluctuating exchange rates may result in spending more (or less) than expected when the item eventually shows up on a statement.

Emergencies

Assuming you know someone who is prepared to send you money in a crisis, the quickest way is to have them take the cash to the nearest ***Western Union*** office and have it instantaneously **wired** to the office nearest you, subject to the deduction of 10 percent commission. Money wired via *Western Union* can be received at many small convenience stores and cheque-cashing stores throughout the city. **American Express Moneygram** offers a similar service.

It's also possible to have money wired directly from a bank in your home country to a bank in the US, although this is somewhat less reliable because it involves two separate institutions. If you go this route, the person wiring the funds to you will need the telex number of the bank the funds are being wired to. Having money wired from home is never convenient or cheap, and should be considered a last resort.

If you have a few days' leeway, sending a postal money order, exchangeable at any post office, through the mail is cheaper still. The equivalent for foreign travellers is the **international money order**, for which you need to allow up to

Exchange Offices

American Express, 237 Post St (Mon–Fri 9am–5pm, Sat 10am–5pm; ☎981-5533).

Thomas Cook, 75 Geary St (Mon–Fri 9am–5pm; ☎362-3452).

Wire Services

Australia
American Express Moneygram within Sydney (☎9886-0666); elsewhere (☎1-800/230100); *Western Union* within Brisbane (☎3229-8610); elsewhere, free call (☎1-800/649565).

Britain
American Express Moneygram (☎0800/894887); *Western Union* (☎0800/833833).

New Zealand
American Express Moneygram Auckland (☎09/379-8243); Wellington (☎04/499-7899 or ☎473-7766); *Western Union* Auckland (☎09/302-0143).

USA and Canada
American Express Moneygram (☎1-800/543-4080); *Western Union* (☎1-800/325-6000).

seven days in the international air mail before arrival. An ordinary cheque sent from overseas takes 2–3 weeks to clear.

British travellers in difficulties have the final option of throwing themselves on the mercy of the **British Consulate**, 1 Sansome St (☎981-3030), who won't be at all pleased to see you but may deign to offer assistance. In worst cases only, they may repatriate you, but they will never, under any circumstances, lend you money.

Crime and personal safety

Though no one could pretend that San Francisco is trouble-free, by and large the worst areas for crime are also the most unusual places for tourists to visit, so you're unlikely to have to deal with any of the threatening environments of some other US cities. Most of the violent crime that does occur is drug-related and generally concentrated in deprived areas such as Hunter's Point, on San Francisco's southeast waterfront, or West Oakland. In Downtown San Francisco, only the Tenderloin and quieter spots of SoMa need a bit of extra vigilance. By being careful, you're unlikely to have problems even in these places, though you may well feel distinctly uncomfortable.

Mugging and theft

The biggest problem for most travellers is the threat of **mugging**. It's impossible to give hard and fast rules about what to do if you're confronted by a mugger. Whether to run, scream or fight depends on the situation – but most locals would just hand over their money.

Of course, the best strategy is simply to **avoid being mugged**. Following a few basic rules helps minimize the danger: *don't* flash money around; don't peer at your map (or this

Main SF and Bay Area Police Stations

San Francisco Police Dept 850 Bryant St, SoMa	☎553-1373
Central Station, 766 Vallejo St North Beach	☎553-1532
Mission Station, 630 Valencia St Mission District	☎558-5400
Northern Station, 1125 Fillmore Western Addition	☎553-1563
Golden Gate Park Station Stanyan and Waller streets	☎753-7280
Potrero Station, 2300 Third St Hunter's Point	☎553-1021
Richmond Station 461 Sixth Ave	☎553-1385
Oakland Police Dept 455 Seventh St	☎510/238-3744
Berkeley Police Dept 2171 McKinley Ave	☎510/644-6743

book) at every corner, thereby announcing you're a lost stranger; even if you're terrified or drunk (or both), *don't* appear so; *avoid* dark streets, especially ones you can't see the end of; and in the early hours stick to the roadside edge of the pavement so it's easier to run into the road to attract attention.

If **the worst happens** and your assailant is toting a gun or a knife, try to stay calm: remember that he (for this is generally a male pursuit) is probably scared, too. Keep still, don't make any sudden movements – and hand over your money. When he's gone you'll be shocked, but try to find a cab to take you to the nearest police station, or **phone ☎911** and the police will send an officer to the scene, who'll take you to the nearest station. Here, report the theft and get a reference number on the report to claim insurance (see "Insurance and Health", p.19) and traveller's cheque refunds. For advice specifically for women in case of mugging or attack, phone the Rape Crisis Line (☎647-7273).

Another potential source of trouble is having your **hotel room burgled**. Always store valuables in the hotel safe when you go out; when inside keep your door locked and don't open it to anyone you are suspicious of. If they claim to be hotel staff and you don't believe them, call reception on the room phone to check.

Stolen passports

Needless to say, having bags snatched which contain travel documents is a big headache, none more so for foreign travellers than **losing your passport**. If the worst happens, go to the nearest consulate (see p.17) and get them to issue a **temporary passport**, basically a sheet of paper saying you've reported the loss, which will get you out of America and back home. Go along (9am–noon & 2–4pm) with any remaining ID – plane tickets, driving licence, etc, and they will issue you with an emergency passport or, if more time is available, have one issued from Washington, DC.

Stolen Traveller's Cheques and Credit Cards

Keep a record of the numbers of your **traveller's cheques** separately from the actual cheques; if you lose them, ring the issuing company on the toll-free number below.

They'll ask you for the cheque numbers, the place you bought them, when and how you lost them and whether it's been reported to the police. All being well, you should get the missing cheques reissued within a couple of days – and perhaps an emergency advance to tide you over.

Emergency Numbers

Mastercard (*Access*)	☎1-800/999-0454
American Express	
(TCs)	☎1-800/221-7282
(credit cards)	☎1-800/528-4800
Diners Club	☎1-800/234-6377
Thomas Cook	☎1-800/223-7373
Visa (TCs)	☎1-800/227-6811
Visa Credit Card	☎1-800/847-2911

Car crime

Crimes committed against tourists driving **rental cars** in the US have garnered headlines around the world in recent years. In major urbanized areas, any car you rent should have nothing on it – such as a particular licence plate – that makes it easy to spot as a rental car. When driving, under no circumstances stop in any unlit or seemingly deserted urban area – and especially not if someone is waving you down and suggesting that there is something wrong with your car. Similarly, if you are "accidentally" rammed by the driver behind, do not stop immediately but drive on to the nearest well-lit, busy area and **phone ☎911 for assistance**. Keep your doors locked and windows never more than slightly open. Do not open your door or window if someone approaches your car on the pretext of asking directions. Hide any valuables out of sight, preferably locked in the trunk or in the glove compartment (any valuables you don't need for your journey should be left in your hotel safe).

Getting around the city

Getting around San Francisco is simple. In spite of the literally breathtaking hills, the city centre is small enough to make walking a feasible way to see the sights and get the feel of things. In addition, the excellent system of public transportation is cheap, efficient and easy to use, both in the city and the more urbanized parts of the surrounding Bay Area – though to go any further afield you'd do well to rent a car. Cycling, and – outside the city centre – mountain biking, is a good option too, though you'll need stout legs to tackle those hills.

Points of arrival

The airports

All international and most domestic flights arrive at **San Francisco International Airport** (SFO), about fifteen miles south of the city. Each of the many ways of getting into town from here is clearly signed from the baggage reclaim areas. The least expensive is to take a San Mateo County Transit (*SamTrans*) **bus**, leaving from the lower level of the airport. The #7F express takes around forty minutes to reach downtown but only allows one small piece of hand luggage (every 30min; $1.75); the slower #7B stops everywhere and takes over an hour but allows any amount of baggage (every 30min; 85¢); and a shuttle runs to the Daly City *BART* station (every 20min; 85¢). The **San Francisco Airporter** bus ($8 one-way, $14 return) picks up from outside each baggage claim area every fifteen minutes and travels to Union Square and the Financial District in about forty minutes. The blue **Supershuttle** and the **Yellow Airport Shuttle** minibuses, which cost a little more, can be quicker if you're the first dropoff – they pick up every five minutes from outside the baggage claim area and will take you and up to five other passengers to any city centre destination for around $12–15 per head. Be ruthless, though; competition for these is fierce.

Taxis from the airport cost $30–35 (plus tip) for any downtown location, more for East Bay and Marin County, and are only worth considering if there's more than one of you or you're so tired after a long flight you don't care about the money. If you're planning to drive, there's the usual clutch of **car rental** agencies at the airport. All operate shuttle buses that circle the top departure level of the airport road, and take you to their depot free of charge.

A number of domestic airlines (*America West* and *Continental* are two) fly into **Oakland International Airport** (OAK; see p.143 for details), across the bay. This airport is just as close to downtown San Francisco as SFO, and efficiently connected with the city by the $2 *AirBART* shuttle bus from the Coliseum *BART* station. The third

Bay Area airport, **San Jose *MUNI*cipal** (SJO), also serves domestic arrivals, but is only worth considering if flights into the other two are booked up (see p.168 for more).

By bus and train

All San Francisco's **Greyhound** services use the **Transbay Terminal** at 425 Mission St (☎558-6789), south of Market Street, near the Embarcadero *BART* station; the old Seventh Street Terminal was closed by the 1989 earthquake. **Green Tortoise** buses (☎1-800/227-4766) disembark behind the Transbay Terminal on First and Natoma. **Amtrak** trains stop across the bay in **Richmond** (with easy *BART* transfers) and continue to Oakland, from where free shuttle buses run across the Bay Bridge to the Transbay Terminal.

By car

The main route by car from the East is I-80, which runs via Sacramento all the way from Chicago. The main north–south route through California, I-5, passes by fifty miles east, and is linked to the Bay Area by I-580. US-101 and Hwy-1, the more scenic north–south routes, pass right through downtown San Francisco.

MUNI

The city's public transportation is run by the **San Francisco Municipal Railway**, or *MUNI* (☎673-6864), and is made up of a comprehensive network of **buses**, **trolley buses** and **cable cars**, which run up and over the city's hills, and underground **trains**, which become **streetcars** when they emerge from the downtown metro system to split off and serve the suburbs. On buses and trains there's a flat **fare** of $1; $3 on cable cars. With trains, you must purchase tickets from the machines to get through the barriers before descending to the platforms; on the buses, correct change is required on boarding. *MUNI* Passports are valid for one day and can be used on all *MUNI's* services except the cable cars, and cost $6. Three-day passes are available for $10 and seven-day passes for $15.

If you're staying more than a week and need to rely heavily on public transportation, get a **Fast Pass**, which costs $35 and is valid for unlimited travel on the *MUNI* system and *BART* stations (see below) within the city limits for a full calendar month. Fast Passes are available from most supermarkets and newsagents and all *MUNI* stations.

MUNI trains run **throughout the night** on a limited service, except on the M-Ocean View line,

Useful Bus Routes

#38 from Geary Street via Civic Center, west to the ocean along Geary Boulevard.

#5 From the Transbay Terminal, west along the north side of Golden Gate Park to the ocean.

#7 From the Ferry Terminal (Market St) along Haight Street to the ocean.

#24 From Castro Street north along Divisadero Street to Pacific Heights and Marina.

#37 From Market Street to Twin Peaks.

#30 From the CalTrain depot in SoMa, north to Fisherman's Wharf via the Financial District, Chinatown and North Beach.

#22 From the Mission along Fillmore Street north to Pacific Heights.

#15 From Third Street (SoMa) to Pier 39, Fisherman's Wharf, via the Financial District and North Beach.

#20 (Golden Gate Transit) From Civic Center to the Golden Gate Bridge.

MUNI Train Lines

***MUNI* N-JUDAH LINE** From downtown west to Ocean Beach, via the Haight.

***MUNI* J-CHURCH LINE** From downtown to Mission and East Castro.

***MUNI* L-TARAVAL LINE** From downtown west to the zoo and Ocean Beach.

***MUNI* K-INGLESIDE LINE** From downtown to Balboa Park.

***MUNI* M-OCEAN VIEW** From downtown west to Ocean Beach.

Cable Car Routes

Powell–Hyde from Powell Street along Hyde through Russian Hill to Fisherman's Wharf.

Powell–Mason From Powell Street along Mason via Chinatown and North Beach to Fisherman's Wharf.

California St From the foot of California Street in the Financial District through Nob Hill to Polk Street.

which stops around midnight; buses, too, run all night, again at greatly reduced levels. For **more detailed information** pick up a *MUNI* map ($2) from the Visitor Information Center or bookstores, though it's unlikely that you'll need to be familiar with more than a few of the major bus routes, the most important of which are listed on p.31. See also the route map overleaf, which details all major bus and *MUNI* lines.

Other public transportation services

A number of **other public transportation networks** run into San Francisco, though these are most useful as connections with the rest of the Bay Area. Along Market Street downtown, *MUNI* shares the station concourses with ***BART*** (☎992-*BART*), the Bay Area Rapid Transit system, linking major points in San Francisco with the East Bay and outer suburbs. The **CalTrain** (☎1-800/660-4287) commuter railway (their depot is at Fourth and Townsend streets, South of Market) links San Francisco with points along the Peninsula south to San Jose. **Golden Gate Ferry** (☎923-2000) boats leave from the Ferry Building on the Embarcadero, crossing the bay past Alcatraz to Marin County. For more details see the "Getting Around" sections of the various Bay Area chapters.

Driving – taxis and cars

There are over 3000 **taxis** in San Francisco, though you can often be hard pushed to find one. As in most American cities, they are normally coloured yellow – though there are variants – but don't trawl the streets in San Francisco as they might elsewhere. If you want a cab and you're not in a busy part of town or near a big hotel you'll probably have to telephone: try *Veterans* (☎552-1300) or *Yellowcab* (☎626-2345). Fares work out at approximately $1.90 for the first mile, $1.50 a mile thereafter.

You don't need a **car** to get around San Francisco, but if you're staying some way out from the centre, it can make life easier – especially if you want to see something of the Bay Area while you're here. The only special rules to **driving** in the city are designed to contend with its often very steep gradients; you are obliged to turn your wheels to the kerb when parking on hills. Bear in mind that **driving while intoxicated (DWI)** is a very serious offence. If a police officer smells alcohol on your breath, he/she is entitled to administer a breath, saliva or urine test. If you fail, you'll be locked up with other inebriates in the *drunk tank* of the nearest jail until you sober up. Your case will later be heard by a judge, who can fine you $200 or, in extreme (or repeat) cases, imprison you for thirty days.

It can be maddeningly difficult to find a place to leave the car, but don't lose your cool. **Parking restrictions** in San Francisco are strictly enforced, and traffic officers will cheerfully ticket you in a matter of seconds – which, at an average of $40 per ticket, can get expensive; worse, they'll sometimes tow your car away. A number of **parking lots** in the South of Market industrial area charge $8 per day; more central ramps charge that much per hour. Of these, the best deals are to be had in the multistorey ramp at Sutter and Stockton, and the parking lots under Union Square downtown, under Portsmouth Square in Chinatown, and at Ghirardelli Square near Fisherman's Wharf.

Driving for foreign visitors

UK nationals can **drive** in the US on a full UK driving licence (International Driving Permits are not always regarded as sufficient). Fly-drive deals are good value if you want to **rent** a car (see box), though you can save up to sixty percent simply by booking in advance with a major firm. If you choose not to pay until you arrive, be sure you take a written confirmation of the price with you. Remember that it's safer not to rent a car straight after a long transatlantic flight, and that standard rental cars have **automatic transmissions**.

As for **rules of the road**, you must drive on the right and front-seat passengers must always

Road Conditions

The California Department of Transportation (aka CalTrans) operates a **toll-free 24-hour information line** (☎1-800/427-ROAD) giving up-to-the-minute details of road conditions throughout the state. On a touch-tone phone simply input the number of the road ("5" for I-5, "29" for Hwy-29, etc) and a recorded voice will tell you about any relevant weather conditions, delays, detours and snow closures, etc. From out of state, or without a touch-tone phone, similar information is available on ☎916/445-1534.

Car Rental

Toll-free numbers for the big international **car-rental firms** are listed below; all have outlets at the airport, and compete with bargain rates and special offers. **Unlimited mileage** is fairly standard, so you can plan long trips without fear of punitive mileage rates. Bear in mind that any insurance included in the rental is probably only basic third-party coverage (a legal requirement for all drivers), to cover damage to other vehicles. Read the small print carefully for details on **Collision Damage Waiver (CDW)**, also known as Liability Damage Waiver (LDW), that specifically covers the car you are driving. Although not usually included with the initial rental charge, it is well worth considering. At $9–13 a day, it can add substantially to the total cost, but without it you're liable for every scratch to the car – even those that aren't your fault. Some credit card companies offer automatic CDW coverage to anyone using their card; read the fine print beforehand in any case.

You should also check your **third-party liability**. The standard policy often only covers you for the first $15,000 of the third party's claim against you, a paltry sum in litigation-conscious America. Companies strongly advise taking out third-party insurance, which costs a further $10–12 a day but indemnifies the driver for up to $2,000,000.

Companies are becoming more particular about checking up on the driving records of would-be renters and refusing to rent to high-risk drivers. As a result, it has become increasingly difficult to rent a car unless you are over 25 – rates for people younger than this can go through the roof. If you are tied into any **AirMiles** scheme, check the special offers on car rental, good discounts and special deals are offered by most airlines in conjunction with the major car-rental firms. Prices quoted below are for the smallest compact vehicles, usually always four-door and not that small.

If you **break down** in a rented car, there'll be an emergency number pinned to the dashboard.

San Francisco Offices

Alamo, 687 Folsom St ☎882-9440
Good rates, from $179 per week.

Avis, 675 Post St ☎885-5011
Week-long deals start at around $200.

Dollar, 364 O'Farrell St ☎771-5300
Good rates from $26.95 per day or $149 per week.

Enterprise, 1133 Van Ness Ave ☎441-3369
From $33 per day or $159 per week.

Hertz, 433 Mason St ☎771-2200
Weekly deals from $250.

Reliable, 349 Mason St ☎928-4414
$22 per day.

Thrifty, 520 Mason St ☎788-8111
From $43 per day or $190 per week.

In North America

Alamo ☎1-800/354-2322
Avis ☎1-800/331-1212
Budget ☎1-800/527-0700
Dollar ☎1-800/421-6868
Enterprise ☎1-800/325-8007
Hertz ☎1-800/654-3131
in Canada ☎1-800/263-0600
National ☎1-800/227-7368
Payless ☎1-800/729-5377
Rent-a-Wreck ☎1-800/535-1391
Snappy ☎1-800/669-4800
Thrifty ☎1-800/367-2277
Value ☎1-800/327-2501

In the UK

Alamo ☎0800/272200
Avis ☎0181/848 8733
Budget ☎0800/181181
Dollar (Eurodollar) ☎01895/233300
Hertz ☎0345/555888
Holiday Autos ☎0990/491 1111
National (Europcar/InterRent) ☎0181/300400

In Australia

Avis ☎008/225533
Budget ☎13/2848
Hertz ☎13/1918

In New Zealand

Avis ☎09/525 1982
Budget ☎09/275 2222
Fly and Drive Holidays ☎09/366 0759
Hertz ☎09/309-0989

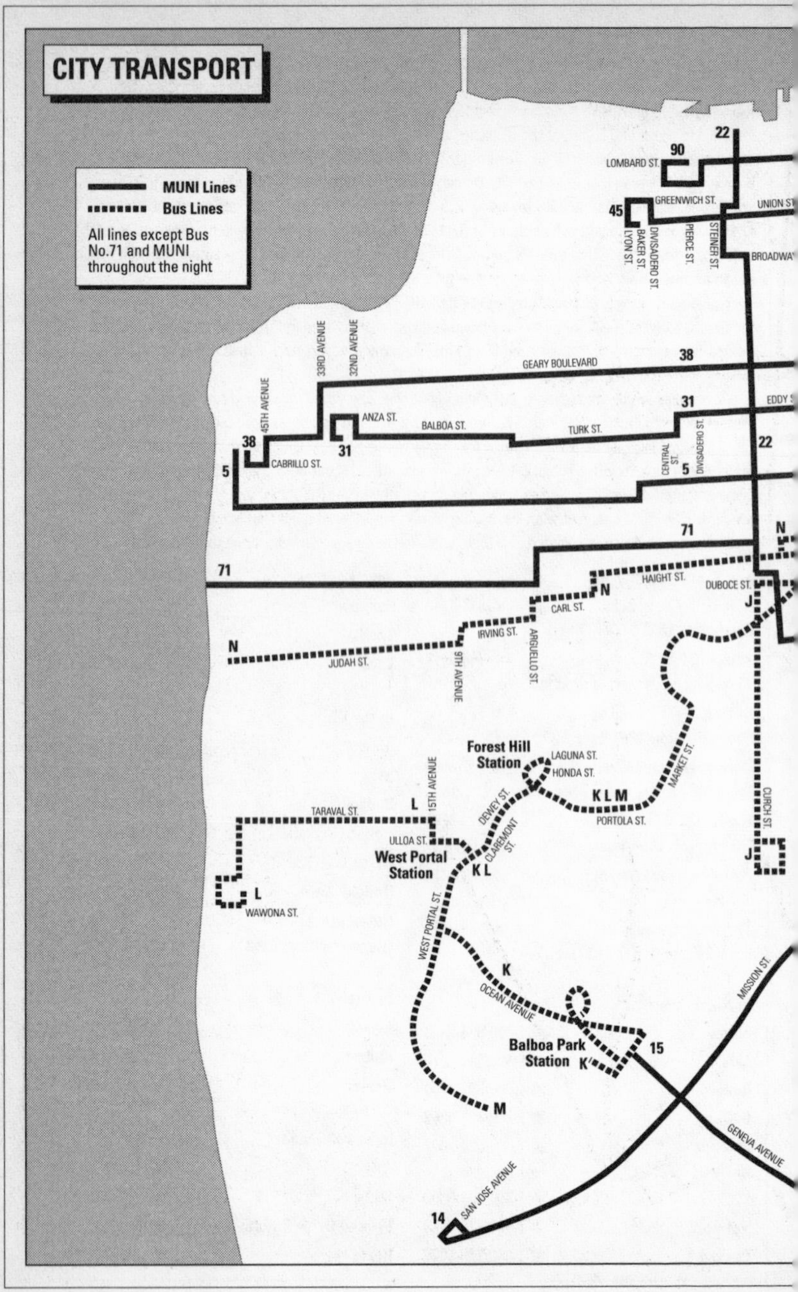

CITY TRANSPORT
MUNI Lines
Bus Lines
All lines except Bus No.71 and MUNI throughout the night
LOMBARD ST.
GREENWICH ST.
UNION ST
BROADWAY
BAKER ST.
LYON ST.
DIVISADERO ST.
PIERCE ST.
STEINER ST.
GEARY BOULEVARD
33RD AVENUE
32ND AVENUE
45TH AVENUE
ANZA ST.
BALBOA ST.
TURK ST.
EDDY ST
CABRILLO ST.
CENTRAL ST.
HAIGHT ST.
DUBOCE ST.
CARL ST.
IRVING ST.
JUDAH ST.
9TH AVENUE
ARGUELLO ST.
Forest Hill Station
LAGUNA ST.
HONDA ST.
MARKET ST.
PORTOLA ST.
CURCH ST.
TARAVAL ST.
15TH AVENUE
ULLOA ST.
DEWEY ST.
CLAREMONT ST.
West Portal Station
WAWONA ST.
WEST PORTAL ST.
OCEAN AVENUE
Balboa Park Station
MISSION ST.
GENEVA AVENUE
SAN JOSE AVENUE

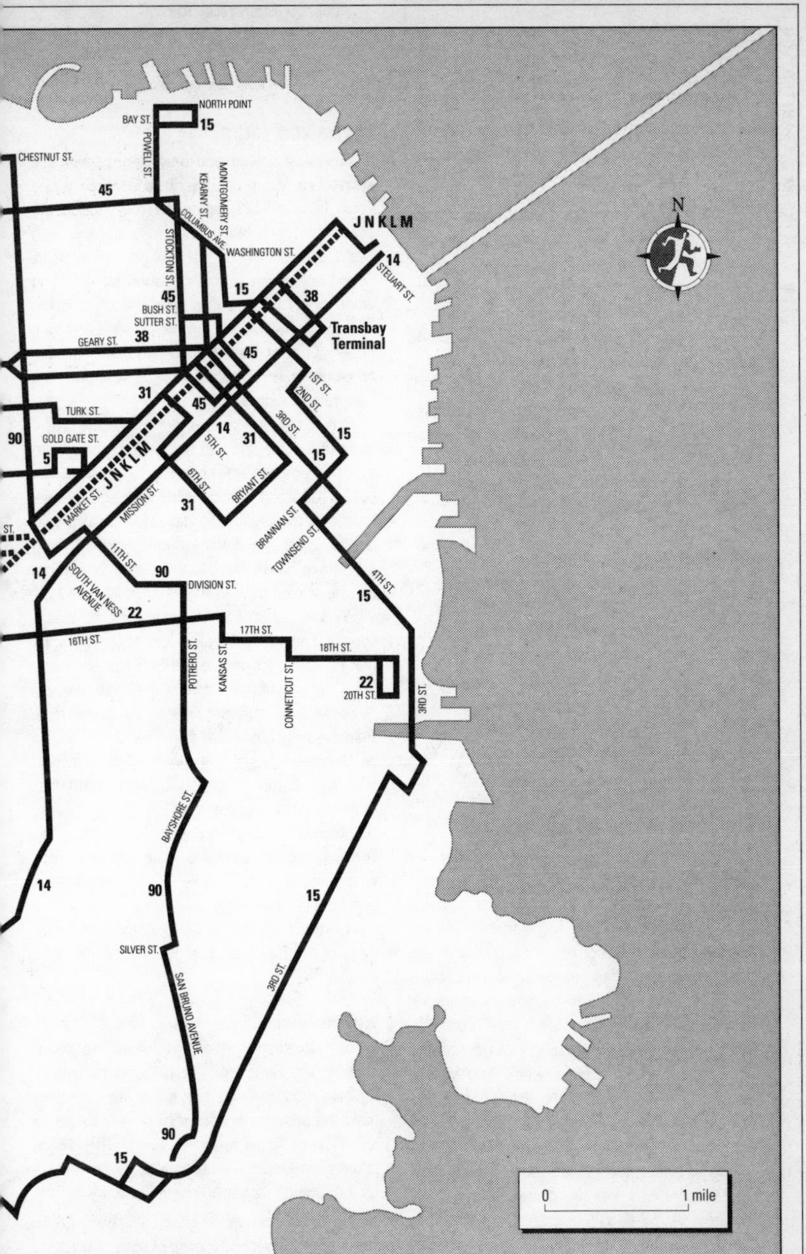
NORTH POINT
BAY ST.
15
POWELL ST.
CHESTNUT ST.
45
MONTGOMERY ST.
KEARNY ST.
COLUMBUS AVE.
STOCKTON ST.
WASHINGTON ST.
JNKLM
14
STEUART ST.
N
15
38
45
BUSH ST.
SUTTER ST.
Transbay Terminal
GEARY ST.
38
45
1ST ST.
2ND ST.
31
45
TURK ST.
3RD ST.
14
31
15
90
GOLD GATE ST.
5TH ST.
15
5
JNKLM
6TH ST.
BRYANT ST.
MARKET ST.
MISSION ST.
31
BRANNAN ST.
ST.
TOWNSEND ST.
11TH ST.
14
90
DIVISION ST.
4TH ST.
SOUTH VAN NESS AVENUE
15
22
16TH ST.
17TH ST.
18TH ST.
POTRERO ST.
KANSAS ST.
CONNETICUT ST.
22
20TH ST.
3RD ST.
BAYSHORE ST.
14
90
15
SILVER ST.
SAN BRUNO AVENUE
3RD ST.
90
15
0
1 mile

Hitching

The usual advice given to **hitchhikers** is that they should use their common sense; in fact, of course, common sense should tell anyone that hitchhiking in the US is a **bad idea**. We do not recommend it under any circumstances.

wear seat belts. There are several **types of road** – the wide, straight and fast **Interstate Highways** (prefixed "I"); **State Highways** (ie Hwy-1); and **US Highways** (ie US-101) – though in San Francisco and the more built-up parts of the Bay Area most roads are better known by their local name. Hwy-1, for instance, is known as 19th Avenue. The speed limit in the city and other built-up areas is 30–35 mph; otherwise, it's a maximum of 55–70mph, depending on the highway or interstate. Keep an eye on signposted limits – there are no **spot fines**, but if given a **speeding** ticket, reckon on a fine of at least $75.

Driveaways

One variation on renting is a **driveaway**, whereby you drive a car from one place to another on behalf of the owner, paying only for the gas you use. The same rules as for renting apply, but look the car over before you take it, as you'll be lumbered with any repair costs, and a large fuel bill if the vehicle's a big drinker. The most common routes are between California and New York, although there's a fair chance you'll find something that needs shifting up the coast, from Los Angeles to San Francisco. See p.13 for further details.

Cycling

In general, **cycling** is a cheap and healthy method of getting around San Francisco and the Bay Area, some parts of which have cycle lanes; local buses are often equipped to carry bikes strapped to the outside. In **country areas**, there's much scenic, and largely level, land, especially around the Wine Country. Bikes can be **rented** for $25 a day, $70–100 a week, from outlets usually found close to beaches, university campuses or simply in areas which are good for cycling; see the appropriate sections of the *Guide*, or contact local visitor centers. Good-value city rental shops include **Waller Sports** (1749 Waller St ☎752-8383); which provides mountain bikes for $12 per hour, $25 a day, and offers weekly rates from $120.

Dubbelju Motorcycle Rentals (271 Clara St, ☎495-2274) can help you realize your *Easy Rider* fantasies by renting you BMW or Harley Davidson bikes from around $75 per day.

Organized tours

If you've just arrived, you may want to orientate yourself by taking an **organized tour**. *Gray Line Tours* (☎558-9400) will whip you around the city in three fairly tedious hours, stopping at Twin Peaks and Cliff House, for around $26 a head. Skip it unless you're really pushed for time and want to get a general idea of the city's layout with minimal effort. For a more personalized tour, *Roger's Custom Tours* (☎742-9611) offer private or group tours to places that interest you and start from around $25.

Excruciatingly expensive but spectacular **aerial tours** of the city and Bay Area in light aircraft are available from several operators. *Bay Aero Tours* (☎207-0044) offer good-value spectacular aerial tours over the city for $55 per person with a third person going for free, including pick-up from downtown hotels. More exciting aerial opportunities are offered by *Mile High Airlines* (☎510/713-2359) who specialize in fantasy flights where couples can enjoy "privacy and elegance while making love high above the San Francisco Bay Area". You might prefer one of the more leisurely two-hour **bay cruises** operated by the *Blue & Gold Fleet* (☎705-5444) from Pier 39 for $15 – be warned, though, that famous San Francisco fogs may shroud the sights. A cheesy, but rather romantic, way to see the Bay is to take a *Hornblower Dining Cruise*, Pier 33, The Embarcadero (☎788-8866), who take you for a whiz around the bay while you eat dinner and enjoy the on-board entertainment.

For **tours of the Wine Country and other parts of the Bay Area**, see the relevant Bay Area chapters.

Walking tours

Various excellent personalized **walking tours** explore San Francisco. The better ones usually have no more than five to a group and can often make an informative and efficient way to get to know a particular area of town. The Visitor Information Center will be able to give you a full list, but among those you might like to try are:

All About Chinatown, 812 Clay St; ☎982-8839. Three-hour tours conducted by Chinatown native Linda Lee: includes all the sights, history and anecdotes you can absorb, as well as a dim sum lunch, all for $35.

City Guides, ☎557-4266. The most extensive range of guided walks, sponsored by the San Francisco Public Library and all free.

Cruisin' the Castro, 375 Lexington St; ☎550-8110. The Supreme Champion of the walking tour circuit in San Francisco, Trevor Hailey, a resident of San Francisco's gay community for fifteen years, takes you on a fascinating tour of this small area. Her knowledge includes everything from politics to the best parties and she embellishes her three-and-a-half-hour tour with funny stories. $25 per person includes breakfast. Worth every cent.

Flower Power Haight-Ashbury Tour, 520 Shrader St; ☎221-8442. Relive the Summer of Love, see where the Grateful Dead used to live and hear endless stories of the exploits of San Francisco's most notorious period in modern history. An enjoyable, non-gruelling two-hour tour that comes packed with recommendations about where to eat, drink and have fun in the Haight.

Friends of Recreation and Parks, MacLaren Lodge, Stanyan and Fell streets; ☎221-1311. Tour Golden Gate Park with trained guides pointing out the park's flora, fauna and history. Free guided tours every weekend rain or shine – call for meeting times.

Helen's Walk Tour: ☎510/524-4544. Helen Rendon, a four-feet-ten-inch dynamo, specializes in personalized tours and uses her extensive knowledge of the city to reveal to you the areas that are of particular interest.

Javawalk, 1899 California St; ☎674-WALK. An insider's guide to the city's coffee-house culture which starts in Union Square and winds through Chinatown and Jackson Square and ends in the coffee houses of North Beach. Tour takes two hours and costs $15.

Travelling with children

Visiting San Francisco with your kids is no more difficult than in any major city, but parents need to be aware that away from the major sights this is very much a place for adults – more so than, say, LA – and there aren't many things to occupy young ones. Mercifully, there is always something that children will want to eat – burgers, hot dogs, french fries and ice cream are in abundance. Hotels are more of a worry; only the larger (and more expensive) establishments will have facilities and play areas for children.

Activities

Of San Francisco's few specifically child-oriented attractions – all of which are listed in the relevant chapters of this book – the *Exploratorium* in the Marina District is excellent, as is the *Steinhart Aquarium* in Golden Gate Park, and the *Lawrence Hall of Science* in Berkeley will captivate any young mind. Pier 39 at Fisherman's Wharf is always good for children with its sea lions, giant aquarium and the *San Francisco Experience* (☎983-1394) which has a thirty-minute widescreen multimedia extravaganza that recreates the earthquakes of 1906 and 1989. For more organized distractions, try the *Great America* amusement park in San Jose, or the animal-themed *Marine World/Africa USA* in Vallejo, accessible by transbay ferry. Young children will enjoy the *San Francisco International Toy Museum*, at 2801 Leavenworth St in the Cannery. It's a wonderland of building toys, stuffed animals, dolls, trains and 100,000 pieces of *Lego* that the children are encouraged to play with and, best of all, that you don't have to clear up afterwards. For general child entertainment, the **Golden Gate Park** is your best bet. As well as the aforementioned *Steinhart Aquarium*, it holds the *Children's Playground* located on the Lincoln Avenue side of the park, which has the standard swings and climbing frames, and features the slide with the fastest ride in the West. Other traditional forms of amusement include the **San Francisco Zoo** (see p.134), where children can enjoy such hands-on exhibits as petting tarantulas and feeding the big cats. Finally, if you want to take your children on a **boat ride**, the best value is the *Golden Gate Ferry* to Larkspur or Sausalito, which departs from the Ferry Building at the foot of Market Street; children can ride for around $3. Slightly older, technology-enthusiastic children will get a kick out of *Cybermind*, the Virtual Reality Video Center on the second floor of the Embarcadero One building (☎693-0348).

Getting around

On most international and domestic routes, children less than two years old are classified as "lap children". Provided they stay on your lap, they can fly for free. Discounts of up to fifty percent apply to children below the age of twelve, but over that the full standard fare is applicable.

For travelling around the city, the ***MUNI*** system is by and large clean, efficient and safe, and children travel for a fraction of the cost of an adult ticket. If you want to travel beyond the city limits it is usually easier to bundle children into a **car**.

Gay and lesbian San Francisco

San Francisco's reputation as a city for gay celebration is not new. This is the most "out" city in the world and its gay community is both respected and the wielder of considerable economic and political power. It is claimed that no politician in San Francisco can survive without the gay vote. In the face of a massive AIDS crisis, San Francisco got smart and lobbied hard for health care and research. A staggering death-toll of over 100,000 and rising has led to a vigorous defence of the gay community, uniting the often disparate worlds of lesbian and gay culture. The exuberant energy that went into the posturing and parading of the 1970s has taken on a much more sober, down-to-business attitude, and these days you'll find as many political activists organizing conferences as drag queens throwing parties. Things have changed and, despite the tragedy of AIDS, much of it for the better – discrimination has waned in the face of consistent gay-awareness campaigns, and education and research about HIV is second to none on this earth.

From its beginnings as a Gold Rush town, when scores of men unaccompanied by their womenfolk came to San Francisco, an exclusively male culture has, not surprisingly, thrived. More significantly, the 1940s saw a big increase in the gay population, when a military purge of homosexual soldiers resulted in several thousand – who were serving in the South Pacific – being booted out at San Francisco. Unable to return home with the stigma and shame of their expulsion, many stayed. Since that time gays have been coming here to make their homes away from the prejudice and isolation of the rest of the US, much of which still hasn't changed a great deal – 23 states still outlaw homosexuality, with penalties ranging from a $200 fine in Texas to twenty years' imprisonment in Georgia. San Francisco is still America's most liberal city for gay men *and* women, who, it's true to say, can genuinely enjoy their sexuality openly and without fear. The moral backlash provoked by AIDS in other parts of the world, never really got a foothold in San Francisco – the basic principles of tolerance and support endure and have even, in some senses, been reinforced. It's inter-

Specifically **gay accommodation** is listed on p.217, the best of San Francisco's **gay and lesbian bars and clubs** are detailed under the relevant sections of the "Listings".

esting to note that on the same day the homophobic "Clause 28" bill was being rushed through Parliament in Britain, San Francisco's former mayor, Art Agnos, rode through the streets of San Francisco in support of the Gay and Lesbian Freedom Day Parade. The annual parade in June draws in excess of half a million people a year and is the largest queer pride event in the world.

Certainly, post-AIDS, San Francisco's gay scene is a different way of life altogether. The 1970s were notorious for the bar and bathhouse culture and the busy and often anonymous promiscuity which went with it, but this toned down abruptly when AIDS first became a problem in the early 1980s. This wasn't a foregone conclusion by any means. Many men saw the closure of the bathhouses as an infringement on their civil liberties and the gay community has become a much more politicized grouping, directing its energies towards fund-raising and programmes for AIDS patients.

Socially, San Francisco's gay scene has also mellowed, though in what is an increasingly conservative climate in the city generally, gay parties, parades and street fairs still swing better than most. Like any well-organized section of society, the gay scene definitely has its social season, and if you're here in June, you'll coincide with the Gay and Lesbian Film Festival, Gay Pride Week, the Gay Freedom Day Parade and any number of conferences. Come October, the street fairs are in full swing and Halloween still sees some of the most outrageous carrying-on.

Though the 1980s saw the flowering of a **lesbian** culture to rival the male 1970s upsurge, by the early 1990s not a single women's bar remained. The explanation may lie in the words of one lesbian bartender, "All the dykes have dried out, honey!". Sobriety has been a keen gay issue (in keeping with California society in general) since the advent of AIDS, and is supposed to represent the much-vaunted new

Gay Contacts and Resources

AIDS Hotline ☎863-2437
24-hour information and counselling.

Bay Area Bisexual Network ☎703-7977
Umbrella group and clearing house of information for bisexuals. Publishes a magazine, *Anything That Moves.*

Bisexual Resource Line ☎703-7977
Bisexual networks and information.

Dignity ☎681-2491
133 Golden Gate Ave; Catholic worship and services.

Femme to Femme ☎510/687-1473 ext 2
An events network that celebrates feminine women.

Gay Cocaine Counselling Service ☎1-800/262-2463

Gay and Lesbian Legal Referral Services ☎621-3900
PO Box 1983 SF, enquiries regarding legal problems and legal representation.

How About Lunch ☎281-5845
Introduction service offered by the Lesbian/Gay Switchboard.

Lesbian/Gay Switchboard ☎510/841-6224
24-hour counselling and advice. Contacts and activities referral service.

Gay Men's Therapy Center ☎673-1160
How to cope with AIDS issues and fears, grief counselling, etc.

Gay Therapy Center ☎558-8828
3393 Market St; counselling and help with coming out.

SF AIDS Foundation ☎487-8000
10 United Nations Plaza, in the 1100 block of Market. Major fund-raiser and organizer of support groups.

San Francisco Sex Information ☎989-7374
Gay and lesbian issues, HIV and health, anything you want to talk about (Mon–Fri 3–9pm).

Shanti Project ☎777-1162
525 Howard St; AIDS support group that offers care of PWAs, advice, testing and counselling.

SOL (Slightly Older Lesbians) ☎510/841-6224
Pacific Center, 2712 Telegraph Ave, Berkeley, CA 94705; drop-in group meets Thurs 7.30–9.45pm.

personal responsibility ethic. Fortunately, at exclusively female club nights around the city – which have flowered exponentially in the 1990s – good-humoured lesbians can still be found drinking, dancing and carousing into the small hours (see p.264).

Neighbourhoods and publications

Traditionally, *the* area for gay men has been the **Castro**, together with a few bars and clubs around **SoMa** – though gay life these days is much less ghettoized and there are bars and clubs all over town. Rent boys and pimps prowl **Polk Street**, not the safest area at 2am, but hardly a danger zone if you use common sense. Lesbian interests are more concentrated in the East Bay than the city, although women's activities thrive in the **Mission**.

New clubs and groups spring up all the time and you should keep an ear to the ground as well as referring to the many free gay publications available: *Coming Up, the Bay Area Reporter* and *Bay Times* all give listings of events, services, clubs and bars in the city and Bay Area. Two slightly racier, off-the-wall publications to look out for are *Oddysey* and *Oblivion,* also free and found in bars and cafés around the city. Women should also keep an eye out in bookstores for *On Our Backs* and *Bad Attitude*, two magazines that often have useful pointers to lesbian organizations in town. Also useful for both men and women is *The Gay Book*, a telephone-cum-resource book that's available in gay bookstores. For a complete gay guide, you might try *Damron's Address Book* (PO Box 422458, San Francisco, CA 94142; ☎1-800/462-6654 or 255-0404), and the *Women's Traveller*, again available from gay bookstores, which has complete listings of gay accommodation, bars, clubs and stores in California; the *Women's Traveller* provides similar listings for lesbians. But for something outrageous, you should get a copy of *Betty & Pansy's Severe Queer Review*, $10.95, from gay bookstores, a cult publication that pulls no punches in its assessments of San Francisco gay entertainment – hysterically funny and frank. *Out & About Inc.* (8 W 19th St, Suite 401, New York, NY 10011; ☎212/645-6922; e-mail: outndabout@aol.com.) is a privately printed resource for lesbian and gay travellers, giving very useful information free from advertising bias.

Women's San Francisco

In contrast to the hostility you can experience in urban centres such as New York or Los Angeles, San Francisco has a friendly, non-threatening atmosphere that is particularly reassuring for travellers who are new to the city. Like any major city, it does of course have its trouble spots, but as these places have nothing you'd particularly want to see anyway, there is no need for undue caution.

Women in particular enjoy San Francisco; in the West Coast's most progressive city, women are treated with respect and courtesy almost everywhere and commonly hold positions of power and authority. The gains of the last twenty years are considerable and visible. San Francisco's large lesbian community is further

Specific **accommodation** options for women are listed on p.218.

proof that backward attitudes are hard to come by. Naturally, common sense still applies; look as if you know where you are going, take taxis at night and **never** hitch – women travelling alone are not at all unusual but the successful ones learn to deal with any harassment firmly and loudly. Rape statistics are high and, while there is more chance of being mugged than raped, you may feel safer if you carry whistles, gas and sprays; useless in the event of real trouble but a confidence booster that can ward off creeps.

The flip side of San Francisco's gay revolution has, in some women's circles, led to a separatist culture, and women's resources and services are sometimes lumped together under the lesbian category. While this may be no bad thing, it can be hard to tell which organizations exist irrespective of sexuality. Don't let this stop you from checking out anything that sounds interesting, especially with regard to the bars and clubs in the gay and lesbian sections of the "Listings". Nobody is going to refuse you either entry or help if you're not a lesbian; support is given to anybody who needs it. Similarly, women's health care is very well provided for in San Francisco and there are numerous clinics you can go to for routine gynecological and contraceptive services. Payment is usually on a sliding scale according to income, but even if you're flat broke, you won't be refused treatment.

Women's Contacts and Resources

Bay Area Resource Center
318 Leavenworth St ☎474-2400
Services, information and clothing.

Lyon-Martin
1748 Market St ☎565-7667
Sliding scale for general and gynecological treatment.

Osento
955 Valencia ☎282-6333
The heart of SF's women's community – a bathhouse where everyone gets their kit off and has a good chat.

Planned Parenthood
Clinics at:
Civic Center, 815 Eddy St ☎441-5454
Financial District,
222 Front St ☎765-6905
Birth control and general gynecological services.

Radical Women
523a Valencia St ☎864-1278
Socialist-feminist organization dedicated to building women's leadership and achieving full equality. Meetings held on the second and fourth Tuesday of each month.

Rape Crisis Line ☎647-RAPE
24-hour switchboard.

Women's Building
3543 18th St ☎431-1180
Central stop in the Mission for women's art and political events. A very good place to get information also – the women who staff the building are happy to deal with the most obscure of enquiries. Don't be afraid to ask.

Women's Needs Center
1825 Haight St ☎487-5607
Low-cost health care and referral service.

Festivals and holidays

Someone is always celebrating something in San Francisco, and, while many of these are uniquely local affairs, most have their roots in the ethnic or national holidays of other countries, highlighting the region's diverse background. Street fairs and block parties take place all over the city throughout the summer months and, at the bigger events, like the Chinese New Year parade in February or Gay Freedom Day in June, it seems as if the entire city is joining in.

Festivals

The first big event in San Francisco's festival season is the **Chinese New Year** celebration, usually at the end of January or early February, depending on the Chinese calendar. A week of low-key activities in and around Chinatown culminates in the Golden Dragon Parade, in which hundreds of people march through downtown leading a 75-foot-long dragon. To find out more, contact the *Chinatown Chamber of Commerce*, (730 Sacramento St; ☎982-3000).

A month later, on March 17, the whole city dresses up in emerald hues to celebrate **St Patrick's Day**, which is marked by excessive consumption of green-tinted beer and by a lengthy parade through downtown. The Shannon Arms (915 Taraval; ☎665-1223) is a relatively unknown dive packed shoulder to shoulder with many of SF's Irish.

Other celebrations continue the international flavour, starting with late April's low-key **Cherry Blossom Festival** in Japantown and picking up steam around the **Cinco de Mayo**, celebrating the Mexican victory at the battle of Puebla with a 48-hour party in the Mission over the weekend nearest to May 5.

June is the biggest party month, with the boisterous, music- and fun-filled **Festival on the Lake** on Oakland's Lake Merritt, followed by numerous San Francisco **street fairs** – the **North Beach Fair** and the **Haight Street Fair** to name two of the biggest – and the lively **Carnaval** happenings in the Mission. The month's main event is the **Lesbian and Gay Freedom Day Parade**, held in June, when crowds of up to a half a million pack Market Street for the city's biggest parade and party. The bands and dancers converge on City Hall afterwards for a giant block party, with outdoor discos, live bands and numerous craft and food stands.

Apart from the **4th of July** fireworks at Crissy Field in the Presidio, for the rest of the year the streets are comparatively quiet, except of course for the city's predominantly gay areas – the **Polk Street Fair** at the end of July, for example, which brings out the black leather brigades. Many of these celebrants resurface for the end-of-summer **Castro Street Fair**, early in October, and at the end of the month when there's one last burst of pre-winter activity on **Halloween** (October 31). Locals dress up and strut their stuff, promenading from bar to bar. Halloween also provides the basis for one of the Bay Area's most unexpected events, the **Pumpkin Festival** in Half Moon Bay, when local farmers open their fields to jack-o'-lantern hunters and host a range of pumpkin-based cooking and eating competitions. Usually held over the fourth weekend of September at Fort Mason is the **San Francisco Blues Festival** featuring local and national acts. Finally, before the city gears up for the Christmas celebrations, **Mexico's Day of the Dead** is celebrated on the first Thursday of November in the Mission, where people costumed to look like skeletons parade the streets.

Public holidays

Banks and offices, and many but not all stores, will be closed for the full day on the following **public holidays**:

January 1 **New Year's Day**

January 15 **Martin Luther King Jr's Birthday**

Third Monday in February **Presidents' Day**

Easter Monday

Last Monday in May **Memorial Day**

July 4 **Independence Day**

First Monday in September **Labor Day**

Second Monday in October **Columbus Day**

November 11 **Veterans' Day**

Fourth Thursday in November **Thanksgiving Day**

December 25 **Christmas Day**

The media

San Francisco is a bit of a media backwater compared to Los Angeles or New York City, but what it lacks in high-power status it makes up with in-depth coverage of local news and features. The provincialism of its daily newspapers – about half the stories in the main *San Francisco Chronicle* are straight reprints from other US papers – is a continual source of embarrassment, but there are dozens of free weekly newspapers, focusing in on the city or parts of the Bay Area, that are informative and entertaining. San Francisco's television is much the same as anywhere else in America, but the city's radio stations are excellent, offering an amazing range of music, the best of which is commercial-free, 24 hours a day.

Newspapers

San Francisco's major **daily newspapers** are the *San Francisco Chronicle* (50¢) in the morning and, in the afternoon, the revamped *San Francisco Examiner* (25¢), which made great efforts to capture the liberal market with in-depth reporting and, in the case of Hunter S. Thompson, some controversial columnists, but there are rumours that it may fold anyway. On Sundays the two papers are published as a very large combined edition ($1), most of which can be discarded, with the exception of the very useful "Datebook" (also known as the "Pink Pages") which gives detailed listings of arts, clubs, films and forthcoming events. Perhaps the best daily paper for straight coverage of local, national and international events is the *San Jose Mercury-News* (35¢), based in the Silicon Valley but available all over the Bay Area.

There's also an abundance of **free publications**, led by the *San Francisco Bay Guardian*, which has 100 pages of lively reporting and invaluable listings every week. Other San Francisco freesheets to look out for (cafés and record stores are likely places) include the *SF Weekly* and the lesbian, gay and bisexual-orientated *Bay Times*, which has tons of listings and the best personal ads.

For listings of what's on in lively Oakland and Berkeley, and yet more voyeuristically interesting personal ads, the weekly *East Bay Express* is unsurpassed, while the Berkeley-based *Poetry Flash* has details of poetry readings, workshops and other literary events. If you're interested in more active pursuits, the monthly *City Sports* has rundowns of upcoming running and cycling and similar events in the Bay Area. There are dozens more locally based newspapers throughout the Bay Area, available at cafés, newsstands and some bookshops.

Television

San Francisco **TV** is pretty much the standard network barrage, frequently interrupted by hard-sell commercials. Game shows and talk shows fill up most of the morning schedule until lunchtime, when you can take your pick of any of a dozen daily soaps. Most hotels provide access to **cable networks** such as CNN, the round-the-clock news channel, and the mainstream pop of MTV.

San Francisco TV

2 KTVU Fox	7 KGO ABC
4 KRON NBC	9 KQED PBS
5 KPIX CBS	

Radio

Bay Area **radio**, in contrast, is probably the best in the US, with some eighty stations catering to just about every conceivable taste. **AM** stations tend to be either all news, chat and phone-in shows or shit-kicking c'n'w tunes for truckers. A better option is the **FM** band, which is broadcast in stereo. The bulk of these stations are commercial, but by far the best are the dozen non-commercial stations, located at the far left end of the radio dial (88–92 FM). Most of these are affiliated with a college or university, and in the main their programming is anarchically varied, from in-depth current affairs discussions to mind-boggling industrial thrash.

San Francisco Radio

KSFO 560 AM Oldies music and Bay Area sporting events.

KCBS 740 AM News, talk shows and excellent commentaries.

KGO 810 AM News, and the most intense talk shows.

KNEW 910 AM Country and western music.

KQED 88.5 FM Classical music, talk, community affairs.

KPOO 89.5 FM Community-based radio – blues, reggae, soul.

KUSF 90.3 FM Excellent college station with rock, news and offbeat issues.

KALX 90.7 FM Voted best US college station most years for its blend of anything-but-mainstream rock and reggae, though the UC Berkeley-based signal rarely makes it across the bay.

KCSM 91.1 FM Diverse but consistently high-quality programming, especially good for late-night jazz.

KPFA 94.1 FM Long-running, listener-supported station known for its in-depth investigative reporting as well as arts programmes.

KSAN 94.9 FM Modern country and western music.

KRQR 97.3 FM Album rock.

KSOL 98.9 FM Soul and mellow dance music.

KBLX 102.9 FM "The Quiet Storm": soul, jazz and lots of house.

104.1 FM Free Radio Berkeley. Pirate radio featuring political talk shows and independent, non-programmed music.

KFOG 104.5 FM Best of the rock stations with lots of oldies and the best of newies.

KITS 105.3 FM "Live 105": popular modern rock/pop station.

KMEL 106.1 FM Soul, house. Very funky.

KKHI 100.7 FM Classical music.

KYLD 107.7 "Wild 107" is the source for dance and rap music.

Directory for overseas visitors

ADDRESSES When pinpointing an **address** verbally, to a cab driver or when giving directions, San Franciscans always give the crossroad rather than the number (ie Valencia and 18th), and you'd do well to follow their example. You may, however, see numbered addresses written down (in this *Guide*, for example), in which case there is a formula for working out where it is on the city's very long thoroughfares. All streets work on blocks of 100 from their downtown source, which on north–south streets is Market Street, on east–west streets it is either Market Street or, above here, the Embarcadero. For example, 950 Powell Street is on the tenth block of Powell north of Market; 1450 Post Street is on the fifteenth block of Post west of Market; 220 Castro Street is on the third block of Castro south of Market. Unlike many American cities, most streets have names rather than numbers, the only grid of numbered streets being that radiating into the docks area south of Market. Further out from downtown, in the Richmond and Sunset, the avenues all have their origin at the foot of the Presidio and travel south in increasing blocks of 100.

AIDS FOUNDATION TRILINGUAL HOTLINE ☎1-800/FOR-AIDS.

AIRPORT TAX $6–14, depending on the airline, but always included in the price of your ticket.

APARTMENT HUNTING If you decide that you love San Francisco so much that you can't leave, be reassured that looking for somewhere to live is not the nightmare it is in New York or London: rented accommodation is plentiful but not cheap – the absence of housing associations and co-ops means that there is very little really cheap accommodation anywhere. Accommodation is almost always rented unfurnished, so you'll have to buy furniture. In general, expect to pay $600–700 a month for a studio apartment in the cheaper parts of town, $800–900 for somewhere a bit smarter. One bedroom apartments range from $850 to $1400 depending on where you want to live. two or three bedrooms will set you back upwards of $1500, again depending on your neighbourhood. Shared housing is a more affordable solution and roommate ads abound in the local press. Most landlords expect one month's rent as a deposit, plus one month in advance. Utilities, such as gas and electricity, are all charged monthly. To find a place, scour the *San Francisco Chronicle*, or, more usefully, the many free papers such as the *Bay Guardian* or the *East Bay Express* – and, for women, *Bay Area Women's News*. **Housing agencies** require two weeks' rent as a finding-fee.

BABY-SITTING *Bay Area Babysitting Agency* ☎991-7474.

CIGARETTES AND SMOKING Cigarettes are sold in virtually any food store, drugstore or bar, and are also available from vending machines on the outside walls of these establishments. A packet of twenty costs around $2 – much cheaper than in Britain – though most smokers buy cigarettes by the carton for around $17. You should be aware that smoking tobacco is greatly frowned upon in San Francisco: all movie houses, theatres and even restaurants are non-smoking. Smoking is universally forbidden on public transportation and in elevators.

CITY CLINIC 356 Seventh St ☎487-5500. STD testing $10 a visit.

CONSULATES See p.17.

DATES Are written month/date/year, so in the American style, 1/8/96; means January 8, not August 1.

DENTISTS Contact the *Dental Society Referral Service* ☎421-1435.

DRUG CRISIS LINE ☎362-3400.

DRUGS Possession of under an ounce of the widely consumed marijuana is a non-criminal offence in California, and the worst you'll get is a $200 fine. Being caught with more than an ounce, however, means facing a criminal charge for dealing, and a possible prison sentence. Other drugs are, of course, completely illegal and it's a much more serious offence if you're caught with any. Of the most widespread, crack and PCP ("angel dust") are confined to ghetto areas and the only contact you'll have with them will be if an addict tries to rob or kill you (statistically improbable). Ordinary cocaine, by contrast, is still the drug of the rich, though the sharp decrease in its street price means it's much more prevalent than it was. The fad for designer drugs such as Ecstasy continues unabated and there are now even legal, so-called herbal substitutes around, though side effects are common to all.

ELECTRICITY 110V AC. All plugs are two-pronged and rather insubstantial. Some travel plug adapters don't fit American sockets.

EMERGENCIES Dial ☎911 for police, fire or ambulance services.

FLOORS The *first* floor in the US is what would be the ground floor in Britain; the *second* floor would be the first floor, and so on.

ID Should be carried at all times. Two pieces of identification should diffuse any suspicion, one of which should have a photo: driving licence, passport and credit card are your best bets.

LAUNDRY All but the most basic hotels do laundry; a wash and dry in a laundromat costs a lot less (about $1.50). *Brainwash,* 1122 Folsom St in SoMa, is a combo bar-and-laundromat: not a bad way to pass the time.

LEGAL ADVICE *Lawyer Referral Service* ☎764-1616.

MEASUREMENTS AND SIZES The US has yet to go metric, so measurements are in inches, feet, yards and miles; weight in ounces, pounds and tons. American pints and gallons are about four-fifths of imperial ones. Clothing sizes are always two figures less than what they would be in Britain – a British women's size 12 is a US size 10 – while British shoe sizes are one and a half below American ones.

PHARMACIES *Walgreen's,* 498 Castro St ☎861-6276, is open 24 hours every day.

POISON CONTROL ☎1-800/523-2222.

PUBLIC TOILETS There are no public toilets as such, although there is a French-style public toilet on Market Street. Bars, and to a lesser extent restaurants and fast food outlets, are your best bets, although technically you should be a customer. If you're desperate, department stores all have rather smart lavatories.

SEX INFORMATION LINE ☎989-7374. Mon–Fri 9am-9pm.

SEXUALLY TRANSMITTED DISEASE (STD) HOTLINE ☎1-800/227-8922.

SUICIDE PREVENTION ☎781-0500.

TAX Be warned that sales tax is added to virtually everything you buy in a store, but isn't part of the marked price. In San Francisco sales tax is 8.5 percent, East Bay 8.25 percent, Marin County 7.25 percent. Hotel tax will add 12 percent on to your bill.

TEMPERATURES Always given in Fahrenheit.

TICKETS For music, theatre, sports and camping reservations, use a charge-by-phone agency, such as *BASS* ☎776-1999. For half-price theatre tickets, try the *Tix Bay Area* booth on the Stockton Street side of Union Square ☎433-7827.

TIME The West Coast runs on Pacific Standard Time (PST), eight hours behind GMT in winter and three hours behind the East Coast. British Summer Time runs almost concurrent with US Daylight Saving Time – implemented between the last Sunday in April and the last Sunday in October – though there's a seven-hour time difference for two weeks of the year.

TIPPING Many first-time visitors to the US think of tipping as a potential source of huge embarrassment. It's nothing of the sort; tipping is universally expected, and you quickly learn to tip without a second thought. You really shouldn't depart a bar or restaurant without leaving a tip of *at least* 15 percent (unless the service is absolutely terrible). The whole system of service is predicated on tipping; not to do so causes a great deal of resentment, and will result in a short pay packet for the waiter or waitress at the end of the week. About the same amount should be added to taxi fares – and round them up to the nearest 50¢ or dollar. A hotel porter who has lugged your suitcases up several flights of stairs should get $3 to $5. When paying by credit or charge card, you're expected to add the tip to the total bill before filling in the amount and signing.

TRAVEL AGENTS *Council Travel,* 530 Bush St, Suite 700 ☎415/421-3473, and 2486 Channing Way, Berkeley ☎848-8604; *STA Travel,* 51 Grant St, ☎391-8407.

VIDEOS The standard format used for video cassettes in the US is different from that used in Britain. Recorded videos bought in the US are not compatible with video players bought in Britain, though blank tapes will work in video cameras.

The City

SAINT BENEDICT SCHOOL
DUFFIELD ROAD
DERBY DE22 1JD

Chapter 1

Introducing The City

Surrounded by the shimmering waters of the Bay, San Francisco's land mass is packed onto and around the four dozen steep hills which give the city its unique and beautiful setting. More than this, its hills serve as useful markers between San Francisco's shifting moods and, more significantly, its class distinctions. As a rule of thumb, the higher up you live, the more coveted your property will be and the better off you are. Commercial square-footage is thoughtfully confined to downtown areas, which is key to the city's appeal. San Francisco's charm is borne out of its residential nature, making it a world-class city that people actually want to live in.

Surprisingly, San Francisco's often dramatic undulations were not taken into account when its streets were laid out. Oblivious to topography, they follow a conventional grid pattern, and thus will frequently climb straight up one side of a precipitous slope to plummet down the other. In fact, Nob Hill, Russian Hill and Telegraph Hill, to name only the best known, are so steep that pavements often turn into stairways.

See Chapters Twelve to Seventeen for comprehensive details of accommodation, restaurants and other facilities in San Francisco.

The best way to get a grip on what makes the city so extraordinary is to walk. Armed with a good map, you could plough through much of the city centre in a day, although it's better to roam, unbound by itineraries. San Francisco's diverse attractions are often best found just dawdling, rather than by frenzied sightseeing. The most interesting districts, certainly, merit at least half a day each of just roaming about.

Downtown San Francisco, the obvious focus for your initial explorations, is examined in detail in Chapter Two. This usefully compact area is composed of three contradictory square miles crowded into the northeastern corner of the peninsula, between the hills and the Bay. Situated on the north side of diagonal **Market Street**, the city's main commercial artery, its high-class stores and fancy hotels sit somewhat strangely between the poor, rather sleazy districts to the west and the New-World skyscrapers of the **Financial District**. Most prominent in the skyline is the

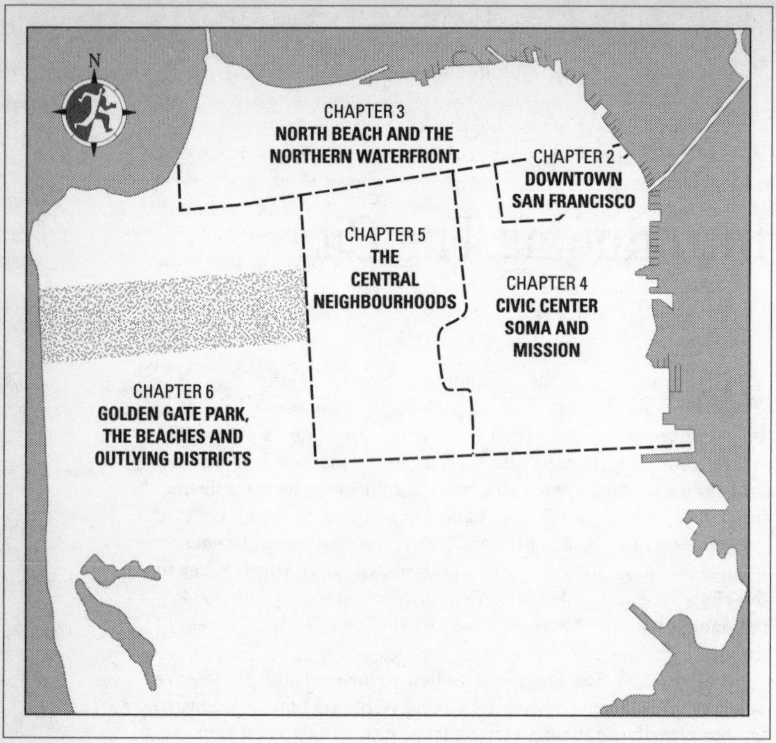

Transamerica Pyramid, which can be seen from almost anywhere in the city, and is a useful landmark for your explorations. Just a few blocks from here and you enter the more chaotic enclave of **Chinatown**, above which sits the otherworldly wealth of San Francisco's most famous peak, **Nob Hill**, a good place to view the downtown expanse.

Chapter Three has a more diverse collection of neighbourhoods, beginning just north of downtown, at the tip of the peninsula with the old Italian enclave of **North Beach**. Despite gentrification, this popular neighbourhood still harbours a vaguely bohemian population – a hangover from the days when the major Beat figures lived here. It's a good place for eating and drinking, with some of the city's best bars and restaurants. Just north of here hugging the Bay is the unbridled kitsch of **Fisherman's Wharf**, which, is the city's number one tourist magnet, thronged by crowds jostling to cruise the Bay, visit Alcatraz and buy souvenirs. While by no means essential viewing, the Wharf provides access to a lengthy Bay-front promenade, which takes you past exclusive, lofty neighbourhoods such as **Pacific Heights** before leading into the rugged expanse of cypress-lined avenues and windswept bluffs of the **Presidio**, ideal for long, secluded walks and ocean-gazing across the orange pilings of San Francisco's most famous landmark, the **Golden Gate Bridge**.

Far from homogenized, San Francisco shocks you every time you turn a corner: changes are abrupt and often unannounced. The **Civic Center**, for example, a little way west of downtown and the starting point for Chapter Four, may be San Francisco's municipal and arts nucleus, holding some of the city's most grandiose architecture, but is usually thronged by a good number of the city's homeless, and sits rather incongruously on the edge of two transitional neighbourhoods. Across the other side of Market Street, the formerly industrial **SoMa** (South of Market) neighbourhood, renowned for its clubs and bars, has had a major injection of life since the arrival of the new Museum of Modern Art and the Yerba Buena Gardens. Neon-lit and buzzing by night, it is now a cultural destination by day. Further south and a whole lot funkier, you find yourself among the bars and restaurants of the vigorously Latin, non-stop, low-rent **Mission** district.

Away from downtown and the commercial hubbub, San Francisco becomes acutely residential. Looking at the largely desirable patchwork of small and self-sufficient communities, frequently defined by their distinct social and ethnic characteristics, you begin to see the attraction of making a home here. Among the **Central Neighbourhoods** explored in Chapter Five, the **Castro** has long been San Francisco's primary gay district - affluent, gentrified and, despite the sobering effects of AIDS, still boasting a high-energy bar and shopping scene with some good eating options. For voyeuristic strolling, the **Haight-Ashbury** is no less rewarding. Formerly the epicentre of San Francisco's 1960s counter-culture, its enduring air of radicalism is manifest in its left-wing bookshops, tastefully scruffy café society, and a smattering of residents still flying a slightly limp freak flag.

For an explanation of how to interpret addresses in San Francisco see p.25.

Finally, Chapter Six leads through the welcome tranquillity of **Golden Gate Park** – a gargantuan urban oasis that incorporates fine art museums, flower gardens and some convincingly bucolic open spaces – to some of San Francisco's most enthralling stretches of coastline, including the city's only **beaches**.

The 49-Mile Drive

If you have your own vehicle, you can orientate yourself – and see some of the best of San Francisco – by way of the **49-Mile Drive**, a route laid out around the city that takes in the most important scenic and historic points in about half a day. Marked by the blue and white seagull signs, it circuits the Civic Center, Japantown, Union Square, Chinatown, Nob Hill, North Beach and Telegraph Hill, before skirting Fisherman's Wharf, the Marina and Palace of Fine Arts – after which it passes the southern approach of the Golden Gate Bridge and winds through the Presidio. From here it sweeps along the ocean, past the zoo and doubles back through Golden Gate Park, vaulting over Twin Peaks and dipping down to Mission Dolores and back to the waterfront for a drive by the Bay Bridge, Ferry Building and Financial District. Free maps of the entire route are available from the Visitor Information Center on Market Street at Powell where the cable cars turn around.

Chapter 2

Downtown San Francisco

San Francisco spreads fairly evenly over most of its 49 square miles, but the main concentration of activity is in its oldest and easternmost plot, jammed between the waterfront and the steeply rising hills. It's difficult to draw clear borders, as the parameters shift according to continuous development and whoever you ask, but most of what the locals call **downtown** is clustered within a square mile around the northern side of **Market Street** – San Francisco's main commercial and traffic drag, which bisects the northeastern corner of the peninsula. The area ends abruptly at the edge of the bay, where the vistas have been greatly improved by the recent tearing down of the Embarcadero Freeway.

In keeping with its quirky history and unique personality, downtown San Francisco is a real mixed bag, conforming to no overall image. One block may be thronged with multinational banks and the young executives who work in them, another home to Chinese markets and sidewalk evangelists, turn the next corner and you'll find upscale department stores, private clubs, smart restaurants and all the hallmarks of an affluent city.

The nearest thing to a centre is **Union Square**, San Francisco's liveliest urban space, populated in equal degree by high-style shoppers, eager street musicians and out-of-it tramps and beggars. As the city's main hotel and shopping district, and the junction of its major transportation lines, it makes a logical starting point for downtown wanderings. Leading off from the **Financial District** at the bottom of the hill (San Francisco's only real high-rise quarter) is the oldest part of town – **Jackson Square**, and the historic **Barbary Coast**, nesting inconspicuously in the shadows of the modern city. The up-and-coming **Embarcadero** or **City Front District** as it is also known, hugs the northeastern tip of the peninsula where downtown meets the bay with a smart collection of hotels, bars and desirable urban dwellings. On the opposite side of the city centre, and worlds away from the glitz and glamour, sits **Chinatown**, a dense and bustling warren of tacky stores and tasty restaurants that's home to the second largest Chinese community outside Asia.

As with most of central San Francisco, **walking** is the best way of seeing all this, though from Union Square – or even better, California Street – you can hop on a cable car up the steep incline of **Nob Hill** to check out the grand mansions of old San Francisco's moneyed elite. It's possible, if exhausting, to cover the entire downtown area in a day, but unless you're on the tightest of schedules you'll get much more out of downtown (and indeed all of San Francisco) just mooching around.

Union Square and around

Though the area around **UNION SQUARE** may not top your list of places to see in San Francisco, as home to most of the city's hotels, department stores and some noteworthy bars and restaurants, it is certainly its heart. As a result, it's usually thronged with tourists and locals in equal numbers. During lunch hour, office workers spread out across its palm-fringed square with a picnic to watch the street performers who gather. The square is also the centre of the city's shopping district, drawing a fairly ritzy crowd: limousines are bumper-to-bumper on the surrounding streets – Powell, Geary, Post and Stockton – and the well-heeled pop in and out of pricey depart-

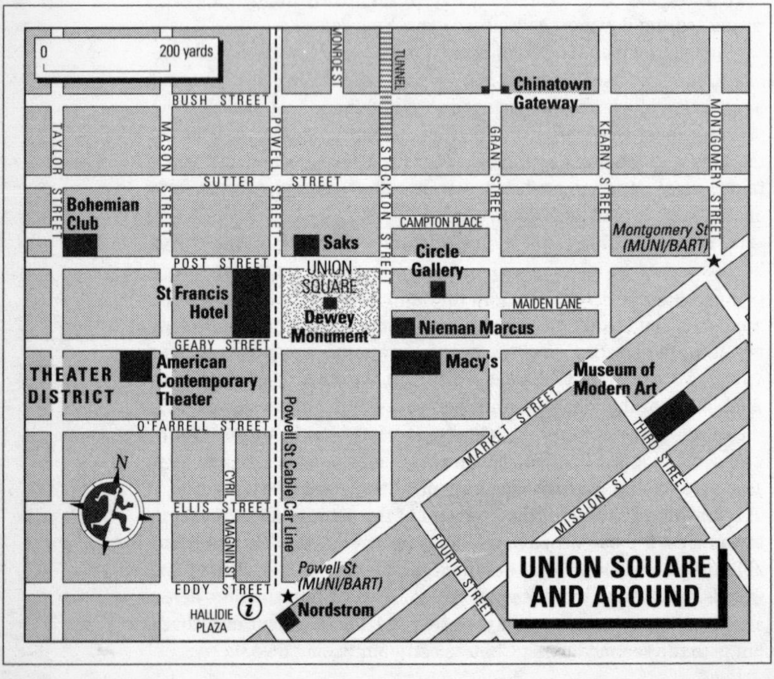

ment stores. It certainly acts as a magnet to the bums and winos from the nearby Tenderloin – not to mention the increasing numbers of homeless people who hope to do a brisk trade panhandling from passing shoppers.

Union Square takes its name from the mass meetings held here on the eve of the Civil War to pledge loyalty to the Union. The modern-day square also sees its fair share of protests and, given its strategic commercial and transportation location, a well-organized demonstration (often by the gay community) can usually draw traffic to a halt. Simply landscaped, apart from a few palms, and mostly paved over, its main feature is the **Dewey Monument**, a pigeon-crowded Corinthian column in the centre, topped by a miniature statue of winged Victory put up in 1904 to mark Admiral Dewey's naval successes in the Spanish–American War.

For much of the nineteenth century, Union Square was home to the more elite Protestant churches and the principal Jewish synagogue, but the transformation to the Union Square of today began with the building of the exclusive **St Francis Hotel** on Powell Street. The hotel features regularly in local folklore – Al Jolson died here while playing poker and Sarah Jane Moore, a member of the Manson "family", attempted to assassinate President Gerald Ford outside. Though its status as the city's premier hotel has dwindled somewhat, it remains a regular temporary home to visiting dignitaries, changing its flags to honour the country of its more important guests. Nothing so flash for Queen Elizabeth II, who had to be put up at the less grand **Sir Francis Drake Hotel**, one block up Powell, when the *Britannia* broke down during a West Coast tour in the late 1970s.

The *St Francis* was a location in Francis Ford Coppola's paranoid post-Watergate film *The Conversation*, in which surveillance expert Gene Hackman spied on lovers strolling in the square from his hotel room. The hotel played a similar role in many of **Dashiell Hammett**'s detective stories, as well as in his own life. In the 1920s Hammett worked there as an operative for the Pinkerton Detective Agency, investigating the notorious rape and murder case against the silent movie comedian Fatty Arbuckle. When Hammett later came to write *The Maltese Falcon* and other classic tales, he modelled many of the locations on the *St Francis*, though nothing in the hotel makes anything of the connection. One of surprisingly few ventures that does capitalize on the Hammett link is *John's Grill* at 63 Ellis St. It's been there since 1908 and looks it, with walls covered in Hammett memorabilia.

The sort of shady characters who inhabited Hammett's fictional world would today be more at home west of Union Square along Geary Street in what's optimistically called the **THEATER DISTRICT**. As in New York's Times Square, or London's Soho, the mainstream culture of San Francisco's Theater District shares space with less rarefied entertainment, namely porn and prostitution, that

PACIFIC STREET
PHOENIX ST
JOHN ST
TRENTON ST
JACKSON STREET
ROSS ALLEY
Cable Car Barn
WASHINGTON STREET
PORTSMOUTH SQUARE
SPOFFORD ST
WAVERLEY PL
WALTER LUM ST
NOB HILL
CLAY STREET
JONES STREET
TAYLOR STREET
MASON STREET
POWELL STREET
JOICE STREET
STOCKTON STREET
GRANT AVENUE
COMMERCIAL
SACRAMENTO STREET
Huntington Park
Grace Cathedral
CHINATOWN
CALIFORNIA STREET
California St Cable Car Line
TUNNEL
QUINCY ST
ST MARY'S SQUARE
PINE STREET
Powell St Cable Car Line
Chinatown Gateway
BUSH STREET
SUTTER STREET
COSMO PL
ISADORA DUNCAN COURT
POST STREET
Circle Gallery
THEATER DISTRICT
SHANNON ST
UNION SQUARE
MAIDEN LANE
LEAVENWORTH STREET
GEARY STREET
O'FARRELL STREET
CYRIL MAGNIN ST
ELLIS STREET
MARKET STREET
Moscone Center
Powell St (MUNI/BART)
EDDY STREET
HALLIDIE PLAZA
MISSION STREET
0
200 yards

PACIFIC STREET
GOLD ST
JACKSON STREET
COLUMBUS AVE
JACKSON SQUARE
N
EMBARCADERO
WASHINGTON STREET
Trans America Pyramid
MERCHANT ST
Ferry Building
Embarcadero Center
CLAY STREET
JUSTIN HERMAN PLAZA
KEARNY STREET
STREET
MONTGOMERY STREET
SANSOME STREET
BATTERY STREET
FRONT STREET
DAVIS STREET
DRUMM STREET
SACRAMENTO STREET
SPRING ST
STEUART ST.
Embarcadero (MUNI/BART)
CALIFORNIA STREET
FINANCIAL DISTRICT
22
15 & 17
Federal Reserve Bank
SPEAR STREET
PINE STREET
BELDEN ST
MAIN STREET
BUSH STREET
MARKET STREET
MISSION STREET
Transbay Terminal
FIRST STREET
HOWARD STREET
Montgomery St (MUNI/BART)
SOUTH OF MARKET (see Chapter Four)
33
Palace Hotel
SECOND ST.
NEW MONTGOMERY
Museum of Modern Art
THIRD STREET
DOWNTOWN ACCOMMODATION
1 Adelaide Inn
2 Alexander Inn
3 Amsterdam Inn
4 Andrews Hotel
5 Beresford Arms Hotel
6 Campton Place Hotel
7 Cartwright Hotel
8 Commodore International Hotel
9 Cornell Hotel
10 Dakota Hotel
11 Hotel David
12 Fairmont Hotel
13 Gates Hotel
14 Grant Plaza Hotel
15 Harbor Court Hotel
16 Hotel Bedford
17 Hotel Griffin
18 Hotel Monaco
19 Hotel Triton
20 Huntington Hotel
21 Hyde Plaza Hotel
22 Mandarin Oriental
23 Mark Hopkins
24 Monticello Hotel
25 Nob Hill Hotel
26 Nob Hill Lambourne
27 Pacific Bay Inn
28 Pan Pacific Hotel
29 Petite Auberge
30 Prescott Hotel
31 Raphael Hotel
32 Ritz Carlton
33 San Francisco Marriott
34 Sheehan Hotel
35 Villa Florence
36 Westin St Francis
37 White Swan Hotel
38 York Hotel

spill over from the neighbouring Tenderloin section near the Civic Center. In fact, the legitimate theatre scene here is small and not highly rated (San Francisco has always been much better at the extremes – at the cutting edge of avant-garde performance, or in high-powered opera productions – than it has at mimicking Broadway). The flagship *American Conservatory Theater* playhouse at 415 Geary St recently reopened following a major restructuring to repair damage from the 1989 quake that almost rocked it to its foundations; the city's best theatrical space, its return was most welcome.

Music, theatre and dance options are detailed from p.258 onwards.

Also part of this district, just north of the Square along Post and Sutter, are downtown's least visible landmarks – though the casual visitor might never suspect their existence, some fourteen private clubs are hidden away behind these discreet facades. Money isn't the only criterion for membership of these esteemed institutions, though being *somebody* usually is. Most notorious is the **Bohemian Club** at Post and Taylor. Better known for its *Bohemian Grove* retreat at the Russian River, where ex-presidents and corporate giants get together for Masonic rituals and schoolboy larks, the club is housed in a Lewis Hobart Moderne-style building that includes a large theatre, as well as more predictable amenities like a bar and good restaurant. Organized in the late 1800s by newspapermen and artists, it evolved into a businessmen's club with an arty slant (during its golden age, members included Frank Norris, Ambrose Bierce and Jack London), though these days the all-male membership includes some of America's biggest political and business movers and shakers. A bronze cornerstone bears an owl (the club's emblem) and the motto "Weaving Spiders Come Not Here".

Union Square's claim to fame as a **shopping** heaven is supported by the presence of large department stores such as *Macy's*, *Saks Fifth Avenue* and *Neiman Marcus* – the latter worth a look for its marvellous stained-glass rotunda, preserved from the old *City of Paris* store which stood on the site until Philip Johnson did an uninspired job of designing the new store in 1982. The city's most beautiful high-end emporium, *I Magnin*, was abruptly closed in 1995 to make way for a new *Macy's* home furnishings store. Some say this has sounded the death knell for truly classy consumerism, and with the recent arrival of *Planet Hollywood* and a vast *Nike Town* emporium in the works, it's certainly looking that way, though a few old-world survivors cling on. The unlikely named *Gump's*, at 135 Post St, just off the Square, is San Francisco's home-grown equivalent of *Liberty's* in London, specializing in Oriental fabrics and Art Nouveau objects, and renowned for its museum-worthy collection of jade figures. Elsewhere on this block you'll find the likes of *Gucci*, *Tiffany* and *Cartier*, though the most attractive place to window-shop is undoubtedly **Maiden Lane**, a chic little urban walkway that leads out of the Square half a block south. Before the 1906 earthquake and fire this was supposedly one of the city's roughest areas, where homicides averaged around ten a month, and prostitutes displayed themselves behind open windows. Nowadays, aside from some prohibitively expensive boutiques, its main feature is San Francisco's only Frank Lloyd Wright building, the exclusive **Circle Gallery** at no. 140. A try-out for the Guggenheim in New York, a gently curving ramp rises towards the skylighted ceiling past some expensive artwork, while in the cases on the lower floor fine china and crystal command equally high prices.

If you're moving on from Union Square, **cable cars** run along the Powell Street side of Union Square but are usually too packed to board. If you want to ride one up to Nob Hill – or on to the waterfront – try squeezing on a block or so up the hill, or line up with everybody else at the Market Street start, near the **Visitor Information Center**. Better still, wander east into the Financial District's looming forest of steel and glass towers and catch the California Street cable car.

The Financial District

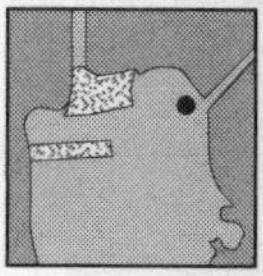

The **FINANCIAL DISTRICT** is San Francisco's most highly charged neighbourhood and the city's phenomenal development is never more apparent than in these few small blocks, which contain over 38 million square feet of office space. As financial centres go, San Francisco's is not unattractive and the area does constitute a virtually comprehensive library of architectural styles and periods, from Palladian piles to postmodern redoubt. The old-style banking halls were overshadowed during the frenetic building boom of the 1970s, when they became flanked by newer, taller structures. To avert the wholesale demolition of the area for more profitable towers, the city nowadays directs new development south of Market Street.

Scattered among the banks and insurance companies are the copy centres and computer stores that serve the offices above, with an occasional restaurant of note. Jam-packed at lunchtimes, by nightfall the area is practically deserted and especially so at weekends. Sharp-suited workers clog the streets in well-mannered, rush-hour droves, racing between the Montgomery *BART/MUNI* station on Market Street and their offices. Notwithstanding its architectural fascination, there's not a great deal to see. However, San Francisco's movers and shakers distinguish themselves from the rest of the American financial community on the last business day of the year, when local custom dictates that office workers throw their desk calendar pages out of the window. Standing on the street and looking skywards, the scene is reminiscent of a ticker-tape parade – not to be missed if you're in town for New Year.

The bars and restaurants of downtown San Francisco are detailed on the map on p.224.

Montgomery Street has been at the heart of San Francisco's business life since the Gold Rush, when it formed the young town's waterfront. To capture the trade of arriving prospectors, canny

The Financial District

merchants built long wharves from their Montgomery Street warehouses across the mud flats which stretched out into the bay. Since then, the shoreline has been filled in and built on. Many of the cross streets – Commercial, Clay and Washington – were simply constructed on top of the old docks, and today's steel and glass towers conceal the remains of over one hundred wooden vessels abandoned in the haste to get to the mines. Nowadays tagged "the

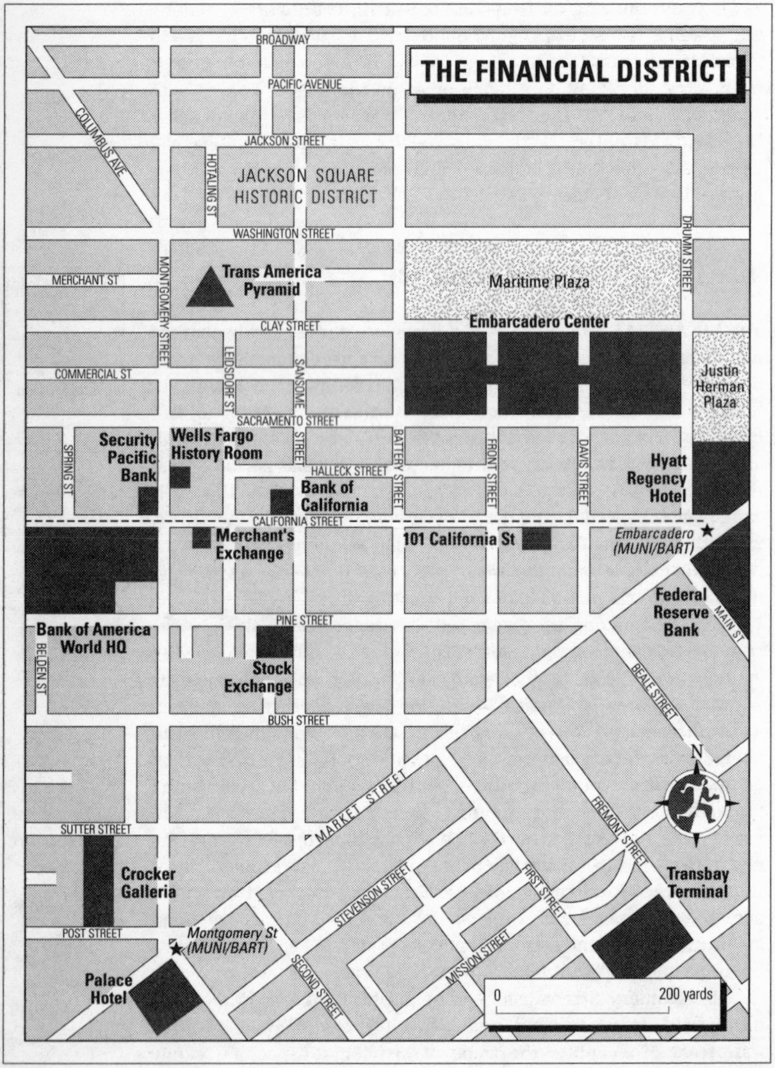

Wall Street of the West", Montgomery Street is still the main artery of the Financial District, but the contrast between generations is stark. The Ionic columns and robust stone details of the 1922 **Security Pacific Bank**, at Montgomery and California, are thoroughly overpowered by the ominous hulk of the **Bank of America** headquarters (California's biggest financial institution) across the street. Though not the tallest, this broad-shouldered monolith of dark-red granite dominates the San Francisco skyline and has divided the city into fans and those who would like to see it razed to the ground. Finished in 1971, it challenged the city not only with its size, but also with the startling contrast of its hue – San Francisco used to be known as "a city of white" – but with time it has assimilated well and even become the subject of admiration. At the top of the building is the handsome *Carnelian Room* (6–10.30pm) which is a great place to go for drinks and sweeping vistas, though be warned; this is a jacket and tie affair. On the California Street side of the tower is a small plaza with a sleek, granite sculpture grandly entitled *Transcendence*, more commonly dubbed "The Banker's Heart".

The Financial District's third largest landmark after the Transamerica Pyramid and the Bank of America Headquarters is **101 California Street** between Front and Davis streets. Despite a somewhat graceless greenhouse-style entrance, the magic of this structure is its luminescence at dusk when the silvery reflective glass shimmers. Further along California Street between Battery and Sansome streets, the **First Interstate Center** is a distinctive piece of modernism, with the luxury *Mandarin Oriental Hotel* sitting atop some prime office space and its twin towers connected by bridges.

Surprisingly, some fine **art** is tucked away in hidden corners of the district. Several blocks north, the **Merchants' Exchange Building** at 465 California St was designed by Willis Polk and has a series of nineteenth-century marine paintings by Irish painter William Coulter. At the entrance of its **Grain Exchange Hall** are four huge columns, beyond which the six vast oil canvases depict the history of San Francisco as a seaport. This room was the original centre of commercial life in the city, monitoring the comings and goings of every Pacific Coast ship. It was also the place where shippers, warehousemen and traders would gather to do their bidding.

If you want to get a better sense of San Francisco's historic importance as the financial centre of the West, a handful of places deserve a quick look. Though not tall, the old **Pacific Coast Stock Exchange** building at 301 Pine St forms the heart of the Financial District. Sadly closed to the public, it's an impressive Art Deco monument from the outside, fronted by muscle-bound figures. The **Wells Fargo History Room**, 420 Montgomery St (Mon–Fri 10am–5pm; free), details the origins of San Francisco's banking and financial boom with exhibits from the days of the Gold Rush. Mining equipment, gold nuggets, photographs and even an old stagecoach show the far-from-slick roots of the city's big money. The **Museum of the Money of the American West**, in the Bank of California at 400 California St (Mon–Thurs 10.30am–3pm; free), offers a similar range of gold nuggets and the like and, for a more hands-on grasp of the dynamics of modern finance, you should try the Economics Gallery in the **Federal Reserve Bank** (see p.68).

If negotiating the charging throngs down on the street is too much, you can always just gaze down on them from the relative tranquillity of the **Crocker Galleria** rooftop garden at 50 Post St. Skip the three floors of expensive boutiques and opt for a packed lunch with the office workers.

The Transamerica Pyramid

The landmark **Transamerica Pyramid**, indisputably the signature of San Francisco's skyline, serves as a useful dividing point between the various downtown areas. Though the streets around it are oddly quiet considering the vitality of surrounding districts, the 855ft tower, San Francisco's tallest, is a hinge marking the transition from the towers of the Financial District to the low-level tangle of North Beach and Chinatown. The pyramid arose amid a city-planning furore that earned it the name of "Pereira's Prick", after its LA-based architect William Pereira. Since then it has been accepted as a notable addition, in these days of plump speculative buildings, a rare example of an architecture which sacrifices the pragmatic to the symbolic. The 48-storey structure is capped by a colossal architectural ornament – a slender 212ft hollow spire, lit from within. As the building tapers upwards, the floors that fetch the highest rents diminish in area; in other words, the pyramid, from a real-estate perspective, would be far more valuable upside down.

Regular art exhibits are displayed in the lobby, there's an observatory on the 27th floor (Mon–Fri 9am–4pm; free) and it's well worth a ride up in the elevator to check out the cityscape from a great height. Look in also on the small **redwood grove** on the east side of the building, landscaped with eighty redwoods from the Santa Cruz mountains, giving the building the appearance of an artificial mountain with its own forest at its feet. Recently opened on the ground floor is *Vertigo* (see p.225), the Financial District's smartest new eatery where locals can be found talking shop when the working day ends.

A brass plaque in the lobby is the sole reminder that this was once the site of San Francisco's prime literary and artistic crossroads, the **Montgomery Block**. From 1853, when it was built, until 1959, when it was torn down and made into a parking lot, the four-storey Montgomery Block was the city's most important meeting place. Though built as an office block for lawyers, doctors and businessmen, it was soon taken over by writers and newspapermen, and evolved into a live-in community of bohemian poets, artists and political radicals. Ambrose Bierce, Bret Harte and Joaquin Miller were frequent visitors to its bar and restaurant, and Mark Twain met a fireman named **Tom Sawyer** – who later opened a popular San Francisco saloon – in the basement steam baths. Later habitués included George Sterling, Maynard Dixon and **Sun Yat-sen**, who devised the successful overthrow of the Manchu Dynasty while running a local newspaper, *Young China*, from his second-floor office.

Jackson Square: the Barbary Coast

A century or so ago, the eastern flank of what is now the Financial District formed part of the **"Barbary Coast"**, a rough-and-tumble waterfront district packed with saloons and brothels where hapless young male visitors were given "Mickey Finns" and "shanghaied" into involuntary servitude on merchant ships. It was also home to *The Dash*, the city's first gay bar which opened in 1908, wild for its time indeed. The district centred on Pacific Street, which was known as "Terrific Street" until World War II, when its wicked reputation made it off-limits to military personnel. Many of the old dives died a death, but a few structures survived the 1906 earthquake and fire and, during the 1930s, the Barbary Coast became a low-rent district that attracted artists and writers, including Diego Rivera who had a studio on Gold Street at the height of his fame as the "communist painter sought after by the world's biggest capitalists". Most of these old structures have since been restored and preserved as the **Jackson Square Historic District** – a rectangle formed by Jackson, Montgomery, Gold and Sansome streets, making up a few dense blocks of low-rise, mostly brick buildings that now house the offices of advertising agencies and design firms, as well as some fairly smart restaurants and watering holes that feed the style-conscious workers therein.

It's more a place for aimless wandering – **Gold Street** and **Hotaling Place**, the narrow alleys off Jackson Street, are best – than for searching out specific highlights, but it does hold a few noteworthy sights. Now an office block, 415 Jackson St was the original Ghirardelli chocolate factory, later moved north to what's now Ghirardelli Square, close by Fisherman's Wharf. At the heart of the district, the survival of **Hotaling's Whisky Distillery** at 455 Jackson St inspired this post-earthquake poetic ditty:

If, as they say, God spanked the town
for being over frisky
Why did He burn His churches down
and save Hotaling's Whisky?

Pacific Avenue, originally Pacific Street, the old heart of the Barbary Coast, is now perhaps the most anodyne stretch of the Jackson Square district, though Montgomery Street, at its western edge, holds a number of handsome facades, many with further literary and libertine associations.

Just down from Jackson Street, 732 Montgomery St was the home of San Francisco's first literary magazine, the *Golden Era*, founded in the 1850s, which helped launch the careers of Bret Harte and Mark Twain. Writers John Steinbeck and William Saroyan later spent many a night drinking in the vanished *Black Cat Café* down the street. In the middle of the block, **722–728 Montgomery Street** has had its original stucco stripped and been done up in overwrought Victorian mode. In its time, the building has been a theatre, Turkish bath, tobacco warehouse and auction room; today you can peer through the windows and see the fascinating, if excessive, clutter and career mementoes of flamboyant San Francisco lawyer, Melvin Belli, which fill the place.

The Embarcadero

At the northeastern edge of the Financial District, the small waterfront district known as **THE EMBARCADERO** separates the city from the bay and has become a magnet for restaurateurs and hoteliers of repute, taking advantage of the wonderful vistas from its bayfront windows. Recently tagged **City Front District** (in an attempt to distance itself from the Embarcadero Center association no doubt) the area is experiencing a dramatic regeneration, and after years of languishing as an abandoned waterfront strip things are beginning to hum. During the 1930s, before the building of the bridges that connect the city to Oakland and Marin County, the Embarcadero was the main point of arrival for 50,000 cross-bay commuters a day. It's still a transportation hub, but the main focus of the area is now a satellite city of offices, hotels and stores housed in four huge modern blocks, recently freed from the shadow of the contentious freeway that shared its name.

The Embarcadero Freeway was badly weakened during the 1989 earthquake. Its subsequent fate aroused passionate debate between the traders who relied on its capacity to move traffic around town, and the aesthetes who thought it spoiled the view of the bay. There was never any question about its efficiency, and driving across it at night, approximately level with the tenth floor of the skyscrapers, was something of a thrill. But, typically, the citizens of San Francisco put beauty first and after some fierce debating down it finally came in 1992.

Commuters from Marin County still arrive at the **Ferry Building** at the water's edge, near the foot of California Street. Modelled on the Moorish cathedral tower in Seville, this small-scale dignified structure is positively dwarfed by the looming towers of the Financial District; and although recently freed from the obscurity imposed by the Embarcadero Freeway, there is not much to suggest its former importance.

North and south from the foot of Market Street (which focuses on a fine view of Twin Peaks at the end) stretches San Francisco's once-vital five-mile-long **waterfront**. It was alive during the first half of the century to the sights and sounds of huge ships loading and unloading cargo at what was still the main point of arrival for goods and people to the city. The area experienced something of a slump after the war but recent development, including the building of a new *MUNI* station and the extension of the cable car lines, is beginning to herald something of a renaissance. On Saturdays the area vibrates to the sound of live bands who play while the **Ferry Plaza Farmers' Market** sets up its stalls for a morning's brisk trading. The pick-of-the-crop produce at knock-down prices always draws a crowd.

The Financial District

The waterfront was also the site of one of the more notorious episodes of twentieth-century San Francisco, when, on the eve of America's involvement in World War I, on July 22, 1916, ten members of a massive pro-war demonstration were killed by a bomb. Though there was no tangible evidence of any link, opposition to US intervention in the war led to the city's union leaders being held responsible for the attack, charged, and found guilty (on perjured testimony) of murder. Tom Mooney, a prominent longshoremen's activist, was sentenced to death, and it took twenty years of lobbying and protest before he was freed and his name cleared. His alleged co-conspirator, Warren Billings, spent most of his life behind bars before being pardoned in 1961. The site of the bombing is now filled by the brick fortress headquarters of the **Southern Pacific Railroad Corporation**.

The bars and restaurants of downtown San Francisco are detailed on the map on p.224.

A couple of blocks from the waterfront you can wander inside the angular **Hyatt Regency** hotel and gaze up into its twenty-storey-high atrium lobby, filled with plants, trees and a fountain sculpture set in a reflecting pool. An amusing novelty is the rooftop *Equinox* revolving bar. The hotel is part of the enormous **Embarcadero Center** development, sponsored by the celebrated eastern Rockefeller family and originally to have borne their name. Somehow "Rockefeller Center West" was an appellation that didn't sit so well on the Barbary Coast; San Francisco sees itself in no sense as subordinate to the Big Apple and is only begrudgingly part of the same state as the Big Orange. The Center's four slender towers rise from a multi-level base of offices, stores and cafés that stretch for several blocks east around the **Justin Herman Plaza**. A large paved space, this is largely unused except for the skateboarders who alone can appreciate such vast stretches of concrete, although it did see some excitement when U2 staged an unannounced concert here in February 1988. For the best part of the day the city came to a standstill as people left their offices and abandoned their shopping, hoping to catch a glimpse of the visiting megastars. Someone hung a banner from an office window that read "SF loves U2" – lead singer Bono misinterpreted the SF for Sinn

Fein and after a vitriolic outburst threatened to cancel the gig. Whoops.

If the shopping opportunities afforded by the Embarcadero don't interest, visit the **Cybermind Virtual Reality Center**, One Embarcadero (Mon–Thurs 10am–11pm, Fri & Sat 10am–1pm, Sun noon–9pm; free) where you can fight marauding pterodactyls, fly fighter planes or just surf the Net. Also worth a look, the **Jewish Museum**, 121 Steuart St (10am–5pm; donations), is a little-known place tucked discreetly into a nondescript building. Far from being the sombre trudge through history its name might suggest, it has an impressive collection of contemporary work by Jewish artists.

Nearby, at 101 Market St, the **Federal Reserve Bank** (Mon–Fri 10am–4pm; free) is an unbeatable amusement if you're at all interested in the machinations of money in the city. Computer games allow you to engineer your own stock-market disasters, while gallery exhibits detail recent scandals and triumphs in the financial world.

Outside the bank is the starting point of the **California Street cable car line**, which leads you out of the Financial District, past Chinatown and up to Nob Hill, though it is a more thrilling ride back down Nob Hill away from the quiet mansions, swooping into the high-rise dynamism of the Financial District.

Nob Hill

Nob Hill, the hill of palaces, must certainly be counted the best part of San Francisco. It is there that the millionaires are gathered together vying with each other in display. From thence, looking down over the business wards of the city, we can decry a building with a little belfry, and that is the stock exchange, the heart of San Francisco: a great pump we might call it, continually pumping up the savings of the lower quarter to the pockets of the millionaires on the hill.

Robert Louis Stevenson

If the Financial District is where money is made in the city, the smart hotels and Masonic institutions of **NOB HILL**, just above, are where it is shown off. In a city famous for its hills, this one tops the lot. It is, as Joan Didion wrote, "the symbolic nexus of all old California money and power". Maintaining San Francisco's most-revered address, its mansions, exclusive hotels and restaurants look snootily down over the lower areas of the city. Traditionally, San Francisco's moneyed elite preferred level streets, and it was the invention of the cable car in the 1870s that turned this from an inaccessible backwater into a slice of prime real estate. At its summit, the hill is 376 feet above sea level, offering fantastic views of the city below. Until the Gold Rush brought new fortunes seeking expression, the hill was scrubland occupied only by sheep.

While the Nob Hill area may hold few real sights as such, just nosing around, or calling into the hotels for a drink in their rooftop bars, is pleasant enough, taking in the aura of privilege and luxury that distinguishes the neighbourhood and enjoying the views over the city and beyond.

When the Transcontinental Railroad barons made their fortune, they had no doubts about where to invest it. Originally called the California Street Hill, the area became known as Nob Hill after **the Big Four** robber-baron industrialists, Collis P Huntington, Charles Crocker, Mark Hopkins and Leland Stanford, who had made millions on the Central Pacific Railroad, and the bonanza kings of the silver mines of the Comstock Lode, built their mansions here in the 1880s. Sadly, only one of these ostentatious piles survived the 1906 fire, the brownstone mansion of James C Flood, which cost a cool million dollars in 1886 – now the **Pacific Union Club**, a private retreat for the ultra-rich on California Street at Mason. Behind the club sits **Huntington Park**, not the finest of San Francisco's small parks but a good place to watch nannies push the power-brokers of the future around in their prams. The mansions of other Nob Hill denizens were not so fortunate, and their former sites now hold some of San Francisco's grandest **hotels**: along California Street, the *Mark Hopkins*, with its spectacular rooftop bar, the *Stanford Court*, the elegant

The Cable Cars

The invention that made high-society life on the hills possible and practical, the **cable car** (the sort that runs along the ground, not swings precipitously from mountainsides) is another of Nob Hill's dominant features. Since 1873, when Scotsman Andrew Hallidie piloted the first of these little trolleys up the Clay Street hill to Portsmouth Square, they have been an integral part of life in the city. At their peak, just before the 1906 earthquake, over 600 cable cars travelled 110 miles of track throughout the city, though by 1955, their usage had dwindled to such an extent that they were due to be closed altogether until nostalgic citizens voted to preserve the remaining seventeen miles of track as a moving historic landmark. The streets along which the tracks lie were due for a multi-million-dollar refit in 1984, and because of the high cost involved city officials again considered abandoning the system. But public indignation (and some worried manoeuvring by the tourist industry) set the restoration in motion. Today some forty-odd cars are in daily operation along three lines, two from Powell Street to Fisherman's Wharf, and the steepest one climbing Nob Hill along California Street from the Embarcadero. The lines cross at the crest of Nob Hill, at California and Powell.

To climb the hills, the cable cars have to fasten onto a moving two-inch cable which runs beneath the streets, gripping on the ascent then releasing at the top and gliding down the other side. These cables are hauled along by huge motorized pulleys which you can see in the **Cable Car Barn**, two blocks from Grace Cathedral at Washington and Mason. This 1887 building has been renovated as a working **museum** (daily 10am–6pm; free) with exhibits of vintage cable cars and associated memorabilia.

Huntington and the strikingly lobbied *Fairmont* all quietly compete for the top-dollar trade.

Impressive though they are, none of these buildings can compete for effect with the hill's biggest hunk of aspirational architecture, the sham-Gothic **Grace Cathedral** across Huntington Park from the Pacific Union Club (daily 7am–6pm; free tours Mon–Fri 1–3pm, Sat 11.30am–1.30pm, Sun 12.15–2pm – the highlight is definitely the choral service on Sundays at 11am, an occasion that could move the un-Godly). Originally, the block the Cathedral stands on was occupied by the homes of the Crocker family, who donated the site to the Episcopal Church after losing their houses in the 1906 fire. Construction began soon after, though most of it was built of faintly disguised reinforced concrete in the early 1960s. A recent lavish renovation makes the Cathedral a mightily impressive sight. The interior shelters an eleventh-century French altar and Renaissance reredos, but the carillon in the bell tower is a contemporary addition from Croydon, England. One part that's worth a look is the entrance, adorned with faithful replicas of the doors of the Florence Baptistry; do also study, the allegorical stained glass around the Cathedral walls.

Chinatown

Hemmed in by prosperity, plumb at the foot of Nob Hill and just three blocks from Union Square, the two dozen square blocks of seeming chaos that make up **CHINATOWN** are completely distinct from any other neighbourhood in the city. The gateway arches that mark Chinatown's borders seem barely able to contain the district, and it's by far the city's most thickly populated quarter, with over 80,000 residents in a quarter-mile area. Alhough home to the second largest community of Chinese outside Asia, it's no longer solely Chinese: Vietnamese, Thai, Filipinos and Koreans have all made inroads over recent years, further adding to the dynamism of the neighbourhood. Noisy, smelly, colourful and overcrowded, Chinatown manages to retain a degree of genuine autonomy, despite an obvious reliance on the tourist dollar, with its own schools, banks and newspapers alongside the predictable morass of souvenir stores. Fortunately, most of the tourist pandering goes on along the main street, Grant Avenue, off which dark, gloomy alleyways thread between buildings that house the real Chinatown of grocery stores, laundries, temples and bakeries. Looming ominously and casting tall, dark shadows over the small, often unkempt buildings are the massive gleaming monoliths of the Financial District. Contrasts don't come much cruder.

The first Chinese arrived in Northern California in the late 1840s, many of them fleeing famine and the Opium Wars at home and seeking the easy fortunes of the Gold Rush. Later, in the 1870s, thousands more came across to build the Transcontinental Railroad. At first the Chinese, or "coolies" as they were called (taken from the words *ku li*, meaning "bitter toil"), were accepted as hard-working labourers, but as the railroad neared completion and unemployment rose, many moved to San Francisco, swelling what was already a sizable community. The city didn't extend much of a welcome; jingoistic sentiment turned quickly into a tide of racial hatred, manifest in sometimes vicious attacks that bound the Chinese defensively into a solid, homogenous community.

The population stagnated until the 1960s, when the lifting of the anti-Chinese immigration restrictions swelled numbers to close on 160,000. Chinatown's history is well documented in the **Chinese Historical Society of America** at 650 Commercial St (Tues–Sat noon–4pm; donations), which traces the beginnings of the Chinese in the US and has a small, but worthy, collection of photographs, paintings and artefacts from the pioneering days of the last century.

Nowadays the Chinese and other Asians are the city's most affluent ethnic groups, mainly thanks to their attitudes to education and a willingness to work all hours. By day the area seethes with activity and congestion, by night the traffic moves a little easier, but the blaze of neon and marauding diners gives the feeling that it just never lets up. Overcrowding is compounded by a brisk tourist trade, but, while Chinatown boasts some of the most egregiously tacky shops and facades in the city, genuine snatches of ethnicity shine through.

Chinatown's restaurants are listed on p.230.

You can approach Chinatown from all sides: Nob Hill drops down to its centre, North Beach blends into its upper reaches and the Financial District flanks it to the east. Coming from the south and Union Square, you enter through the large **dragon-clad archway** that crosses the intersection of Bush Street and **Grant Avenue** – a gift from the Government of Taiwan and, judging by the look of it, not one that broke the bank. Once through here, Grant Avenue seems suddenly much narrower, crowded with gold-ornamented portals and brightly painted balconies which sit above the souvenir stores and restaurants. Plastic Buddhas, floppy hats and chopsticks are much in evidence. The least obviously Chinese of these false fronts, a horseshoe-shaped funnel at 916 Grant Ave, marks one of the very few **bars** in Chinatown – *Li Po's*, named after the great Chinese poet and still something of a literary hang-out. Some of the **restaurants**, too, are historical landmarks, none more so than *Sam Woh's* at 813 Washington St; cheap and churlish ex-haunt of the Beats and still a popular late-night hang-out in which, legend has it, Gary Snyder taught Jack Kerouac to eat with chopsticks and had them both thrown out for his loud and passionate interpretation of Zen poetry.

Before the days of brisk commerce, Grant Avenue was known as Dupont Street, an ensemble of opium dens, bordellos and gambling huts terrorized by *tongs* – **gangs** who took it upon themselves to police and protect their district in any (usually violent) way they saw fit. Their original purpose was to retaliate against racial hooliganism, but this developed quickly into Mafia-style family-feuding – as bloody as any of the Chicago gangland wars. These days there isn't much trace of them on the streets, but the mobs continue to operate, battling for a slice of the lucrative West Coast drug trade.

Parallel to Grant Avenue, **Stockton Street** is closer to the real thing – Chinatown's main street, crammed with exotic fish and fruit and vegetable markets, bakeries and spice stores; your dollar will go further here than anywhere else in the neighbourhood and your search for the authentic face of Chinatown will be better rewarded, especially if you can manage an early rise. Between Grant and Stockton, at the centre of Chinatown, jumbled alleys hold the most worthwhile stops in the area. The best of these is **Waverly Place**, a two-block corridor of brightly painted balconies that was lined with brothels before the 1906 catastrophe and is now the site of most of Chinatown's many family associations and community support groups. It's also home to two opulently decorated but skilfully hidden **temples** (nos. 109–111 and 123–129), their interiors a riot of black, gold and vermilion. They're still in use today and open to visitors, but the variable opening times mean you'll have to take pot luck to get in, or take the Saturday tour at 2pm, organized by the **Chinese Cultural Center**, tucked away inside the *Holiday Inn* at 750 Kearny St (Tues–Sat 10am–4pm). The Center also runs a regular programme of art shows, mostly contemporary, that give much-needed exhibition space for the Chinese artistic community. If your mind is not on worship or even appreciation, an amusing diversion is a trip to *Golden Gate Fortune Cookies*, 56 Ross Alley, off Jackson, who do a nice sideline in X-rated fortune cookies as well as the regular variety.

Another, more accessible, point of interest is the **Buddha's Universal Church** at 720 Washington St, where America's largest Zen sect give tours on the second and fourth Sunday of each month. This five-storey building was painstakingly built by the sect-members from an exotic range of polished woods, adorned everywhere by mosaic images of the Buddha. Across the street at 743 Washington, the triple-tiered pagoda of the **Bank of Canton** once housed the multilingual operators of the Chinatown telephone exchange. The bank's site was previously the home of the *California Star* newspaper – the city's first daily, and the one that announced the discovery of gold in 1848.

Across a concrete footbridge sits the larger of Chinatown's two green spaces, **Portsmouth Square**. This was the old centre of the city, and indeed its Mexican era birthplace, as well as the place where Sam Brannan announced the discovery of gold – an event that transformed San Francisco from a sleepy Spanish pueblo into a frontier town. Though not the most attractive of parks, it's an oasis in a very cramped part of town. Old men come to play chess while younger ones fly past on skateboards. In the northwest corner there's a statue of the galleon *Hispaniola* from *Treasure Island*, a monument to Robert Louis Stevenson, who, while waiting for his lover's divorce to come through in 1879, used to come here and write. More recently, sculptor Thomas Marsh's bronze *The Goddess of Democracy* was erected here after an unsuccessful stay in Tiananmen Square, Beijing in the Spring of 1989.

The other, smaller park, **St Mary's Square**, two blocks south, is dwarfed by a wall of Financial District skyscrapers and marks the western edge of their permissible development. The square holds a bold, modernist sculpture of Sun Yat-sen, founder of the Chinese republic. Its modern lines would look misplaced anywhere in the neighbourhood, but do so particularly here, where the little old ladies do their modest Tai Chi routines in the morning.

Chapter 3

North Beach and the Northern Waterfront

From patrician elegance to downright gaudiness, San Francisco's **northern waterfront** is a comprehensive study of what you can do, for better or worse, with a spare stretch of shoreline. Before the area came to rest on landfill, the original waterfront was the aptly named **North Beach**, a sunny neighbourhood in a wind-sheltered valley between two hills in the northeastern corner of the peninsula which, despite gentrification, has managed to weather the changes with its Italian foundations intact. As one of the city's oldest neighbourhoods, it has an appealing worn-in feeling; it's a wonderful area for just hanging around cafés and bars and weaving through its gently sloping streets.

Within walking distance, flanking either side of North Beach, **Russian** and **Telegraph hills** are more residential in flavour, with steep streets that turn into steps, beautiful homes and hidden gardens. Good for strolling and taking in the views of the waterfront, they are an attractive pocket of the city on the whole, apart from the masts and bunting that signal the city's number one crowd-puller, **Fisherman's Wharf**. Each year, some twelve million visitors have to plough through a lot of overpriced tat and commercial gimmickry to find what remains of the almost obsolete fishing industry.

As you move west from the Wharf, things improve dramatically. **Aquatic Park** is a small **beach** that draws a few hardy bathers, though it's better known as the home of the **Maritime Museum**. It's used as a walk-through on the way to **Fort Mason** – an old military installation that was rescued from the clutches of development and now has an impressive grouping of small museums, workshops, theatres and an excellent youth hostel. Continuing west, the waterfront becomes a focus for the fancy yacht clubs that make up the northernmost tip of the **Marina** district and the adjacent **Pacific Heights**, a desirable neighbourhood which thrives on its exclusivity and has little to offer the visitor beyond a mild envy and the distinctive **Palace of Fine Arts**, rising majestic and surreal above a skyline of elegant homes. If you're a keen walker, you may want to trudge the extra mile to the vast tract of open green space dominating the remainder of the northern shoreline, known as **The Presidio**. A former army base turned over to public use, it is a good example of the city's ability to combine beauty with utility – its 1500 acres harbour walking trails, cycling routes and picnic spots with panoramic views. Its eucalyptus groves provide a well-needed dose of scented air and an inspiring approach to the orange spires of the city's most famous landmark, the **Golden Gate Bridge**.

North Beach

Starting from the base of the Transamerica Pyramid, **Columbus Avenue** cuts diagonally through the heart of one of San Francisco's most wanderable quarters, **NORTH BEACH**. This was indeed a beach before landfill pushed back the bay. Nowadays, resting in the hollow between Russian and Telegraph hills, North Beach is the lovably raffish, unconventional centre of San Francisco, its restaurants and cafés are constantly thronged and its drinking joints full of disreputable characters. As the Puritanism which has swept California makes inroads into the city's habits, North Beach is staunch in its defence of the pleasure principle. Originally, it was the city's Italian quarter, with more than 60,000, mostly northern, Italians living within its boundaries at its peak during the 1940s. With the increased prosperity and mobility that followed the war, many left the area, and as rents came down the disenchanted children of postwar America moved in. Since this migration of the 1950s, when the more prominent figures of the **Beat movement** gathered here, it has been among the city's most sought-after sectors for anyone vaguely artistic or counter-cultural. It still has a certain Italian slant, and is home to some of the city's best bars and restaurants. Rocketing real-estate prices levelled off in the 1980s and the die-hard free-thinkers wrestled to maintain their territory amidst the growing numbers of sharp-suited young professionals slumming it at North Beach's traditionally scruffy cafés. But, whoever claims it as home, it is still a most likeable neighbourhood, inhabited by a solid core of people who remember what bohemia was really like. The anecdotes connected with North Beach remain legion – get chatting to any barfly over fifty, they seem to know them all.

The bars and restaurants of North Beach are detailed on the map on p.229.

The southern edge of the district is visually anchored by the green flatiron **Columbus Tower**, situated on the island formed by Columbus Avenue and Kearny and Jackson streets, dwarfed and somewhat surreal set against the backdrop of the Financial District skyline. A much-loved San Francisco building with its white tile and green-copper windows, it was saved from demolition by San

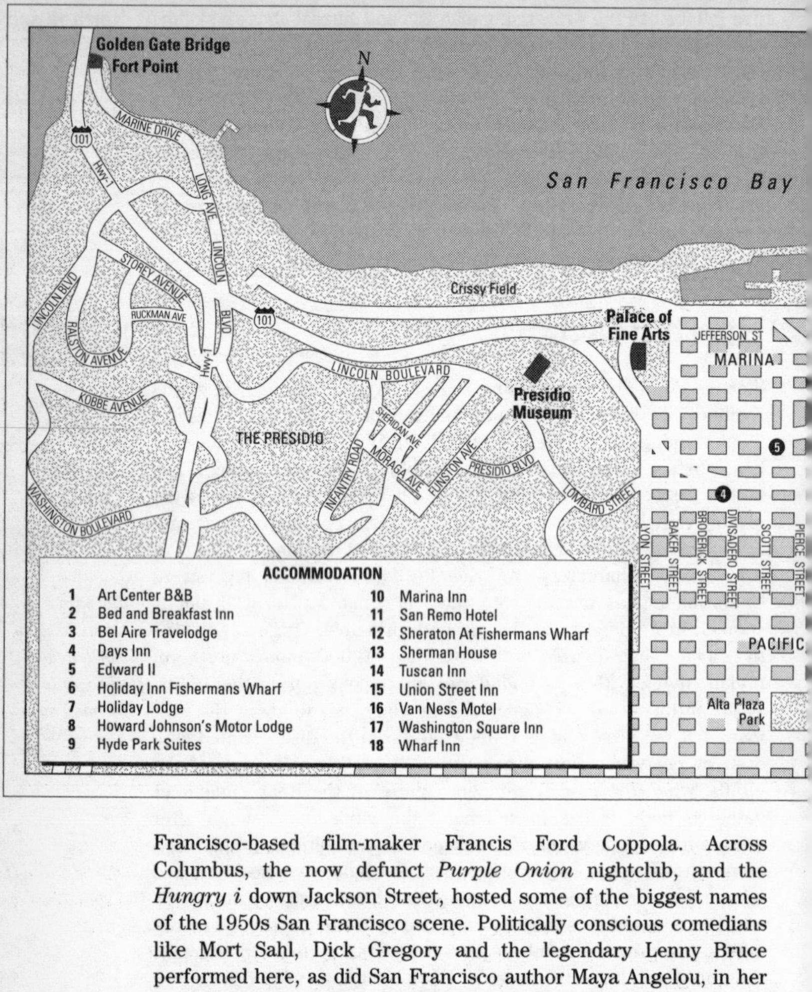

Francisco-based film-maker Francis Ford Coppola. Across Columbus, the now defunct *Purple Onion* nightclub, and the *Hungry i* down Jackson Street, hosted some of the biggest names of the 1950s San Francisco scene. Politically conscious comedians like Mort Sahl, Dick Gregory and the legendary Lenny Bruce performed here, as did San Francisco author Maya Angelou, in her earlier guise of singer and dancer. These landmarks have now closed or changed beyond recognition, but the district still trades on a reputation earned decades ago.

Another North Beach literary landmark, the **City Lights Bookstore**, stands two blocks up at 261 Columbus Ave, where it meets Broadway. The nation's first all-paperback bookstore, established in 1953 and still owned by the poet and novelist Lawrence Ferlinghetti, it's open until midnight seven days a week, and its vast collection of avant-garde, contemporary and Beat writings keep it very much at the core of the San Francisco literary scene. To encourage the creative juices, almost every local with literary aspira-

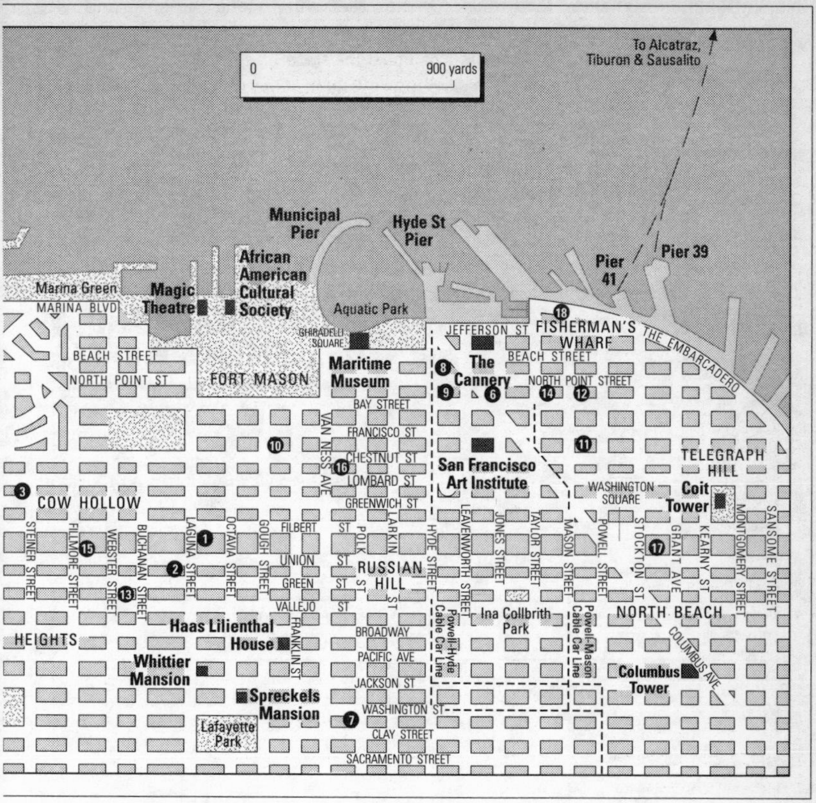

tions has spent some time at **Vesuvio's**, handily placed next door. The likes of Dylan Thomas and Jack Kerouac regularly got loaded here, and while times have changed considerably since then, it remains a haven for the lesser-knowns to get ploughed with impunity and pontificate on the state of the arts. On the other side of Columbus the other Beat bar, *Tosca Café*, should satisfy all but the most unquenchable thirst. See North Beach listings for details, p.250.

For more on the City Lights, see p.278.

Assuming you leave either of these places with your senses intact, you'll find yourself at the crossroads of **Columbus and Broadway**, where poetry meets porn in a raucous assembly of declining strip joints, rock clubs and drag queens. Most famous of these is the *Condor Club*, where the sight of Carol Doda's silicone-implanted breasts thrilled a decade of voyeurs before she quit the stage for a quieter life. Her nipples, once immortalized in neon above the door as a tribute to the years of mammary fascination, have ceased to flash with the conversion of the club into a café,

Carol Doda now sells lingerie at Carol Doda's Champagne and Lace Lingerie Boutique *(no. 1 1850 Union St, ☎415 776-6900).*

signalling lean times for the other clubs along the strip and what seems to be the long, slow demise of the sex-club era.

For a city that is in a constant state of gentrification, the seedy side of Broadway resists improvement. One survivor, the **Finocchio Club** at 506 Broadway, was a speakeasy during prohibition which nowadays offers polished drag acts. Beat tourists will want to stop for a look at the building two blocks down, on the northeast corner of Broadway and Montgomery, where Allen Ginsberg lived during 1955 when he wrote the definitive Beat poem, *Howl*.

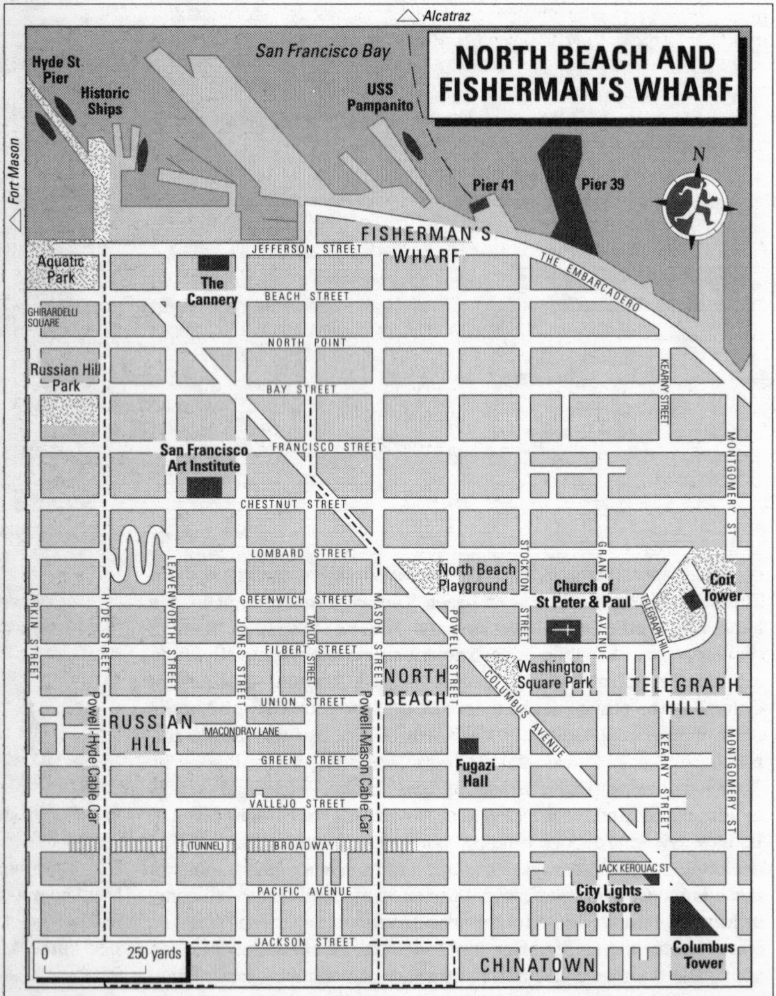

Continuing north on Columbus the bright lights fade and you enter the heart of the old Italian neighbourhood, an enclave of restaurants, cafés and delicatessens set against a background of narrow streets and leafy enclosures. Like all good Italian neighbourhoods, North Beach has its rightful share of opulent places of worship; **St Francis of Assisi Roman Catholic Church**, at 610 Vallejo St off Columbus, to name one. After the Spanish missions, this was the first Roman Catholic parish to be established in California and was an important focal point for the local community – how times change. It is now, due to falling attendances, considered obsolete by the church authorities, closed for worship and awaiting its fate; though, visually at least, it remains central to the neighbourhood. Other landmarks include the **Café Trieste** at 601 Vallejo St, a literary waking-up spot since the days of the Beats and still a reminder of more romantic times; the jukebox blasts out opera classics to a heavy-duty art crowd toying with their cappuccinos and browsing slim volumes of poetry.

Fugazi Hall at 678 Green St, between Columbus and Powell, is another of the neighbourhood's symbols of Italian pride. Donated to the community in 1912 by their most prominent figure, John Fugazi, a banker who founded the Transamerica Corporation, this elaborate terracotta ornamented building is now host to San Francisco's longest-running show, *Beach Blanket Babylon*. An upper-floor room holds photographs depicting the history of the local Italian community. Other memorabilia can be found at the intimate **North Beach Museum**, on the mezzanine level of the *Eureka Bank*, 1435 Stockton, near Columbus. Filled with old photographs and heirlooms, it is the best peep into the area's unique history of the Italian and Chinese Americans.

For more on Beach Blanket Babylon, *see p.267.*

Across the street, at Columbus Avenue and Union Street, **Washington Square Park** is not, with its five sides, much of a square, but the pale, light-reflecting buildings that line it and the simple landscaping of this admittedly not very big space, lend it a tranquil, rather graceful air. It is that rare thing in a large US city, a park used by the people and not dominated by gangs; elderly Italians rest on the benches and the neighbouring Chinese go through their Tai Chi routines on a Sunday morning. On the Columbus Avenue side of the park stands one of heiress Lily Coit's many tributes to her fascination with firemen: a large bronze of volunteer firemen holding hoses – the monument has a certain macho charm. On the north side of the park the lacy spires of the **Church of St Peter and Paul**, where local baseball hero Joe DiMaggio married Marilyn Monroe, dominate "the square". Inside this stately Romanesque totem to local dignity (it also has a very good school built around it) is a wonderful painting, *La Madre del Lume*, of a Madonna, child on hip, reaching into the inferno to pull out a sinner – makes you wonder what was going through Marilyn's mind as she made her vows. More puritanical than holy, the statue

The Beat Generation

North Beach has always been something of a literary hang-out, but it was the emergence of the **Beat Generation** in the late 1950s that really put the place on the map, focusing media attention on it as literary capital of California. The first Beat writers – Jack Kerouac, Allen Ginsberg and others – came out here from New York City; like many, they were frustrated by the conservative political climate of the time, and their lifestyle and values emphasized libertarian beliefs that America wasn't perhaps ready for. Nothing really crystallized, however, until they moved out West, settling in North Beach and linking up with an esoteric cluster of writers, poets, musicians and inevitable hangers-on around the *City Lights* bookstore.

It wasn't long before the Beats were making news. In 1957, a storm of controversy rose up when police moved in to prevent the sale of Ginsberg's poem *Howl* under charges of obscenity – an episode the press latched onto immediately, inadvertently hyping the Beats to national notoriety, as much for their hedonistic antics as for their literary merits. Within six months, Jack Kerouac's *On the Road* – inspired by his friend Neal Cassady's Benzedrine monologues and recorded in a marathon two-week session in New York six years earlier – shot to the top of the best-seller lists, having been previously rejected by all the publishers he had offered it to.

As well as developing a new, more personalized style of fiction and poetry, the Beats eschewed most social conventions of the time, and North Beach soon became a virtual symbol of their wild and subversive lifestyle, the road trips and riotous partying, the drug-taking and embrace of Eastern religion revered and emulated nationwide. Whether the Beat "message" was an important one is a moot point; in any case, the movement – and Kerouac in particular – became more of an industry than anything else, and whatever impact the Beats might have had was quickly trivialized as tourists poured into North Beach for "Beatnik Tours" and the like. But the legend has yet to die, not least in North Beach itself, where – in a campaign vigorously led by Lawrence Ferlinghetti – many streets have been renamed to honour the famous figures who have graced the neighbourhood: the small alley which runs down the side of *City Lights* is called "Jack Kerouac Street".

of Benjamin Franklin in the centre of the park was donated by a dentist and active prohibitionist, H D Cogswell, who installed taps at the base of the monument in the unlikely hope that people would drink water from them rather than try to get their hands on bootleg liquor. A futile gesture.

It is behind the square and along the backstreets of Grant and Vallejo that you find the **bars** and **unusual shops** that sustain this diverse community. *The Lost and Found Saloon*, half a block up Grant next to the ancient *Fugazi Hardware Store*, is another great survivor – a favourite with the jazz-and-poetry brigades. There are dozens of bars and cafés jumbled throughout the neighbourhood, the best of which are listed in *Restaurants* and *Nightlife*, see Chapters Thirteen and Fourteen.

Before you enter the movement of the Columbus and Broadway junction once again, stop at the **Tattoo Museum**, 841 Columbus, and check out Lyle Tuttle's bizarre collection of the flesh canvases that have fallen under his needle. This is a working tattoo parlour, where the renowned tattooist is happy to execute your own designs.

Russian Hill and Telegraph Hill

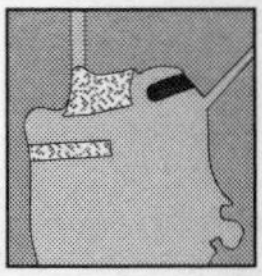

The two hills that rise steeply to either side of Columbus Avenue are where the bar- and café-hoppers go home to. To the west of Columbus Avenue, **Russian Hill** is known to some for the much-photographed curves of Lombard Street – and to others as the home of writer Armistead Maupin's *Tales of the City* crew. To the east, the narrow alleys and eclectic architecture of **Telegraph Hill** – named after an old communications station that once stood here, and now capped by Coit Tower – are perched on 45-degree inclines. Both hills have the some very desirable residences, and if you've got strong legs the network of enticing paths, leafy alleys and stairways that climb, their heights can make for a great afternoon's wander.

Russian Hill

Bounded by North Beach to the east and Nob Hill to the south, **RUSSIAN HILL** is an immaculately maintained residential neighbourhood of steep slopes and small parks, whose population could be termed the high end of bohemia. At its western edge is the lively Polk Street strip of movie houses, cafés and small offbeat stores which start out smart and degenerate as you descend south toward the rent-boy hang-out approaching Civic Center.

The hill takes its name from a mysterious legend that tells of a group of Russian sailors who died and were buried here during a fur-trading expedition in the early 1800s. Excavations carried out some years ago uncovered some unidentified graves, but no tangible proof exists either to deny or confirm the story. At its summit, the hill is some 295ft high and no houses were built until cable-car lines crossed it during the 1880s. Since that time, it has had an artistic reputation supported only by a few literary inhabitants – Jack Kerouac, Ambrose Bierce, Joaquin Miller, Frank Norris and California's first poet laureate, Ina Coolbrith – and its art institute. For the most part it's a quiet, fairly wealthy enclave in a crowded corner of town; figuratively, and literally, above it all. A sensible city ordinance prohibits tour buses, and the most you'll see of other visitors will be those hanging off the Powell–Hyde cable car that traverses Russian Hill on its way to Fisherman's Wharf.

Whether you tour the area by day or night, **Hyde Street** makes a sensible point of reference. It's central to anything you might want to see as well as being well served from downtown and the waterfront by cable cars. Come before nightfall, if only to visit the **San**

Francisco Art Institute at 800 Chestnut St (galleries open Tues–Sat 10am–5pm; free) on the eastern slope. As the oldest art school in the Western United States, the institute has been central to the development of the arts in the Bay Area. Housed in a hybrid structure, one part Mission-style from the 1920s and another part concrete brutalism from the 1960s, it has four galleries, three dedicated to painting and one to photography, mainly exhibiting the work of the students and rotated on a regular basis. The highlight of the institute is unquestionably the **Diego Rivera Gallery**, which has an outstanding mural done by the painter in 1931 at the height of his fame. The **cafeteria** on a deck at the back of the building is a cheap place to refresh yourself and enjoy the great views of North Beach, Telegraph Hill and the bay.

Two blocks away on the 1000 block of Lombard Street at Hyde, you'll run into the cars lining up to drive down the **"Crookedest Street in the World"** – a narrow, tightly curving street with a five mph speed limit to make descending its steep gradient less hazardous. It's featured as often as the Golden Gate Bridge in publicity shots for the city, and is usually surrounded by camera-toting tourists by day – better to see it at night after they're gone and city lights twinkle below. Its contours make for a thrilling descent by car. At the top of the street is the tiny but immaculate **Alice Marble Park**, good for taking a breather and stretching out in the sun. To continue on from here, head south to Union Street and then one block east until you come to **Macondry Lane**, a walkway made famous as "Barbary Lane" in Armistead Maupin's *Tales of the City*. The lane's leafy enclosure makes for a pleasant stroll across the cobbles, leading to a rickety old staircase that descends to the intersection at Taylor Street, also featured prominently in Maupin's narrative.

From here it's a demanding two-block uphill walk to **Russian Hill Place**, off Vallejo between Jones and Taylor. After ascending the steep staircase at the summit of the hill, you're rewarded with a 180° view of the city that includes the skyscrapers of the Financial District, the candy-coloured houses of North Beach and Telegraph Hill, the Bay Bridge and, of course, the shimmering bay. After all the climbing you'll probably be eager to get back to Hyde and recover on a cable car, but before leaving you should take a walk down **Russell Street**, a small lane west of Hyde between Green and Union streets. Check out the modest (by San Francisco standards) little house at no. 29, where Jack Kerouac lived in Neal and Carolyn Cassady's attic for six months in 1952. It was here, with Neal's encouragement, that Kerouac began an affair with Carolyn that endured for many years. Kerouac produced some of his best work during this period, inspired by tape-recorded sessions with Neal Cassady, and went on to write *Doctor Sax*, *Visions of Cody*, as well as revising earlier versions of *On the Road*. Carolyn Cassady's own rich memoir, *Heartbeat*, chronicles this period, with some vivid physical descriptions of the city itself.

The prolific turn-of-the-century San Francisco architect **Willis Polk** lived nearby, at the head of the Vallejo Street staircase between Jones and Taylor, in an attractive, shingled house of his own design. Not the work of Willis Polk, but worth a peek, is the 1000 block of Green Street, where one of the city's few remaining octagonal houses survives thanks to the Colonial Dames of America. The **Feusier Octagon House**, built in the 1870s, is sadly not open to the public, but its outside still merits a look. An alternative to taking the Hyde Street cable car back downtown is to walk a couple of blocks east to the Powell–Mason cable car line, passing on the way the **Ina Coolbrith Park**, another postage-stamp piece of greenery, but quiet and pretty enough for a sit-down before negotiating the crowds.

Telegraph Hill

Once an extension of the wilder North Beach territory, but now a firmly settled community in its own right, the pastel clapboard homes of **TELEGRAPH HILL** dangle precipitously from steep inclines. Apart from the stiff walk, there's no easy way up, unless you're willing to sit on *MUNI* bus #39 while it makes the slow climb through the usually packed tourist traffic, and anyway the walk may make you appreciate the dramatic panorama – from the famous Golden Gate Bridge at the northern edge, all the way east to the more seductively simple lines of the Bay Bridge and beyond to the hills of Berkeley.

The most direct path to the top of the hill is to take **Filbert Street**, a steep climb from Washington Square Park past the flowery gardens of a line of cottages, up to Telegraph Hill Boulevard. The best viewpoint is from the top of **Coit Tower** (daily 10am–5pm; $3), another Lily Coit monument to the firefighters who doused the flames of 1906, this one soaring skywards in the form of a single 210-foot reinforced concrete column designed by Arthur Brown, the architect of City Hall. Lily Coit bequeathed $100,000 after her death in 1929 "to be expended in an appropriate manner for the purpose of adding to the beauty of the city which I have always loved" .

While waiting for the lift to the top of the tower, dawdle about and look at the marvellous social-realist Works Progress Administration **murals**, inspired and supervised by Diego Rivera. All the frescoes are thematically linked, though styles vary greatly. One section depicts muscle-bound Californians working on the land; another shows a man reading Marx in front of a wall of books by left-leaning authors like Upton Sinclair and Jack London, while others contemplate apocalyptic newspaper headlines. The murals were completed in 1934, during a longshoremen's dispute that escalated into a general strike after two union members were killed by police during demonstrations. When rumours about the "subversive" frescoes reached the authorities, the Art Commission ordered that a hammer and sickle be removed from one and even tried to close the tower until tempers had cooled. A picket of the tower was mounted by local unions, keeping it in the headlines until the authorities gave in and allowed it to open several months later.

Heading back downhill, you may feel more able to stop and savour the subtle charms of the hill's many fine houses, and there are a few places you definitely won't want to miss. The fine Art Moderne apartment block in which Lauren Bacall lived in the classic Bogart and Bacall film *Dark Passage* still stands just down from Coit Tower on the eastern side of the hill at 1360 Montgomery St. From Montgomery the beautifully landscaped **Filbert Steps** drop steeply down, looking out over the Bay Bridge and giving access to narrow footpaths such as **Darrell Place** and **Napier Lane** that cut off to either side. Napier Lane is one of the few remaining boardwalks in the city, lined with bucolic cottages and overflowing greenery.

Fisherman's Wharf and Alcatraz

Restaurants in the Fisherman's Wharf area are reviewed from p.228 onwards.

On the whole, San Francisco cultivates an admirable "take us as you find us" attitude, but at **FISHERMAN'S WHARF** they're after your tourist dollar with a vengeance, pulling in millions of visitors each year with its crowded and sometimes hideous ensemble of waterfront kitsch and fast-food stands. A series of refurbished piers have been converted into souvenir complexes and points to pick up a pleasure cruise around the bay; stalls selling sweatshirts and baseball caps dominate and, while there are a few windy bluffs, interesting old ships and quiet spots, all in all it makes for a misleading introduction to the charms of San Francisco.

The area was transformed with the tourist industry in mind thirty years ago from a once busy shipbuilding and industrial site, and though it might seem hard to believe now, this was originally a serious fishing port. The few fishermen that can afford the exorbitant mooring charges these days are usually finished by early morning, and get out before the tourists arrive. There are a few good seafood restaurants and a handful of mildly interesting spots, but crowd-weary families do little to add to the ambience and frankly, unless you have restless children to amuse, the best thing you can do with the Wharf is skip it altogether.

Details of bay cruises can be found on p.36.

At the eastern edge of the Wharf, **Pier 39** marks the beginning of a high-volume strip that continues for eight blocks west. You can take a boat from here and cruise the bay. Although the central focus is a large complex of stores and restaurants, an accidental attraction has popped up slightly west of the pier. A large herd of California sea lions has taken a fancy to the marina and their loud barks can be heard from quite a distance. More animal magic can be found at the new **Underwater World**, Pier 39 at Beach Street and

Embarcadero (daily 10am–10pm; $12.50 adults, $6.50 kids; reservations available ☎623-5300), the result of a part of a $40 million dollar improvement programme. Visitors can see over 10,000 Pacific Coast marine creatures while through a 400-foot acrylic viewing tunnel.

A cluster of pricey museums and exhibitions along Jefferson Street – known as the **Amusement Zone** – are designed to relieve you of more money: a **Wax Museum** (daily 9am–10.30pm; $7.95) with laughable replicas – the one of Cleopatra is uncannily like that of Elizabeth Taylor; **Ripley's "Believe It or Not" Museum** (Sun–Thurs 10am–10pm, Fri & Sat 10am–midnight; $6); even a **Guinness World of Records Museum** (daily 10am–10pm; $5.95). Sadly, even for people with kids to amuse, none are really worth the expenditure of very much energy or money. Things improve the further west you walk – **Pier 45** at the foot of Taylor Street has the last vestiges of the working wharf. It still pulls in some twenty million pounds of fish a year, although up to ten times that amount arrives by truck to serve the restaurants of the Bay Area. Unless you're there early in the morning, you won't see much action, but the boats and storage sheds are there to poke around in, and **Fish Alley** (officially called Tonquin Street) across from the foot of Jones Street provides a backstage glimpse that few make the effort to see. At the very end of the pier is the *USS Pampanito* (daily 9am–9pm; $5), a submarine that sank five Japanese ships during its operation in World War II. While hardly a must, it rates highly as an attraction compared to other sights in the area.

Of the Wharf's two refurbished **shopping complexes**, the first, **The Cannery** on Jefferson Street at Leavenworth, was part of the turn-of-the-century industrial wharf, a fruit-packing factory that was done up in the 1960s when the tourism drive really took off. Escalators take you up and around the three floors of shops, restaurants, a movie theatre and a small museum – **The Museum of the City of San Francisco**, third floor (Wed–Sun 10am–4pm; free), which is not the exhaustive collection the name suggests, but has some interesting pieces if you tire of shopping. The Cannery does have one magnificent feature – a Jacobean staircase that was originally built in the 1600s by Inigo Jones, but which seems misplaced in what is essentially a shopping complex. **Ghirardelli Square** at 900 N Point St marks the western edge of the Wharf, a boutiquey mall that is a far cry from its days as a chocolate factory, though its handsome red-brick facade and red neon sign remain a landmark. A little more upmarket than The Cannery, its careful refurbishment took six years, and to its credit contains some very good restaurants and one thing you don't need money to enjoy. The non-profit **California Crafts Museum** (daily noon–6pm; free) is better than its name suggests. A far cry from the batik and macramé knick-knacks you might expect, it has some innovative stuff, exhibiting work in media (wood, metal, glass and clay) that are often unrecognized by galleries. In addition to the more traditional ceramics and suchlike, you'll be able to see some designer furniture and unusual sculpture. If this is as much of the wharf as you can take and you travel back downtown, either catch the downtown loop bus #19 at Hyde and Beach streets or catch the cable car at the turnaround in **Victorian Park**, at the same junction. Prettily landscaped with benches, it offers a peaceful respite while you wait for your ride back.

The **Maritime Museum**, on Beach Street at the foot of Polk (daily 10am–6pm; free), is housed in a great Moderne building known as the – Aquatic Park Casino or "Boathouse" – a bold, Art Deco, streamlined imitation of a luxury liner, with three curving levels, steel railings and porthole windows. Permanent WPA exhibits inside trace the saga of the people and merchant ships that shaped the development of the city back in the days of the Barbary Coast. Hundreds of artefacts, photographs and documents chart San Francisco's seafaring history, but the most interesting item is Hilaire Hiler's 1939 **mural** in the main room, symbolizing the lost continent of Atlantis in 37 individual hallucinogenic panels.

More seafaring vessels are on display at the **Hyde Street Pier** at the foot of Hyde Street (daily 8am–5pm; $3). Originally the pier was used to serve the Sausalito ferries before the opening of the Golden Gate Bridge; today it boasts a collection of five historic ships, three of which are open to the public. The *Balclutha* is the most interesting, a hard-working ship of the late 1800s that journeyed round Cape Horn, returning with wine and spirits from London, coal from Wales and hardware from Antwerp. She was put into retirement in the 1930s, to be dragged out and done up for bit parts in such films as *Mutiny on the Bounty* before her current job as a showboat. The *Eureka*, once the largest passenger ferry in the world, is now loaded with a fleet of vintage cars and trucks; the *Alma* is a flat-bottomed workhouse that used to carry hay and lumber around the bay.

Alcatraz

Boats to Alcatraz leave hourly from Pier 41, from 8.15am onwards; the last boat back leaves at around 6pm ($8.75 per person, including audio tour).

Visible from the waterfront, its beacon flashing eerily in the fog, the prison island of **ALCATRAZ** is commonly known as "The Rock". A craggy little islet rising out of the bay that was originally home to nothing more than thousands of pelicans, thus inspiring the Spanish name *Isla de los Acatraces* ("Pelican Island"). In the late nineteenth century, the island became a military fortress, and in 1934 it was converted into America's most dreaded high-security prison, in an attempt to restrain the hitherto uncontrollable heavyweights of the penal system. Surrounded by freezing, impassable water, it was an ideal place for a jail, and safely kept some of America's most wanted criminals behind bars – Al Capone and Machine Gun Kelly were just two of the villains imprisoned here, and Robert "Bird Man" Stroud had a film made about him and his time here.

The conditions were about as inhuman as you'd expect: most inmates were kept in solitary confinement, in cells no larger than five by nine feet – some without light, they were not allowed to converse with the guards, read newspapers, play cards or even talk to the other inmates, and relatives were allowed to visit for only two hours per month. The psychological toll it took on the prisoners is said to have been devastating. Frustration culminated in several riots, including one particularly bloody affair that ended in the deaths of several guards and inmates. Despite many ingenious attempts, no successful escape was ever verified: of the 36 men who tried, some were shot, most were captured in the water and five vanished, presumed dead.

For all its usefulness as a jail, however, the island turned out to be a fiscal as well as penitential nightmare and, after years of generating massive running costs, not to mention whipping up a storm of public protest when it started to imprison petty criminals, it closed in 1963. The remaining prisoners were distributed among decidedly less horrific detention centres, and the island remained abandoned until 1969, when a group of Native Americans staged an occupation as part of a peaceful attempt to claim it for their people – citing treaties which designated all federal land not in use as automatically reverting to their ownership. Using all the bureaucratic trickery they could muster, the government finally ousted them in 1971, claiming the operative lighthouse qualified Alcatraz as active. Nowadays, the island's sole function is as a tourist attraction. You can wander about on your own if you wish, but many of the annual 750,000 visitors join the excellent hour-long audio-tours of the abandoned rows of cells. On the tape are sharp anecdotal commentaries by several of the surviving inmates, recalling the horror and desperation of their time and the conditions of the prison. The area around the main prison building is, in parts, strangely pretty, and the views of the city from the island are impressive. Speculation about the future of the island has included plans to turn it into an offshore gambling haven (gambling is illegal in California), although the latest proposal – and one that looks set to stick – is a scheme to let the island revert to its natural state and develop a series of hiking trails.

Fort Mason and the Golden Gate National Recreation Area

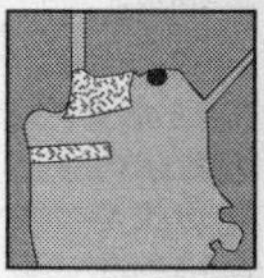

A little way west of Fisherman's Wharf, the area known as the **Golden Gate National Recreation Area** was organized in 1972 to provide much-needed central park space for the city by pulling together vacant parts of the waterfront. The most visited national park in the nation, it encompasses almost seventy beautiful square

Fort Mason and the Golden Gate National Recreation Area

miles of waterfront property, from the beach areas to the south, right up to the cliffs of Marin County on the other side of the Golden Gate Bridge. By claiming this property for public use, commercial enterprise has been pushed back, and the waterfront feels very much on the fringes of the city. Just a few blocks can take you from urban density to seafront expanse.

At the foot of Hyde Street, stretching over 1800ft in a long curve from **Aquatic Park,** where a small beach provides swimming for all-weather types, is the elegant **Municipal Pier** – a quiet spot favoured by lone fishermen and strollers – which adds real beauty to an otherwise crowded area. Few brave the choppy waters of the bay, however, and most use the beach as a sunny spot to walk dogs, take picnics and generally laze about. At weekends, salsa and reggae bands set up on the broad semicircle of steps above it and entice crowds away from the congestion of the Wharf. The three-and-a-half-mile scenic walk that begins here – the **Golden Gate Promenade** – wraps along the waterfront to the Golden Gate Bridge, passing through attractive spots like Marina Green and the Palace of Fine Arts (see p.91).

For details of Fort Mason's hostel, see p.219.

Fort Mason, adjacent to the park, can be reached by car via Bay and Franklin streets, or by climbing a spectacular flight of stairs up to the bluff from the foot of Van Ness Avenue. This military site, dating originally from the late 1700s, was manoeuvred into public hands in 1972, when a powerful congressman and environmentalist, Philip Burton, blocked plans to turn the land over to private speculation. Initially used by Spanish soldiers from the Presidio in 1797, it came under the auspices of the US Army in 1850, but failure to occupy the land immediately led squatters to build homes here. The squatters took thirteen years to evict, in a gradual programme of building, but the Fort was to shelter the homeless again as a refugee centre after the 1906 earthquake and fire. It saw its greatest action during World War II, when 1.6 million soldiers passed through on their way to the Pacific War Zone, and again in the early 1950s during the Korean War, when it was a logistical support centre.

Today Fort Mason is known locally as "Fort Culture", its old shed-like buildings housing an assortment of non-profit arts organizations known collectively as the **Fort Mason Center**. The fruit of pressure for free or low-cost cultural activities in the city, the complex has grown tenfold since its opening in 1976. It also holds a **hostel**, workshops, a few stores and several **museums** staging a mixture of permanent and temporary exhibitions. **African American Historical and Cultural Society** in Building C (Wed–Sun noon–5pm; free) is dedicated to preserving the history of black Americans. As well as a library, gift store and meditation room, a **gallery** shows excellent work by new and master artists of

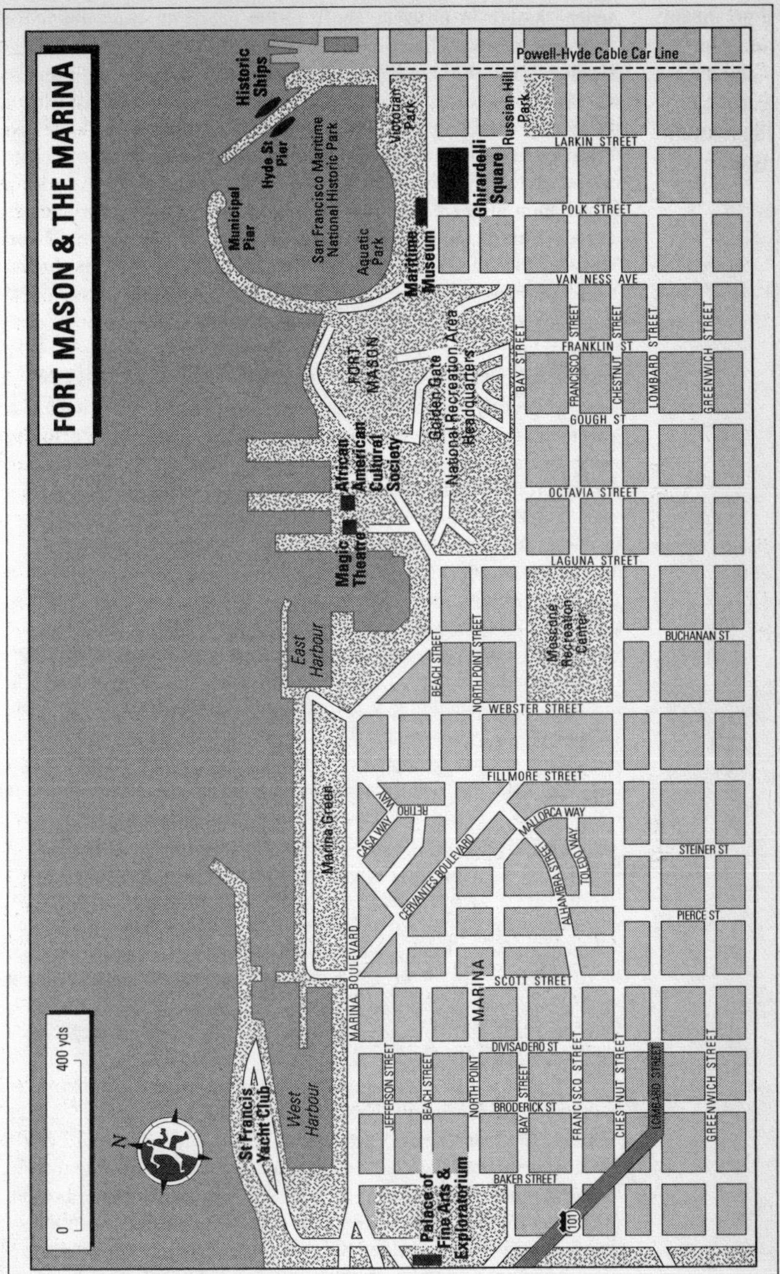
FORT MASON & THE MARINA
0
400 yds
N
Historic Ships
Hyde St Pier
Municipal Pier
San Francisco Maritime National Historic Park
Aquatic Park
Victorian Park
Russian Hill Park
Ghirardelli Square
Maritime Museum
Powell-Hyde Cable Car Line
LARKIN STREET
POLK STREET
VAN NESS AVE
FRANKLIN ST
GOUGH ST
OCTAVIA STREET
LAGUNA STREET
BUCHANAN ST
WEBSTER STREET
FILLMORE STREET
STEINER ST
PIERCE ST
SCOTT STREET
DIVISADERO ST
BRODERICK ST
BAKER STREET
BAY STREET
FRANCISCO STREET
CHESTNUT STREET
LOMBARD STREET
GREENWICH STREET
FORT MASON
Golden Gate National Recreation Area Headquarters
African American Cultural Society
Magic Theatre
East Harbour
BEACH STREET
NORTH POINT STREET
Moscone Recreation Center
Marina Green
RETIRO WAY
CASA WAY
CERVANTES BOULEVARD
MALLORCA WAY
ALHAMBRA STREET
TOLEDO WAY
MARINA BOULEVARD
MARINA
JEFFERSON STREET
NORTH POINT
West Harbour
St Francis Yacht Club
Palace of Fine Arts & Exploratorium
101

Fort Mason and the Golden Gate National Recreation Area

African-American descent, and a rather academic **museum** holds specialist artefacts and archival materials. **The San Francisco Museum of Modern Art Rental Gallery** (Tues–Sat; free) focuses on work by lesser-known northern Californian artist in a frequently changing series of exhibitions and the **San Francisco Craft and Folk Art Museum** (Tues–Sun 11am–5pm) has a large collection locally made crafts.

Though the Fort is predominantly a daytime attraction, crowds come here by night for performances at the acclaimed **Magic Theater**, one of the oldest and largest theatre companies on the West Coast. At night, the Fort's always pretty bluff becomes one of the most irresistibly romantic spots in the city.

For more on the Magic Theater, see p.267.

The Marina, Palace of Fine Arts and Union Street

Perched prettily on the edge of the bay, with its tastefully arranged Mediterranean revival houses and shops, the **MARINA** is a fitting neighbourhood for the young, image-conscious, money-no-object sort of professionals who inhabit it. Flanked by The Presidio to the west and Fort Mason to the east, it's one of the city's greenest districts, and its prestigious yacht club, joggers and kite-flyers all add to the ambience of a neighbourhood that would rather be a resort. Ironically, the Marina, built specifically to celebrate the rebirth of the city after the massive earthquake of 1906, was the worst casualty of the earthquake of 1989 – tremors tore through fragile landfill and a good number of homes collapsed into a smouldering heap. Rebuilding was immediate, however, and the only reminders of the destruction are the obviously new structures that went up to replace the lost dwellings. Even disaster was not enough to bring rents down, and the Marina remains, despite its hazardous foundations, home to a well-heeled and very smart young set.

The Marina's commercial centre runs along **Chestnut Street** between Broderick and Fillmore. As a neighbourhood, it has a reputation for being something of a haven for swinging singles; the local watering holes are known as "High-intensity breeder-bars" and even the local *Safeway* has been dubbed "The Body Shop" because of the inordinate amount of cruising that goes on in the aisles. Union Street (see below) is better for ordinary shopping, but Chestnut is just the job if you all you want to do is grab a bite to eat, have a drink and look at the locals.

Before the 1915 Panama Pacific International Exhibition to commemorate the rebuilding of the city after the 1906 earthquake and fire, the Marina didn't exist at all. On the bay north of Pacific Heights, a sea wall parallel to the shoreline was built and the marshland in between was filled in by pumping up sand from the bottom of the ocean. Dredging left enough deep water for the creation of the **St Francis** and **Golden Gate Yacht Clubs**, which occupy a prestigious spot at the foot of Baker Street. Slightly to the east is

Marina Green, a large stretch of turf frequented for the most part by fitness fanatics. For less strenuous exercise, walk the **Golden Gate Promenade** which runs parallel to Marina Boulevard and runs for a couple of miles before reaching the bridge.

The Palace of Fine Arts and Exploratorium

Marking the westernmost point of the neighbourhood is the Marina's most notable landmark, the magnificent **Palace of Fine Arts** at Baker and Beach. It is not, as the name suggests, a museum, but a huge, freely interpreted classical ruin by Bernard Maybeck, whose dream-like columns and rotunda were also created for the Panama Pacific Exhibition in 1915. The weeping figures on the colonnade, by sculptor Ulric Ellerhusen, are said to represent the melancholy of life without art. Whatever the implicit message, the lachrymose ladies are the ultimate decorative detail on a structure conceived out of great optimism for post-earthquake San Francisco. It was saved from immediate demolition after the exhibition by sentimental San Franciscans, and crumbled with dignity until the late 1950s when a wealthy resident put up the money for its reconstruction. It's the sole survivor of many such triumphal structures built for the Exhibition, which stretched from here all along the waterfront to Fort Mason. Surrounded by Monterey cypresses, a swan-filled lagoon and other nice touches of urban civility, it beats Marina Green hands down as a picnic spot and makes for the best idling in the neighbourhood.

Like the Palace of Fine Arts, the rather unsightly hangar-like **Exploratorium** next door (summer daily 10am–5pm, Wed 10am–9.30pm; rest of year Tues–Sun, 10am–5pm; $8.50, $4.50 children), is a product of high ideals, founded in 1969 on the idealistic premise that a better understanding of the sciences is the key to solving the world's problems. More than 700 exhibits explore light and colour, sound and music, patterns of motion, language and other natural phenomena. Each year over half a million people come to peer through lenses, look in mirrors, stare through filters, experiment with magnets and electricity, spin wheels, swing pendulums and supposedly, in the process, "learn more about their environment and themselves". It makes a good pacifier for restless children, although some of the exhibits can be a bit tedious for anybody with an elementary grasp of science.

Union Street

Known by some as **Cow Hollow**, **Union Street** is the busy commercial strip which rests between the Marina and its slightly wealthier neighbour, Pacific Heights, to the south. It takes its name from the days when cows rather than shoppers grazed the valley between Russian Hill and the Presidio, and washerwomen would bring their loads to what was one of the very few sites of fresh water in the city. Problems with open sewage, and complaints from the neighbours up on Pacific Heights about the stench from the cows, brought its pastoral days to an end, and these days cattle markets of an altogether different variety set the tone. Union Street, like the Marina, is quite the place for single straight people come sundown, when the bars fill with well-paid young professionals, dressed to the nines and very expectant, slinging down cocktails and waiting for their luck to change.

Indeed, despite stumbling across some attractive flower-filled courtyards, shopping and bar-hopping is what Union Street is all about. Second only to the downtown area, the seven-block stretch between Fillmore and Franklin is crammed with boutiques, fancy restaurants, antique stores, cafés and bars. Even the most faint-hearted consumer will find it hard to ignore the bookshops and classy Italian designer shops.

Pacific Heights

Sharply defined by California Street to the south, Van Ness Avenue to the east, the Marina to the north and the hulking green landmass of the Presidio to the west, **PACIFIC HEIGHTS** is a beautifully poised millionaires' ghetto. It's a common source of amusement that when the bright young things of the Marina grow up and have kids they climb the hill to Pacific Heights and look down on all the fun they used to have. Even when these were bare hills back in the 1860s, their panoramic views of the ocean earmarked them as fashionable territory as soon as the gradient-conquering cable cars could link them with downtown. Lavishly proportioned mansions teeter precipitously atop hills that are the chosen domain of the stockbroker, business magnate and the odd best-selling novelist. Erle Stanley Gardner, the creator of Perry Mason, set up his one-man fiction factory here, producing 82 novels that sold some three hundred million copies.

The neighbourhood is neatly divided by Fillmore Street: to the west are the large dwellings that earned the neighbourhood its reputation; to the east swanky Art-Deco apartment buildings that do little to damage it. Known as the **Upper Fillmore**, the stretch of Fillmore Street above California Street is where locals go to shop, dine and generally lash their cash – a street that merits your exploration if you're to get a clear idea of exactly the kind of people who can afford to live here. Approaching the area from the south where California crosses Fillmore, you should ascend the latter through the maze of fancy pet stores, florists and restaurants towards the more residential territory to the north, taking in the air of casual wealth and sophistication. The stores, while pricey, are not remarkable and, unless you're a shopaholic, skipping the boutiques and heading straight for a walk around the mansions would not constitute a loss.

The western portion of the neighbourhood is centred around the quiet and restful **Alta Plaza Park**, one block west of Fillmore at Clay and Steiner streets. A lovely piece of urban landscaping, this is where local dog-walkers earn their keep, exercising pretty pooches, and you can enjoy good views of St Mary's Cathedral and Civic Center from its crest. Streisand fans will recognize the park as the site of the famous scene in *What's Up Doc?*, in which she drives the car down the steps on the south side of the park. Close inspection reveals cracks left in the steps after shooting the scene. North of the park, the territory becomes solidly residential, home to well-tended gardens around immaculately maintained houses, apart from one rogue structure on the southwestern corner of Baker and Broadway. This Italian Renaissance Palace, probably built around the turn of the century, is in a romantic stage of decay and from its fancy perch overlooks the Getty Mansion down the street. One block over, at the intersection of Broadway and Lyon, you'll reach the fenced-off Presidio and won't be able to go any further west. From here, a set of steps leads south down a steep incline and out to the water's edge, passing grandiose homes and presenting a magnificent view of the Palace of Fine Arts and the bay.

Pacific Heights

To do anything other than mooch about, you'll need to cross Fillmore and explore the eastern side of the neighbourhood, filled for the most part with luxury apartment buildings that replaced the great Victorian piles the modern rich found too gloomy to live in. There are, however, still a couple where you can actually get a look around the inside. The **Whittier Mansion**, 2090 Jackson St (Wed, Sat & Sun 1.30–3pm; free) was for many years home to the *California Historical Society* (now moved to Yerba Buena Center) and has a good collection of nineteenth-century Californian art and immaculate Queen Anne furniture. One block east, the **Haas-Lilienthal House**, 2007 Franklin St (Wed noon–4pm, Sun 11am–4.30pm; $3), is the headquarters for the *Foundation for San Francisco's Architectural Heritage* – a fully furnished Queen Anne-style house with more than its fair share of gingerbread trim, turrets, cupolas and filigree. The unchallenged star, but unfortunately one you can't venture inside, is the **Spreckels Mansion** at Gough and Washington, whose ostentatious faded elegance, grand in every detail, is as unrestricted in its design as in its decay. Follow the house around to its lovely sloping back garden and look at it in its entirety – pulp-romance writer Danielle Steele took over the empty mansion several years ago, and despite a spending programme on the inside that made her the darling of the interior design industry, the outside has mercifully yet to be tackled and crumbles gracefully on its majestic perch.

The Presidio

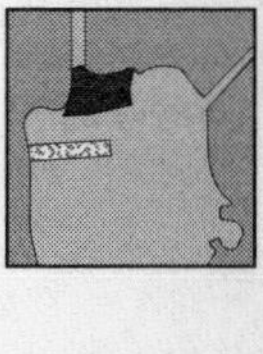

Occupying most of the northwest tip of the San Francisco peninsula, the **PRESIDIO** covers some 1500 acres and is home to 75 miles of forested roads. After a hundred years of sporadic US military use, in October 1994 it became a national park. City wrangles continue over speculation to sell off parts of the new national park for development, though it seems unlikely that San Franciscans would stand for it. Blissfully free of "attractions", the Presidio offers little more than taking a drive through its eucalyptus-scented highways or choosing a section to hike through. Also a favourite spot with cyclists, the Presidio lacks the congestion of Golden Gate Park, and makes for a pleasant, if lengthy, stroll on the way to the beaches and some incredible views from its windy bluffs.

San Francisco's beaches are covered in Chapter Six.

In the 1770s, the Presidio was founded as a frontier station for the Spanish Empire, which garrisoned the distant peninsula to forestall British and Russian claims on the San Francisco Bay. In 1822, it became the northernmost outpost of the new Mexican republic who abandoned it in 1835 to move north to Sonoma. By 1846, it was occupied by the American armed forces, who billeted their soldiers here for the Modoc War in 1870 and their campaigns against the Apaches in the southwest. The US Army started to develop the inherited adobe structures, but the Presidio didn't take on its present appearance until the 1880s, when an environmentally minded major initiated a programme of forestation that changed it from a windswept, sandy piece of coastline into the dense thicket it is today. Afterwards it served mainly as a medical and administrative army base; the only time its harbour defences were activated was for a brief period during World War II. Today, almost thirty acres of the Presidio is given over to the **San Francisco National Military Cemetery** – a sobering sight.

The main entrance to the Presidio is by way of Lombard Street, west of Pacific Heights and the Marina. A huge gate bearing the figures of Liberty and Victory leads you inside to the main quadrangle of buildings that functioned as the military headquarters. There's a small chapel and adobe officers' mess, but the only thing you can actually visit is the **Presidio Museum**, on Lincoln Boulevard and Funston Avenue (Tues–Sun 10am–4pm; free) – it's the original hospital building, converted into exhibition space. In addition to military history, detailed models and maps trace how San Francisco's appearance has changed over the centuries, showing which parts of the city were wiped out by the 1906 earthquake.

You may recognize Fort Point as the site of Kim Novak's suicide attempt in Alfred Hitchcock's Vertigo.

The Presidio's (and perhaps even San Francisco's) most dramatic location is the **Fort Point National Historic Site** (at the head of Marine Drive, daily 10am–5pm; free), a brick fortress seawall built in the 1850s to guard the bay. From here, where the surf crashes and the Pacific stretches interminably, you get a good sense of the Presidio as the westernmost frontier of the nation. It was originally to have been demolished to make way for the Golden Gate Bridge, but the redesign of the southern approach left it intact. It's a theatrical site, with the ocean pounding away beneath the great span of the bridge high above. Supposedly, the water here makes for one of the best (if most foolhardy) local surfing spots.

The Golden Gate Bridge

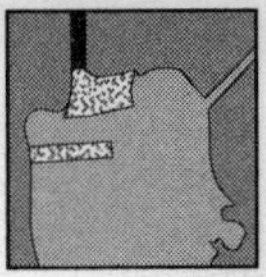

The orange towers of the **Golden Gate Bridge** – probably the most beautiful, certainly the most photographed, bridge in the world – are visible from almost every point of elevation in San Francisco. The only cleft in Northern California's 600-mile continental wall, for years this mile-wide strait was considered unbridgeable. As much an architectural as an engineering feat, the Golden Gate took only 52 months to design and build, and was opened in 1937. Designed by Joseph Strauss, it was the first really massive suspension bridge, with a span of 4200ft, and until 1959 ranked as the world's longest. It connects the city at its northwesterly point on the peninsula to Marin County and Northern California, rendering the hitherto essential ferry crossing redundant, and was designed to withstand winds of up to a hundred miles an hour and to swing as much as 27ft. Handsome on a clear day, the bridge takes on an eerie quality when the thick white fogs pour in and hide it almost completely.

You can either drive or walk across. The drive is the more thrilling of the two options as you race under the bridge's towers, but the half-hour walk across it really gives you time to take in its enormous size and absorb the views of the city behind you and the headlands of Northern California straight ahead. Pause at the midway point and consider the seven or so suicides a month who choose this spot, 260ft up, as their jumping-off spot. Monitors of such events speculate that victims always face the city before they leap. In 1995, when the suicide toll from the bridge had reached almost 1000, police kept the figures quiet to avoid a rush of would-be suicides going for the dubious distinction of being the thousandth person to leap. Perhaps the best-loved symbol of San Francisco, in 1987 the Golden Gate proved an auspicious place for a sunrise party when crowds gathered to celebrate its fiftieth anniversary. Some quarter of a million people turned up (a third of the city's entire population); the winds were strong and the huge numbers caused the bridge to buckle, but fortunately not to break.

SAINT BENEDICT SCHOOL
DUFFIELD ROAD
DERBY DE22 1JD

Chapter 4

Civic Center, South of Market and the Mission

While much of San Francisco is depicted as some kind of urban utopia – not always erroneously – the districts of the **Civic Center**, **South of Market** and the **Mission** reveal a city of harsher realities. Pretty, tree-lined streets, hills and stunning views are conspicuously absent down here, and for the most part these areas are a gritty, blue-collar reminder that not everybody in San Francisco has it easy. The Civic Center, supposedly the bastion of civic pride, has big problems. The offices of the mayor overlook a park that for several years, between evictions, has been the chosen abode of hundreds of homeless people, much to the embarrassment of City Hall. Immediately north of the Civic Center, **Polk Gulch** on the other hand, thrives on its slightly seedy edge, with a flourishing commercial strip of bars, theatres and shops that nicely balance the comparatively staid nature of gay life in the Castro. Running parallel to Polk Gulch, north of the Civic Center, the main north–south city artery of **Van Ness Avenue**, a traffic-swarmed stretch of Highway 101, runs along the westernmost edge of downtown and makes the clearest division between San Francisco's commercial and residential districts.

Tucked between the southern end of Van Ness Avenue and downtown, the **Tenderloin** is San Francisco's most notorious neighbourhood. Despite attempts at gentrification and the arrival of Vietnamese families with their small businesses, it remains a stronghold of low-rent dwellings, the homeless, and the soup kitchens and shelters that sustain them. This district is relatively small and nowhere near as menacing at its LA counterparts, though you shouldn't expect to walk around and not be hassled for money. South of Market (SoMa), the large chunk of land that takes its name from its position immediately south of Market Street, has responded rather better to recent investment and has even effected a transformation. An industrial wasteland turned hip club turf, SoMa's once fairly empty blocks are changing beyond recognition by bold commercial and housing initiatives. Its biggest boost came in January 1995, when the new **Museum of Modern Art** opened its doors as part of the thriving **Yerba Buena Center** cultural project. The last part of SoMa to change will be the old docklands around **Mission Rock** and **China Basin** – still romantically desolate, save the odd waterfront location for a beer and burger. In sharp contrast, the large, lively, low-rent Mission has long been the city's first stop for immigrants. Home to many different nationalities over the years, for the last couple of decades it has been solidly and increasingly Hispanic. A recent smattering of smart new bars and restaurants has created a hip pocket of the neighbourhood known as the **Valencia Corridor**. Nestling in a hilly corner west of the Mission, **Potrero Hill** couldn't be more different. A small enclave of brightly painted houses on slopes offering panoramic views of downtown and the waterfront, it is determinedly village-like and resistant to change.

Civic Center

Born out of a grand, celebratory architectural scheme, the **CIVIC CENTER**, a little way southwest of the downtown area, is an impressive layout of majestic federal and municipal Beaux Arts buildings focusing on the grand dome of **City Hall**, designed by Arthur Brown and completed in 1915, just in time for the Panama Pacific International Exhibition. The surrounding complex is a watered-down version of planner Daniel Burnham's ambitious schemes for the city, which would have seen grand avenues fanning out across San Francisco, including one extending to the Panhandle of Golden Gate Park. Drawn up with the help of architect Willis Polk, the plans won the wholehearted approval of city leaders, only to be delayed by the massive earthquake and fire of 1906. Political difficulties after the quake delayed the project further, and although Burnham doggedly pursued his vision of a "City Beautiful", the project was only finished after his death. He no doubt would be saddened by the complex today: it's still a fine collection of buildings, but the elegant layout has become the focus of San Francisco's most glaring social problem – the homeless. Periodically, police evict the hundreds of street people who set up makeshift homes on the plaza opposite City Hall and on the grass verges around the quadrangle, moving them to temporary shelters in response to a growing rage at the lack of decent public housing in the city. Being San Francisco's centre for the performing arts – by night, beautifully lit and swarming with dinner-suited San Franciscans heading in and out of the opera, ballet and symphony – the problem was not one that could be easily hidden, and although the authorities have since established a number of shelters, the Civic Center, along with the adjacent Tenderloin, remains the most intensely down-and-out area of town.

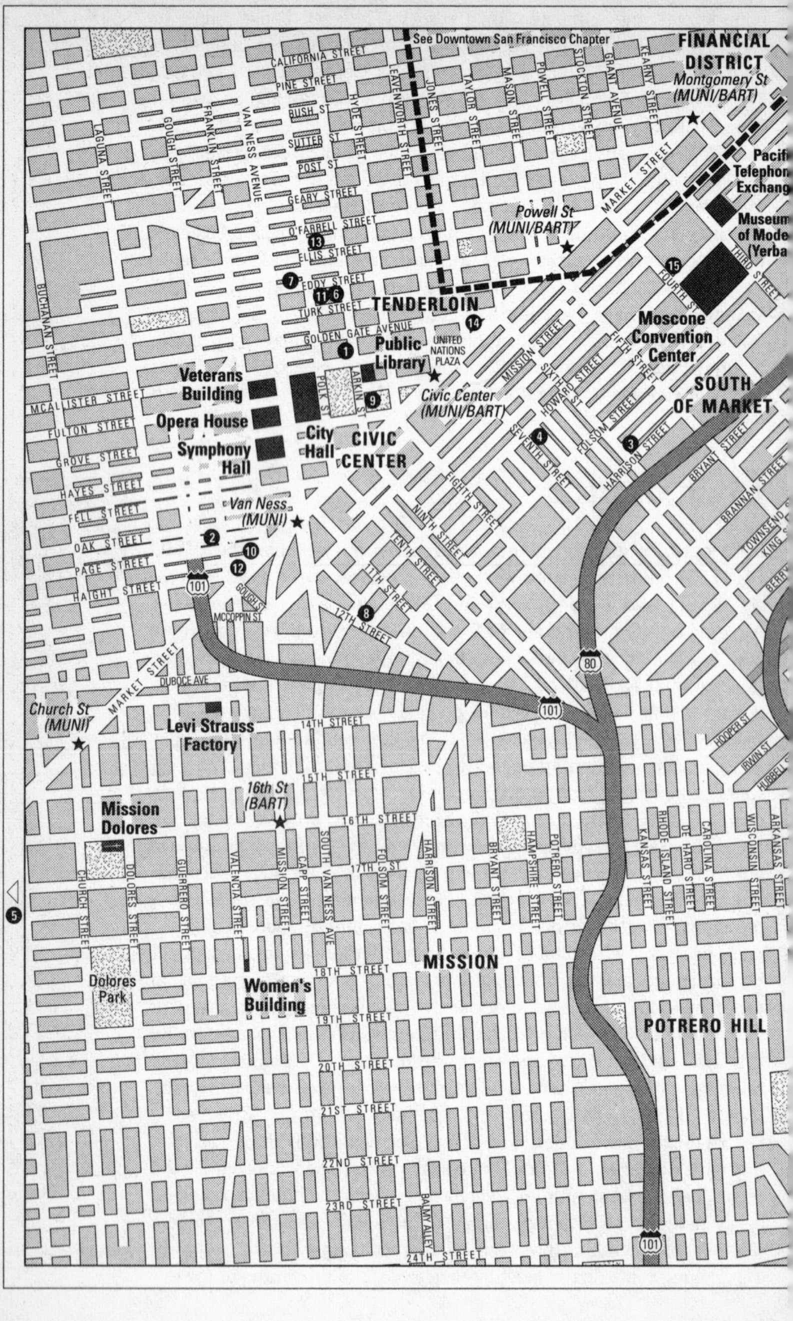
See Downtown San Francisco Chapter
FINANCIAL DISTRICT
Montgomery St (MUNI/BART)
Pacifi Telephon Exchang
Museum of Mode (Yerba
Powell St (MUNI/BART)
TENDERLOIN
Moscone Convention Center
SOUTH OF MARKET
Public Library
UNITED NATIONS PLAZA
Civic Center (MUNI/BART)
Veterans Building
Opera House
Symphony Hall
City Hall
CIVIC CENTER
Van Ness (MUNI)
Church St (MUNI)
Levi Strauss Factory
16th St (BART)
Mission Dolores
Dolores Park
Women's Building
MISSION
POTRERO HILL
CALIFORNIA STREET
PINE STREET
BUSH ST
SUTTER ST
POST ST
GEARY STREET
O'FARRELL STREET
ELLIS STREET
EDDY STREET
TURK STREET
GOLDEN GATE AVENUE
MCALLISTER STREET
FULTON STREET
GROVE STREET
HAYES STREET
FELL STREET
OAK STREET
PAGE STREET
HAIGHT STREET
MCCOPPIN ST
DUBOCE AVE
MARKET STREET
14TH STREET
15TH STREET
16TH STREET
17TH ST
18TH STREET
19TH STREET
20TH STREET
21ST STREET
22ND STREET
23RD STREET
24TH STREET
LAGUNA STREET
GOUGH STREET
FRANKLIN STREET
VAN NESS AVENUE
HYDE STREET
LEAVENWORTH STREET
JONES STREET
TAYLOR STREET
MASON STREET
POWELL STREET
STOCKTON STREET
GRANT AVENUE
KEARNY STREET
BUCHANAN STREET
POLK ST
LARKIN ST
MISSION STREET
HOWARD STREET
SIXTH ST
FIFTH STREET
FOURTH ST
THIRD STREET
SEVENTH STREET
EIGHTH STREET
NINTH STREET
TENTH STREET
11TH STREET
12TH STREET
FOLSOM STREET
HARRISON STREET
BRYANT STREET
BRANNAN STREET
TOWNSEND
KING
BERRY
HOOPER ST
IRWIN ST
HUBBELL
GOUGH ST
CHURCH STREET
DOLORES STREET
GUERRERO STREET
VALENCIA STREET
MISSION STREET
CAPP STREET
SOUTH VAN NESS AVE
FOLSOM STREET
HARRISON STREET
BALMY ALLEY
BRYANT STREET
HAMPSHIRE STREET
POTRERO STREET
KANSAS STREET
RHODE ISLAND STREET
DE HARO STREET
CAROLINA STREET
WISCONSIN STREET
ARKANSAS STREET
101
80
1
2
3
4
5
6
7
8
9
10
11
12
13
14
15

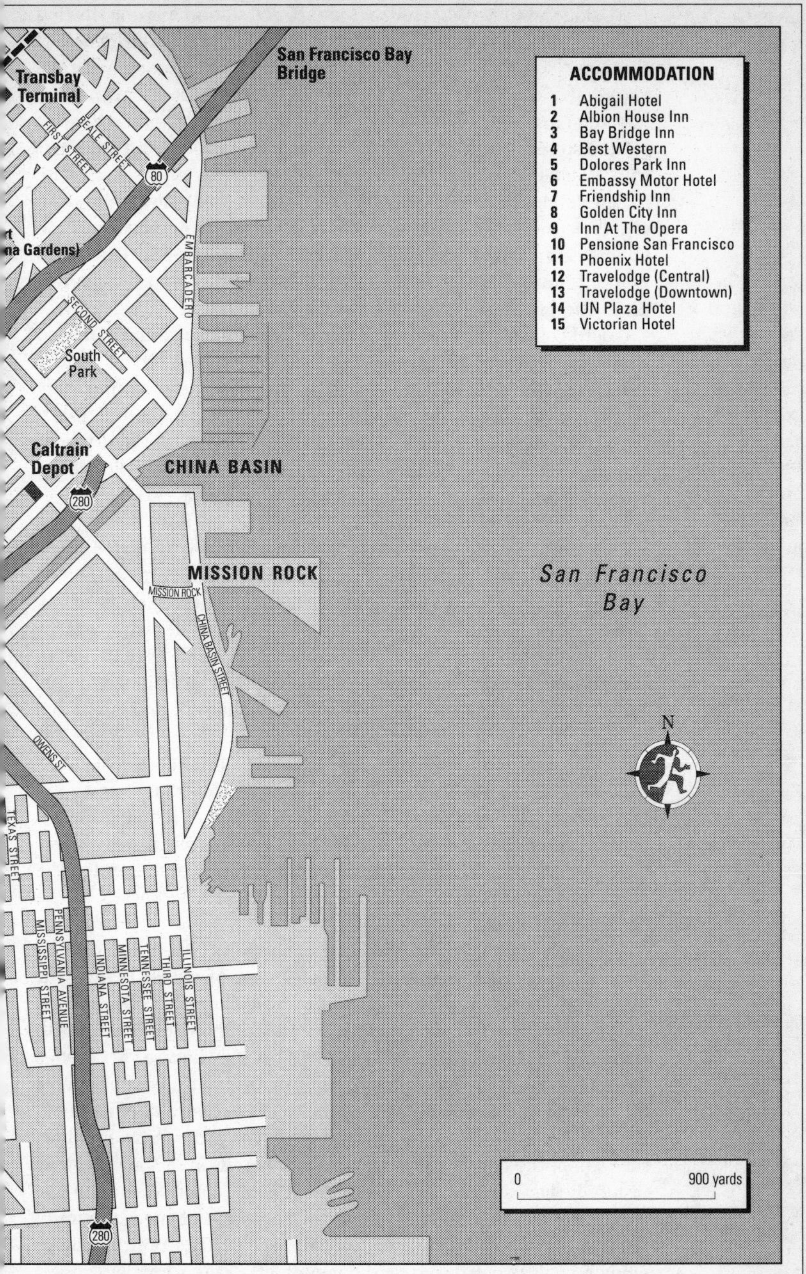
San Francisco Bay Bridge
Transbay Terminal
FIRST STREET
BEALE STREET
80
na Gardens)
EMBARCADERO
SECOND STREET
South Park
Caltrain Depot
CHINA BASIN
280
MISSION ROCK
MISSION ROCK
CHINA BASIN STREET
OWENS ST
TEXAS STREET
PENNSYLVANIA AVENUE
MISSISSIPPI STREET
INDIANA STREET
MINNESOTA STREET
TENNESSEE STREET
THIRD STREET
ILLINOIS STREET
280
San Francisco Bay
N
ACCOMMODATION
1 Abigail Hotel
2 Albion House Inn
3 Bay Bridge Inn
4 Best Western
5 Dolores Park Inn
6 Embassy Motor Hotel
7 Friendship Inn
8 Golden City Inn
9 Inn At The Opera
10 Pensione San Francisco
11 Phoenix Hotel
12 Travelodge (Central)
13 Travelodge (Downtown)
14 UN Plaza Hotel
15 Victorian Hotel
0
900 yards

Civic Center

Using the Civic Center *MUNI* and *BART* station as your starting point, you'll emerge from underground facing the **United Nations Plaza** just south of the main quadrangle. Built to commemorate the founding of the UN here in 1949, it is an attractive design with fountain and flags which has become the largest public urinal in the city – if the stench doesn't deter you, the characters who hang around it will. Wednesdays are the exception, when the site serves **The Farmer's Market,** the city's largest and most inexpensive fruit and vegetable market. Moving north, you enter the main square of the Civic Center, where, on McAllister and Larkin, the **San Francisco Public Library** is three floors of regal turn-of-the-century architecture. The classical columns adorning the entrance guard a fairly standard collection of reading material, although the **San Francisco History Room and Archives** on the third floor is excellent (Tues–Sat 10am–6pm; free). In this quiet, crowd-free space, used mainly as a research library, the books are primarily of scholarly interest, but some fascinating glass cases are packed with bits and pieces evoking the history of the city: newspaper cuttings, old coins, photographs and paraphernalia from the Gold Rush years.

Once the new library next door is completed, the old building will house the Asian Art Museum, now in Golden Gate Park – see p.128.

Dominating the quadrangle at its far end on Polk Street, **City Hall** is arguably the best-looking building in town. Modelled on St Peter's Cathedral in Rome, this grandiose copper-green-domed baroque structure of granite and marble forms the nucleus of the Civic Center. The interior is as grand as its facade, with a large baroque marble staircase dominating the centre, leading up to opulent arches and balustrades, all beneath a gold-inlaid dome. Sadly, the building closed in 1995 for a seismic refit and is not due to open again until 1999. It was here in 1978 that Dan White got past metal-detecting security by climbing through a basement window and assassinated Mayor George Moscone and gay Supervisor Harvey Milk. Later, when White was found guilty of manslaughter (not murder), it was the scene of violent demonstrations, as gay protesters set fire to police vehicles and stormed the doors of City Hall – an event that has come to be known as the "White Night Riot".

For more on the assassination of Harvey Milk, see p.117.

Directly behind City Hall on Van Ness Avenue are San Francisco's cultural mainstays, most elegant of which is the **War Memorial Opera House**, home to the *San Francisco Opera* and *Ballet*. A suitably refined structure, its understated grandeur puts to shame the giant Modernist fishbowl of the **Louise M Davies Symphony Hall** one block down. Built in 1980, at a cost of almost $35 million, the symphony hall has none of the restraint of its dignified neighbour, and despite having fans in the progressive architecture camp, the consensus is that it's an aberration of the otherwise tastefully harmonious scheme of the Civic Center. (Between the two, The Veteran's Building is the former home of the Museum of Modern Art, which has moved to SoMa; see p.105.) Both buildings enjoy a healthy patronage, and come nightfall the formally dressed arrive by the busload. Sadly, few performances are subsidized, so prices remain generally high. Until 1997, the War Memorial Opera House will also be closed for earthquake-proof engineering work and the ballet and opera will be performing in selected venues around the city.

Civic Center

See p.265 for details of ballet and opera performances.

If your budget doesn't stretch to a night at the opera, you can at least get a sense of its history and success at the **San Francisco Performing Arts Library and Museum**, 399 Grove St (Mon–Fri noon–5pm; free), around the corner between the opera house and symphony hall. Housing the largest collection of performing arts material outside of New York, the museum has over a million painstakingly collected programmes, photographs, posters and press clippings concentrating on music, dance, theatre and opera. Performing arts fans could spend hours raking through the memorabilia, the highlight of which is the Isadora Duncan collection, focusing on the influential dancer who was born in the city in 1877.

Nearby, at 155 Grove St, the gallery of the **San Francisco Arts Commission** is the foremost exhibition space for up-and-coming artists in the Bay Area. Less prestigious, but worth a look, is the **San Francisco Women Artists Gallery** at 370 Hayes St, concentrating

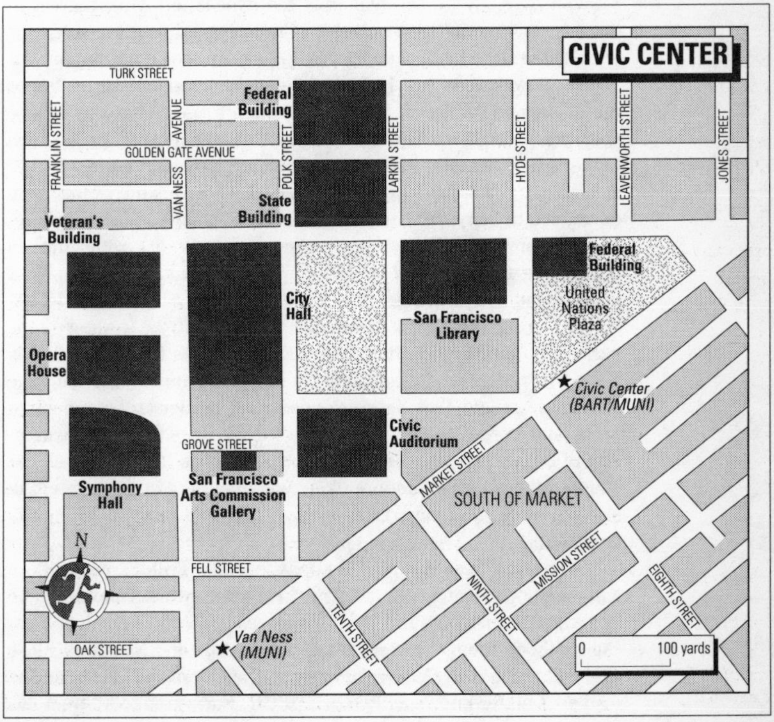

mostly on photographs, alongside some paintings and crafts. By far the most superior commercial gallery is the **Vorpal Gallery** at 393 Grove St – a large space with fine contemporary work that merits a browse.

Beginning to evolve on the western fringes of the Civic Center is a clutch of fashionable restaurants and bars known locally as **Hayes Valley**, as most of them are centred along Hayes Street (see *Restaurants* and *Bars and Cafés* pp.231 & 250).

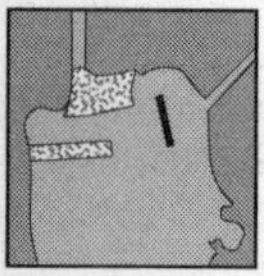

Van Ness Avenue and Polk Street

Running parallel to each other from Market Street near the Civic Center, north to the waterfront, the major thoroughfares of **Van Ness Avenue** and **Polk Street**, though no more than a block apart, have quite distinct characters. Each has enough movie houses, restaurants, bars and stores to count as an autonomous strip, and strict social distinctions can be made between those who shop and dine on one as opposed to the other. They may not be at the top of your sightseeing list, but you'll certainly use them at some point to traverse the city.

Van Ness, by far the busier of the two, is the widest street in the city, and as the major carrier of northbound traffic headed for the Golden Gate Bridge and beyond, it rarely sees a quiet moment. Traffic flows pretty much 24 hours per day and the street is not recommended for casual strolling. Though it seems hard to believe now, when originally laid out in 1854 this was a quiet, prestigious boulevard of graceful mansions, which were dynamited in 1906 to ebb the fire that had raged through downtown and would have consumed the city had the firefighters not managed to stop it here. The few surviving houses were used as temporary retail outlets during the rebuilding of downtown, and apart from a couple of condominium complexes, the avenue has not been residential since. During the 1920s, a stately row of luxury car showrooms were built and these remain today as the places to shop for Rolls Royces, Jaguars and Cadillacs. Most interesting is the Cadillac showroom at **901 Van Ness Ave**, designed by Bernard Maybeck in 1928, and a temple-like construction for the worship and consumption of luxury automobiles. It's doubtful that you'll find yourself car shopping, however; it's more likely you'll be here at night to eat in one of Van Ness's many restaurants or take in a movie at one of its theatres.

While Van Ness is a place to pass through, **Polk Street** is more a place to pause, and can make a refreshing contrast to some of the city's stuffier neighbourhoods. It improves the further north you go, especially on the southwestern side of Russian and Nob hills, close to the junction with California Street at the end of the cable-car line – an area better known as **POLK GULCH**. For years Polk Street has been home to the sleazier side of the city's gay culture, but apartment prices here are beginning to rival the more expensive city addresses, and the strip looks set for big changes.

Polk Gulch is still a centre for interesting and affordable small shops, several good movie theatres, San Francisco's best oyster bar and some rollicking good drinking holes. The characters who hang out here are far from dull – the poet John Wieners wrote the *Hotel Wentley* poems in Polk Gulch, Frank Norris lived here for a while and now has a small side street off the strip named after him – and it still nurtures a small contingent of poets in its diners and coffee shops, muttering at their notebooks. Go by day for inexpensive snooping around its bookstores and clothing shops, but Polk Street is best appreciated at night when the streets fill up with people eating on the cheap, going to the movies, or visiting the neighbourhood's **gay bars**, which have a raw (though not inhospitable) edge and still rock to a beat more reminiscent of the free-wheeling 1970s. It's hardly intimidating, but if the thought of open solicitation bothers you you're probably better off giving it a miss. A famous neighbourhood spot is the **Mitchell Brothers O'Farrell Theatre**, 895 O'Farrell St. This San Franciscan institution is notorious for its sexual entertainment and entered into local legend several years ago when one of the Mitchell brothers murdered the other.

If you're here at the end of June or beginning of July, make an effort to attend the **Polk Street Fair**, possibly the largest assembly of leather-clad gay men you're ever likely to see (see "Festivals and Holidays", p.42) as they gather for a weekend of gay celebration and high-spirited revelry.

The Tenderloin

The **TENDERLOIN**, squashed on the north side of Market Street between Union Square's Theater District and the Civic Center, is a small, uninviting area measuring no more than four blocks by five. Despite its prime location beneath Nob Hill, this remains one of the shabbiest – and poorest – spots in town. The streets are the dirtiest and most litter-strewn in the whole city, and form a kind of base for increasing numbers of homeless, who cram the local soup kitchens and flophouses, while between the poorhouses and the porn shops prostitutes do a brisk trade. Despite complaints from the recent wave of Vietnamese and Laotian immigrants who have moved in with their young families, nothing seems likely to change, at least in the immediate future. That's a pity, as the Tenderloin holds some of San Francisco's least expensive hotels, and many travellers on limited budgets find themselves staying here. If you are among them, it's best to treat this area simply as a place to sleep, and move on to the more interesting parts of town for your entertainment.

For columnist Herb Caen's account of the Tenderloin, see p.298.

The Tenderloin

Smack in the middle of town, the Tenderloin is at least convenient, and most things you'll want to see will be within walking distance; also, thanks to the Vietnamese immigrants, there are several places for ultra-cheap food-on-the-run. There are some lively, if grimy, bars a few blocks away in the Theater District. Partly as an attempt to spruce the area up for the immigrant influx, the city has gone to great lengths to design a "bum-proof" park on Jones and Eddy streets, replete with every imaginable barrier to dissuade the locals from establishing residence – on a good day, and with heavy patrolling by local police, it can claim to be a success.

Efforts to dignify the strip of **Taylor** around **Eddy** and **Turk** have been less successful; despite the constant police patrols, and city programmes to make the streets safer, drug dealers and prostitutes have made this their territory. Lingering is not recommended.

South of Market

As Market Street bisects the city, the division it makes is more than simple geography. Its north side, with perhaps the exception of the Tenderloin, is affluent, bristling and lively; the south side, from just beyond the Embarcadero to about 12th Street was, until very recently, a half-used industrial and transportation area with cheap residential hotels, and on the face of things, one of the city's least appealing quarters. This is **SOMA** (South of Market), a district of old factory spaces that in the last fifteen years or so have been converted into galleries, fashionable restaurants and nightclubs, bringing about a dramatic renaissance, and thriving in the 1990s with an altered reputation. The biggest change was the recent arrival of the new **Museum of Modern Art**, part of the Yerba Buena Center. Culture aside, SoMa is the only place any serious San Franciscan night owl will be seen after dark. It's reminiscent, in a way, of New York's SoHo, and by night it can fairly claim to be the epicentre of San Franciscan clubland.

The first factories and foundries appeared as early as the 1850s, but the area boomed as an industrial base in the 1940s after World War II and, with its extensive docks and railyards, became the largest transportation hub on the West Coast. The decline of shipping and the rail freight system in the 1960s left much of the area desolate. Ironically, the cheap hotels that housed many of SoMa's residents have been razed to the ground in order to build the Yerba Buena Center; homelessness has increased dramatically, taking the edge off the area's "improvements".

SoMa divides roughly into four areas: the increasingly developed area **around the Transbay Terminal** and the **Moscone Convention Centre**, named after the mayor who was assassinated along with Harvey Milk; the **nightclub plexus** around 11th and Folsom streets; the area between Third and Fourth streets, home of the new **Yerba Buena Center** and another nucleus of activity; and, finally, the as-yet-undeveloped dockland areas of **Mission Rock** and **China Basin**.

The Museum of Modern Art, Yerba Buena Center and around

Of all the recent SoMa arrivals, none is more exciting than the new home of the **Museum of Modern Art**, 151 Third St (Tues–Sun 11am–6pm, Thurs 11am–9pm, closed Mon; $7), which has doubled its former exhibition space and – optimists predict – will make San Francisco the foremost centre for contemporary art on the West Coast. The $62 million building was designed by Swiss architect Mario Botta, and the allegation that the building is far more beautiful than anything inside is hard to dispute. Flooded with natural light from a soaring truncated, cylindrical skylight, it's a sight to behold in the often tatty streets of SoMa.

The permanent collection is distinguished by some major paintings from the **American Abstract Expressionist** school, most notably Clyfford Still, Jackson Pollock and Philip Guston. Other strong areas include **German Expressionism**, **Fauvism** and **Mexican painting** by Frida Kahlo and Diego Rivera. There's also a smattering of works by Dali, Matisse, Picasso, O'Keefe and Kandinsky, but by no means their best. The museum excels most with its collection of twentieth-century **photography**, which includes work by both European and American photographers: Cartier-Bresson, Alfred Stieglitz, Brassai, as well as Man Ray and Ansel Adams, along with a strong collection of modern works by Asian photographers. The most expanded part of the museum is its **architecture** and **design** collection, with models and drawings associated with the West Coast and the Pacific Rim by Timothy Pflueger, Charles Moore, William Turnbull and Shiro Kuramata. A burgeoning **media** arts department boast some very progressive video installations by pioneers like Bill Viola, Dan Graham and others who have over two-thousand square feet of specially designed gallery space to present their works.

But perhaps the museum's strongest suit is its calendar of temporary exhibitions made possible by their newly acquired financial muscle. By appointment, there's also access to an exhaustive **Fine Arts Library** with over 12,000 volumes for the committed archivist, though most will be happy with the **bookstore**'s exhaustive stock of posters and art-related literature.

Opposite the museum is another new totem of civic pride, the **Yerba Buena Center**, bounded by Third, Fourth, Mission and Folsom streets. Its premise is to provide a forum for the work of San Francisco's diverse artistic and ethnic communities, and features a theatre and visual arts centre. The work is rather provincial compared to the stuff in the modern museum– if you've ever wondered what a gay Korean baker's interpretation of life in San Francisco might be, wonder no more. Recently moved from Fort Mason to the Center, the **Mexican Museum** is a cut above. It houses a small, but important, collection of pre-Hispanic, colonial and folk art. But the Center's best feature is its setting in five and a half acres of lovely gardens, with a fifty-foot Sierra granite waterfall memorial to Martin Luther King Jr. Also around this area of Fourth Street are a couple of independent museums worth taking a look at. The **Cartoon Art Museum,** 814 Mission St (Wed–Fri 11am–5pm, Sat 10am–5pm, Sun 1–5pm; $3.50) is dedicated to the preservation, collection and appreciation of original cartoons and is a treasure trove for fans of this unique art form. At 250 Fourth St, the **Ansel Adams Center** (Tues–Sun 11.00am–5pm; first Thurs of Month 11am–8pm; $4) has a permanent collection of the work of the famed California photographer as well as four other galleries dedicated to photographic and mixed media installations.

The Transbay Terminal and around

The corner of SoMa closest to the Embarcadero holds a large concentration of buildings that were prohibited residence in the Financial District. The densest part of SoMa, this includes the **Transbay Terminal** at First and Mission, swarming twice daily with commuters, and the first in a proposed series of yuppie housing developments, **Bayside Village**. City ordinances state that any commercial downtown developer must make funds available for medium- to low-cost housing for the extra workforce that is drawn to the city. With rents starting at $1000 per month, it's a questionable definition of low-cost housing, though terrifically handy for the Financial District whiz kids who have only a ten-minute walk to work. Recently, the area has spawned a few lively bars and restaurants (see Chapters Thirteen and Fouteen), which help to minimize its desolate feeling by night.

The **Rincon Center**, 101 Spear St, was originally San Francisco's main post office, but has been tastefully converted into a shopping centre. It is worth a look, not just for its Art Deco architectural interest but for the permanent exhibition of murals by Anton Refregier. In all, 27 murals depict life during the Depression and industrial themes; they were inspired by Diego Rivera, who left his mark in several sites around the city during the 1920s and 1930s. Walking west from the Rincon Center along Mission, you hit the 200 block of New Montgomery Street and the **Pacific Telephone Building**, a product of architecture's golden age in the 1920s. It's a gently tapered, subtly shadowed mountain, detailed in terracotta – really just another office building, but one that aspires to greatness.

Though most people only visit at night, a daytime stroll will reveal some interesting, if unexpected, corners of SoMa. Nestled between

Brannan and Bryant, and Second and Third streets, **South Park** is an odd fish in the heavy industrial landscape, a small open space designed by an English architect to mimic the squares of London. The construction of the Bay Bridge – which has its western foot just a block away – spelt the end of this as a residential neighbourhood and the smart set high-tailed it to Pacific Heights and Nob Hill.

The few surviving bits have been recently rediscovered and increasingly house the offices of architects and designers, who can be seen lunching at the chic and genuinely French *South Park Café* on the square. Around the corner, where Third Street meets Brannan, a **plaque** marks the birthplace of *Call of the Wild* writer Jack London, though he soon escaped what were then pretty mean streets, enjoying his better days in Oakland and the valleys of Sonoma.

The South Park Café *is reviewed on p.251.*

Folsom Street

Folsom Street between Seventh and 11th streets is the main artery of clubland. A former gay strip, it was once the centre for much lewder goings-on than the now mainly respectable Castro. A few gay clubs and bars remain, but for the most part the mix is pretty diverse and you should expect to find everything except the very tame. The kernel of activity is around Folsom and 11th streets, where the largest grouping of clubs and bars draw crowds who don't mind the long waits at weekends. Comparatively little traffic uses this intersection during the day, and it comes as a surprise to see the bumper-to-bumper and double-parked vehicles after midnight. If you find yourself here during the day and want to check out the area, take a walk along Folsom to the block between Seventh and Eighth streets. *Brainwash* at 1122 Folsom St is the epitome of SoMa, a café where you can also do your laundry; opposite, *Buster's Newsstand* has an exhaustive collection of magazines and guides to SoMa and the nightlife scene. Rising impressively out of the desolation of the area, the **Old Mint Museum** at Fifth and Mission streets is an unexpected sight. Classically styled from brick and stone, the building is no longer used as a mint, or even a museum after earthquake damage, but it lends a little hauteur to a gritty neighbourhood.

Mission Rock and China Basin

With all the new development in progress, it can be hard to imagine what SoMa looked like before. But the real spirit of blue-collar, industrial San Francisco can still be found around the abandoned docks and old shipyards known as **Mission Rock** and **China Basin**. They cover a large area on the eastern edge of the peninsula, and unless you're wildly energetic, you'll probably need a car to get the best out of them. Deserted, apart from a few spots along the water, it's strange to think that this was once the busiest port along the

West Coast, employing thousands of men, most of whom were members of San Francisco's radical Longshoremen's Union. Few of the docks are operational now, and the most the area is good for is an indolent stroll, taking in the views of the East Bay across the water and stopping off for a drink at the couple of places along the shoreline.

The easiest way to reach the district is to follow Third Street south from Market as it curves round to meet the dock area. Starting at the **switchyards** where the drawbridge crosses China Basin Channel at Third Street, you'll see a small hut-like building on the south side of the bridge – formerly *Blanche's*, a tiny café that drew attention to the problems of development here when the city tried to get Blanche to move. Despite having her trading licence taken away, she opened up the small pier, which juts out over the channel switchyards, for all-comers to bring their sandwiches and wine at lunchtime and look at her collection of antiques from the mills of San Francisco's boomtown days. Sadly, financial deprivation pushed Blanche into retirement and the site has now been taken over by a Vietnamese family who can never quite capture *Blanche's* ambience. It was on the switchyards below that Jack Kerouac worked as a brakeman in the 1950s for Southern Pacific – at the same time writing the material that was later to appear in *Lonesome Traveller*, detailing scenes of SoMa skid-row hotels, drunks and whores.

A short walk south takes you to the heart of China Basin, the old water inlet and Mission Rock – the old Pier 50 that juts out into the bay. This was the focus of the old port where freight ships used to dock from Asia. Occasionally the odd ship will sail by, but these days military ships from the Oakland Naval Base are more likely to be cruising the bay than the freight liners that once jammed the waterways. A few, small boat clubs have sprung up along the waterfront, but most people come to visit the *Mission Rock Resort*, a creaky wooden structure that is a local landmark. Locals are determined that the *Mission Rock* should not be sacrificed in the rush for development, but frankly its chances of survival are slim once the Mission Bay Project picks up steam. At the northern end of the docks around Third and 16th streets, behind the *Esprit* outlet, *42 Degrees* is the last word in fashionable San Francisco dining.

For more on 42 Degrees, *see p.233.*

The Mission

Low-rent, hip, colourful, occasionally dangerous and solidly Hispanic working-class, the **MISSION** is what's known as San Francisco's *transitional* neighbourhood. Positioned way south of downtown, it is also the city's warmest, avoiding the fogs which blanket most of the peninsula during the summer. Stretching from the southern end of SoMa down to Army Street in the south, the

The Mission

Mission is a large district, although with *BART* stations at each end getting here isn't a problem. Most of the action takes place in the eight blocks between the two *BART* stations (16th and 24th streets) along Mission, Valencia and Dolores. The streets are lined with thrift stores, bookstores, cafés and bars in which it isn't difficult to empty your pockets. The famous transition the neighbourhood is allegedly undergoing has recently included a clutch of trendy restaurants and bars referred to as the **Valencia Corridor**, which pull in people from all over the city. Overall, though, it remains a noisy melange of garages, furniture and junk stores, old movie houses and parking lots. Inexpensive food and a fair concentration of lively nightspots make the Mission a good place to plan a night out.

As a first stop for arriving immigrants to the city, the Mission is something of a microcosm of the history of San Francisco. It was first inhabited by the Scandinavians and Germans, later the Irish, then the Italians, and most recently and significantly, it has been the home of San Francisco's Hispanic population. There's a marked political edge to the area, with active Hispanic campaigning and a multitude of **murals** depicting aspects of the Latin American struggle. Sadly, it is also one of the few areas in town where women are likely to encounter the cat-calling and hissing of Latin men. It is also ironically something of a lesbian stronghold, with feminist bookstores and meeting places dotting the streets. There is, too, a flourishing arts scene – theatre groups, cultural centres and a thriving Latin literary network, possibly San Francisco's most vibrant since the Beats, that feels far away from the middle-class complacency of much of the rest of the city.

The bars and restaurants of the Mission (and the Castro) are detailed on the map on p.235.

The district takes its name from the **Mission Dolores** on 16th and Dolores streets (daily 9am–4pm; $2), San Francisco's oldest building, its fragile adobe structure survived the earthquakes of 1906 and 1989. Founded in 1776, it was the sixth in a series of Spanish missions built to consolidate Spain's claim to California. Distorted as it is in pious romanticism, the true story of California's Mission period is often hard to uncover. Tales of kindly Franciscan friars coming to save the native peoples are misguided fantasy, and in reality the Spanish Franciscans all but obliterated the Native Americans in San Francisco and, indeed, California. The eerie, still, cool interior of the mission is filled with paintings, with an old Mexican statue of St Francis tucked away in one corner. Few reminders remain of the Costanoans who were enslaved here, and little in the adjoining cemetery indicates that over five thousand of them are buried here. As well as the Costanoans, the gravesites are occupied by Spanish, Mexican and Yankee pioneers, California's first governor and San Francisco's first mayor. During the day, tour buses are double-parked outside and if you really want to get the feel for this lovely old mission, the 7.30am Mass or the noon service in Spanish is a better bet. The **Basilica** adjacent to the mission is hardly worth entering, but its Churrigueresque Revival design makes it one of the most beautiful block-fronts in town.

Dolores Street itself is an attractive boulevard divided by a line of palm trees along the western border of the neighbourhood. High on a hill, **Dolores Park** commands the best view of the downtown skyline – a pretty, quiet place to rest during the day, plagued though it is with children on BMX bikes and defecating doggies. Its southern bank has earned the tag **"Dolores Beach"** because of the crowds of semi-naked gay men who gather on warm days to work on their tans and gaze at their fellow men; it's quite a scene. By night, it's a little more sinister and has a reputation for being one of the central exchanges for San Francisco's drug trade.

The Modern Times *bookstore on Valencia Street is reviewed on p.279.*

Valencia Street is a curious mix of housing projects, groovy bars, chronically low-profit, progressive **bookstores** (including the great *Old Wives Tales* at no. 1009 and *Modern Times*, at no. 888 Valencia St) and restaurants. There are few sights proper along here, but the **Levi Strauss & Co Factory** at 250 Valencia St (free tours Wed 10am & 1pm, reserve on ☎565-9159), where you can see how the world's most famous jeans are made, is definitely worth a visit. The Levi Strauss empire started in the Gold Rush days when leftover tent material was used to make work jeans, and has gone on to become the biggest manufacturer of jeans in the world. Tours of the plant include a look at the cutting and sewing operations, and advice on how to "stonewash" your new pair to make them look old.

Two blocks up at 446 Valencia St, **Intersection for the Arts** is a non-profit organization that hosts cultural and theatrical events. The programme changes constantly, but occasionally they have good exhibitions of local artists and it's worth popping in just to see what's on. Similarly the **Women's Building** at 3543 18th St supports gay, lesbian, peace and progressive groups and often has interesting lectures and exhibitions. Across the first floor of the building a mural depicts local feminist heroines. Women's interests generally are well-represented in the neighbourhood with their bookstores and cafés, but nowhere are the needs of a woman better catered to than at **Good Vibrations** at 1210 Valencia St. It's something of a San Francisco institution; see p.279 for details.

Mission Street is a slightly more congested version of Valencia and, unless you're bargain hunting in the thrift stores (see p.275) or hanging around its bars, you should take it as far as **24th Street** – the axis of Latino shopping, with Nicaraguan, Salvadorian, Costa Rican, Mexican and other Latin American stores and restaurants. Apart from being the most authentic Latin street in the neighbourhood, it's a good place to start a self-guided tour of the Mission's 200-odd **murals**, the fruits of a City Hall scheme to occupy the creative talents of the Mission's poor and not unusually disaffected youth before their energies were channelled into criminal activities. Now the major attraction in a neighbourhood that until recently rarely saw tourists, hundreds are peppered all over the Mission. The biggest concentration is along 24th Street between Mission and South Van Ness. The largest is a tribute to local hero **Carlos Santana**, adorning three buildings where 22nd Street meets South Van Ness; for more controversial subject matter, take a walk down **Balmy Alley** between Folsom and Harrison off 24th Street, where every possible surface is covered with murals depicting the political agonies of contemporary Central America. It was started in 1973 by a group of artists and community workers and has become the most quietly admired public art in San Francisco.

More Latin artwork is on display at the **Mission Cultural Center**, 2868 Mission St (daily 10am–6pm), founded in 1977 with the aim of preserving and promoting Latino cultural arts. As well as theatrical productions, poetry readings and classes, there is a large exhibition space for the changing contemporary exhibitions of local paintings and drawings.

Potrero Hill

Cut off from the rest of the Mission by the freeway, rising above San Francisco General Hospital, **POTRERO HILL** is a tiny community that's easy to miss. Its quiet streets and brightly painted houses sit high on a hill overlooking the Mission to the west and the SoMa docks to the north. Unpretentious and solidly residential, it's a peaceful neighbourhood that prides itself on its isolation, a lack of tourist traffic and a pace more evocative of a country village than a major city – it even has its own weekly newspaper. There's precious little to do, but its leafy streets are perfect for a morning stroll, taking in the views of downtown and the docks and pausing for a coffee. There are also several excellent **restaurants** in the area with the notable *Slow Club* (see p.261), which draws an appreciative crowd for the nightly live jazz and tapas-style dining.

Chapter 5

The Central Neighbourhoods

Residential, well tended and, for the most part, almost anodyne in their pleasantness, San Francisco's **CENTRAL NEIGHBOURHOODS** don't have the cachet or excitement of downtown; nor, on the whole, the hip quota of North Beach or South of Market, but they're the main reason San Franciscans find their city so easy to live in. Self-sufficient and independent, each of these inviting hamlets has its own distinct ethnic and social identity, the result of years of immigrant waves and political activity. Bounded by the fancy reaches of Pacific Heights and the Presidio to the north, and stretching from the Civic Center to the Pacific Ocean beaches, they sit snugly in a series of sunny valleys and gentle slopes that make up the core of living space in San Francisco. Their ornate Victorian architecture is interspersed with open spaces and parks, sidewalk cafés and small stores, revealing something of the city's true identity as a remarkably civilized place to call home.

The area as a whole is definitely not poor. The largest and most depressed neighbourhood, the **Western Addition** is shrinking piecemeal, as money from Pacific Heights trickles down in the search for real estate. Its borders are regularly redefined by a creeping gentrification that pays little heed to recession. In its northern reaches, the pristine enclave known as **Japantown** has been spruced up by affluent Japanese families who have bought up lots, opened stores and transformed the streets. South of here, dilapidated housing estates give way at Haight Street to the eponymous **Lower Haight**, another slightly depressed, but inexorably trendy, neighbourhood that almost rivals its famous neighbour to the west, the **Haight-Ashbury**.

The Haight is long past its 1960s heyday of druggy hedonism, but traces of its anti-Establishment past linger in bookstores and cafés that continue to draw a steady subculture. The Haight's biggest appeal, apart from its bars and history, is perhaps its proximity to the urban idyll of **Golden Gate Park**, which stretches west for two miles until it meets the Pacific Ocean.

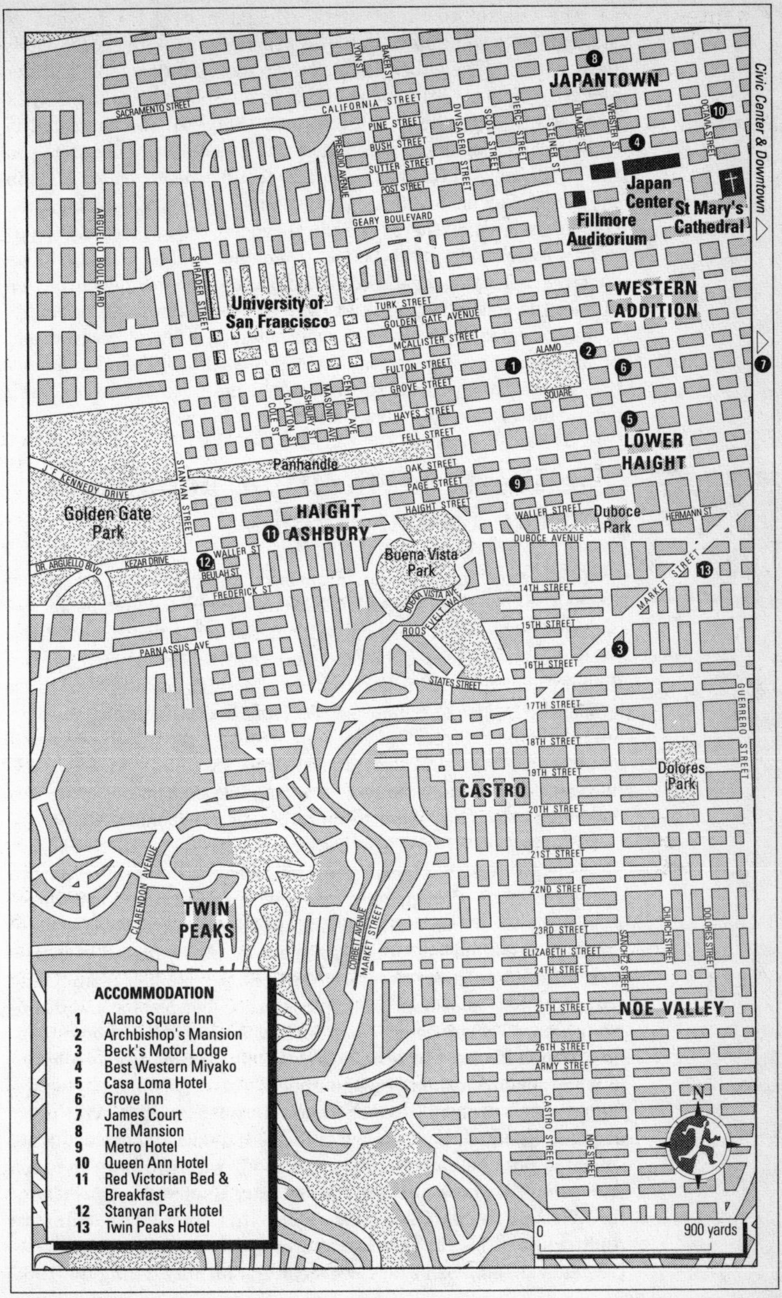

JAPANTOWN
Japan Center
St Mary's Cathedral
Fillmore Auditorium
WESTERN ADDITION
University of San Francisco
ALAMO SQUARE
LOWER HAIGHT
Panhandle
Golden Gate Park
HAIGHT ASHBURY
Duboce Park
Buena Vista Park
CASTRO
Dolores Park
TWIN PEAKS
NOE VALLEY
Civic Center & Downtown
ACCOMMODATION
1 Alamo Square Inn
2 Archbishop's Mansion
3 Beck's Motor Lodge
4 Best Western Miyako
5 Casa Loma Hotel
6 Grove Inn
7 James Court
8 The Mansion
9 Metro Hotel
10 Queen Ann Hotel
11 Red Victorian Bed & Breakfast
12 Stanyan Park Hotel
13 Twin Peaks Hotel
0
900 yards
N

The **Castro**, southeast of the Haight and at the far end of Market Street from downtown San Francisco, is perhaps the city's most distinctive neighbourhood, though more for its people than for any great sights. As the focus of San Francisco's gay community, it has been through the struggles of the 1960s which culminated in widespread recognition, acceptance and a whole lot of decadence in the 1970s, only to be knocked off its feet by the advent of AIDS in the 1980s. Gay pride was not lost for long, though, and amongst the younger generation there is a radical caucus, though the neighbourhood's freewheeling days belong to another era. In a sunny valley over the hill from the Castro, **Noe Valley** is a restful, attractive district that has changed little over the years until very recently. Family-oriented, with a rooted suburban feel, a few chic stores and boutiques are now emerging. **Twin Peaks**, the city's most distinctive summit, looms over Noe Valley and the Castro, offering fresh air and unbeatable 360°-views over the city below.

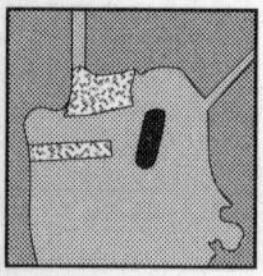

The Western Addition, Japantown and the Lower Haight

Looking at any map of San Francisco, you'll see several blocks labelled the **WESTERN ADDITION**, smack in the middle of the peninsula – a central position which belies its status as one of the city's most relentlessly poor neighbourhoods. Also known as "the Fillmore" after its main thoroughfare, the large, mostly black area spreads both sides of Fillmore Street from Geary Boulevard south to around Haight Street, marked by block after block of semi-abandoned housing projects and low-rent dwellings, where unemployment, drugs and violence are tangible indications that this community does not share in the prosperity that much of the city visibly enjoys.

Over the last few years the city has taken steps to improve conditions here, though only by moving the problem elsewhere. Whole blocks of the Western Addition have been demolished and crime-infested housing projects ripped out and replaced with new structures. In an effort to reform the area, private blocks are being sold on the basis of their proximity to the Civic Center and downtown areas. They're built, claim officials, for middle-income families, though it's hard to imagine any family wanting to buy a house in what remains a slum neighbourhood. This leaves the city with a bigger social problem than the one it's trying to cure, with poor, dispossessed and now homeless black families inevitably being squeezed out and empty units that nobody wants to buy. The area ends abruptly where Fillmore meets Geary Boulevard at the site of the Western Addition's great claim to fame, **The Fillmore Auditorium**. This large, three-storey yellow-brick building was crucial in shaping San Francisco's cultural identity during the 1967

"Summer of Love", when Bill Graham leased the hall and staged acid-drenched concerts by the likes of Jimi Hendrix, Janis Joplin and Jefferson Airplane – often on the same bill – and innovated the light shows that were to become the hallmark of psychedelia. An unofficial city landmark, it was central to San Francisco's emergence as the leader of 1960s culture.

San Francisco can alter dramatically within a few blocks and never is this more visible than where the Western Addition gives way at Geary Boulevard to **JAPANTOWN.** This immaculate community covers the area between Fillmore and Webster streets, with Geary Boulevard marking its southern border and Pine Street separating it from Pacific Heights. Japanese immigrants first came to the area via Hawaii, where they worked on sugar plantations at the turn of the century. Slowly, the businesses they built up in the Western Addition grew to occupy some forty blocks, but the Japanese were obliged to sell their property, reluctantly and in haste, when anti-Japanese hysteria swept California in response to the Pearl Harbor bombing. Several years later, some Japanese drifted back and tried to pick up the threads, but found their old neighbourhood occupied by the black community who now inhabit most of the surrounding area. The limits of the Japanese occupation now looks confined to six blocks.

In contrast to the old, ad hoc and concentrated development of Chinatown, Japantown is well tended and new – and really quite American. Ethnicity is more evident in Spring when the **Cherry Blossom Festival** brings Japanese culture onto the streets. Japantown is something of a misnomer for what is basically a shopping centre – the Japanese Cultural and Trade Center (*Nihonmachi*) – albeit one with a distinctly Eastern flavour and a five-tiered, one hundred-foot pagoda at its heart. Better known as the **Japan Center**, it's home to Japanese restaurants and stores, the Japanese Consulate and, more interestingly, the excellent **Kabuki Complex** – an ultra-modern industrial design in glass with eight movie screens. For most of the year these show current-release and popular films, but at the beginning of May they host the **San Francisco Film Festival** which runs for about three weeks. The Japan Center's other highlight is the **Kabuki Hot Springs** at 1750 Geary Blvd (daily 10am–10pm; ☎922-6000). These genuine community baths offer shiatsu massage, steam baths and other luxuriating facilities for around $35 a session.

There's more on San Francisco's festivals on p.42.

Away from the Japan Center complex there are some signs of a more traditional Japanese lifestyle working alongside the new. Over on Pine Street at Octavia, the **Buddhist Church of San Francisco** has a multiracial congregation and offers services in both English (Sun 10am) and Japanese (Sun 1pm) to cater to the diversity of San Franciscans who have chosen Buddhism as their faith. The plainness of the building itself gives little indication of the sumptuous temple inside, filled with what are claimed to be relics of the

Buddha, donated by the King of Siam in 1935. Two blocks over, where Geary Boulevard meets Gough, is the monumental **St Mary's Cathedral**. Visible from the heart of downtown, St Mary's is San Francisco's newest Roman Catholic cathedral. Built in 1971, it is elaborate and ostentatious, with a comparatively functional, modern exterior. Take a walk around the inside and look up into the 190-foot dome.

Another, much more sinister quasi-religious relic once stood on the now-empty lot six blocks to the west on Geary Boulevard, between Scott and Steiner streets. This was the site of the **People's Temple**, in which, during the 1970s, the Reverend Jim Jones established the cult that was later to go and live in "Jonestown", Guyana – an attempted utopia of common-living and egalitarian principles. The mass suicide in 1978 that came to be known as the "Jonestown Massacre" involved mainly San Franciscans, and had a devastating effect on the city just as it was trying to come to terms with the assassinations of George Moscone and Harvey Milk. Today, there is little reference to Jones in San Francisco, and rumours that the old temple was jinxed seem to have had some supporting evidence. Several years after the Jonestown Massacre, a wealthy, anonymous man filled the temple with riches, priceless antiques and artwork that the public could visit free of charge. After a series of small mishaps and accidents, a mysterious fire burned it to its foundations several years ago – no great loss for superstitious San Franciscans.

Heading back south on Fillmore Street, through the heart of the Western Addition (*MUNI* bus #23 runs all day and night), you pass through one of the few parts of San Francisco that survived the 1906 earthquake and fire. For a few years afterwards, Fillmore Street was the city's main commercial stretch, with houses turned into hotels and front rooms converted into banks and grocery stores. As the rest of San Francisco returned to normal, however, the Fillmore area was abandoned, a trend which has continued more or less to the present day. But, despite the general shabbiness, it's safe enough to walk through – during the day, at least. Should you do so, divert a block west of Fillmore along Fulton Street to **Alamo Square**. This small gem of a park is quiet, pastoral and at its peak has one of the city's nicest views. Sit on the crest and look east across Steiner Street at the multicoloured **Painted-Ladies**, six identical, marvellously restored 1894 Victorian houses set against the skyline of the Financial District, which feature in most brochures on San Francisco.

Lower Haight is home to some of the city's best bars and meeting places – *see p.251.*

The few newcomers, particularly around the junction of Fillmore and Haight streets, have had an effect, but have so far managed to strike the right balance of bringing better stores and restaurants to the area without evicting its residents or radically changing its character. The truth is, there just isn't enough money or traffic to effect a full-scale transformation. Nowadays, the area known as the **LOWER HAIGHT**, has, after a period of transition, become a stomping-ground for the sort of fashion-conscious crowd usually spotted hanging out South of Market. There's a growing mix of ethnic restaurants, and, given its good access to downtown and proximity to the Castro and Haight-Ashbury, its desirability as a place to live for good-time boys and girls on a budget is undeniable – a fine place to get a cheap breakfast, browse the bookstores, rake through vintage clothing stores and drink yourself silly.

The Castro

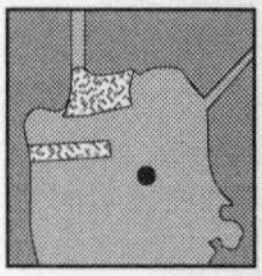

Arguably San Francisco's most progressive, if no longer most celebratory, neighbourhood, the **CASTRO** is the city's avowedly queer-capital and, as such, the best barometer for the state of the gay scene. People say many things about the changing face of the Castro, some insist it still ranks as one of the wildest places in town, others reckon it's a shadow of its former self. But all agree that things are not the same. As a district, the Castro occupies a large area, stretching from Market Street as far south as Noe Valley (see below), but in terms of visible street life, the few blocks from Market Street to 20th Street contain about all there is to see. These streets, once brimming with gay emancipation and riotous partying, have evolved into a rather nice place to shop. A walk down the Castro fifteen years ago would have had you gaping at the non-stop revelry, and while most of the same bars and hang-outs still stand, they're host to an altogether different, younger and more conservative breed these days. It is still undeniably the province of the gay man, (and to a lesser extent, the gay woman), but the energy that was once invested in hard-won, open hedonism has been squarely diverted to the formation of AIDS support groups, care for the sick, and enough political dexterity to maintain a mainstream influence in the city's political arena. It is claimed that no politician in San Francisco can survive without the gay vote.

The bars and restaurants of the Castro (and the Mission) are detailed on the map on p.235.

The Castro *MUNI* station at Market Street is about the best place to begin a tour, at **Harvey Milk Plaza**, dedicated to the extremely popular gay city supervisor who, before his assassination in 1978, owned a camera store on Castro Street and was the community's most prominent figure. Milk's and Mayor George Moscone's assailant, Dan White, was a disgruntled ex-supervisor who resigned when the liberal policies of Moscone and Milk didn't accord with his conservative views. A staunch Catholic, White was a spokesman for San Francisco's many blue-collar Irish families and, as an ex-policeman, saw himself as the vanguard of the family values he believed gay rights were damaging. He later tried to get his post back but was refused by Moscone, and soon after climbed through a basement window in City Hall, sauntered into their offices and shot them both dead. At the trial, during which the prosecution never once used the word "assassination" or recognized a political motive for the killings, White pleaded temporary insanity caused by harmful additives in his fast-food diet – a plea which came to be known as the "Twinkie defence" – and was sentenced to five years' imprisonment for manslaughter. The gay community reacted angrily to the brevity of White's sentence and the riots that followed were among the most violent San Francisco has ever witnessed, with protesters marching into City Hall, turning over and burning police cars as they went. White was released in 1985 and moved to Los Angeles, committing suicide shortly afterwards. The anniversary of the murders, **November 27**, is marked by a candlelight procession from the Castro to City Hall.

Before heading down the hill into the heart of the Castro, take a short walk across Market Street to the headquarters of the **Names Project** at 2362 Market St (daily 10am–7pm). The organization was founded in the wake of the AIDS crisis and sponsored the creation of "The Quilt" – a gargantuan patchwork composed of panels, each six feet by three feet (the size of a gravesite) and bearing the name of a loved one lost to the disease. Made by their lovers, friends and families, the panels are stitched together and regularly toured around the country; it has been spread on the Mall in Washington DC several times to bring the impact of the epidemic home to the government. Sections of the quilt, too large to be exhibited in any one place in its entirety, continue to tour the world to raise people's awareness of the tragedy, as well as funds to help keep the care programmes alive. Inside the showroom are the thousands of panels stored on shelves: some are hung up for display and machinists tackle the endless task of stitching the whole thing together. Sharing space with the *Names Project*, **Under One Roof** is a shop that has been set up as an additional fund-raising aid for the fifty or so participating Northern California AIDS service organizations, selling books, T-shirts and gift items.

For more on the Castro Theater, see p.269.

Back on Castro Street, one of the first things you see is the **Castro Theater**, self-described as "San Francisco's landmark movie palace" and undeniably one of San Francisco's better (if not best) movie houses, as popular for its pseudo-Spanish baroque interior as it is for its billing, which includes revival programmes, twenty-minute performances on a Wurlitzer organ and plush, velvet surroundings.

Half a block down the hill, the junction of **Castro and 18th streets**, known as the "gayest four corners of the earth", is the heart of the Castro, and the site of much political activity, particularly at weekends, when people set up petition stands, canvass for votes and the bums hang out capitalizing on the throng. **The Sisters of Perpetual Indulgence**, a now world-famous group of local figures who won their notoriety by dressing up as nuns and roaring about on motorbikes and roller skates, spend a lot of time at this junction canvassing for some cause or other, usually in full regalia and always surrounded by an amused crowd. Cluttered with bookstores, clothing stores, cafés and bars, this junction is as packed as the neighbourhood gets, and a sure sign that, despite the losses of the last few years, the survival of this community is assured. The best way to get the measure of this unique pocket of gay life is to walk its streets with a veteran – Trevor Hailey's *Cruisin the Castro* walking tour (see "Walking Tours", p.37) is a fun way to spend a morning, mooching around and learning from Ms Hailey's sharp anecdotal and informed commentary about the people and places that have made the Castro so famous.

See p.279 for more on the Castro's noteworthy gay and lesbian bookstores.

Noe Valley

NOE VALLEY, immediately south of the Castro, was, until very recently, remarkable only for its insignificant status in the pantheon of San Francisco neighbourhoods; in fact, it was so good at failing to capture imaginations that it was fondly tagged "Noewhere Valley". Snug in a sunny valley, the main vein of which runs along 24th Street from the borders of the Mission, this relaxed urban village has an air of rugged unfashionableness, manifest in clean streets, visible signs of family life, blue-collar sports bars, small, human-scale stores and a noticeable lack of street crime and vagrancy. Such urban utopias do not go unnoticed, however, and the last few years has seen a smattering of boutiquey shops and delicatessens springing up to serve the new wave of well-to-dos that tired of the city's busier neighbourhoods and have chosen this idyllic neighbourhood as home.

A good balance of commercial activity along 24th Street gives you reason enough to spend an afternoon wandering in and out of the book and record shops, good delicatessens and clothing stores. The neighbourhood is served by the J-Church streetcar, which, from downtown, winds prettily past Dolores Park and around leafy, curving hills before stopping at Church and 24th streets. It is surprisingly close to the centre of town, and with San Francisco real-estate prices climbing way beyond the means of most, it was perhaps only a matter of time before the rents squeezed out the families to make room for wealthy professionals.

As well as the 24th Street strip, Church Street between 24th and 30th streets has an unusual (and thankfully uncrowded) hodgepodge of weird little junk stores, nail parlours and hair salons. Noe Valley is *the* place to get your appearance sorted out. There are about seven hairdressers between 24th and 30th streets alone, and all along 24th Street beauty salons vie for your business with some pretty cut-throat prices. There's even a **hot tub** and sauna place called *Elisa's Health Spa*, at 4026 24th St, where you can get half an hour in an outdoor hot tub for $7.50 and half an hour's shiatsu massage for $20.

Diverting slightly onto Sanchez Street, the **Noe Valley Ministry**, 1021 Sanchez St, is a place to look out for. Originally built in the late nineteenth century as a Presbyterian church, this attractive Gothic-style building now serves as the neighbourhood community centre. In addition to providing a forum for worship, lectures and a nursery school, it also hosts a good programme of concerts each Saturday, ranging from classical and chamber choir to modern jazz and soul.

Twin Peaks

Real-estate prices in San Francisco are gauged in part by the quality of the views, so it's no surprise that the curving streets that wind around the slopes of **TWIN PEAKS** hold some of the city's most outrageously-unaffordable homes. If the peaks themselves were up for sale, they'd command millions, but fortunately they're among the few hills in San Francisco that have been saved from being entirely covered with houses, and so offer spectacular, 360°-views that you should make every effort to see.

It's a stiff, but rewarding, climb or bike ride up Twin Peaks Boulevard from the top of Market Street (*MUNI* bus #37 saves most of the work), or you can join one of the many guided **bus tours** of the city – they all stop here. It makes a beautiful drive by night as well, though it can get terribly cold and windswept. Should you not want to share the experience with the tour buses, there is a promontory just beneath the famous peaks known as **Tank Hill** at the end of Belgrave Street, just off 17th. Almost always deserted, it's a nice place to dawdle away from the crowds, and the views of the city are just as impressive.

Before the skyscrapers went up downtown, Twin Peaks were San Francisco's most distinctive landmark – Market Street was laid out expressly to focus sightlines on the voluptuous symmetry. Before that, local Native Americans related that the slopes were created when a married couple argued so violently that the Great Spirit separated them with a clap of thunder. Spanish explorers later tagged them "Breasts of the Indian Girl", but Americans finally settled on the more literal name of Twin Peaks. Architect Daniel Burnham spent time here in 1905, working on a master plan for the city that would have replaced the relentless urban grid with more curving streets and broad parkways. Despite the opportunity offered by the earthquake and fire of the following year, commercially minded civic authorities lacked the vision to carry it out, and the ideas were largely forgotten, except for his plans for the Civic Center.

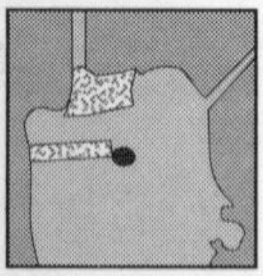

Haight-Ashbury

Two miles west of downtown San Francisco, the **HAIGHT-ASHBURY** neighbourhood lent its name to an era, giving it a fame that far outstrips its size. Small and dense, "The Haight" spans no more than eight blocks of attractive Edwardian and Victorian buildings, centred around the junction of Haight and Ashbury streets. Since it emerged in the 1960s as the Mecca of the counter-cultural scene, it has gone slightly upmarket, but still remains one of San Francisco's most racially and culturally mixed neighbourhoods, with radical bookstores, laid-back cafés, record stores and second-hand clothing boutiques recalling its days of international celebrity.

Until 1865, the Haight was no more than a pile of sand dunes, claimed in part by squatters. Then a forward-thinking Supervisor called Frank McCoppin spearheaded the development of the dunes into the area now known as Golden Gate Park. The landscaping of the Panhandle that leads into the park, the creation of a cable-car line along Haight Street, and an amusement park drew people out to the western edge of town. Development continued, and by the 1890s, the Haight was a thriving middle-class neighbourhood. After the 1906 earthquake, new building gathered pace and the neighbourhood's desirability grew. That was checked by the 1930s Depression, which turned many of the respectable Victorian homes into low-rent rooming houses. The 1950s saw inroads of students from the then nearby San Francisco State College, and a youth culture began to develop that later blossomed into Flower Power, the hippies and the Summer of Love.

The first hippies were an offshoot of the Beats, many of whom had moved out of their increasingly expensive North Beach homes to take advantage of the low rents and large spaces in the run-down Victorian houses of the Haight. The post-Beat bohemia that subsequently began to develop here was a small affair at first, involving the use of drugs and the embrace of Eastern religion and philosophy, together with a marked anti-American political stance. Where Beat philosophy had emphasized self-indulgence, the hippies, on the face of it at least, attempted to be more embracing by emphasizing such concepts as "universal truth" and "cosmic awareness". The use of drugs was crucial and seen as an integral, and positive, part of the movement – LSD especially, the effects of which were just being discovered, despite an esoteric following in psychoanalytical circles for decades before.

Hunter S Thompson's seminal 1967 article The "Hashbury" is the Capital of the Hippies *is reprinted on p.300 of this book.*

Naturally, it took a few big names to get the ball rolling, the pivotal occasion coming in January 1966, when Ken Kesey and his Merry Pranksters hosted a "Trips Festival" in the Longshoremen's Hall at Fisherman's Wharf. Attended by thousands, most of whom had dropped acid, it set a precedent for wild living, challenging authority and dropping out of the social and political establishment. At the time, LSD was not illegal and was being hyped by groups like the Pranksters as an avant-garde art form, consciousness-raising in its effects. Pumped out in private laboratories and promoted by the likes of Timothy Leary with the prescription "Turn on, tune in, drop out", LSD galvanized a generation into believing that it could be used to raise the creativity of one and all. Before long, life in the

Haight took on a theatrical quality: Pop Art found mass appeal, light shows became legion, dress flamboyant and behaviour untethered from any notion of respectability. The Grateful Dead (who lived in 710 Ashbury St – site of a famous drugs bust in 1967), Jefferson Airplane and Big Brother and the Holding Company began to make names for themselves, and, backed by the business weight of Bill Graham, the psychedelic music scene became a genuine force nationwide.

It wasn't long before large numbers of kids from all over America started turning up in the Haight for the free food, free drugs . . . and free love. Money became a dirty word, the hip became "heads", the others "straights", and by the time of the massive "Be-In" in Golden Gate Park in 1966 and the so-called "Summer of Love" the following year, this busy little intersection had attracted no fewer than 75,000 transitory people in its short life as the focus of alternative culture.

But along with all the nice middle-class kids who simply wanted to get stoned, came the outcasts, the crazies and the villains. Charles Manson recruited much of his "family" in the Haight and the enormous flow of drugs through the neighbourhood made it inviting prey for organized crime. Hunter S Thompson, too, spent his time here researching and writing his book *Hell's Angels*, and was notorious for inviting Angels to his apartment at 318 Parnassus St for drinking and drug-taking sessions which were noisy, long and sometimes – given Thompson's penchant for firearms – even dangerous.

The Haight today has few real sights, relying instead on the constant turnover of hip clothing stores, popular cafés and bookstores to sustain its legend. Two blocks east of the Haight-Ashbury junction, **Buena Vista Park** is a mountainous forest of Monterey pines and California redwoods, used by dog walkers and other people who go to enjoy the stunning views of the city, but come nightfall the locale of much sex-in-the-shrubbery. Around the park are examples of some of the most lavish Victorian architecture to be found in the city, many lavished with turrets, false gables, columns, corner towers and elaborate window design. Indeed for all its hipness and supposed disdain for bourgeois living, the Haight has all the makings (or at least the architecture) of an exclusive, chi-chi community.

A worthy 1960s hangover is the **Haight-Ashbury Free Clinic** at 558 Clayton St. By American standards, it's quite a phenomenon, providing free health care since the 1960s when drug-related illnesses became a big problem in the Haight. It survives – barely – on contributions and continues to treat drug casualties and the poor, both disproportionately large groups in this part of the city.

The best use of your time is to stroll along the Haight and take advantage of what is still one of the best areas in town to **shop**. It shouldn't take more than a couple of hours to update your record collection, dress yourself up, buy non-traditional smoking accoutrements and blow money on good books. If you're looking for food, some interesting restaurants are starting to appear along Haight Street, although there's still a better line in bakeries, cafés and lunch-type places. For some serious fun, try **Rock & Bowl** at 1855 Haight St. Ostensibly a bowling alley, this is the site of much beer-swilling and dancing around to music videos – great if you're with a group that needs entertaining.

Haight-Ashbury

Moving west along Haight Street, things get livelier the nearer you approach the **Panhandle**, the finger-slim strip of greenery that eventually leads to Golden Gate Park but is generally considered to be part of the Haight. The Panhandle was landscaped before the rest of the park back in the 1870s, and for a while was the focus for high society carriage rides, where the well-dressed would go to look and be looked at. In post-quake 1906, it became a refuge for fleeing families, with some thirty thousand living in tents. During the 1960s, it was the scene for outdoor rock concerts which caused considerable wear and tear on the delicate landscape. Today it's rather seedy: home to vagrants and the few guitar-strumming hippies that remain.

Chapter 6

Golden Gate Park, the Beaches and Outlying Districts

Beyond downtown and the central neighbourhoods, San Francisco's **Outlying Districts** may lack much of the character that has helped define the city, but they constitute a good part of what makes it such a wonderful place to live. These peripheral areas resemble suburbs common to many American cities, providing a feeling of openness and room to breathe, even though they are often shrouded in fog. Few cities have a magnificent shoreline at the edge of the Pacific Ocean that is a mere twenty-minute drive from downtown, but it is this convenient geography that makes San Francisco at once cosmopolitan and bucolic. The area also benefits from an abundance of large green spaces, most famous of which is the magnificent **Golden Gate Park**. Its museums, gardens and lakes are something of an oasis for San Franciscans struggling to find relief from the congestion of downtown. Beautifully landscaped and immaculately maintained, its vast grounds have room aplenty for the joggers, bike-riders and busloads of tourists who flock here.

As you'd expect, the area around the park is predominantly residential, inhabited by families and those who either can't afford – or don't care – to live downtown. Whichever way you look at it, it's unlikely to be at the top of your agenda on a short visit, even though public transportation connections are frequent and reliable. If you have the time, you should definitely explore the city's **beaches**. The most popular of these, **Baker Beach**, and the less-visited **China Beach**, are easily accessible from downtown, curving around the peninsula from the Golden Gate Bridge to meet **Lands End** – a usually uncrowded set of hiking trails and cliffs above the shoreline that make for a perfect break from the city. A little way inland, the **Palace of the Legion of Honor**, San Francisco's finest arts museum, stands in majestic isolation on a bluff near the ocean.

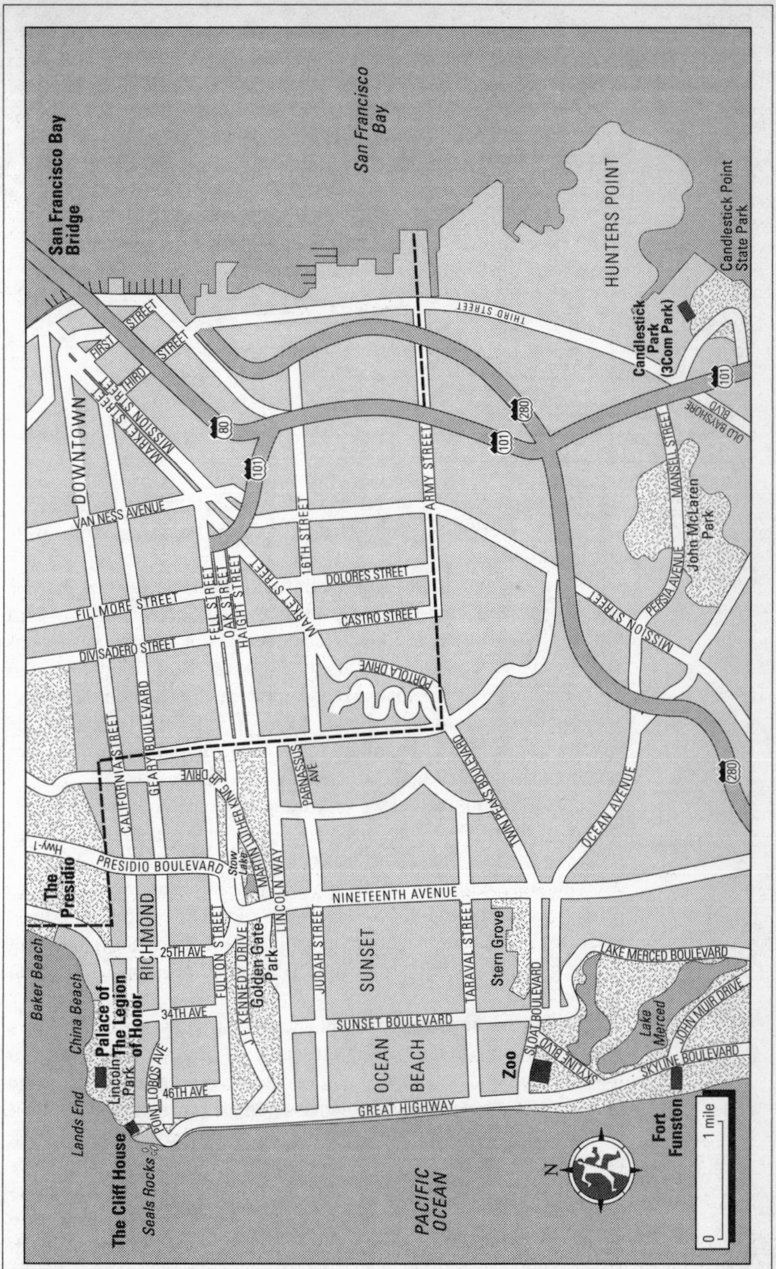

San Francisco Bay Bridge
San Francisco Bay
HUNTERS POINT
Candlestick Point State Park
Candlestick Park (3Com Park)
THIRD STREET
FIRST STREET
DOWNTOWN
MARKET STREET
MISSION STREET
80
101
280
ARMY STREET
OLD BAYSHORE BLVD
MANSELL STREET
John McLaren Park
PERSIA AVENUE
VAN NESS AVENUE
16TH STREET
DOLORES STREET
CASTRO STREET
FILLMORE STREET
DIVISADERO STREET
FELL STREET
OAK STREET
HAIGHT STREET
PORTOLA DRIVE
CALIFORNIA STREET
GEARY BOULEVARD
MARTIN LUTHER KING JR DRIVE
PARNASSUS AVE
TWIN PEAKS BOULEVARD
OCEAN AVENUE
Hwy-1
PRESIDIO BOULEVARD
The Presidio
Stow Lake
LINCOLN WAY
NINETEENTH AVENUE
RICHMOND
25TH AVE
FULTON STREET
J F KENNEDY DRIVE
Golden Gate Park
JUDAH STREET
SUNSET
TARAVAL STREET
Stern Grove
SLOAT BOULEVARD
LAKE MERCED BOULEVARD
Lake Merced
JOHN MUIR DRIVE
SKYLINE BOULEVARD
SKYLINE BLVD
Zoo
Baker Beach
China Beach
Palace of The Legion of Honor
34TH AVE
SUNSET BOULEVARD
OCEAN BEACH
Lincoln Park
POINT LOBOS AVE
46TH AVE
GREAT HIGHWAY
Lands End
The Cliff House
Seals Rocks
PACIFIC OCEAN
N
Fort Funston
0
1 mile

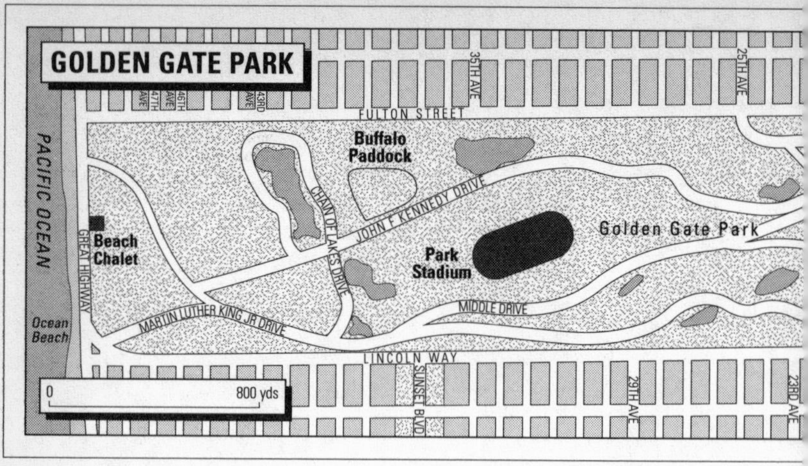

The least patronized of all the city's museums, its high-calibre collection merits an unhurried half-day's browsing, free from jostling crowds.

Around Point Lobos, the peninsula's westernmost tip, parked tour buses and camera-toting tourists signal arrival at the **Cliff House, Sutro Baths** and **Seal Rocks** – a trio of seaside attractions that form the busiest point along the coast. Stretching for miles from here is the vast expanse of **Ocean Beach**. Better suited to dog-walking than sun-worship, it's not a crowd-puller and is used mostly by the residents of the often fog-bound **Richmond** and **Sunset** neighbourhoods that hug the ocean's edge nearby.

Further south, the city's prettily landscaped **zoo** and the leafy ravine of **Stern Grove** are both good options for restless children, either to see the animals or just kick a ball around. Similarly, **Lake Merced**, a little further south, is a fine place to stop for lunch, take a boat out or sit around waiting for the fog to lift. Better still, head west to reach the beautiful cragginess of **Fort Funston**, San Francisco's southernmost and probably most attractive stretch of beach.

You're considerably less likely to visit notorious **Hunter's Point**, over on the southeastern edge of the peninsula near a massive US Navy shipyard – a run-down neighbourhood with some of the city's worst urban problems – though you may find yourself travelling through on your way to **Candlestick Park** or **3COM Park** as it is now called, thanks to new sponsorship. This is the city's main outdoor sports arena, where local heroes the San Francisco 49ers (football) and their baseball equivalents, the San Francisco Giants, keep the city's sporting morale intact with a regular string of victories.

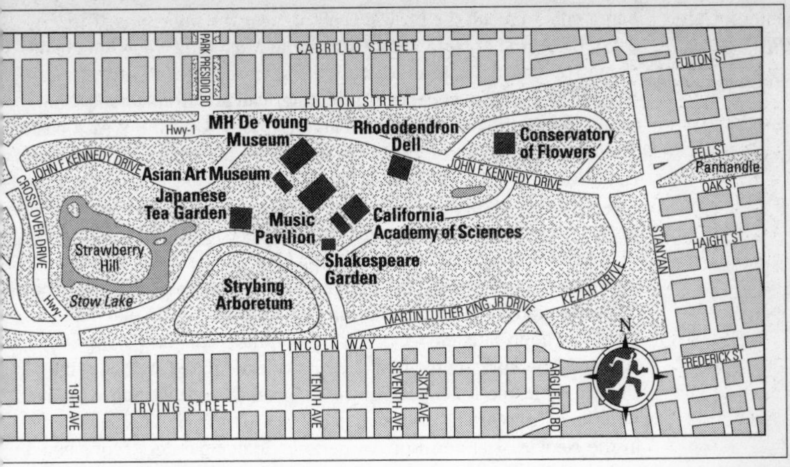

Golden Gate Park

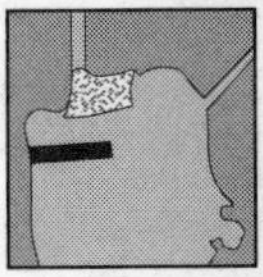

Unlike most American cities, San Francisco is not short on green space, but **GOLDEN GATE PARK** is its largest, providing a massively pastoral antidote to the city centre. Despite the throngs of joggers, polo players, roller skaters, cyclists and strollers, it never gets overcrowded, and you can always find a spot to be alone. Inspired by Frederick Law Olmsted, creator of Central Park in New York, and designed by park engineer William H Hall in 1871, it's one of the most beautiful and safe corners of the city, with none of the menace of New York's park. Spreading three miles or so west from the Haight to the Pacific, it was constructed on what was then an area of wild sand dunes buffeted by the spray from the nearby ocean, with the help of a dyke to protect the western side from the sea. John McLaren, the Scottish park superintendent for 56 years, planted several thousand trees here and it's nowadays the most peaceful and most skilfully crafted spot to relax in the city. McLaren died while still in office, aged 93.

Exploration of all the corners of this huge park could take days of footwork, though it's best to wander aimlessly, getting lost and seeing what you can stumble across. Sloping gently from east to west, it divides roughly into two sections. The eastern side, nearest the Haight, has all the main attractions – art and science museums, horticultural palaces, tea gardens and bandstands. The west is fairly isolated, with more open space and a less sculpted landscape better suited to horse riding and other sporting activities.

Fell Street runs along the side of the Panhandle, becoming John F Kennedy Drive where it enters the park – though you should note that John F Kennedy Drive is closed to traffic on Sundays. Follow this for half a mile to reach the busiest section, near the **museums**. The largest of these, the **M H de Young Memorial Museum** (Wed–Sun 10am–5pm; $5, free Sat am and first Wed of month), is the city's most diverse; its permanent collection of American art, from colonial times to the twentieth century, is rated among the best on the West Coast. The museum had its origin in the California Midwinter International Exposition of 1894, a venture that was so successful that the Fine Arts Building (around which the current museum was built) was turned over to newspaper publisher M H de Young with the purpose of establishing a permanent museum. Overall the collection is very impressive, in particular the core of over a hundred paintings from the collection of Mr and Mrs John D Rockefeller III that features works by John Singleton Copley, Rembrandt Peale and John Singer Sargent. The works in the new British Galleries date from the reign of George III in the latter half of the eighteenth century and continue into the early years of the nineteenth – an era of potent achievement in the Neoclassical and Rococo periods. Major painters represented include John Constable, Sir Joshua Reynolds, Thomas Gainsborough and Henry Raeburn. Least interesting is the museum's showing of the traditional arts of Africa, Oceania and the Americas, with the ancient arts of Egypt, Greece and Rome slightly better represented.

The Asian Art Museum is scheduled to move in 1997; see p.100.

Next door, the **Asian Art Museum** (Wed–Sun 10am–5pm; $5, free Sat am and the first Wed of each month) opened in 1966 after Avery Brundage, long-time head of the International Olympic Committee, donated his world-famous collection to the city of San Francisco. The largest museum in the Western world devoted exclusively to Asian art, its sheer size precludes the display of the whole lot at once; instead works are rotated periodically. Highlights include the **Jade Room**, in which the pieces date back as far as 3500 years, and the oldest-known **Chinese Buddha** image (338 AD). The addition of a new **Indian Gallery** has done much to improve the museum, with over twenty miniature paintings, heavy stone sculptures from the Jain period, and textiles.

Opposite is the **California Academy of Sciences** (daily 10am–5pm; $7, children under 6, free), perfect for inquisitive children. The natural history museum holds a thirty-foot skeleton of a 130-million-year-old dinosaur and life-size replicas of humans throughout the ages. You can look at stars and ride an earthquake, but the show-stealer is the collection of 14,500 specimens of aquatic life in the **Steinhart Aquarium** (same times and ticket). The feeding of the seals and dolphins at 10.30am is always worth seeing, as is the doughnut-shaped tank known as the Fish Roundabout; the viewing area is in the centre of this 200ft-circumference tank and the impression of being underwater with the fish swimming all about you is uncanny. Reptile fans will enjoy watching the scaly beasts in The Swamp – a simulated habitat for lizards, alligators and tortoises. Adults will get more out of a trip to the Academy of Sciences if they can catch the **Morrison Planetarium** at the right time (schedule varies; ☎387-6300). Laser light shows and rock music often draw an acid-crazed crowd for the evening performances.

Slightly west of the museums is the usually crowded **Japanese Tea Garden** (daily 8am–6pm; $3 admission charged 9am–5pm). Built in 1894 for the California Midwinter Exposition, the garden was beautifully landscaped by the Japanese Hagiwara family, who looked after the garden until World War II when, along with other Japanese Americans, they were sent to internment camps. A massive bronze Buddha dominates the garden, and all around are the bridges, footpaths, pools filled with shiny carp, bonsai and cherry trees that – but for the busloads of tourists that pour in regularly throughout the day – lend a peaceful feel. The best way to enjoy the garden is to get there around 8am when it first opens and have a breakfast of tea and fortune cookies in the tea house.

Considering the general abundance of flowers throughout the park, it would seem that an enormous exhibition space for them was unnecessary, but the **Conservatory of Flowers** on John F Kennedy Drive (daily 10am–5pm; free), a huge Victorian glass palace modelled on the Palm House at England's Kew Gardens, has an impressive collection of tropical plants and flowers. Still, it seems a bit foolish to endure the heat of this giant greenhouse when you can stroll the park, free of crowds, and see more or less the same thing. Two of the hundreds of flower gardens are particularly lovely. **Rhododendron Dell**, where John F Kennedy Drive meets Sixth Avenue, is a twenty-acre memorial to John McLaren, filled with over 500 species of his favourite flower, as well as statues of McLaren and his favourite poet, Robert Burns. The **Shakespeare Garden**, where Middle Drive meets Martin Luther King Jr Drive, has every flower or plant ever mentioned in the writer's plays.

The best things to do at the park are outdoors and free. On Sundays, in the central space near the museums, **music** can be heard for free at the **Music Pavilion** bandstand; to enjoy the quieter corners of the park, head west through the many flower gardens and eucalyptus groves towards the ocean. Although most people head for the western end of the park to do nothing whatsoever, activities are many, and quite cheap, if you're feeling energetic. **Boat rental** on the beautiful, vast and marshy **Stow Lake** costs around $10 per hour, and is most enjoyable midweek when the place is almost deserted. In the middle of the lake, the large artificial mountain **of Strawberry Hill** is perfect for a picnic and a laze in the sunshine.

Perhaps the most unusual thing you'll see in the park is the substantial herd of bison, roaming around the **Buffalo Paddock** off JFK Drive near 38th Avenue; you can get closest to these shaggy giants at their feeding area, at the far west end. Moving towards the edge of the park at Ocean Beach, passing a tulip garden and large windmill, you'll come to the **Beach Chalet** facing the Great Highway. This two-storey, white-pillared structure designed by Willis Polk is home to some of San Francisco's lesser-known public

Five Golden Gate Park cultural attractions now offer a single admission when you buy a Culture Pass for $10 – good for admission to the Asian Art Museum, California Academy of Sciences, Conservatory of Flowers, de Young Museum and Japanese Tea Garden. The passes are available from the Visitor Information Center at Hallidie Plaza, TIX Bay Area at Union Square, McLaren Lodge in the Park and all participating attractions.

Despite the widely prevalent belief that fortune cookies are Chinese, they were in fact invented by the Hagiwara family in 1909.

art. A series of frescoes painted in the 1930s depict the growth of the city and the creation of Golden Gate Park.

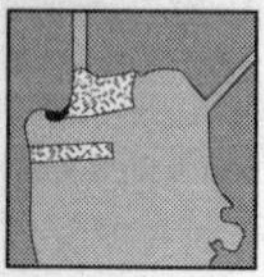

Baker Beach and China Beach

Partly due to the weather, partly due to the people, **beach** culture doesn't exist in San Francisco the way it does in Southern California; people here tend to watch the surf rather than ride it. Powerful currents and very cold water make it almost impossible to swim comfortably and with any degree of confidence outside high summer (though people *do* swim all year round) and, more often than not, nude sunbathing is as adventurous as it gets. As a result, San Francisco's beaches are blissfully uncrowded, free from parading dollies and the surf mobs they follow.

Baker Beach extends for almost a mile along the jagged cliffs below the Presidio, great for walking or fishing but not recommended for swimming. *MUNI* bus #29 will bring you here; but, if you're driving or cycling, approach from the Golden Gate Bridge. It's a breathtaking route along winding and cypress-shaded Lincoln Boulevard, with the green hills of the Presidio to your left and the crashing Pacific Ocean to your right. Far from being a pleasure zone, Baker Beach was originally used as the hiding place for an enormous 95,000-lb cannon that the army placed in an underground concrete bunker just above the strand in 1905 to protect the bay from intruders. When aircraft began to replace the army's land defences, the cannon was decreed obsolete and after World War II was melted for scrap, having never seen a day's active service in its forty-year career. A replacement cannon (for exhibition purposes only) was set up on the site in 1977, and at weekends the rangers give a brief demonstration of how the huge thing would have been aimed and fired. Most people who come here seem quite happy to ignore the massive lump of iron and steel, preferring to laze about taking in the fantastic views of the ocean and bridge.

Southwest of Baker Beach, **China Beach** is a tiny cove nestling at the bottom of the exclusive Sea Cliff neighbourhood. It takes its name from the 1870s, when Chinese fishermen camped along its crescent and fished its comparatively calm waters. Later, when the government slapped immigration restrictions on the Chinese, China Beach was supposedly used to smuggle people into San Francisco. During the 1920s there was much wrangling over developing the beach and the land above, but busy campaigning won the day and the beach remained in public hands. These days it is San Francisco's safest swimming beach, but despite this is seldom used, with most people opting for the much larger and more easily accessible Baker Beach. During good weather, however, you should make the effort to get there – changing rooms, showers and deck chairs are all freely available, making it the best option if you want to spend a whole day sunning and swimming.

Lands End and the Palace of the Legion of Honor

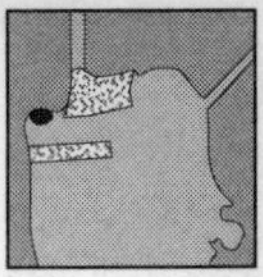

Balanced precariously at the city's edge, **Lands End** is as wild and remote as its name implies. Situated on the tip of land that divides Baker and China from Ocean Beach to the south, this lonely bluff has hiking trails and a sublime lookout across the ocean. Beneath the jagged cliffs are the shells of ships which fell foul of the treacherous waters – when the tide is out you can see the wreckage. This is one of the few wilderness areas left in the city, ice plant grows across the sandy cliffs and dazzling wild flowers appear in random clumps; catch it with a good sunset and the experience is quite humbling. A mile-long circular trail that snakes through the cypress groves and along the grassy cliffs is a popular cruising spot for gays, who favour the privacy it offers – but, apart from a few lurkers, expect to be alone.

At the south end of the Lands End trail, the **Palace of the Legion of Honor** (☎750-3600; call for times) is a white-pillared twin of the more famous Légion d'Honneur in Paris. Arguably San Francisco's best museum, it is indubitably its most beautifully located – the romantic setting, graceful architecture and colonnaded courtyard with Rodin's *Thinker* in the middle combine to lend a truly elegant impression. After an extensive three-year restoration programme, the museum has opened its doors again, and looks more beautiful than ever.

Built from a donation from the wealthy San Franciscan Spreckels family, the Legion of Honor was built in 1920, and dedicated on Abraham Lincoln's birthday in 1921. Its permanent collection includes a strong **Renaissance** contingent, represented with the works of Titian, El Greco and sculpture from Giambologna. Great canvases by Rembrandt and Hals are highlights of the seventeenth-century Dutch and Flemish collection, as is Rubens' magnificent *Tribute Money*. The **impressionist** and **post-impressionist** galleries contain works by Courbet, Manet, Monet, Renoir, Degas and Cézanne, and there's also one of the world's finest assemblies of **Rodin** sculptures, with bronze, porcelain and stone pieces such as *The Athlete*, *Fugit Amor*, *The Severed Head of John the Baptist* and *Fallen Angel*, as well as a small cast of *The Kiss*.

There's another impressive Rodin collection in Stanford University's art museum; see p.171.

Cliff House, Sutro Baths and Seal Rocks

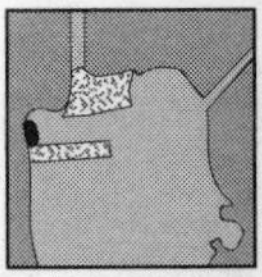

About a mile southwest along the coast from the tip of Lands End, the **Cliff House**, judging by the number of tour buses parked outside, is one of the top sightseeing spots in the city. At the edge

Cliff House, Sutro Baths and Seal Rocks

of the Pacific Ocean, 1090 Point Lobos Ave, the house itself is not spectacular (or even authentic), but its setting on a mammoth rock perched over the Pacific, with the broad strand of Ocean Beach stretching for miles to the south, is memorable. The original building on this site in the 1850s, Seal Rock House, was used by hiking and horse-riding San Franciscans as a rest spot after the long journey from downtown. It closed at the end of the 1850s, but the idea for a seaside resort stuck, and with the completion of the first road from the city to the beach, the first Cliff House was constructed, thriving for two decades as an exclusive resort for the leisure classes – the Stanfords, Crockers and Hearsts of late-nineteenth-century San Francisco – and soon earning a reputation for gambling and prostitution. A Prussian immigrant, Adolph Sutro bought the original Cliff House, only to watch it burn to the foundations in 1894, and it was he who built the Cliff House that is best remembered today. A stunning Gothic monolith of glass and spires, it had dozens of dining rooms, an art gallery and twenty private luncheon rooms, enjoying a much celebrated existence until it, too, was destroyed by fire in 1907. Sadly, today's Cliff House can't compare – though the **view** from the bar at sunset makes it worth braving the hordes.

Adolph's other opulent creation, the **Sutro Baths**, was more enduring; 100,000 feet of stained glass covering over three acres of sculpted swimming pools and tanks of fresh and salt water. It came to be known as California's "Tropical Winter Garden", and for 10c you could enter through a Classical pillared entrance that led to gardens of fountains, flowers and trees, and swim all day amid sculptures, tapestries and ancient artefacts that Sutro had collected from around the world. It all got to be too expensive to maintain, and the baths crumbled elegantly until they were razed by a fire in 1966. Today, some very ancient-looking ruins remain, and if you can manage the clamber down the steep staircase down the cliff face, it makes for an interesting, if occasionally wet, trek through the old ramparts and tunnels. At night, when the surf really starts to crash, things can get a bit frightening here, but there's a certain romance too, and on a rare warm evening it becomes one of the city's favourite snogging spots. By day, you'll get the best and closest view of **Seal Rocks**, the clump of boulders a little way out to sea that have been coloured white by the hundreds of seagulls. The rocks take their name from the population of seals that are forever competing for the sunniest spots.

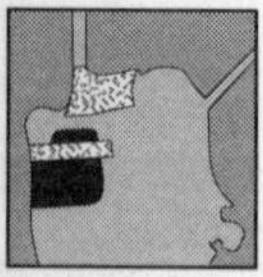

The Richmond, Sunset and Ocean Beach

Quite apart from entailing long journeys on public transportation, the **Richmond** and **Sunset** districts, often referred to as "The

Avenues", are disappointing for the tourist. Large neighbourhoods, populated for the most part by families, are neat, clean, respectable – and terrifically dull. Divided by Golden Gate Park, they have many similarities: flat, often fog-bound, orderly avenues surrounded by some great open spaces. Stretching north to the Presidio and south of the Golden Gate Park, they extend westwards for miles before ending abruptly at the ocean's edge.

The Richmond

Solidly middle class, the **RICHMOND** was first settled by Russian and Eastern European Jews after World War I. Later came the Japanese and now, most predominantly, Chinese families are moving their businesses here away from the overcrowding and noise of Chinatown, lending the area the name "New Chinatown". It's a vast neighbourhood, divided into **inner** and **outer** districts, separated by Park Presidio Boulevard (Hwy-1). The outer portion is only for passing through on your way out to Sutro Baths and the Cliff House and, assuming that you're going to bother with it at all, you should confine your wanderings to the inner Richmond around **Clement Street**, between Arguello Street and Eighth Avenue. This is the neighbourhood's commercial strip, with some good Asian restaurants, a couple of cafés, a movie theatre and some rowdy Irish pubs.

Sunset and Ocean Beach

Few places in San Francisco could be termed unpleasant, but neighbourhoods like the **SUNSET** can certainly be described as monotonous – clean, quiet streets, spread out across a large area, and leading eventually to **Ocean Beach**, the largest and least arresting stretch of San Francisco's shoreline. Some surfing and fishing goes on, but mostly the beach is the domain of dog-walkers and strollers out for some fresh air. Strong undertow and unexpected riptides render swimming out of the question, and the often grey colour of the sand makes sunbathing unappealing. The beach improves as you head south, (see Fort Funston overleaf).

Like Golden Gate Park and the Richmond district, the Sunset was once just windswept sand dunes, until a massive Federal Housing Administration programme after World War II paved over the area and put up houses that then cost $5000 each. The same modest structures, which are occupied largely by the original owners (the Sunset has the highest population of residents over 60), are reckoned to be fetching around half a million at today's prices.

There's a buildup of stores and a few restaurants around the area of Judah and Ninth avenues, but nothing worth making an effort for; indeed if you never saw the neighbourhood you wouldn't be missing a thing.

The Zoo, Lake Merced and Fort Funston

There may be precious little to do in the Sunset, but if you journey a short way **south** your options widen considerably. Some of the city's prettiest green spaces are locked into a square bordered by Hwy-1 to the east, the San Francisco county line to the south and the best part of Ocean Beach to the west. Take a picnic and spend a day exploring San Francisco's least-visited attractions.

Where Sloat Boulevard meets the Pacific coast, just off the end of the *MUNI* L Taraval trolley line, **San Francisco Zoo** (daily 10am–5pm; $7, under-12s free) is a small but expertly designed institution, organized around the principle that the animals should be housed in an environment most closely resembling their natural habitat. Rather than the usual spectacle of animals listlessly slumped in their small cages, the thousand or so exotic beasts at San Francisco Zoo swing happily from trees, roam across fields and lounge on islands. One of the most innovative enclosures is the **Primate Discovery Center**, a complex of fenced-in atriums in which you can get intimate with sixteen playful varieties of primate. It also has an interactive computer facility where you can design a primate to your own specification. There are also the more standard exhibits of lions and tigers, a special **Children's Zoo** ($1) where the under-12s can go and feed a barnyard full of domestic animals, and a **Zebra Zephyr Train** that will take them on an informative tour of the entire zoo.

A little way east, where Sloat Boulevard crosses 19th Avenue (Hwy-1), **Stern Grove** is a leafy ravine of eucalyptus, redwood and fir trees that shelters a natural amphitheatre. For most of the year it's used by picnickers and schoolchildren on nature rambles, but, during the summer between June and August, **free concerts** are held each Sunday at 2pm; check local listings for details. An excellent assortment of programmes from classical to jazz are presented – take a picnic and get there early to be sure of a good spot.

For something more active, head south along Skyline Boulevard to **Lake Merced**. A standby reservoir for the city, this large freshwater lake is a peaceful, uncrowded spot to rent a rowing boat or have a picnic. The bar and restaurant at the **boathouse** offer a welcome opportunity to sit out on the deck overlooking the lake and have a cheap lunch while waiting for the fog to lift. Seldom used, it's a great place for isolation-seekers and those who need a large open space to let their children run wild.

Even if you skip all of the above, it's well worth making the effort to visit **Fort Funston**, at the southernmost point of the city's coastline and above its most windswept and beautiful stretch of beach. Wild flowers grow along the craggy cliff tops, and on a sunny day it's nice to clamber down the cliff face, lie on the fine white sand, and gaze up at the hang-gliders as they leap off the cliffs to soar above the ocean's edge.

Hunter's Point and 3COM Park

San Franciscans speak of **HUNTER'S POINT** with some trepidation. The neighbourhood has the city's largest concentration of public housing, and is rife with the social problems that ail many such projects. Situated south of the SoMa docks on its own mini-peninsula, in the far southeast corner of San Francisco, it was chosen as the site of a major US Navy shipyard during World War II. The temporary housing that went up to shelter the 35,000 employees who came to work in the war effort is still in use, and this is perhaps the city's most isolated and forgotten corner. The entire area has a distinct air of neglect about it, plagued by unemployment, crime and drug abuse. Few outsiders ever venture into the neighbourhood, and to be honest, as a visitor, there's little reason to come.

About the only occasion you're likely to pass through this part of town is if you're trying to beat the often blocked-up traffic on the Bayshore Freeway (US-101) – the main route to and from the airport – or if you're taking Third Street to a Giants or 49ers game at **3COM (Candlestick) Park**, just south of Hunter's Point. *MUNI* puts on special buses on game days, and most take this route. It was here at Candlestick during the World Series that the big 1989 earthquake hit. The panic of the startled crowds in the shaking stadium was broadcast nationwide – hardly what they'd expected but certainly something they'll never forget.

For tickets to see the 49ers, call ☎468-2249; for the Giants, call ☎467-8000; see also p.283.

A walk around **Candlestick Point State Park** reveals a fine example of the 1970s asphalting craze, when hitherto unkempt pieces of land were paved into fitness courses, with trails that lead you from push-up bench to pull-up bar, with markers for you to gauge your progress. Skip that and walk towards the pier at the easternmost point of the park, where old men and young boys fish indolently and share the views over the quiet stretch of the bay. To describe the park as beautiful, or even attractive, would be pushing it, but it's a pleasant enough place to picnic or just lie about and enjoy the peace.

Part 3

Out of the City

Chapter 7

Introducing the Bay Area

While San Francisco proper occupies only 48 hilly square miles at the tip of a slender peninsula, the metropolitan **Bay Area** sprawls out far beyond these narrow confines, north and east across the impressive Golden Gate and Bay bridges, and to the south along the peninsula. There's no doubt about the supporting role these places play in relation to San Francisco – always "The City" – but each contributes in its own way to making the Bay Area one of the country's most desirable places to live or visit.

Across the grey steel Bay Bridge, eight miles from downtown San Francisco, the **East Bay** – covered in Chapter Eight – is the biggest and perhaps the most interesting segment of the bay, home to the lively, left-leaning cities of Oakland and Berkeley, which have some of the best bookshops and restaurants and most of the live music venues in the greater Bay Area. The weather is generally much sunnier and warmer here, too, and it's easy to reach by way of the space-age *BART* trains that race under the bay. The rest of the East Bay is filled out by Contra Costa County, which includes the short-lived early state capital of California – the near ghost town of Benicia – as well as the homes of writers John Muir and Eugene O'Neill.

Full listings of accommodation, restaurants and other facilities in the Bay Area are provided in Chapters Twelve to Seventeen.

South of the city, and the focus of Chapter Nine, the **Peninsula** holds some of San Francisco's oldest and most upscale suburbs, reaching down into the computer belt of the Silicon Valley around San Jose, California's fastest-growing city; though, apart from some fancy houses, there's not a whole lot to see. The beaches, however, are excellent – sandy, clean and surprisingly uncrowded with the added bonus of a couple of youth hostels set in old lighthouses at the edge of the Pacific.

For some the most beautiful land- and seascapes in California, cross the Golden Gate Bridge or ride a ferry across the bay to **Marin County**, explored in Chapter Ten. This mountainous peninsula is half wealthy suburbia and half unspoiled hiking country, holding the coastal wildernesses of Muir Woods and the Point Reyes National Seashore. The redwood forests that rise sheer out of the thundering ocean are separated from the yacht clubs and plush, bay-view houses of Sausalito and Tiburon by a range of 2500-foot peaks.

North of Marin County, at the top of the Bay, and still within an hour's drive of San Francisco, is the **Wine Country**. Dotted with hundreds of prestigious wineries, Napa Valley in particular provides dozens of places where you can sample fine wines, enjoy a four-star meal or simply soak your weary bones in one of the many local hot springs. Its neighbour, the Sonoma Valley, is more rural and informal. Together they make an excellent day or two away from the San Francisco hustle. Chapter Eleven suggests some possible itineraries.

Public **transport** around the Bay Area is quite good by US standards, although it is primarily aimed at commuters not visitors. Unless you have more time than money, you'll probably do best to rent a car; many of the best places are simply inaccessible without one.

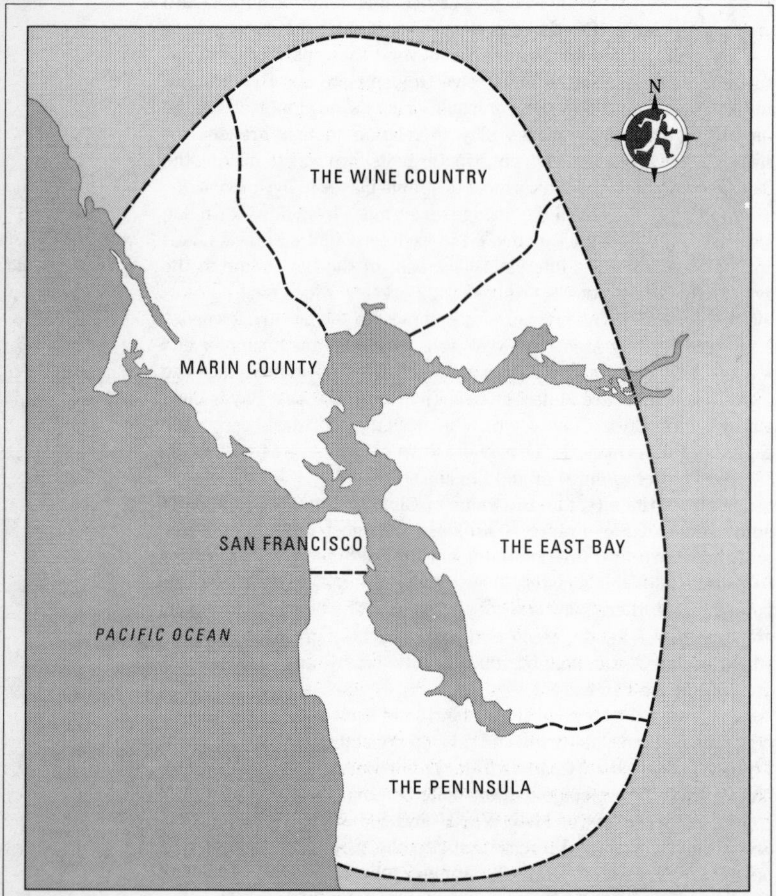

Chapter 8

The East Bay

The largest and most-travelled bridge in the US, the **Bay Bridge** heads east from downtown San Francisco, part graceful suspension bridge and part heavy-duty steel truss. Built in 1933 as an economic booster during the Depression, the bridge is made from enough steel cable to wrap around the earth three times. Completed just seven months before the more famous (and better-loved) Golden Gate, the Bay Bridge works a whole lot harder for a lot less respect; a hundred million vehicles cross the bridge each year, though you'd have to search hard to find a postcard of it. Indeed, its only claim to fame – apart from the much-broadcast videotape of its partial collapse during the 1989 earthquake – is that **Treasure Island**, where the two halves of the bridge meet, hosted the 1939 World's Fair. During World War II the island became a Navy base, which it remains. Just inside the gates there's a small **museum** (daily 10am–3pm; free) with pictures of the Fair amid maritime memorabilia. The island also offers great views of San Francisco and the Golden Gate.

The Bay Bridge – and the *BART* trains that run under the bay – finish up in the heart of the East Bay in **Oakland**, a hard-working, blue-collar city that earns its livelihood from shipping and transport services based at the massive Port of Oakland, whose huge cranes dominate the place. Oakland spreads north along wooded foothills to **Berkeley**, an image-conscious college town that looks out across to the Golden Gate and collects a mixed bag of pinstriped Young Republicans, ageing 1960s radicals, and Nobel Prize-winning nuclear physicists in its many cafés and bookstores.

Berkeley and Oakland blend together so much as to be virtually the same city, and the hills above them are topped by a twenty-mile string of forested **regional parks**, providing much needed fresh air and quick relief from the concrete grids below. The rest of the East Bay is filled out by **Contra Costa County**, a huge area that contains some intriguing, historically important waterfront towns – well worth a detour if you're passing through on the way to the Wine Country region of the Napa and Sonoma valleys – as well as some of the Bay Area's most inward-looking suburban sprawl.

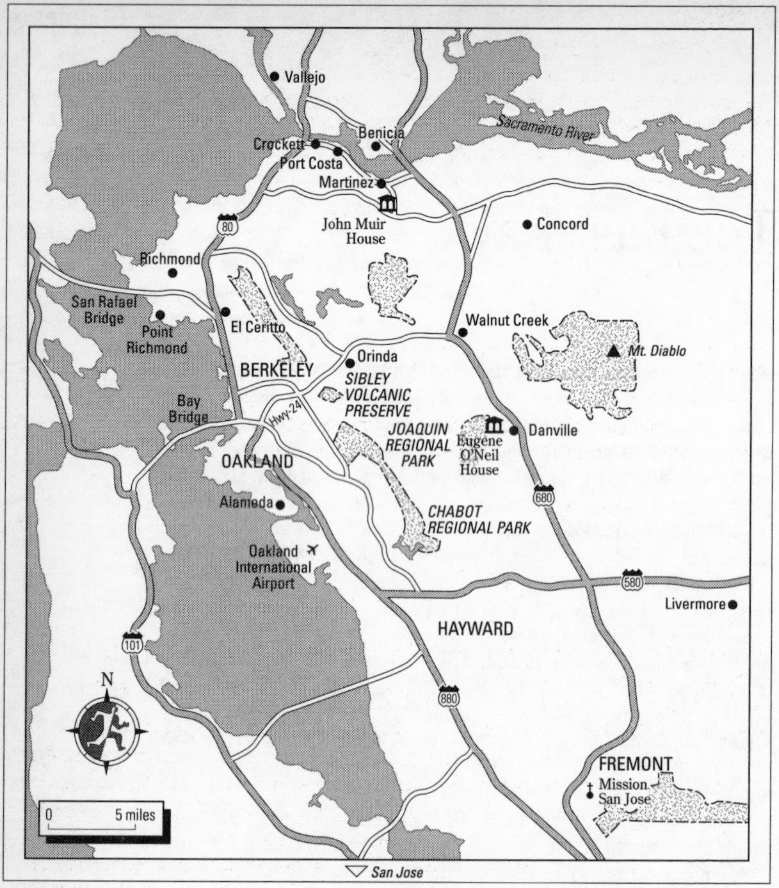

For East Bay accommodation, see Chapter Twelve; restaurants are on p.238; and cafés and bars on p.252.

Curving around the **North Bay** from the heavy-industrial landscape of Richmond, and facing each other across the narrow **Carquinez Straits**, both Benicia and Port Costa were vitally important during California's first twenty years of existence, after the 1849 Gold Rush; they're now strikingly sited but little-visited ghost towns.

In contrast, standing out from the soulless dormitory communities that fill up the often baking hot **inland valleys**, are the preserved homes of an unlikely pair of influential writers: the naturalist **John Muir**, who, when not out hiking around Yosemite and the High Sierra, lived most of his life near **Martinez**, and playwright **Eugene O'Neill**, who wrote many of his angst-ridden works at the foot of **Mount Diablo**, the Bay Area's most impressive peak.

Arrival

You're most likely to be staying in San Francisco when you visit the East Bay, though it is possible, and sometimes cheaper, to fly direct to **Oakland Airport**, particularly if you're coming from elsewhere in the US. It's an easy trip from the airport into town: take the *AirBART Shuttle* van (every 15min; $2) from outside the terminal direct to the Coliseum *BART* station, from where you can reach Oakland, Berkeley or San Francisco. In addition, various privately operated shuttle buses cost from $10.

Long-distance transport connections to Oakland are detailed from p.10 onwards.

Oakland's *Greyhound* **bus station** is in a dubious part of town, alongside the I-980 freeway on San Pablo Avenue at 21st Street. If you come to the Bay Area **by train**, *Amtrak* terminates at Second Street near Jack London Square, though it's a better option to get off at Richmond and change there onto *BART*.

The most enjoyable way to arrive in the East Bay is to take the commuter **boat** ($3.75 each way) that sails every two hours from San Francisco's Ferry Building to Jack London Square.

East Bay transport

The East Bay is linked to San Francisco via the underground *BART*, the ultra-modern *Bay Area Rapid Transit* system, between 6am and midnight, Monday to Saturday, 9am to midnight on Sundays. Three lines run from **Daly City** through San Francisco and onto Downtown Oakland, before diverging to service East Oakland out to **Fremont**, Berkeley and north to **Richmond**, and east into Contra Costa County as far as **Concord**. Fares range from 85¢ to $3. If you're relying on *BART* to get around a lot, buy a **high-value ticket** ($5 or 10) to avoid having to stand in line to buy a new ticket each time you ride. The cost of each ride is deducted from the total value of the ticket, purchased from machines on the station concourse.

To phone BART from San Francisco dial ☎992-BART; from the East Bay it's ☎510/465-BART.

From East Bay *BART* stations, pick up a free transfer to save 35¢ off the $1.10 fares of ***AC Transit*** (☎510/839-2882), which provides a good bus service around the entire East Bay area, especially Oakland and Berkeley. *AC Transit* also runs buses on a number of routes to Oakland and Berkeley from the Transbay Terminal in San Francisco. These operate throughout the night, and are the only way of getting across the bay by public transit once *BART* has shut down. Excellent **free maps** of both *BART* and the bus system are available from any station.

A smaller-scale bus company that can also prove useful, the ***Contra Costa County Connection*** (☎510/676-7500), runs buses to most of the inland areas, including the John Muir and Eugene O'Neill historic houses.

One of the best ways to get around is **by bike**. A fine cycle route follows Skyline and Grizzly Peak boulevards along the wooded crest of the hills between Berkeley and Lake Chabot. If you don't have your own, touring bikes are available for $15 a day (mountain bikes cost $25) from *Carl's Bikes*, 2416 Telegraph Ave in Oakland (☎510/835-8763), and from *Cal Adventures*, 2301 Bancroft Way on the UC Berkeley campus (☎510/642-4000). For those interested in **walking tours**, the city of Oakland sponsors free "discovery tours" (☎510/238-3234) of various neighbourhoods every Wednesday and Saturday at 10am.

If you're **driving**, allow plenty of time; the East Bay has some of California's worst traffic, with I-80 in particular jam-packed sixteen hours per day.

Car rental companies are listed on p.33.

East Bay information

The **Oakland Convention and Visitors Bureau**, at 550 Tenth St, near the 12th Street *BART* station downtown (Mon–Fri 8.30am–5pm; ☎510/839-9000), offers free maps and information, as does the **Berkeley Convention and Visitors Bureau**, 1834 University Ave (Mon–Fri 9am–4pm; ☎510/549-7040).

If you're spending any time at all in the Berkeley area, pick up a copy of *Berkeley Inside/Out* by Don Pitcher (Heyday Books, $12.95), an informative guide that'll tell you everything you ever wanted to know about the town and its inhabitants. For information on hiking or horse riding in the many parks that top the Oakland and Berkeley hills, contact the **East Bay Regional Parks District**, 11500 Skyline Blvd (☎510/562-7275). The widely available (and free) *East Bay Express* – in many ways the best newspaper in the Bay Area – has the most comprehensive listings of **what's on** in the vibrant East Bay music and arts scene. The troubled daily *Oakland Tribune* (50¢) is also worth a look for its coverage of local politics and sporting events.

Oakland

A quick trip across the Bay Bridge, or on *BART*, brings you to **OAKLAND**, as solidly working class as San Francisco is upwardly mobile: the workhorse of the Bay Area, one of the busiest ports on the West Coast and the western terminal of the railroad network. It's not all hard slog, though; the climate is rated the best in the US, often sunny and mild when San Francisco is cold and dreary. Despite the 1991 fire that ravaged the hills, there's also great hiking around the redwood- and eucalyptus-covered peaks above the city and views right over the entire Bay Area.

Oakland has more historical and literary associations than important sights. **Gertrude Stein** and **Jack London** both grew up in the city, at approximately the same time, though in entirely different circumstances – Stein was a stockbroker's daughter, London an orphaned delinquent. Most of the waterfront where London used to steal oysters and lobsters is now named in his memory, while Stein is

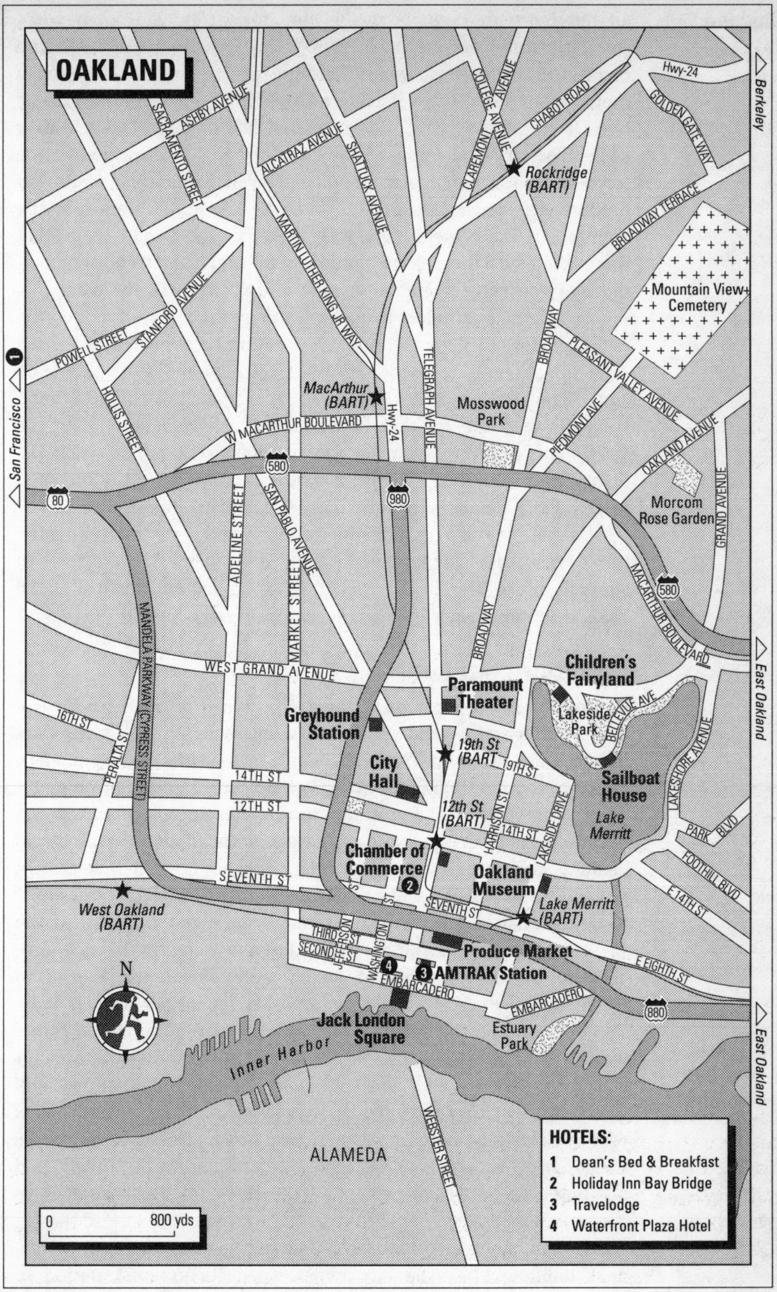
OAKLAND
Berkeley
San Francisco
East Oakland
East Oakland
Rockridge (BART)
MacArthur (BART)
19th St (BART)
12th St (BART)
Lake Merritt (BART)
West Oakland (BART)
Mountain View Cemetery
Mosswood Park
Morcom Rose Garden
Children's Fairyland
Paramount Theater
Greyhound Station
City Hall
Lakeside Park
Sailboat House
Lake Merritt
Chamber of Commerce
Oakland Museum
Produce Market
AMTRAK Station
Jack London Square
Estuary Park
Inner Harbor
ALAMEDA
HOTELS:
1 Dean's Bed & Breakfast
2 Holiday Inn Bay Bridge
3 Travelodge
4 Waterfront Plaza Hotel
0 800 yds
N

all but ignored. Perhaps this is due to her book, *Everybody's Autobiography*, in which she wrote: "What was the use of me having come from Oakland, it was not natural for me to have come from there, yes write about it if I like or anything if I like but not there, *there is no there there*" – a quote that has haunted Oakland ever since. The city's businesses have a history of deserting their home town when the going gets good, and even its football team, the Raiders, defected to Los Angeles for thirteen years. Nonetheless, the majority of Oaklanders stick with the city, and would argue that there is indeed a there there, notably in the small and trendy communities of Rockridge, Piedmont Avenue and the lively Grant Avenue.

Jack London's mildly socialist leanings set a style for the city, and Oakland has been the breeding ground for some of America's most unabashedly revolutionary **political movements** in the years since. The 1960s saw the city's 50-percent black population find a voice through the militant Black Panther movement, and in the 1970s Oakland was again on the nation's front pages when the Symbionese Liberation Army demanded a ransom for kidnapped heiress Patty Hearst in the form of free food distribution to the poor.

Oakland is still very much its own city, and it's worth taking the time to get a feel for its diversity and dynamism. A good place to start, if you're here in the spring, is at the annual Festival at the Lake, celebrated each June on the shores of Lake Merritt.

Downtown Oakland

Coming by *BART* from San Francisco, get off at the 12th Street–Civic Center station and you're in **Downtown Oakland**, a compact district of spruced-up Victorian storefronts overlooked by modern hotels and office buildings that has been in the midst of an ambitious programme of restoration and redevelopment for over a decade. The project has been fraught with allegations of illegal dealings and incompetent planning, and so far it's less than a complete success. To make way for the moat-like I-980 freeway – now the main route through Oakland since the collapse of the Cypress Freeway in the 1989 earthquake – entire blocks were cleared of houses, some of which were saved and moved to **Preservation Park** at 12th Street and Martin Luther King Jr Way. The late nineteenth-century commercial centre along Ninth Street west of Broadway, now tagged **Victorian Row**, underwent a major restoration some years ago, but many of the buildings are still boarded up waiting for tenants. By way of contrast, stroll a block east of Broadway, between Seventh and Ninth streets, to Oakland's **Chinatown**, whose bakeries and restaurants are as lively and bustling – if not as picturesque – as those of its more famous cousin across the Bay.

Oakland's restaurants are detailed on p.241.

Luckily, not all of downtown Oakland has the look of a permanent building site. The city experienced its greatest period of growth in the early twentieth century, and many of the grand buildings of this era survive a few blocks north along Broadway, centred on the awkwardly imposing 1914 **City Hall** on 14th Street. Two blocks away, at 13th and Franklin, stands Oakland's most unmistakable landmark, the chateau-esque lantern of the **Tribune Tower**, the 1920s-era home of the *Oakland Tribune* newspaper.

Further north, around the 19th Street *BART* station, are some of the Bay Area's finest early twentieth-century buildings, highlighted by the outstanding Art Deco interior of the 1931 **Paramount Theater** 2025 Broadway (☎510/465-4600; tours Sat 10am; $5), which shows Hollywood classics on selected Friday nights. Nearby buildings are equally exuberant in their decoration, ranging from the wafer-thin Gothic "flatiron" office tower of the **Cathedral Building** at Broadway and Telegraph, to the Hindu temple-like facade of the magnificent 3500-seat **Fox Oakland** (now closed) on Telegraph at 19th. At the time it was built in 1928, it was the largest movie house west of Chicago. Across the street you'll find the 1931 **Floral Depot**, a group of small Moderne storefronts faced in black-and-blue terracotta tiles with shiny silver highlights.

West of Broadway, the area around the *Greyhound* bus station on San Pablo Avenue is fairly seedy. San Pablo used to be the main route in and out of Oakland before the freeways were built, but many of the roadside businesses are now derelict, especially around the industrial districts of **Emeryville**. Some of the old warehouses have been converted into artists' lofts and studios, though any gentrification there might be is diffused by the scenes on the street, where prostitutes and drug-dealers hang out under the neon signs of the dingy bars and gambling halls like the *Oaks Card Club*, where the father of Oaktown rapper MC Hammer once worked.

Lake Merritt and the Oakland Museum

Five blocks east of Broadway, the eastern third of downtown Oakland is made up of **Lake Merritt**, a three-mile-circumference tidal lagoon that was bridged and dammed in the 1860s to become the centrepiece of Oakland's most desirable neighbourhood. All that remains of the many fine houses that once circled the lake is the elegant **Camron-Stanford House**, on the southwest shore at 1418 Lakeside Drive, a graceful Italianate mansion whose sumptuous interior is open for visits (Wed 11am–4pm, Sun 1–5pm; $2). The lake is also the nation's oldest wildlife refuge, and migrating flocks of ducks, geese and herons break their journeys here. The north shore is lined by **Lakeside Park**, where you can rent canoes and row boats ($4 per hour), and a range of sailboats and catamarans ($4–10 per hour) from the Sailboat House (Summer daily 10am–5pm; rest of year weekends only), provided you can convince the staff you know how to sail. A miniature Mississippi riverboat makes half-hour lake cruises on weekend afternoons ($1), and kids will appreciate the puppet shows and pony rides at the Children's Fairyland (daily 10am–5.30pm; Winter weekends only; $1.50), along Grand Avenue on the northwest edge of the Park. Every year on the first weekend in June the park comes to life during the **Festival at the Lake**, when all of Oakland gets together to enjoy nonstop music and performances from local bands and entertainers.

Two blocks south of the lake, or a block up Oak Street from the Lake Merritt *BART* station, the **Oakland Museum** (Wed–Sat 10am–5pm, Sun noon–7pm; $5) is perhaps a more worthwhile stop, not only for the exhibits but also for the superb modern building in which it's housed, topped by a terraced rooftop sculpture garden that gives great views out over the water and the city. The museum covers many diverse areas: there are displays on the **ecology** of California, including a simulated walk from the seaside through various natural habitats up to the 14,000-foot summits of the Sierra Nevada mountains; state **history**, ranging from old mining equipment to the guitar that Berkeley-born Country Joe MacDonald played at the Woodstock festival in 1969; and a broad survey of works by California artists and craftspeople, some highlights of which are pieces of turn-of-the-century **arts and crafts furniture**. You'll also see excellent **photography** by Eadweard Muybridge, Dorothea Lange and Imogen Cunningham. The museum also has a collector's gallery which loans and sells works by California artists.

The Waterfront, Alameda and West Oakland

Ferry services from San Francisco are detailed on p.143.

Half a mile down from downtown Oakland on *AC Transit* bus #51A, at the foot of Broadway on the Waterfront, **Jack London Square** is Oakland's sole concession to the tourist trade. Also accessible by direct ferries from San Francisco, this somewhat anaesthetic complex of boutiques and restaurants along the harbour was named after the self-taught writer who grew up pirating shellfish around here, but is about as distant from the spirit of the man as it's possible to get. Jack London's best story, *The Call of the Wild*, was written about his adventures in the Alaskan Yukon, where he carved his initials in a small cabin that has been reconstructed here; another survivor is *Heinhold's First and Last Chance Saloon*, a seedy bar where London spent much of his wayward youth.

No Jack London enthusiast should fail to visit his Sonoma Valley ranch – see p.202.

If you're not a keen fan of London, there are still a few worthwhile things to do here. The **Ebony Museum of Arts** at 30 Alice St (Tues–Sat 11am–6pm, Sun noon–6pm; free) is worth a visit for its African art and pop American counter-culture collectibles. Otherwise, walk a few short blocks inland to the **Produce Market**, along Third and Fourth streets, where a couple of good places to eat and drink lurk among the railroad tracks (see p.239). This bustling warehouse district has fruit and vegetables by the forklift-load, and is at its most lively early in the morning, from about 5am.

Alameda

AC Transit bus #51A continues from Broadway under the inner harbour to **Alameda**, a quiet and conservative island of Middle America dominated by an empty naval air base. Massive nuclear-powered aircraft carriers still dock here occasionally. The fine houses along the original shoreline on Clinton Street were part of the summer resort colony that flocked here to the *contra costa* or "opposite shore" from San Francisco, near the now-demolished Neptune Beach amusement park. The island has since been much enlarged by dredging and landfill, and 1960s apartment buildings now line the long, narrow shore of **Robert Crown Memorial Beach**, along the bay – a quiet, attractive spot.

West Oakland

West Oakland – an industrial district of warehouses, railroad tracks, 1960s housing projects and decaying Victorian houses – may be the nearest East Bay *BART* stop to San Francisco, but it's light years away from that city's prosperity. Despite the obvious poverty, it's quite a safe and settled place, but the only time anyone pays it any attention is when something dramatic happens. Two examples are when Black Panther Huey Newton was gunned down here in a drugs-related revenge attack in 1989, and when the double-decker I-880 freeway, which divided the neighbourhood from the rest of the city, collapsed onto itself in the 1989 earthquake, killing dozens of commuters.

Local people have successfully resisted government plans to rebuild the old concrete eyesore (current plans call for it to be re-routed closer to the harbour); the potentially very attractive **Nelson Mandela Parkway** now occupies where the freeway used to run through West Oakland. But otherwise, this remains one of the Bay Area's poorest and most neglected neighbourhoods, and apart from a marvellous stock of turn-of-the-century houses there's little here to tempt tourists.

For a long time West Oakland was known as "the place where the trains stopped". It was the end of the Southern Pacific Railroad from 1869. A new, high-tech station now stands conveniently near Jack London Square. Half a mile south, near the West Oakland *BART* station, Seventh Street was the heart of the Bay Area's most vibrant entertainment district from the end of Prohibition in 1933, until the early 1970s, when many of the bars and nightclubs were torn down in the name of urban renewal. Seventh Street runs west between the docks and storage yards of the Oakland Army Base and the Naval Supply Depot, ending up at **Portview Park**, one of the best places to watch the huge cargo ships that cruise by. The small park stands on the site of the old transbay ferry landing, used by as many as forty million passengers per year at its peak in the 1930s before the Bay Bridge was completed. The park has officially been closed since the earthquake, but you can nip around the fence and join the people fishing from the small pier, or just enjoy the unmatched view of the San Francisco skyline framed by the Bay and Golden Gate bridges.

East Oakland

The bulk of Oakland spreads out along foothills and flatlands to the east of downtown, in neighbourhoods obviously stratified along the main thoroughfares of Foothill and MacArthur boulevards. Gertrude Stein grew up here, though when she returned years later in search of her childhood home it had been torn down and replaced by a dozen Craftsman-style bungalows – the simple 1920s wooden houses that still cover most of **East Oakland**, each fronted by a patch of lawn and divided from its neighbour by a narrow concrete driveway.

A quick way out from the gridded streets and sidewalks of the city is to take *AC Transit* bus #15A from downtown east up into the hills to **Joaquin Miller Park**, the most easily accessible of Oakland's hilltop parks. The park stands on the former grounds of the home of the "Poet of the Sierras", Joaquin Miller, who made his name playing the eccentric frontier American in the literary salons of 1870s London. His poems weren't exactly acclaimed, although his prose account, *Life Amongst the Modocs*, documenting time spent with the Modoc people near Mount Shasta, does stand the test of time. It was more for his outrageous behaviour that he became famous – wearing funny clothes and biting debutantes on the ankle.

Perhaps Joaquin Miller's finest poetic achievement was to rhyme teeth *with* Goethe.

Perched in the hills at the foot of the park, the pointed towers of the **Mormon Temple** look like missile launchers designed by the Wizard of Oz – unmissable by day or floodlit night. During the holiday season, speakers hidden in the landscaping make it seem as if the plants are singing Christmas carols. Though you can't go inside (unless you're a confirmed Mormon), there are great views out over the entire Bay Area, and a small museum explains the tenets of the faith (daily 9am–9pm; free).

Two miles east along Hwy-13 sits the attractive campus of **Mills College**. Founded in 1852 as a women-only seminary, and still decidedly female after a much-publicized recent struggle against plans to make it co-ed, Mills is renowned for its music school, considered one of the best and most innovative in the US, and worth a visit for its **museum** (Sept–June Tues–Sun 10am–4pm; free), which has a fine collection of Chinese, Japanese and pre-Columbian ceramics. A broad stream meanders through the lushly landscaped grounds, and many of the buildings, notably the central campanile, were designed in solid California Mission style by Julia Morgan, architect of Hearst Castle as well as nearly five hundred Bay Area structures. Further east, **Oakland Zoo** in Knowland Park is not worth the entry fee, but you can hire horses from the stables at 14600 Skyline Blvd (☎510/569-4428), and ride around Lake Chabot in the forested hills above.

Along the bay south to San Jose stretch some twenty miles of tract house suburbs, and the only vaguely interesting area is around the end of the *BART* line in **Fremont**, where the short-lived Essanay movie studios were based. The first studios on the West Coast, Essanay made over 700 films in three years, including Charlie Chaplin's *The Tramp* in 1914. Not much remains from these pre-Hollywood days, however, and the only real sight is the **Mission San Jose de Guadalupe** on Mission Boulevard south of the I-680 freeway (daily 10am–5pm; donations), which, in the best traditions of Hollywood set design, was completely rebuilt in Mission style only a few years ago.

North Oakland and Rockridge

The horrific October 1991 **Oakland fire**, which destroyed three thousand homes and killed 26 people, did most of its damage in the high-priced hills of **North Oakland**. It took the better part of two years, but most of the half-million dollar houses have been rebuilt, and though the lush vegetation that made the area so attractive will never be allowed to grow back, things are pretty much back to normal. Which is to say that these bayview homes, some of the Bay Area's most valuable real estate, look out across some of its poorest – the neglected flatlands below, that were the proving grounds of Black Panthers Bobby Seale and Huey Newton in the 1960s.

Broadway is the dividing line between the two halves of North Oakland, and also gives access (via the handy *AC Transit* #51 bus) to most of what there is to see and do. The **Oakland Rose Garden**, on Oakland Avenue three blocks east of Broadway (April–Oct daily dawn–dusk; free), repays a look if you come during the day. One of Oakland's most neighbourly streets, **Piedmont Avenue**, runs in between, lined by a number of small bookstores and cafés. At the north end of Piedmont Avenue, the **Mountain View Cemetery** was laid out in 1863 by Frederick Law Olmsted (designer of New York's Central Park and the city's Golden Gate Park) and holds the elaborate dynastic tombs of San Francisco's most powerful families – the Crockers, the Bechtels and the Ghirardellis. You can jog or bicycle around the well-tended grounds; be sure to have a look at the enormous turtles in the pond.

Back on Broadway, just past College Avenue (see below), Broadway Terrace climbs up along the edge of the fire area to **Lake Temescal** – where you can swim in summer – and continues on up to the forested ridge at the **Robert Sibley Regional Preserve**, which includes the 1761-foot volcanic cone of Round Top Peak and panoramas of the entire Bay Area. Skyline Boulevard runs through the park and is popular with cyclists, who ride the twelve miles south to Lake Chabot or follow Grizzly Peak Boulevard five miles north to Tilden Park through the Berkeley Hills.

Most of the Broadway traffic, and the *AC Transit* #51 bus, cuts off onto College Avenue through Oakland's most upscale shopping district, **Rockridge**. Spreading for half a mile on either side of the Rockridge *BART* station, the quirky stores and restaurants here are, despite their undeniably yuppie overtones, some of the best around and make for a pleasant afternoon's wander. Both in geography and in atmosphere it's as near as Oakland gets to the café society of neighbouring Berkeley.

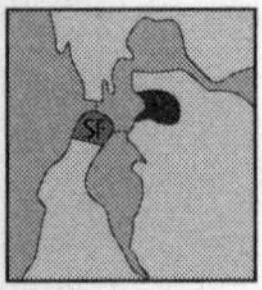

Berkeley

> *This Berkeley was like no somnolent Siwash out of her own past at all, but more akin to those Far Eastern or Latin American universities you read about, those autonomous culture media where the most beloved of folklores may be brought into doubt, cataclysmic of dissents voiced, suicidal of commitments chosen – the sort that bring governments down.*
>
> Thomas Pynchon, *The Crying of Lot 49*

More than any other American town, **BERKELEY** conjures up images of 1960s student dissent. When college campuses across the nation were protesting against the Vietnam War, it was the students of the University of California, Berkeley, who led the charge; gaining a name as the vanguard of what was increasingly seen as a challenge to the authority of the state. Full-scale battles were fought almost daily here at one point, on the campus and on the streets of the surrounding town, and there were times when Berkeley appeared to be almost on the brink of revolution itself: students (and others) throwing stones and gas bombs were met with tear-gas volleys and truncheons by National Guard troops under the nominal command of governor Ronald Reagan.

Such activities were inspired by the mood of the time and, apart from several anti-apartheid rallies in the 1980s, Berkeley politics are nowadays decidedly middle-of-the-road. But – despite an influx of non-rebellious students, a thriving bedrock of exclusive California Cuisine restaurants and the recent dismantling of the city's rent control programme – the progressive legacy lingers, noticeable in the many small bookstores and regular political demonstrations, if not the agenda of the city council.

The centrally located **University of California** completely dominates Berkeley, and makes a logical starting point for a visit. Its many grand buildings and 30,000 students give off a definite energy that spills down the raucous stretch of **Telegraph Avenue**, which runs south from the campus and holds most of the student hangouts, including a dozen or so lively cafés, as well as a number of Berkeley's many fine bookstores.

Older students, and a good percentage of the faculty, congregate in the **Northside** area, popping down from their wooded-

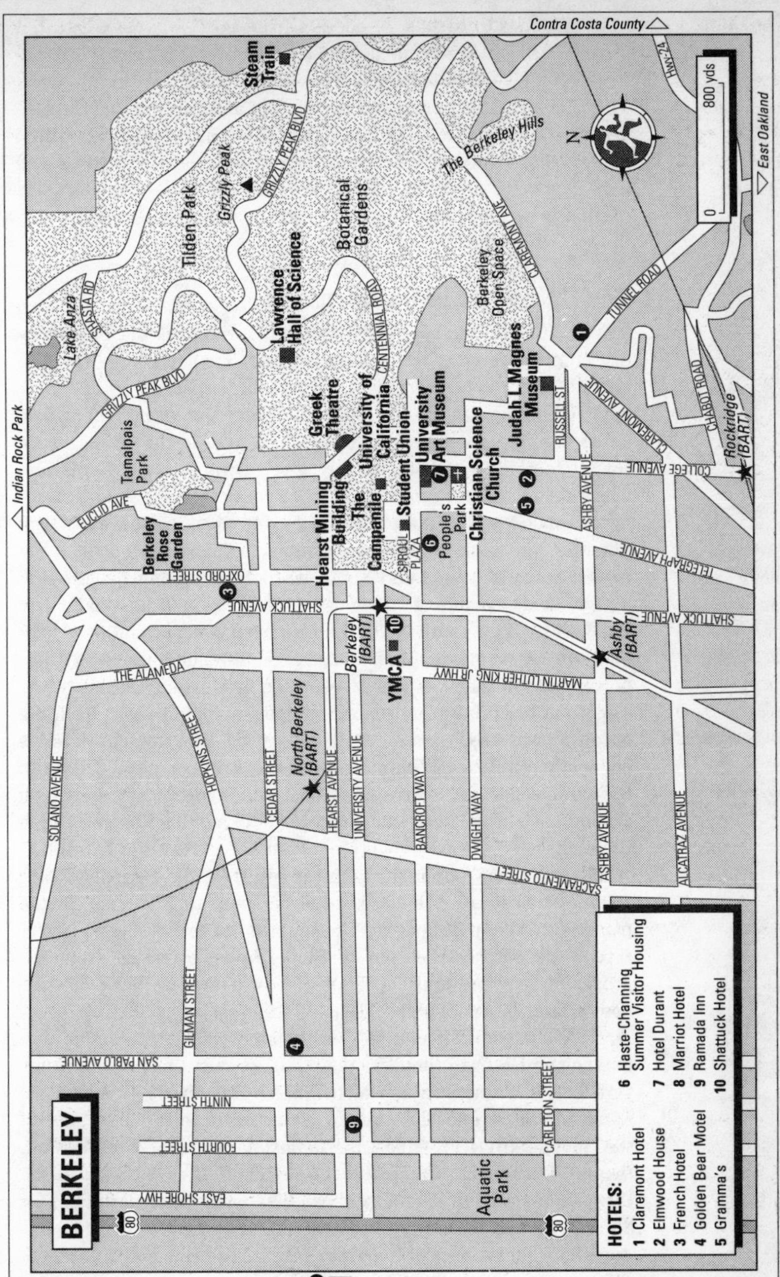
BERKELEY
HOTELS:
1 Claremont Hotel
2 Elmwood House
3 French Hotel
4 Golden Bear Motel
5 Gramma's
6 Haste-Channing Summer Visitor Housing
7 Hotel Durant
8 Marriot Hotel
9 Ramada Inn
10 Shattuck Hotel
Indian Rock Park
Contra Costa County
East Oakland
Tilden Park
Grizzly Peak
Steam Train
Lake Anza
Lawrence Hall of Science
Botanical Gardens
The Berkeley Hills
Berkeley Open Space
Greek Theatre
University of California
Hearst Mining Building
The Campanile
Student Union
University Art Museum
People's Park
Christian Science Church
Judah L Magnes Museum
Tamalpais Park
Berkeley Rose Garden
YMCA
Berkeley (BART)
North Berkeley (BART)
Ashby (BART)
Rockridge (BART)
Aquatic Park
SHASTA RD
GRIZZLY PEAK BLVD
CENTENNIAL ROAD
CLAREMONT AVE
TUNNEL ROAD
Hwy-24
EUCLID AVE
OXFORD STREET
SHATTUCK AVENUE
SPROUL PLAZA
COLLEGE AVENUE
TELEGRAPH AVENUE
RUSSELL ST
ASHBY AVENUE
CLAREMONT AVENUE
CHABOT ROAD
THE ALAMEDA
MARTIN LUTHER KING JR HWY
SOLANO AVENUE
HOPKINS STREET
CEDAR STREET
HEARST AVENUE
UNIVERSITY AVENUE
BANCROFT WAY
DWIGHT WAY
SACRAMENTO STREET
ALCATRAZ AVENUE
GILMAN STREET
SAN PABLO AVENUE
NINTH STREET
FOURTH STREET
CARLETON STREET
EAST SHORE HWY
80
N
0
800 yds

hillside homes to partake of goodies from the "Gourmet Ghetto", a stretch of Shattuck Avenue that collects many of Berkeley's internationally renowned restaurants, delis and bakeries.

Of quite distinct character are the flatlands that spread through **West Berkeley** down to the bay, a poorer but increasingly gentrified district that mixes old Victorian houses with builders' yards and light-industrial premises. Along the bay itself is the **Berkeley Marina**, where you can rent sailboards and sailboats or just watch the sun set behind the Golden Gate.

The University of California

Caught up in the frantic crush of students who pack the **University of California** campus during the semesters, it's nearly impossible to imagine the serene learning environment envisaged by its high-minded founders. When the Reverend Henry Durant and other East Coast academics decided to set up shop here in the 1860s, these rolling foothills were still largely given over to dairy herds and wheat fields, the last remnants of the Peralta family's Spanish land-grant rancho which once stretched over most of the East Bay. Construction work on the two campus buildings – imaginatively named North Hall and South Hall – was still going on when the first 200 students, including 22 women, moved here from Oakland in 1873. Since then, more buildings have been squeezed into the half-mile-square main campus, and the state-funded university has become one of the most highly respected in America. Overcrowding aside, the beautifully landscaped campus, stepping down from the eucalyptus-covered Berkeley Hills towards the Golden Gate, is eminently strollable. With maps posted everywhere, you'd have to try hard to get lost – though enthusiastic students will show you around on a free two-hour tour; drop in at the Student Union Building, 101 University Hall (Mon, Wed & Fri 10am and 1pm).

There are so many Nobel laureates on the University faculty that it's said you have to be awarded one just to get a parking permit.

A number of footpaths climb the hill from the Berkeley *BART* station on Shattuck Avenue, but the best way to get a feel for the place is to follow Strawberry Creek from the top of Center Street across the southeast corner of the campus, emerging from the groves of redwood and eucalyptus trees at **Sproul Plaza**. It's the newest and largest public space on campus, enlivened by street musicians playing for quarters on the steps of the **Student Union** building and conga drummers pounding away in the echoing courtyard below. **Sather Gate**, which bridges Strawberry Creek at the north end of Sproul Plaza, marks the entrance to the older part of the campus. Up the hill, past the imposing facade of Wheeler Hall, the 1914 landmark **Campanile** is modelled after the one in the Piazza San Marco in Venice; you can take an elevator to the top for a great view of the campus and the entire Bay Area (daily 10am–4pm; 25¢). At the foot of the tower stands red-brick **South Hall**, the sole survivor of the original pair of buildings.

San Francisco's bookstores are detailed on p.278.

Berkeley's Bookstores

Berkeley's **bookstores** are as exhaustive as they are exhausting – not surprising for a college town. Perfect for browsing and taking your time, you won't be made to feel guilty or obliged to buy a book you've been poring over for ages.

Black Oak Books, 1491 Shattuck Ave. Huge selection of secondhand and new books for every interest; also holds regular evening readings by internationally acclaimed authors. ☎510/486-0698.

Cody's Books, 2454 Telegraph Ave. The flagship of Berkeley booksellers, with an excellent selection of fiction, poetry and literary criticism. ☎510/845-7852.

Comics and Comix, 2502 Telegraph Ave. Great selection of comic books, both current and classic. ☎510/845-4091.

Easy Going, 1385 Shattuck Ave. The essential bookstore for every traveller. Packed with printed travel paraphernalia, it offers a wide selection of guidebooks and maps for local, countrywide and worldwide exploration. ☎510/843-3533.

Moe's Books, 2476 Telegraph Ave. An enormous selection of new and used books on four floors with esoteric surprises in every field of study; for academics, book-collectors and browsers. There's also an excellent art section on the top floor. ☎510/849-2087.

Serendipity Books, 1201 University Ave. Damp and disorganized, but with an incredible selection of first edition and out of print books. A must for collectors of first editions and obscure fiction and poetry. ☎510/841-7455.

Shakespeare and Company, 2499 Telegraph Ave. Crammed with quality second-hand books at reasonable prices. The best place to linger and scour the shelves for finds. ☎510/841-8916.

Shambala Booksellers, 2482 Telegraph Ave. Have a transcendental out-of-body experience where Eastern and Western religious traditions meet in this cosy store near campus. ☎848-8443.

Inside the plain white building next door, the **Bancroft Library** (Mon–Sat 10am–5pm) displays odds and ends from its exhaustive accumulation of artefacts and documents tracing the history of California, including a faked brass plaque supposedly left by Sir Francis Drake when he claimed all of the West Coast for Queen Elizabeth I. It also contains an internationally important collection of manuscripts and rare books, from Mark Twain to James Joyce – though you have to show some academic credentials if you want to see any of these. Around the corner and down the hill, just inside the arched main entrance to Doe Library, you'll find the **Morrison Reading Room**, a great place to sit for a while and read foreign magazines and newspapers, listen to a CD or just ease down into one of the many comfy overstuffed chairs and unwind.

Also worth a look if you've got time to kill is the **Museum of Paleontology** in the nearby Earth Sciences Building, which details evolutionary concepts with hundreds of fossils, skeletons and geological maps displayed along the corridors on the lower floors. From here it's a quick walk to the collection of cafés and restaurants lining Euclid and Hearst avenues and the beginning of Berkeley's Northside (see p.158).

The Hearst family name appears with disturbing regularity around the Berkeley campus, though in most instances this is due not to the notorious William Randolph Hearst but to his altruistic mother, Phoebe Apperson Hearst. Besides inviting the entire senior class to her home every spring for a giant picnic, she sponsored the architectural competition that came up with the original campus plan, and donated a number of the campus buildings, including many that have since been destroyed. One of the finest that survives, the 1907 **Hearst Mining Building** (daily 8am–5pm) on the northeast edge of the campus, conceals a delicate metalwork lobby topped by three glass domes, above ageing exhibits on geology and mining – which is how the Hearst family fortune was originally made, long before scion William Randolph took up publishing. Another Hearst legacy is the **Greek Theatre**, an open-air amphitheatre cut into the Berkeley Hills east of the campus, which hosts a summer season of rock concerts.

Higher up in the hills, above the 80,000-seat Memorial Stadium, is the lushly landscaped **Botanical Garden** (daily 9am–5pm; free), good for defeating on-campus claustrophobia with its thirty acres of plants and cacti. Near the crest, with great views out over the bay, a full-size fibreglass sculpture of a sei whale stretches out in front of the space-age **Lawrence Hall of Science** (daily 10am–4.30pm; $5, children under 6 $2), an excellent museum and learning centre that features earthquake simulations, model dinosaurs and a planetarium, plus a number of hands-on exhibits for kids in the Wizard's Lab. Both the Gardens and the Lawrence Hall of Science are accessible on weekdays via the free *UC Berkeley Shuttle* bus from the campus or the Berkeley *BART* station.

In the southeast corner of the campus, the **Hearst Museum of Anthropology** in Kroeber Hall (daily except Wed 10am–4pm; $2, free Thurs) holds a variety of changing exhibits as well as an intriguing display of artefacts made by Ishi, the last-surviving Yahi Native American, who was found near Mount Lassen in Northern California in 1911. Anthropologist Alfred Kroeber brought Ishi to the museum (then located on the UC San Francisco campus), where he lived under the scrutiny of scientists and journalists – in effect, in a state of captivity – until his death from tuberculosis a few years later. Also in Kroeber Hall, the Worth Ryder Art Gallery in room 116 shows varying degrees of quality in the work of Berkeley's art students.

Alfred Kroeber was also the father of writer Ursula K Le Guin.

The brutally modern, angular concrete of the **University Art Museum** across Bancroft Way (Wed–Sun 11am–5pm; $5, free Thurs 11am–noon) is in stark contrast to the campus's older buildings. Its skylit, open-plan galleries hold works by Picasso, Cézanne,

Rubens and other notables, but the star of the show is the collection of 1950s American painter Hans Hofmann's energetic and colourful abstract paintings, on the top floor. The museum is renowned for its cutting-edge, changing exhibitions: the main space hosts a range of major shows – such as Robert Mapplethorpe's controversial photographs – while the Matrix Gallery focuses on lesser-known, generally local artists. Works on paper are shown downstairs outside the **Pacific Film Archive**, which shares the building, showing new films from around the world that you won't see elsewhere, as well as revivals from its extensive library.

There's more on the Pacific Film Archive on p.269.

Telegraph Avenue and South Berkeley

Downtown Berkeley – basically two department stores, a few banks, a post office and the City Hall building – lies west of the University campus, around the Berkeley *BART* station on Shattuck Avenue, but the real activity centres on **Telegraph Avenue**, which runs south of the University from Sproul Plaza. This thoroughfare saw some of the worst of the 1960s riots and is still a frenetic bustle, especially the four short blocks closest to the University, which are packed to the gills with cafés and second-hand bookstores. Sidewalk vendors hawk hand-made jewellery and brilliantly coloured T-shirts, while down-and-outs hustle for spare change and spout psychotic poetry.

People's Park, now a seedy and overgrown plot of land half a block up from Telegraph between Haste Street and Dwight Way, was another battleground in the late 1960s, when organized and spirited resistance to the University's plans to develop the site into dormitories brought out the troops, who shot dead an onlooker by mistake. To many, the fact that the park is still a community-controlled open space (and outdoor dosshouse for Berkeley's homeless legions) is a small victory in the battle against the Establishment, though it's not a pleasant or even very safe place to hang about, especially after dark. A mural along Haste Street remembers some of the reasons why the battles were fought, in the words of student leader Mario Savio: "There's a time when the operation of the machine becomes so odious, makes you so sick at heart, that you can't take part, you can't even tacitly take part. And you've got to put your bodies upon the gears and upon the wheels, upon the levers, upon all the apparatus, and you've got to make it stop" – ideals that can't help but be undermined by the state of the place these days. Recent efforts by the University to reclaim the space with volleyball and basketball courts were met with short-lived but violent protests – rioters thrashed Telegraph Avenue storefronts, and a nineteen-year-old woman was shot dead by police while trying to assassinate the Chancellor.

Directly across Bowditch Street from People's Park stands one of the finest buildings in the Bay Area, Bernard Maybeck's **Christian Science Church**. Built in 1910, it's an eclectic but thoroughly modern structure, laid out in a simple Greek cross floor plan and spanned by a massive redwood truss with carved Gothic tracery and Byzantine painted decoration. The interior is only open on Sundays for worship and for tours afterwards at 11am, but the outside is worth lingering over, its cascade of many gently pitched roofs and porticoes carrying the eye from one hand-crafted detail to another. It's a clever building in many ways: while the overall image is one of tradition and craftsmanship, Maybeck also succeeded in inconspicuously incorporating such unlikely materials as industrial metal windows, concrete walls and asbestos tiles into the structure – thereby cutting down costs.

Many of the largely residential neighbourhoods elsewhere in **South Berkeley** (Southside) – especially the Elmwood and Claremont districts around College Avenue – are worth a wander, with a couple of specific sights to search out. One of these is the **Judah L Magnes Museum**, a few blocks south of the campus at 2911 Russell St (daily except Sat 10am–4pm; free). Located in a rambling old mansion, it has California's largest repository of Judaica, and exhibits detail the history of Jewish life from ancient times to the present day. The other Southside attraction is much harder to miss, towering as it does over the Berkeley–Oakland border. The half-timbered castle imagery of the **Claremont Hotel** gives a fairly clear hint as to what's inside – it's now one of the Bay Area's plushest resort hotels, with the three-storey Tower Suite going for a cool $750 per night. Built in 1914, just in time for San Francisco's Panama-Pacific Exposition, the *Claremont* was designed to encourage day-trippers out across the bay in the hope that they'd be so taken with the area they'd want to live here. The ploy worked, and the hotel's owners (who incidentally also owned the streetcar system that brought people here, and all the surrounding land) made a packet.

North Berkeley

North Berkeley (Northside) is a subdued neighbourhood of professors and postgraduate students, its steep, twisting streets climbing up the lushly overgrown hills north of the campus. At the foot of the hills, some of the Bay Area's finest restaurants and delicatessens – most famously *Chez Panisse*, started and run by Alice Waters, the acclaimed inventor of California Cuisine – have sprung up along Shattuck Avenue to form the so-called "Gourmet Ghetto", a great place to pick up the makings of a tasty alfresco lunch.

The restaurants of the "Gourmet Ghetto" are detailed on p.238.

Above the Gourmet Ghetto on Euclid Avenue (if you want to avoid the fairly steep walk, take bus #65 from Shattuck Avenue), there are few more pleasant places for a picnic than the **Berkeley Rose Garden**, a terraced amphitheatre filled with some three thousand varietal roses and looking out across the bay to San Francisco. Built as part of a WPA job-creation scheme during the Depression, a wooden pergola rings the top, stepping down to a small spring. Opposite the Rose Garden, through a pedestrian tunnel, is **Codornices Park**, a broad expanse of manicured lawn edged by a baseball diamond, basketball courts and lots of play equipment, the best of which is a long concrete helter-skelter that's good fun to hurtle down, and not only for kids. A footpath leads up from the park along Codornices Creek, burbling with small waterfalls after a good rain.

Though the hills are steep, the homes here – built in an eclectic range of styles, designed to meld seamlessly into the wooded landscape – are some of the finest and most impressively sited in the Bay Area. All repay many times over the effort it takes to see them, if only for their marvellous setting. Many were constructed by members of the Hillside Club, a slightly bohemian group of turn-of-the-century Berkeleyans who also laid out many of the pedestrian paths that climb the hills. Perhaps the single most striking of these hillside homes, the **Rowell House** – a half-timbered chalet built in 1914 by architect John Hudson Thomas – stands alone at the top of the path up from Codornices Park, where it crosses Tamalpais Road. Many of the other houses nearby were designed and built by Bernard Maybeck, architect of the Palace of Fine Arts, Christian Science Church and other notable Bay Area buildings; the homes he built for himself and his family still stand around the junction of Buena Vista Way and La Loma Avenue, a hundred yards south.

A number of enticing parks, all with great views over the bay, complement the picturesque houses of the Berkeley Hills. The largest and highest of these, **Tilden Park**, spreads along the crest of the hills, encompassing some 2065 acres of near wilderness. You can get there from downtown Berkeley via *AC Transit* #65 bus. Kids can enjoy a ride on the carved wooden horses or a mini-steam train through the redwood trees. In the warm months, don't miss a swim in Lake Anza (lifeguard on duty May–Oct daily 11am–6pm; $2).

Nearer to town, at the north end of Shattuck Avenue and close by the stores and cafés along Solano Avenue, the grey basalt knob of **Indian Rock** stands out from the foot of the hills, challenging rock-climbers who hone their skills on its forty-foot vertical faces. There are steps around its back for those who just want to appreciate the extraordinary view. Carved into similarly hard volcanic stone across the street are the mortar holes used by the Ohlone to grind acorns into flour. In between, and in stark contrast, stands the rusting hulk of a Cold War air-raid siren.

West Berkeley and the waterfront

From downtown Berkeley and the UC campus, **University Avenue** runs downhill towards the bay, lined by increasingly shabby frontages of motels and massage parlours. The liveliest part of this **West Berkeley** area is around the intersection of University Avenue and

San Pablo Avenue – the pre-freeway main highway north – where a community of recent immigrants from India have set up shops and markets and restaurants that serve some of the best of the Bay Area's rare curries.

The area between San Pablo Avenue and the bay is the oldest part of Berkeley, and a handful of hundred-year-old houses and churches – such as the two white-spired Gothic Revival ones on Hearst Avenue – survive from the days when this district was a separate city, known as Ocean View. The neighbourhood also holds remnants of Berkeley's industrial past, and many of the old warehouses and factory premises have been converted into living and working spaces for artists, craftspeople and computer software companies. Along similar lines are the cafés, workshops and galleries built in the late 1970s along **Fourth Street** north of University Avenue, which have since become somewhat yuppified but are still good places to wander in search of handicrafts and household gadgets.

One of the few places you can visit here is the **Takara Sake Tasting Room**, just off Fourth Street south of University Avenue at 708 Addison St (daily noon–6pm; free). Owned and operated by one of Japan's largest producers, this plant is responsible for more than a third of all sake drunk in the US. You can sample any of the five varieties of California-strain sake (brewed from Californian rice), best drunk warm and swallowed sharply. Though no tours are offered, they will show you a slide presentation of the art of sake brewing.

Berkeley Marina

The I-80 freeway, and the railroad tracks that run alongside it, pretty well manage to cut Berkeley off from its waterfront. The best way to get there is to take *AC Transit* bus #51M, which runs regularly down University Avenue. Once a major hub for the transbay ferry services – to shorten journey times, a three-mile-long pier was constructed, much of which still sticks out into the bay – the **Berkeley Marina** is now one of the prime spots on the bay for leisure activities, especially windsurfing. If you're interested in having a try on the boards, contact the *Cal Sailing Club* (see p.284 for details). The surrounding area, all of which is landfill largely owned by the *Southern Pacific* railroad, has long been the subject of heated battles between developers and the environmentalists who want to preserve it as a shoreline park. For the moment, the winds off the bay make it a good place to fly a kite, and there are some short hiking trails.

The North Bay and inland valleys

Compared to the urbanized bayfront cities of Oakland and Berkeley, the rest of the East Bay is sparsely populated, and places of interest are few and far between. The **North Bay** is home to some of the Bay

Area's heaviest industry – oil refineries and chemical plants dominate the landscape – but also holds a few remarkably unchanged waterfront towns that merit a side trip if you're passing by. Away from the bay, the **inland valleys** are a whole other world, of dry rolling hills dominated by the towering peak of Mount Diablo. Dozens of tract house developments have made commuter suburbs out of what were once cattle ranches and farms, but so far the region has been able to absorb the numbers and still feels rural, despite having doubled in population in the past twenty years.

Walnut Creek off Ygnacio Valley Road, is renowned for its restaurants. Put on some nice clothes after a day's hike on Mount Diablo for dinner at Soleil; *see p.241.*

The North Bay

Western Costa County offers a taste of life not dictated by trend-setting students or the high-paced City influence. Beyond the casual mix of new buildings with remains of old, it's easy to find a traditional Californian lifestyle amid the strip malls. Much of the early 1900s character still exists here, mostly untouched by neighbouring glamorous trends.

In **ALBANY**, Golden Gate Fields has horse racing from October to June, and **El Cerrito**'s main contribution to world culture was the band Creedence Clearwater Revival, who did most of their *Born on the Bayou* publicity photographs in the wilds of Tilden Park in the hills above; El Cerrito is still home to one of the best record stores in the US, *Down Home Music* (see p.280 for details).

RICHMOND, at the top of the bay, was once a boom town, building ships during World War II at the Kaiser Shipyards, which employed 100,000 workers between 1940 and its closure in 1945. Now it's the proud home of the gigantic Standard Oil refinery, the centre of which you drive through before crossing the **Richmond–San Rafael Bridge** ($1) to Marin County. As Richmond marks the north end of the *BART* line, the adjacent *Amtrak* station is a better terminal for journeys to and from San Francisco than the end of the line in West Oakland. If you find yourself with time to fill, check out the **Richmond Museum of History** at 400 Nevin Ave (Wed–Sun 1–4pm; free), which exhibits artefacts, photos and antique items illustrating the history of Richmond during the first half of the twentieth century. Also worth a visit, **The National Institute of Art and Disabilities** at 551 23rd St (Tues–Sat 10am–5pm; free) exhibits art created by artists with development and physical disabilities, for view in a kooky warehouse space where the artists are often at work.

Amtrak *services to the San Francisco area are detailed on* *p.12.*

If you're heading from the East Bay to Marin County, **Point Richmond** repays a look. Follow Dorman Drive through a tunnel to Keller Beach, where you can walk along the shore at high tide to Cozy Cove Beach. Further along, Dorman passes Miller Knox Regional Park, with its exotic-bird-populated lagoon, until it eventually turns into Brickyard Cove Road, where modern bay-view condos surround a disused brick kiln. Beyond this is Sandpiper Spit and

Bing Crosby and Trader Vic were known to visit Brooks Island for an occasional hunt.

other planned narrow pieces of landfill created to build unaffordable homes on the waterfront. In the bay, **Brooks Island**, once stocked with wild game, is now inhabited by one employee of the East Bay Regional Parks. In the same bay you can watch the Standard Oil factory receive oil from the enormous ships from all over the world docked at the long wharf.

Also in Point Richmond, take Hwy-580 to the last exit before the Richmond–San Rafael Bridge toward Point Miladi, follow Western Drive out to the deserted **Winehaven**, built in 1908 as the largest winery in the world. A colossal, empty brick castle remains on the water's edge, surrounded by a small, planned mini-community of prefabricated early 1900s homes. Later used as a military barracks, these houses and the great distillery sit lonely in the countryside.

The Carquinez Straits

At the top of the bay some 25 miles north of Oakland, the land along the **Carquinez Straits** is a bit off the beaten track, but it's an area of some natural beauty and much historic interest. The still-small towns along the waterfront seem worlds away from the bustle of the rest of the Bay Area, but how long they'll be able to resist the pressure of the expanding commuter belt is anybody's guess. *AC Transit* bus #70 runs every hour from Richmond *BART* north to **Crockett** at the west end of the narrow straits – a tiny town cut into the steep hillsides above the water that seems entirely dependent upon the massive C&H Sugar factory at its foot, whose giant neon sign lights up the town and the adjacent Carquinez Bridge. Crockett seems mostly closed-down, though a friendly atmosphere makes it comfortable enough to stop for a glance around town. The *Valona Market* at 1317 Pomona St is a fine café with live jazz on weekend nights, or else enjoy food and drinks on the harbour at the *Nantucket*, turn left at the Crockett exit off I-80, take another left down Port Street until you come to the marina.

From Crockett the narrow **Carquinez Straits Scenic Drive**, an excellent cycling route, heads east along the Sacramento River. A turn two miles along drops down to **Port Costa**, a small town that was dependent upon ferry traffic across the straits to Benicia until it lost its livelihood when the bridge was built at Crockett. Often unnoticed on maps and difficult to find off the swerving Carquinez Scenic Road, this small, working-class town is worth a visit. Commanding most of the grain trade in its heyday at the turn of the century, Port Costa was home to twenty saloons, fourteen hotels and eight bordellos. It's still a nice enough place to watch the huge ships pass by on their way to and from the inland ports of Sacramento and Stockton. If you don't have a bike (or a car), you can enjoy the view from the window of an *Amtrak* train, which runs alongside the water from Oakland and Richmond, not stopping until Martinez at the eastern end of the Straits, two miles north of the John Muir house (see p.165).

Benicia

On the north side of the Straits, and hard to get to without a car (see p.32), **BENICIA** is the most substantial of the historic waterfront towns, but one that has definitely seen better days. Founded in 1847, it initially rivalled San Francisco as the major Bay Area port, and was even the state capital for a time; but, despite Benicia's better weather and fine deep-water harbour, San Francisco eventually became the main transportation point for the fortunes of the Gold Rush, and the town very nearly faded away altogether. Examples of Benicia's efforts to become a major city stand poignantly around the very compact downtown area, most conspicuously the 1852 Greek Revival building that was used as the **first State Capitol** for just thirteen months. The building has been restored as a **museum** (daily except Tues & Wed 10am–5pm; $2), furnished in the legislative style of the time, with top hats on the tables and shining spittoons every few feet.

A walking tour map of Benicia's many intact Victorian houses and churches is available from the **tourist office** at 601 First St (☎707/745-2120), including on its itinerary the steeply pitched roofs and gingerbread eaves of the **Frisbie-Walsh house** at 235 East L St – a prefabricated Gothic Revival building that was shipped in pieces from Boston in 1849. Across the City Hall park, the arched ceiling beams of **St Paul's Episcopal Church** look like an upturned ship's hull; it was built by shipwrights from the Pacific Mail Steamship Company, one of Benicia's many successful nineteenth-century shipyards. Half a dozen former brothels and saloons have been renovated along First Street to show the town's history; follow it along down near the serene waterfront, from where the world's largest train ferries used to ply the waters between Benicia and Port Costa until 1930.

An identical house was erected by General Vallejo in Sonoma; see p.202.

In recent years Benicia has attracted a number of artists and craftspeople, and you can watch glass-blowers and furniture-makers at work in the **Yuba Complex**, at 670 East H St (Mon–Fri 10am–4pm). Judy Chicago is among those who work in converted studios and modern light-industrial parks around the sprawling fortifications of the old **Benicia Arsenal** east of the downtown area, whose thickly walled sandstone buildings formed the main Army storage facility for weapons and ammunition from 1851 up through the Korean War. One of the oddest parts of the complex is the **Camel Barn** (Sat & Sun 1–4pm, also Fri in summer; free), now a museum of local history, but formerly used to house camels that the Army imported in 1856 to transport supplies across the deserts of the Southwestern US. The experiment failed, and the camels were kept here until they were sold off in 1864.

Vallejo and Marine World/Africa USA

Across the Carquinez Bridge from Crockett, the biggest and most boring of the North Bay towns – **VALLEJO** – was, like Benicia, an early capital of California, though it now lacks any sign of its historical significance. In contrast to most of the other Gold Rush-era towns that line the Straits, Vallejo has remained economically vital, largely because of the massive military presence here at the **Mare Island Naval Shipyard**, a sprawling, relentlessly grey complex that covers an area twice the size of Golden Gate Park. Its less than glamorous history – the yard builds and maintains supply ships and the like, not carriers or battleships – is recounted in a small **museum** in the old City Hall building at 734 Mare St (Tues–Fri 10am–4.30pm; $1), where the highlight is a working periscope that looks out across the bay. Though no great thrill, it merits a quick stop; it's right on Hwy-29, the main route from the East Bay to the Wine Country, in the centre of town.

The best reason to come to Vallejo is **Marine World/Africa USA** (daily 9.30am–6.00pm; adults $25.95, children under twelve $16.95, under threes free), five miles north of Vallejo off I-80 at the Marine World Parkway (Hwy-37) exit. Operated by a non-profit educational group, it offers a well-above-average range of performing sea lions, dolphins and killer whales kept in approximations of their natural habitats, as well as water-ski stunt shows and the like. It can be a fun day out, especially for children, and it's not bad as these things go: the animals seem very well cared for, their quarters are clean and spacious, and the shows are fun for all but the most jaded. The new shark exhibit lets you walk (through a transparent tunnel) alongside twenty-foot Great Whites, and the tropical butterfly aviary is truly amazing – nearly worth the price of admission.

The most enjoyable way to get to Marine World from San Francisco is to take one of the *Red and White Fleet* **catamaran ferry** boats from Fisherman's Wharf, which take an hour each way and add another $13 to the admission price.

The inland valleys

Most of the inland East Bay area is made up of rolling hills covered by grasslands, slowly yielding to suburban housing developments and office complexes, as more and more businesses abandon the pricey real estate of San Francisco. The great peak of **Mount Diablo** which dominates the region is twice as high as any other Bay Area summit and surrounded by acres of campgrounds and hiking trails; other attractions include two historic homes that serve as memorials to their literate and influential ex-residents, John Muir and Eugene O'Neill.

BART tunnels from Oakland through the Berkeley Hills to the leafy-green stockbroker settlement of **Orinda**, continuing east through the increasingly hot and dry landscape to the end of the line at **Concord**, site of chemical plants and oil refineries and a controversial nuclear weapons depot. A few years ago, a peaceful, civilly disobedient blockade here ended in protestor Brian Willson losing his legs under the wheels of a slow-moving munitions train. The event raised public awareness – before it happened few people knew of the depot's existence – but otherwise it's still business as usual.

Martinez and John Muir's house

From Pleasant Hill *BART*, one stop before the end of the line, *Contra Costa County Connection* bus #116 leaves every half-hour for **MARTINEZ**, the seat of county government, passing the preserved home of naturalist **John Muir** (daily 10am–4.30pm; $1), just off Hwy-4, two miles south of Martinez. Muir, an articulate, persuasive Scot whose writings and political activism were of vital importance in the preservation of America's wilderness, spent much of his life exploring and writing about the majestic Sierra Nevada mountains, particularly Yosemite. He was also one of the founders of the **Sierra Club** – a wilderness lobby and education organization still active today. Anyone who is familiar with the image of this thin, bearded man wandering the mountains with his knapsack, notebook and packet of tea might be surprised to see his very conventional, upper-class Victorian home, now restored to its appearance when Muir died in 1914. The house was built by Muir's father-in-law, and only those parts Muir added to it himself reflect much of the personality of the man, such as the massive, rustic fireplace he had built in the East Parlour so he could have a "real mountain campfire". The bulk of Muir's personal belongings and artefacts are displayed in his study, on the upper floor, and in the adjacent room an exhibition documents the history of the Sierra Club and Muir's battles to protect America's wilderness.

Behind the bell-towered main house is a large, still productive orchard where Muir cultivated grapes, pears and cherries to earn the money to finance his explorations (you can sample the fruits free of charge, pre-picked by staff gardeners). Beyond the orchard is the 1849 **Martinez Adobe**, homestead of the original Spanish land-grant settlers and now a small **museum** of Mexican colonial culture. It's worth a look if you're out here, if only for the contrast between Mexican and American cultures in early California; also, the building's two-foot-thick walls keep it refreshingly cool on a typically hot summer day.

Eugene O'Neill and Mount Diablo

At the foot of Mount Diablo, fifteen miles south, playwright **Eugene O'Neill** used the money he got for winning the Nobel Prize for Literature in 1936 to build a home and sanctuary for himself, which he named **Tao House**. It was here, before 1944, when he was struck down with Parkinson's disease, that he wrote many of his best-known plays: *The Iceman Cometh*, *A Moon for the Misbegotten* and *Long Day's Journey into Night*. Readings and performances of his works are sometimes given in the house, which is open to visitors, though you must reserve a place on one of the free guided tours (Wed–Sun 10am & 12.30pm; ☎510/838-0249). There's no parking on site, so the tours pick you up in the town of **Danville**.

No public transportation serves the park, but the Sierra Club sometimes organizes day trips.

As for **Mount Diablo** itself, it rises up from the rolling ranchlands at its foot to a height of nearly 4000ft, its summit and flanks preserved within **Mount Diablo State Park** ($5 parking; ☎510/837-2525). The main road through the park reaches within 300ft of the top, so it's a popular place for an outing, and you're unlikely to be alone to enjoy the marvellous view: on a clear day you can see over two hundred miles in every direction. The 15,000 acres of parkland surrounding the peak offer many miles of hiking and some of the only **camping** in the East Bay.

Two main entrances lead into the park, both well marked off I-680. The one from the southwest by way of Danville passes by the **ranger station**, where you can pick up a trail map ($1) which lists the best day-hikes. The other runs from the northwest by way of Walnut Creek, and the routes join together five miles from the summit. March and April, when the wild flowers are out, are the best times to be here, and since mornings are ideal for getting the clearest view, you should drive to the top first and then head back down to a trailhead for a hike, or to one of the many picnic spots for a leisurely lunch. In summer it can get desperately hot and dry, so much so that parts of the park are closed because of fire danger.

Livermore and Altamont

The sleepy suburb of **Livermore** has little to offer for any entertainment. One restaurant worth the trip, *Gio's Trattoria*, offers outstanding Italian food in an elegant atmosphere (see p.241). A long, often traffic-filled, car ride from San Francisco might be justified for science buffs. Fifteen miles southeast of Mount Diablo, on the main road out of the Bay Area (I-580), the rolling hills around Livermore are covered with thousands of shining, spinning, high-tech **windmills**, placed here by a private power company to take advantage of the nearly constant winds. It's the largest wind farm in the world, and you'll probably have seen it used in a number of TV ads, as a space-age backdrop to hype flashy new cars or sexy perfumes. Though the Federal government provides no funding for this non-polluting, renewable source of energy, it spends billions of dollars every year designing and building nuclear weapons and other sinister applications of modern technology at the nearby **Lawrence Livermore Laboratories**, where most of the research and development of the nuclear arsenal takes place. A small **visitor center** holds hands-on exhibits showing off various scientific phenomena and devices, two miles south of I-580 on Greenville Road (Mon–Fri 9am–4.30pm, Sat & Sun noon–5pm; free).

Up and over the hills to the east, where I-580 joins I-5 for the 400-mile route south through the Central Valley to Los Angeles, stand the remains of **Altamont Speedway**, site of a nightmarish Rolling Stones concert in December 1969. The free concert, which was captured in the film *Gimme Shelter*, was intended to be a sort of second Woodstock, staged in order to counter allegations that the Stones had ripped off their fans during a long US tour. In the event, it was a complete fiasco: three people died, one of whom was kicked and stabbed to death by the Hell's Angels "security guards" – in full view of the cameras – after pointing a gun at Mick Jagger while he sang *Sympathy for the Devil*. Needless to say, no historical plaque marks the site.

Chapter 9

The Peninsula

The city of San Francisco sits at the tip of a five-mile-wide **Peninsula**. Home of old money and new technology, this stretches south from San Francisco along the bay for fifty miles of relentless suburbia, past the wealthy enclaves of Hillsborough and Atherton, to wind up in the futuristic roadside landscape of the **Silicon Valley** near **San Jose** – though your only glimpse of the area may be on the trip between San Francisco and the airport. There was a time when the region was covered with orange groves and fig trees, but the concentration of academic interest around Stanford University in Palo Alto and the continuing boom in computers – since the 1970s, the biggest local industry – has buried any chances of it hanging onto its agricultural past.

Surprisingly, most of the land along the **coast**, separated from the bayfront sprawl by a ridge of redwood-covered peaks, remains rural and undeveloped; it also contains some of the best **beaches** in the Bay Area and a couple of affably down-to-earth farming communities, all well served by public transit.

Transport and Information

Peninsula accommodation options are listed in Chapter Twelve; restaurants are on p.244, and cafés and bars on p.254.

BART only travels down the Peninsula as far as **Daly City**, from where you can catch *SamTrans* (☎761-7000) buses south to Palo Alto or along the coast to Half Moon Bay. For longer distances, *Caltrain* (☎557-8661) offers an hourly rail service from its terminal at Fourth and Townsend streets in downtown San Francisco, stopping at most bayside towns between the city and San Jose, for between $1 and $5; *Greyhound* runs regular buses along US-101 to and from their San Jose terminal at 70 S Almaden, on the corner of Santa Clara Street (☎408/297-8890). *Santa Clara County Transit* (*SCCT*) (☎408/287-4210) runs buses and modern trolleys around metropolitan San Jose. If you're going to be spending most of your time down here, it's possible to fly direct into **San Jose International Airport** (SJO), alarmingly close to downtown San Jose.

The **Palo Alto Chamber of Commerce**, 325 Forest Ave (Mon–Fri 9am–noon & 1–5pm; ☎324-3121), has lists of local restaurants

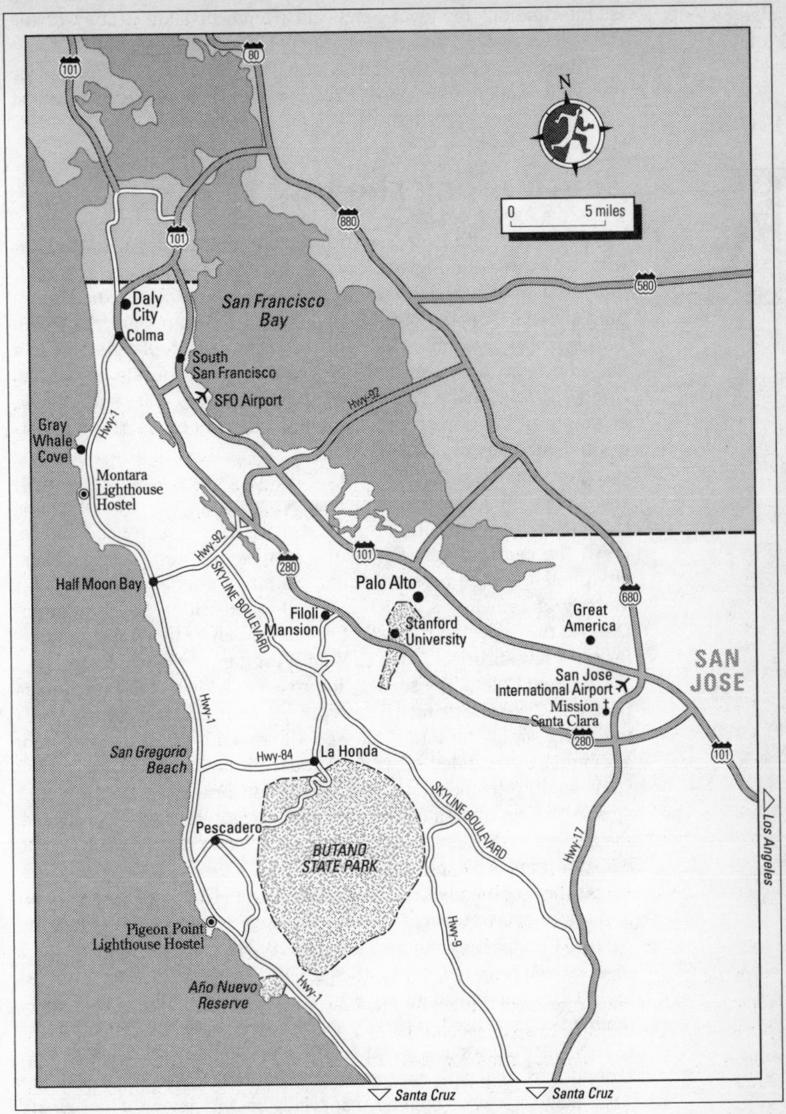

and cycle routes; for information on nearby Stanford University, phone ☎ 723-2560. To find out what's on and where, pick up a free copy of the *Palo Alto Weekly*, available at most local shops.

At the southern end of the bay, the **San Jose Convention and Visitors' Bureau**, 333 W San Carlos St, Suite 1000 (Mon–Sat 9am–5pm; ☎ 408/295-9600 or 1-800/SAN-JOSE), is the best bet for tourist information; for local news and events pick up a copy of the excellent *San Jose Mercury* newspaper or the free weekly *Metro*.

Along the coast, the **Half Moon Bay Chamber of Commerce** gives out walking tour maps and information on accommodation at 520 Kelly Ave (☎ 726-5202).

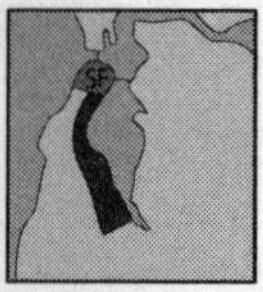

South Along the Bay

US-101 runs south from San Francisco along the bay through over fifty miles of unmitigated sprawl to San Jose, lined by light-industrial estates and shopping malls. The only place worth stopping at is the **Coyote Point Museum** (Wed–Fri 9am–5pm, Sat & Sun 1–5pm; free), four miles south of the airport off Poplar Avenue in a large bayfront park, where examples of the natural life of the San Francisco Bay – from tidal insects to birds of prey – are exhibited in engaging and informative displays, enhanced by interactive computers and documentary films.

A more pleasant drive is via **I-280**, the newest and most expensive freeway in California, which runs parallel to US-101 but avoids the worst of the bayside mess by cutting through wooded valleys down the centre of the Peninsula. Just beyond the San Francisco city limits the road passes through **Colma**, a unique place made up entirely of cemeteries, which are prohibited within San Francisco. Besides the expected roll call of deceased San Franciscans luminaries are a few surprises, such as Wild West gunman Wyatt Earp.

Beyond Colma, the scenery improves quickly as I-280 continues past the **Crystal Springs Reservoir**, an artificial lake which holds the water supply for San Francisco – pumped here all the way from Yosemite. Surrounded by twenty square miles of parkland, hiking trails lead up to the ridge from which San Francisco Bay was first spotted by eighteenth-century Spanish explorers; it now overlooks the airport to the east, but there are good views out over the Pacific coast, two miles distant.

At the south end of the reservoir, just off I-280 on Canada Road in the well-heeled town of **Woodside**, luscious gardens surround the palatial **Filoli Estate** (tours Tues–Sat 10.30am & 1pm; $8; advance reservations required ☎ 364-2880). The 45-room mansion, designed in 1915 in neo-Palladian style by architect Willis Polk, may seem familiar – it was used in the TV series *Dynasty* as the Denver home of the Carrington clan. It's the only one of the many huge houses around here that you can actually visit, although the gardens are what make it worth coming, especially in the spring when everything's in bloom.

Palo Alto and Stanford University

PALO ALTO, just south and three miles east between I-280 and US-101, is a small, leafy community with all the contrived atmosphere you'd expect to find in a college town but little of the vigour of its northern counterpart, Berkeley. Though a visit doesn't really merit the expense of a night's accommodation, you could spend a lazy day in the bookstores and cafés that line University Avenue, the town's main drag. Or, if you're feeling energetic, try cycling around the town's many well-marked bike routes; a range of bikes are available for $12–25 a day from *Action Sports Limited* at 401 High St (☎328-3180), near the *Caltrain* station a block west of University Avenue. Be aware, however, that **East Palo Alto**, on the bay side of US-101, has a well-deserved reputation for gang- and drug-related violence, with one of the highest per capita murder rates of any US city. Founded in the 1920s as the utopian Runnymeade colony, an agricultural, poultry-raising cooperative – the local historical society (☎329-0294) can point out the surviving sites. East Palo Alto, also where Grateful Dead guitarist Jerry Garcia grew up, is about as far as you can get off the San Francisco tourist trail.

Stanford University, spreading out from the west end of University Avenue, is by contrast one of the tamest places you could hope for. The University is among the best – and most expensive – in California, though when it opened in 1891, founded by railroad magnate Leland Stanford in memory of his dead son, it offered free tuition. Ridiculed by East Coast academics, who felt that there was as much need for a second West Coast university (after UC Berkeley) as there was for "an asylum for decayed sea captains in Switzerland", Stanford was defiantly built anyway, in a hybrid of Mission and Romanesque buildings on a huge campus that covers an area larger than the whole of downtown San Francisco.

Stanford, whose reputation as an arch-conservative think-tank was enhanced by Ronald Reagan's offer to donate his video library to the school (Stanford politely declined), hasn't always been an entirely boring place, though you wouldn't know it to walk among the preppy future-lawyers-of-America that seem to comprise the majority of the student body. Ken Kesey came here from Oregon in 1958 on a writing fellowship, working nights as an orderly on the psychiatric ward of one local hospital, and getting paid $75 a day to test experimental drugs (LSD among them) in another. Drawing on both experiences, Kesey wrote *One Flew over the Cuckoo's Nest* in 1960 and quickly became a counter-culture hero. Stanford attracts a more prosaic body of students these days, preferring to bolster its departments in medicine, science and engineering.

Approaching from Palo Alto *Caltrain* and *SamTrans* bus station, which acts as a buffer between the town and the University, you enter the campus via a half-mile-long, palm-tree-lined boulevard which deposits you at its heart, the **Quadrangle**, bordered by the phallic Hoover Tower and the colourful gold-leaf mosaics of the Memorial Church. Free hour-long walking tours of the campus leave from here daily at 11am and 2pm, though it's fairly big and best seen by car or bike.

The **Stanford Museum of Art** between "the Quad" and the town was damaged by the 1989 Loma Prieta earthquake and is scheduled to reopen in 1998. For now, the best reason to come here is to have a look at the distinguished collection of **Rodin sculpture**, including

SAINT BENEDICT SCHOOL
DUFFIELD ROAD
DERBY DE22 1JD

a *Gates of Hell* flanked by a shamed *Adam and Eve*, displayed in an attractive outdoor setting on the museum's south side. Also, if you keep up on the latest trends in sub-atomic behaviour, you won't want to miss the **Stanford Linear Accelerator** (Mon–Fri by appointment only; ☎926-3300), a mile west of the central campus on Sand Hill Road, where infinitesimally small particles are crashed into one another at very high speeds to see what happens.

San Jose

The fastest-growing major city in America's fastest-growing state, **SAN JOSE** is not strong on identity – despite the Burt Bacharach song – though in area and population it's nearly twice the size of San Francisco. Sitting at the southern end of the Peninsula, located almost exactly in the centre of the state, an abundance of cheap land brought developers and businessmen into the area in the 1960s, hoping to draw from the concentration of talent in the commerce-orientated halls of Stanford University. An enormous concentration of the world's technology industry is now located here. Fuelled by the success of computer firms such as Apple, Intel and Hewlett-Packard, in the past 25 years San Jose has emerged as the civic heart of **Silicon Valley**, surrounded by miles of faceless high-tech industrial parks where the next generations of computers are designed and crafted.

Ironically, San Jose is one of the oldest settlements in California, though the only sign of that is at the late eighteenth-century **Mission Santa Clara de Asis**, just south of The Alameda (Route 82). On the grounds of the Jesuit-run University of Santa Clara, two miles northwest of the *Caltrain* station, the **de Saisset Museum** (Tues–Fri 10am–5pm, Sat & Sun 1–5pm; $1) holds a permanent display of objects from the Mission era along with changing shows of contemporary art. Otherwise, there are only a couple of good reasons to subject yourself to San Jose's relentlessly boring cityscape. The main attraction is the **Rosicrucian Museum**, 1342 Naglee Ave (daily 9am–5pm; $4). Languishing in the suburbs, this grand structure contains a brilliant collection of Assyrian and Babylonian artefacts, with displays of mummies, amulets, a replica of a tomb and ancient jewellery. Right downtown, at 145 W San Carlos St, is a more modern magnet, the **Tech Museum of Innovation** (Tues–Sun 10am–5pm; $6), with hands-on displays of high-tech engineering. Otherwise, on a typically hot day, refresh with locals at the modern public fountains at **Caesar Chavez Park** on the corner of Market Street and San Carlos Avenue.

You could also stop off at the **Winchester Mystery House**, 525 S Winchester Blvd, just off I-280 near Hwy-17 (daily 9.30am–4.30pm; $12.50). Sarah Winchester, heir to the Winchester rifle fortune, was convinced by an occultist upon her husband's death that he had been taken by the spirits of men killed with Winchester rifles. She was told that unless a room was built for each of the spirits and the sound of hammers never ceased, the same fate would befall her. Work on the mansion went on 24 hours per day for the next thirty years, with results that need to be seen to be believed – stairs lead nowhere, windows open onto solid brick, and so on. It is, however, a shameless tourist trap, and you have to run a gauntlet of ghastly gift stores and soda stands to get in or out.

One other Peninsula place might exercise a certain attraction, particularly to those fond of roller coasters, log rides and all-American family fun; **Great America** (summer daily 10am–10pm; winter weekends only; $23.95, children under 6 $16.95). This huge, hundred-acre amusement park on the edge of San Francisco Bay, just off US-101 north of San Jose, is not in the same league as Disneyland, but doesn't suffer from the same crowds and lengthy lines, and the range of high-speed thrills and chills – from the loop-the-looping "Demon" to "The Edge", where you free-fall in a steel cage for over a hundred feet – is worth the entry fee, especially on weekdays when you may well have the place to yourself. The whole park is laid out into such heritage-themed areas as "Hometown Square", "Yankee Harbor" and "County Fair", each filled with all sorts of sideshow attractions and funfair games.

The Coast

The **coastline** of the Peninsula south from San Francisco is more appealing than what's on offer inland – relatively undeveloped, with very few buildings, let alone towns, along the 75 miles of coves and beaches that extend down to the resort city of **Santa Cruz**. Bluffs protect the many nudist beaches from prying eyes and make a popular launching pad for hang-glider pilots, particularly at **Burton Beach** and **Fort Funston**, a mile south of the San Francisco Zoo – also the point where the earthquake-causing San Andreas Fault enters the sea, not to surface again until Point Reyes. **Skyline Boulevard** follows the coast from here past the repetitious tracts of proverbial ticky-tacky houses that make up **Daly City**, where it is joined by Hwy-1 (and *SamTrans* bus #1A) for the rest of the journey.

San Pedro Point, a popular surfing beach fifteen miles south of the city proper, marks the southern extent of San Francisco's suburban sprawl. The old **Ocean Shore Railroad Depot** here, now a private residence among the handful of shops in the beachfront town, is one of the few surviving remnants of an ill-advised train line between San Francisco and Santa Cruz. The line was wiped out during the 1906 earthquake, but was in any case never more than a third complete. Its few patrons had to transfer back and forth by ferry to connect the stretches of track that were built, the traces of

SAINT BENEDICT SCHOOL
DUFFIELD ROAD
DERBY DE22 1JD

which you can still see scarring the face of the bluffs. The continually eroding cliffs don't take very well to being built on, as evidenced a mile south by the **Devil's Slide**, where the highway is washed away with some regularity in winter storms. The slide area was also a popular dumping spot for corpses of those who'd fallen foul of rum-runners during Prohibition, and features under various names in many of Dashiell Hammett's detective stories.

Just south of the Devil's Slide, the sands of **Gray Whale Cove State Beach** (daily dawn–dusk; $5 parking) are clothing-optional. Despite the name it's not an especially great place to look for migrating grey whales, but there is a stairway from the bus stop down to a fine beach. Two miles south, the red-roofed buildings of the *Point Montara Lighthouse*, set among the windswept Monterey pines at the top of a steep cliff, have been converted into a youth hostel. There are a few good places to stop for a drink or a bite to eat in the town of **Moss Beach**, across Hwy-1.

For details of the Point Montara Lighthouse *hostel, see p.219.*

South of the Lighthouse, the **James Fitzgerald Marine Reserve** strings along the shore, a two-mile shelf of flat, slippery rocks that make excellent tidal pools. The ranger often gives guided interpretative walks through the reserve at low tide, the best time to explore. At the south end of the reserve, **Pillar Point** juts out into the Pacific; just to the east, along Hwy-1, fishing boats dock at **Pillar Point Harbor**. In the faintly touristy, ramshackle town adjacent to the waterfront, **Princeton-by-the-Sea**, a couple of bay-view restaurants sell fish and fries, sometimes freshly caught. Further along, the best of the local surfing areas is just offshore from **Miramar Beach**; after a day in the water or on the beach, the place to head for is the beachfront *Bach Dancing and Dynamite Society*, an informal jazz club and beer bar that faces the sands.

Half Moon Bay

HALF MOON BAY, twenty miles south of the city and the only town of any size between San Francisco and Santa Cruz, takes its name from the crescent-shaped bay formed by Pillar Point. Lined by miles of sandy beaches, the town is surprisingly rural considering its proximity to San Francisco and Silicon Valley, and sports a number of ornate Victorian wooden houses around its centre. The oldest of these is at the north end of Main Street; built in 1849, it's just across a little stone bridge over Pillarcitos Creek. The smell of the ocean pervades the air in this seaside town, the stereotype of a romantic getaway. Be sure to take a stroll on the beach, even if the weather is cold. The **Chamber of Commerce** on Hwy-1 has free walking tour maps of the town, and information on the two annual festivals for which the place is well known. These are the **Holy Ghost and Pentecost Festival**, a parade and barbecue held on the sixth Sunday after Easter, and the **Pumpkin Festival**, celebrating the harvest of the area's many pumpkin farms, just in time for Halloween, when the fields around town are full of families searching for the perfect jack-o'-lantern to greet the hordes of trick-or-treaters. There are free, primitive campgrounds all along the coast in **Half Moon Bay State Park**, half a mile west of the town.

Half Moon Bay is also the southern end of the *SamTrans* bus #1A route; to continue south, transfer here to route #90C, which runs every three hours to Waddell Creek, twenty miles south. **San Gregorio State Beach**, ten miles south of Half Moon Bay, is at its best in the spring, after the winter storms, when flotsam architects construct a range of driftwood shelters along the wide beach south of the parking area. In summer the beach is packed with well-oiled bodies; the sands around the bluffs to the north are quieter. If bathing suits are undesirable, bathe nude at San Gregario Private Beach; follow Hwy-1 one mile north of San Gregario Road, watch for the white gate that marks the turning. Dunes Beach and Venice Beach are also beautiful expanses of sand and ocean. Ride a horse along the beaches from the Sea Horse Ranch, Hwy-1 one mile north of Hwy-84 ($20 per hour; ☎415/726-2362).

Buy delicious fresh strawberries from roadside farm stands, or pick your own at the Andereatti Family Farm on Kelly Avenue, west of Hwy-1.

The Butano Redwoods and the Año Nuevo State Reserve

If you've got a car and it's not a great day for the beach, head up into the hills above, where the thousands of acres of the **Butano redwood forest** feel at their most ancient and primeval in the greyest and gloomiest weather. About half the land between San Jose and the coast is protected from development in a variety of state and county parks, all of which are virtually deserted despite being within a half-hour's drive of the Silicon Valley sprawl. Any one of a dozen roads heads through endless stands of untouched forest, and even the briefest of walks will take you seemingly miles from any sign of civilization. Hwy-84 climbs up from San Gregorio through the Sam McDonald County Park to the hamlet of **La Honda**, from where you can continue on to Palo Alto or, better, loop back to the coast via Pescadero Road. A mile before you reach the quaint town of **Pescadero**, Cloverdale Road heads south to **Butano State Park**, where you can hike and camp overlooking the Pacific.

Pescadero has one of the best places to eat on the Peninsula – Duarte's. *See p.244 for the review.*

Back on Hwy-1, five miles south of Pescadero is another great place to spend the night, sleeping in the old lighthouse keeper's quarters or soaking your bones in a marvellous hot tub at the **Pigeon Point Lighthouse Hostel**. If you're here in December or January, continue south another five miles to the **Ano Nuevo State Reserve** for a chance to see one of nature's most bizarre spectacles – the mating rituals of the northern **elephant seal**. These massive, ungainly creatures, fifteen feet long and weighing up to three tons, were once found all along the coast, but were nearly hunted to extinction by whalers in the last century. During the mating season the beach is literally a seething mass of blubbery bodies, with the trunk-nosed males fighting it out for the right to sire as many as fifty pups in a season. At any time of the year you're likely to see a half-dozen or so dozing in the sands. The

For more information on the Pigeon Point Lighthouse *hostel, see p.219.*

reserve is also good for bird-watching, and in March there's a chance of getting a good look at migrating gray whales.

The slowly resurgent Año Nuevo seal population is still carefully protected, and during the breeding season the obligatory guided tours – designed to protect spectators as much as to give the seals some privacy – are often oversubscribed (hourly 8am–4pm; ☎879-0227). Otherwise tickets are usually made available to people staying at the *Pigeon Point Lighthouse Hostel*, and *SamTrans* (☎348-SEAL) sometimes runs charter bus tours from the town of **San Mateo** on the bay side of the Peninsula.

On your way back north to San Francisco along a breathtakingly scenic Hwy-1, one stop near the city worth a quick tour is the **Sanchez Adobe**, 1000 Linda Mar Ave, Pacifica (Tues–Thurs 10am–4pm, weekends 1–5pm; ☎359-1462), a 1846 hotel and speakeasy which now contains old-fashioned rooms to tour and various Native American artefacts.

Chapter 10

Marin County

Across the Golden Gate from San Francisco, **Marin County** (pronounced *Ma-RINN*) provides an unabashed introduction to Californian self-indulgence; an elitist pleasure-zone of conspicuous luxury and abundant natural beauty, with sunshine, sandy beaches, high mountains and thick redwood forests. Often ranked as the wealthiest county in the US, Marin's swanky waterside towns have attracted a sizable contingent of northern California's wealthiest young professionals, many of whom grew up during the Flower Power years of the 1960s and lend the place its New Age feel and reputation. Though many of the cocaine-and-hot-tub devotees who populated the place in the 1970s have traded their drug habits for mountain bikes, life in Marin still centres around personal pleasure, and the throngs you see hiking and cycling at weekends, not to mention the hundreds of esoteric self-help practitioners – Rolfing, Re-Birthing and soul-travel therapists fill up the want ads of the local papers – prove that Marinites work hard to maintain their easy air of physical and mental well-being. Simply, Marin is lush and beautiful. It continues to be a place where Bay Area residents wish to move once they succeed financially. Residents are extremely protective of their self-acclaimed county, which can come across as cold and unwelcoming to outsiders. It's possible to receive consciously incorrect directions to such small towns as **Bolinas** or Ross. As long as you don't trespass on private property as you hike, you're likely to have little hassle.

Flashy modern ferry boats, appointed with fully stocked bars, sail across the bay from San Francisco and give a good initial view of the county. As you head past desolate Alcatraz Island, curvaceous **Mount Tamalpais** looms larger until you land at its foot in one of the chic bayside settlements of **Sausalito** or **Tiburon**. **Angel Island**, in the middle of the bay but accessible most easily from Tiburon, provides relief from the excessive style-consciousness of both towns, retaining a wild, untouched feeling among the eerie ruins of derelict military fortifications.

Sausalito and Tiburon, and the lifestyles that go with them, are only a small part of Marin. The bulk of the county rests on the

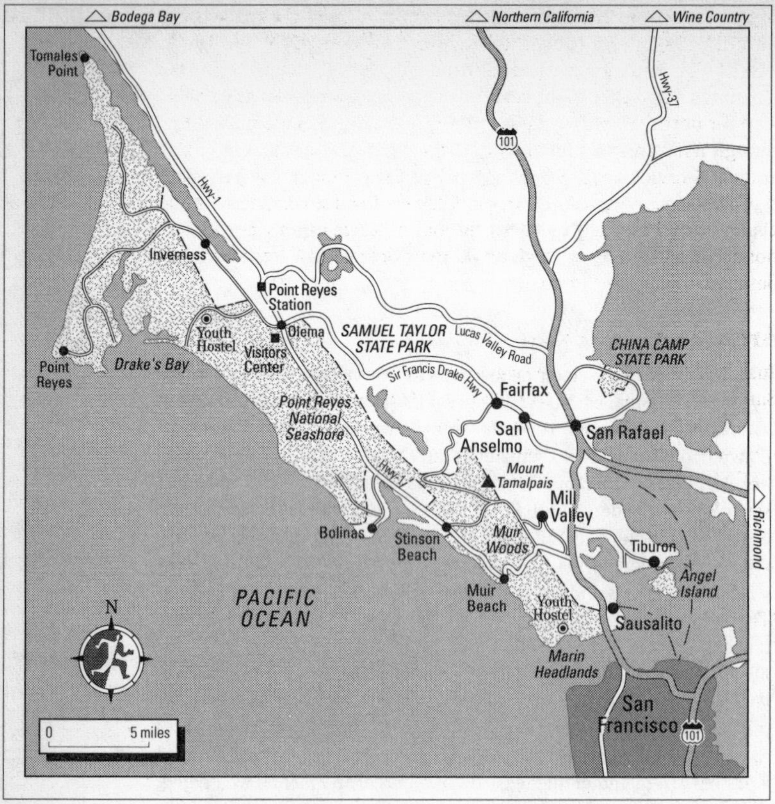

slopes of the ridge of peaks that divides the peninsula down the middle, separating the sophisticated harbourside towns in the east from the untrammelled wilderness of the Pacific coast to the west. The **Marin Headlands**, just across the Golden Gate Bridge, hold time-warped old battlements and gun emplacements that once protected San Francisco's harbour from would-be invaders, and now overlook surfers and backpackers enjoying the acres of open space. Along the coastline that stretches north, the broad shore of **Stinson Beach** is the Bay Area's finest and widest stretch of sand, beyond which Hwy-1 clings to the coast past the rural village of **Bolinas** to the seascapes of **Point Reyes**, where Sir Francis Drake landed in 1579 and claimed all of California for England.

Inland, the heights of Mount Tamalpais, and specifically, **Muir Woods**, are a magnet to sightseers and nature-lovers, who come to wander through one of the few surviving stands of the native coastal redwood trees. Such trees once covered most of Marin, before they were chopped down to build and rebuild the dainty wooden houses of San Francisco. The long-vanished lumber mills of the rustic town of **Mill Valley**, overlooking the bay from the slopes of "Mount Tam", bear the guilt for much of this destruction; the oldest town in Marin County is now home to an eclectic bunch of art galleries and cafés. Further north, Marin's largest town, **San Rafael**, is best passed by, though its outskirts contain two of the most unusual places in the county: **Frank Lloyd Wright**'s peculiar Civic Center complex and the preserved remnants of an old Chinese fishing village in **China Camp State Park**. The northern reaches of Marin County border the bountiful wine-growing regions of the Sonoma and Napa valleys, detailed in Chapter Eleven.

Arrival and transport

Just getting to Marin County can be a great start to a day out from San Francisco. *Golden Gate Transit* **ferries** (☎923-2000) leave from the Ferry Building on the Embarcadero, crossing the bay past Alcatraz Island to **Sausalito** and **Larkspur**; they run from 5.30am until 8pm, approximately every half-hour during the rush hour, less often the rest of the day, and every two hours at weekends and holidays. Tickets cost $4.25 one-way to Sausalito, $2.50 to Larkspur Monday to Friday ($3 weekends). Refreshments are served on board. The more expensive *Red and White Fleet* ($12 round trip; ☎546-2805) sail from Pier 43 1/2 at Fisherman's Wharf to **Sausalito** and to **Tiburon** – from where the *Angel Island Ferry* ($5 round trip, plus $1 per bicycle; ☎435-2131) nips back and forth to **Angel Island State Park** daily in summer, weekends only in the winter.

Golden Gate Transit also runs a comprehensive **bus service** around Marin County and across the Golden Gate Bridge from the Transbay Terminal in San Francisco (in Marin County, call ☎453-2100), and publishes a helpful and free system map and timetable, including all ferry services. Bus fares range from $1 to $3, depending on the distance travelled. Basic *GGT* bus routes run every half-hour throughout the day, and once an hour late at night. *GGT* commuter services, which run only during the morning and evening rush hours, can be the only way to get to some places. Also, San

Marin County accommodation listings are in Chapter Twelve, restaurants are covered on p.245; and cafés and bars on p.254.

Marin County Bus Services

#10: San Francisco–Sausalito–Marin City–Mill Valley–Tiburon.

#20: San Francisco–Marin City–Larkspur–San Anselmo–San Rafael.

#50: San Francisco–Sausalito–Marin City–San Rafael.

#24: San Francisco–San Anselmo–Fairfax–Point Reyes Station; once a day at 5.40pm, weekdays only.

#63: Marin City–Stinson Beach; weekends and holidays only at 8.45am, 9.45am and 10.45am.

#65: San Rafael–Point Reyes; 9am and 4pm, weekends only.

Francisco's *MUNI* bus #76 runs hourly from San Francisco direct to the Marin Headlands on Sundays only.

The only services between Marin County and the East Bay are offered by *Traveler's Transit* minivans (☎457-7080), running between the Richmond *BART* station and downtown San Rafael for $2 a trip.

If you'd rather avoid the hassle of bus connections, *Gray Line* ($37.50; ☎558-9400) offers four-hour **guided bus tours** from San Francisco, taking in Sausalito and Muir Woods, daily at 9am, 11am and 1.30pm; the *Red and White* ferry fleet also has a boat-and-bus trip to Muir Woods, via Tiburon.

One of the best ways to get around Marin is by **bike**, particularly using a mountain bike to cruise the many trails that criss-cross the county. If you want to ride on the road, **Sir Francis Drake Highway** – from Larkspur to Point Reyes – makes a good route, though it's best to avoid weekends, when the roads can get clogged up with cars. All ferry services (except Alcatraz) allow bicycles.

San Francisco–Marin County Ferries

Because ferry schedules change slightly four times a year, please use the following timetable as an estimate of arrival and departure times. Current schedules are always available from the terminals.

***GOLDEN GATE TRANSIT* FERRIES**

San Francisco–Tiburon: depart at 10am, noon, 2pm and 3.45pm daily.

Tiburon–San Francisco: depart at 11am, 1pm, 3pm and 5pm daily.

San Francisco–Larkspur: depart at 6.50am, 7.50am, 8.50am, 10.45am, 12.45pm, 2.45pm, 3.35pm, 4.15pm, 4.50pm, 5.20pm, 6pm, 6.45pm and 8.25pm Mon–Fri; 10.45am, 12.45pm, 2.45pm, 4.45pm and 6.45pm Sat, Sun & holidays.

Larkspur–San Francisco: depart at 6am, 7am, 7.30am, 8am, 8.40am, 9.45am, 11.45am, 1.45pm, 3.45pm, 4.25pm, 5.05pm, 5.40pm and 7.35pm Mon–Fri; 9.45am, 11.45am, 1.45pm, 3.45pm, 5.45pm and 7.45pm Sat, Sun & holidays.

San Francisco–Sausalito: depart at 7.40am, 9.15am, 10.25am, 11.45am, 1.10pm, 2.35pm, 4.10pm, 5.30pm, 6.40pm and 8pm Mon–Fri; 11.30am, 1.00pm, 2.30pm, 4pm, 5.30pm and 6.55pm Sat, Sun & holidays.

Sausalito–San Francisco: depart at 7.05am, 8.15am, 11.05am, 12.25pm, 1.55pm, 3.20pm, 4.45pm, 6.05pm and 7.20pm Mon–Fri; 10.50am, 12.15pm, 1.45pm, 3.15pm, 4.45pm and 6.10pm Sat, Sun & holidays.

***RED AND WHITE FLEET* FERRIES**

San Francisco–Sausalito: depart at 11am, 12.15pm, 1.35pm, 3pm and 4.50pm Mon–Fri; 10.40am, 12.45pm, 2.10pm, 3.45pm and 5.50pm Sat, Sun & holidays.

Sausalito–San Francisco: depart at 11.50am, 1.05pm, 2.20pm, 3.40pm, 5.45pm and 8pm Mon–Fri; 11.15am, 1.10pm, 2.45pm, 4.20pm and 6.25pm Sat, Sun & holidays.

San Francisco–Tiburon: depart at 11am, 12.45pm, 1.35pm, 3pm, 4.05pm and 4.50pm Mon–Fri; 10.40am, 12.35am, 2.10pm, 3.45pm, 5.50pm Sat, Sun & holidays.

Tiburon–San Francisco: depart at 11.25am, 12.40pm, 1.55pm, 3.20pm, 5.25pm and 7.45pm Mon–Fri; 11.40am, 1.35pm, 3.15pm, 5.15pm and 6.50pm Sat, Sun & holidays.

Marin County information

Three main on-the-spot sources can provide further information on Marin County: the **Marin County Visitors Bureau**, 30 N San Pedro Rd, San Rafael (Mon–Fri 9am–5pm; ☎472-7470), the **Sausalito Chamber of Commerce**, at 333 Caledonia St (Mon–Fri 9am–5pm; ☎332-0505), and the **Mill Valley Chamber of Commerce**, 85 Throckmorton Ave (Mon–Fri 9.30am–4pm; ☎388-9700), in the centre of the town.

For information on **hiking** and **camping** in the wilderness and beach areas, depending on where you're heading, contact the Golden Gate National Recreation Area, Building 201, Fort Mason Center (daily 9am–4pm; ☎556-0560), Mount Tamalpais State Park, 801 Panoramic Highway, Mill Valley (daily 9am–5pm; ☎388-2070), or the Point Reyes National Seashore, Bear Valley, Point Reyes (daily 9am–5pm; ☎663-1092). Information on **what's on** in Marin can be found in the widely available local freesheets, such as the down-to-earth *Coastal Post* or the New-Agey *Pacific Sun*.

Marin County Accommodation

You might prefer simply to dip into Marin County using San Francisco as a base, and if you've got a car or manage to time the bus connections right it's certainly possible, at least for the southernmost parts of the county. However, it can be nicer to take a more leisurely look at Marin, staying over for a couple of nights in some well-chosen spots. Sadly there are few **hotels**, and those that there are often charge in excess of $100 a night; **motels** tend to be the same as anywhere, though there are a couple of attractively faded ones along the coast. In any case, the best bet for budget accommodation is a dorm bed in one of the beautifully situated **hostels** along the western beaches. For specific recommendations see the *Accommodation* listings, beginning on p.207.

Across the Golden Gate: Marin Headlands and Sausalito

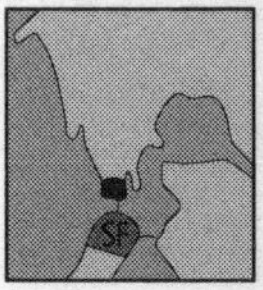

The headlands across the Golden Gate from San Francisco afford impressive views of the bridge and the city behind. Take the first turn past the bridge, and follow the road up the hill into the **Marin Headlands** section of the Golden Gate National Recreation Area – largely undeveloped land, except for the concrete remains of old forts and gun emplacements standing guard over the entrance to the bay. The coastline here is much more rugged than it is on the San Francisco side, and though it makes a great place for an aimless cliff-top scramble, or a walk along the beach, it's impossible not to be at least a little sobered by the presence of so many military relics – even if none was ever fired in anger. The oldest of these artillery batteries dates from the Civil War, while the newest was built to protect against a Japanese invasion during World War II, but even though the huge guns have been replaced by picnic tables and brass plaques – one of the concrete bunkers has even been painted to make a

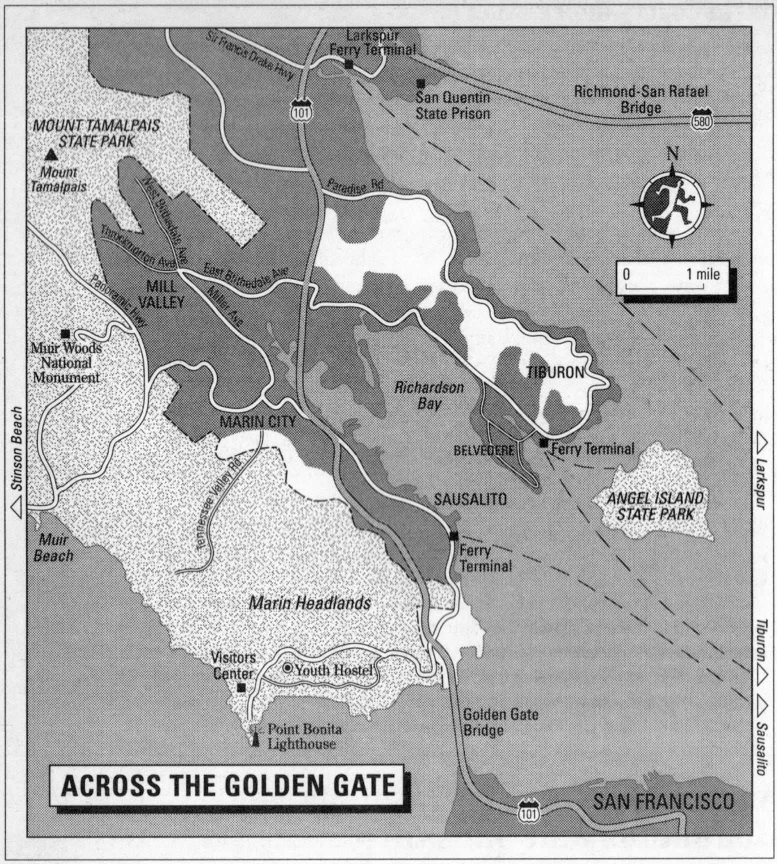

trompe-l'oeil Greek temple – you can't overlook their violent intent. **Battery Wallace**, the largest and most impressive of the artillery sites, is cut through a hillside above the southwestern tip, and the clean-cut military geometry survives to frame views of the Pacific Ocean and Golden Gate Bridge. If you're interested in such things, come along on the first Sunday of the month and take a guided tour of an abandoned 1950s ballistic missile launch pad, complete with disarmed nuclear missiles. The one non-military thing to see, the **Point Bonita Lighthouse**, stands at the very end of the Headlands, where it's open for tours at weekends, except during the winter.

Most of what there is to do out here is concentrated half a mile to the north, around the rocky cliffs and islets of the point. Adjacent to the **Marin Headlands Visitor Center** (daily 8.30am–4.30pm; ☎331-1540), at the end of the *MUNI* bus #76 route from San Francisco (Sun and holidays only), a wide sandy beach fronts the chilly ocean and marshy warm water of **Rodeo Lagoon**. Swimming is prohibited here, in order to protect the nesting seabirds. Next to the center, the **Marine Mammal Center** rescues and rehabilitates injured and orphaned sea creatures, which you can visit while they recover; there's also a series of displays on the marine ecosystem and a bookstore that also sells T-shirts and posters. The largest of the old army officers' quarters in the adjacent **Fort Barry**, half a mile to the east, has been converted into the spacious and homey **Marin Headlands Youth Hostel**, an excellent base for more extended explorations of the inland ridges and valleys.

Full details of the Marin Headlands Youth Hostel can be found on p.220.

Sausalito

SAUSALITO, along the bay below US-101, is a pretty, smug little town of exclusive restaurants and pricey boutiques along a picturesque waterfront promenade. Expensive, quirkily designed houses climb the overgrown cliffs above **Bridgeway Avenue**, the main road and bus route through town. Sausalito used to be a fairly gritty community of fishermen and sea-traders, full of bars and bordellos, and despite its upscale modern face it still makes a fun day out from San Francisco by ferry, the boats arriving next to the Sausalito Yacht Club in the centre of town. Hang out in one of the waterfront bars and watch the crowds strolling along the esplanade, or climb the stairways above Bridgeway and amble around the leafy hills. If you have sailing experience, split the $85 daily rental fee of a four- to six-person sailboat at *Cass's Marine*, 1702 Bridgeway (☎332-6789).

The old working wharves and warehouses that made Sausalito a haven for smugglers and Prohibition-era rum-runners are long gone; most have been taken over by dull steakhouses such as the *Charthouse*. However, some stretches of it have, for the moment at least, survived the tourist onslaught. Half a mile north of the town centre along Bridgeway Avenue, an ad hoc community of exotic barges and houseboats, some of which have been moored here since the 1950s, is being threatened with eviction to make room for yet another luxury marina and bay-view office development. In the meantime, many of the boats – one looks like a South Pacific island, another like the Taj Mahal – can be viewed from the marina behind the large brown shed that houses the Army Corps of Engineers **museum** (Mon–Sat 9am–4pm; free), which features a massive working model of San Francisco Bay, simulating changing tides and powerful currents.

Fifty years ago, Sausalito's waterfront served as one of the settings for Orson Welles' murder mystery, The Lady from Shanghai.

The Marin County Coast to Bolinas

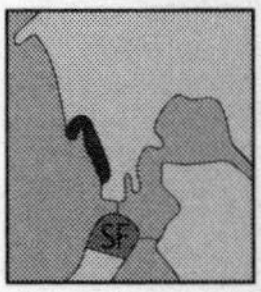

The **Shoreline Highway**, Hwy-1, cuts off west from US-101 just north of Sausalito, following the old main highway towards Mill Valley (see p.186). The first turn on the left, Tennessee Valley Road, leads up to the less-visited northern expanses of the Golden Gate National Recreation Area. You can make a beautiful three-mile hike from the parking lot at the end of the road, heading down along the secluded and lushly green **Tennessee Valley** to a small beach along a rocky cove; or you can take a guided tour on horseback from *Miwok Livery* ($25 per hr; ☎383-8048).

Hwy-1 twists up the canyon to a crest, where **Panoramic Highway** spears off to the right, following the ridge north to Muir Woods and Mount Tamalpais (see p.185); *Golden Gate Transit* bus #63 to Stinson Beach follows this route every hour on weekends and holidays only. Two miles down from the crest, a small unpaved road cuts off to the left, dropping down to the bottom of the broad canyon to the **Green Gulch Farm and Zen Center** (☎383-3134), an organic farm and Buddhist retreat, with an authentic Japanese teahouse and a simple but refined prayer hall. On Sunday mornings the centre is opened for a public meditation period and an informal discussion of Zen Buddhist practice, after which you can stroll down to Muir Beach. If you already have some experience of Zen, enquire about the centre's Guest Student Program, which enables initiates to stay from three days to several weeks at a time (it costs about $10 a night). If you just want a weekend's retreat, you can also stay overnight in the attached *Lindisfarne Guest House* for about $50 a night including meals, and take part as you choose in the communal life. Residents of the centre rise well before dawn for meditation and prayer, then work much of the day in the gardens, tending the vegetables that are eventually served in many of the Bay Area's finest restaurants (notably *Greens*, in San Francisco's Fort Mason Center – see p.190).

You'll find further details about the Lindisfarne Guest House on p.216.

Beyond the Zen Center, the road down from Muir Woods rejoins Hwy-1 at **Muir Beach**, surprisingly dark and usually uncrowded, around a semicircular cove. Three miles north, **Steep Ravine** drops sharply down the cliffs to a small beach, past very rustic $30-a-night cabins and a $9-a-night campground, bookable through Mount Tamalpais State Park (see opposite). A mile on is the small and lovely **Red Rocks** nudist beach, down a steep trail from a parking area along the highway. **Stinson Beach**, which is bigger, and more popular despite the rather cold water (it's packed at weekends in summer, when the traffic can be nightmarish), is a mile further. You can rent boogie boards and wet suits for $10 a day from the *Livewater Surf Shop* 3448 Shoreline Hwy (☎868-0333), along the highway at the south end of a short block of stores. Another aquatic alternative is to rent kayaks for $35–50 per day a bit further down the road at the *Stinson Beach Health Club*, 3605 Shoreline Hwy (☎868-2739).

Bolinas and Southern Point Reyes

At the tip of the headland, due west from Stinson Beach, is the village of **BOLINAS**, though you may have a hard time finding it – road signs marking the turn-off from Hwy-1 are removed as soon as they're put up, by locals hoping to keep the place to themselves. The campaign may have backfired, though, since press coverage of the "sign war" has done more to publicize the town than any road sign ever did; to get there, take the first left beyond the estuary and follow the road to the end. Bolinas is completely surrounded by federal property: the Golden Gate National Recreation Area and Point Reyes National Seashore. Even the lagoon was recently declared a national bird sanctuary. The village itself is a small colony of artists and writers (the late trout-fishing author Richard Brautigan and basketball diarist Jim Carroll among them), and there's not a lot to see – though you can get a feel for the place (and pick up tasty sandwiches and bags of fresh fruit and vegetables) at the *Bolinas People's Store* in the block-long village centre.

Beyond Bolinas there's a rocky beach at the end of Wharf Road west of the village; and **Duxbury Reef Nature Reserve**, half a mile west at the end of Elm Road, is well worth a look for its tidal pools, full of starfish, crabs and sea anemones. Otherwise, Mesa Road heads north from Bolinas past the **Point Reyes Bird Observatory** (☎868-0655) – open for informal tours all day, though best visited in the morning. The first bird observatory in the US, this is still an important research and study centre. If you time it right you may be able to watch, or even help, the staff as they put coloured bands on the birds to keep track of them. Beyond here, the unpaved road leads onto the **Palomarin Trailhead**, the southern access into the Point Reyes National Seashore (see p.190). The best of the many beautiful hikes around the area leads past a number of small lakes and meadows for three miles to **Alamere Falls**, which throughout the winter and spring cascade down the cliffs onto Wildcat Beach.

Mount Tamalpais and Muir Woods

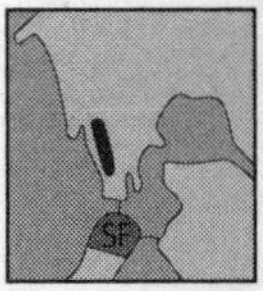

Mount Tamalpais dominates the skyline of the Marin peninsula, hulking over the cool canyons of the rest of the county in a crisp yet voluptuous silhouette and dividing the county into two distinct parts: the wild western slopes above the Pacific Coast and the increasingly suburban communities along the calmer bay frontage. Panoramic Highway branches off from Hwy-1 along the crest through the centre of **Mount Tamalpais State Park**, which has some thirty miles of hiking trails and many campgrounds, though most of the redwood trees that once covered its slopes have long since been chopped down to form the posts and beams of San Francisco's Victorian houses. One grove of these towering trees does remain, however, protected as the **Muir Woods National Monument** (daily 8am–sunset; free), a mile down Muir Woods Road from Panoramic Highway. It's a tranquil and majestic spot, with sunlight filtering through the 300-foot trees down to the laurel- and fern-covered canyon below. The canyon's steep sides are what saved it from Mill Valley's lumbermen, and today this is one of the few first-growth redwood groves between San Francisco and the fantastic forests of Redwood National Park, up the coast near the Oregon border.

Its location close to San Francisco makes Muir Woods is a popular target. The trails nearest the parking lot have been paved and are often packed with bus-tour hordes. However, if you visit during the week, or outside midsummer, it's easy enough to leave the crowds behind, especially if you're willing to head off up the steep trails that climb the canyon sides. More secluded hiking paths include the **Matt Davis Trail**, leading south to Stinson Beach and north to Mount Tamalpais. Winter is a particularly good time to come, as the streams are gurgling – the main creek reaches down to Muir Beach, and salmon have been known to spawn in it – and the forest creatures are more likely to be seen going about their business. Keep an eye out for the various species of salamanders and newts that thrive in this damp environment; be warned, though, that some are poisonous and will bite if harassed. Other colourful Muir Woods occupants include the colonies of ladybugs that spend their winter huddling in the rich undergrowth.

One way to avoid the crowds, and the only way to get here on public transportation, is to enter the woods from the top, by way of a two-mile hike from the **Pan Toll Ranger Station** (☎388-2070) on Panoramic Highway – which is a stop on the *Golden Gate Transit* #63 bus route. As the state park headquarters, the station has maps and information on hiking and camping, and rangers can suggest hikes to suit your mood and interests. From here, the **Pan Toll Road** turns off to the right along the ridge to within a hundred yards of the 2571ft summit of Mount Tamalpais, from where there are breathtaking views of the distant Sierra Nevada and close-ups of red-necked turkey vultures, listlessly circling the peak.

Mill Valley

From the East Peak of Mount Tamalpais, a quick two-mile hike downhill follows the **Temelpa Trail** through velvety shrubs of chaparral to the town of **MILL VALLEY**. The oldest and most enticing of the inland towns of Marin County is also accessible every half-hour by *Golden Gate Transit* bus #10 from San Francisco and Sausalito. Originally a logging centre, it was from here that the destruction of the surrounding redwoods was organized, though for many years the town has made a healthy living out of tourism. The **Mill Valley and Mount Tamalpais Scenic Railroad** – according to the blurb "the crookedest railroad in the world" – was cut into the slopes above the town in 1896, twisting up through nearly three hundred tight curves in under eight miles. The trip proved so popular with tourists that the line was extended into Muir Woods in 1907, though a combination of road-building and fire put an end to the railroad by 1930. You can, however, follow its route from the end of Summit Avenue in Mill Valley, a popular trip with daredevils on all-terrain bikes. More sporting activity goes on here each June, when runners and assorted masochists come together for the **Dipsea**, a fiercely competitive seven-mile, cross-country race over the mountains through Muir Woods to Stinson Beach.

Though much of Mill Valley's attraction lies in its easy access to hiking and mountain-bike trails up Mount Tam, its compact yet relaxed centre collects a number of cafés and some surprisingly good shops and galleries. The *Book Depot and Cafe* is an especially popular bookstore, café and meeting place on Throckmorton and Miller (daily 7am–10pm). Next door, the **Chamber of Commerce** (Mon–Sat 9am–5pm; ☎1-800/388-9701), has maps and restaurant listings, as well as information on the wide range of local entertainment, including summer plays in the outdoor *Mountain Theater* and a world-class **film festival** in October.

All-terrain or mountain bikes were, incidentally, invented in Mill Valley.

Tiburon and Angel Island

TIBURON, at the tip of a narrow peninsula three miles east of US-101, is, like Sausalito, a ritzy harbourside village to which hundreds of people come each weekend, many of them via direct *Red and White Fleet* **ferries** from Pier $41^1/_2$ in San Francisco's Fisherman's Wharf. It's a relaxed place, less touristy than Sausalito, and if you're in the mood to take it easy and watch the boats sail across the bay, sitting out on the sunny deck of one of many cafés and bars can be idyllic. There are few specific sights to look out for, but it's quite pleasant just to wander around, calling into the odd gallery or antique store. The best of these are grouped together in **Ark Row**, at the west end of Main Street, where the quirky buildings are actually old houseboats that were beached here early in the century. On a hill above the town stands **Old St Hilary's Church** (tours Wed & Sun 4–6pm), a Carpenter Gothic beauty that should be visited in the spring, when the surrounding fields are covered with multicoloured buckwheat, flax and paintbrush.

If you're feeling energetic, rent a bicycle from *Bike Sport*, 1701 Tilburon Blvd (☎435-5064), and cruise around the many plush houses of **Belvedere Island**, just across the Beach Road Bridge from the west end of Main Street, enjoying the fine views of the bay and Golden Gate Bridge. More ambitious cyclists can continue along the waterfront bike path, which winds from the bijou shops and galleries three miles west along undeveloped Richardson Bay frontage to a bird sanctuary at **Greenwood Cove**. The pristine Victorian house here is now the western headquarters of the National Audubon Society and open for tours on Sundays (10am–4pm);

there's also a small interpretive centre with displays on local and migratory birds and wildlife.

Another fine ride heads east from Tiburon along winding Paradise Road, around the mostly undeveloped headland three and a half miles to **Paradise Beach**, a county park with a fishing pier and close-up views of passing oil tankers heading for the refinery across the bay in Richmond. If you want to make a full circuit, Trestle Glen Boulevard cuts up and over the peninsula from near Greenwood Cove, linking with Paradise Road two miles northwest of Paradise Beach.

Angel Island

The pleasures of Tiburon are swiftly exhausted, and you'd be well advised to take the hourly *Angel Island Ferry* ($5 round trip, plus $1 per bicycle; ☎435-2131) a mile offshore to the largest island in the San Francisco Bay, ten times the size of Alcatraz. **Angel Island** is now officially a state park, but over the years it's served a variety of purposes, everything from a home for Miwok Native Americans to a World War II prisoner-of-war camp. It's full of ghostly ruins of old military installations and, with oak and eucalyptus trees and sagebrush covering the hills above rocky coves and sandy beaches, feels quite apart from the mainland. The island offers some relaxing bike rides: a five-mile road rings the island, and an unpaved track (plus assorted hiking trails) leads up to the 800ft hump of **Mount Livermore**, which gives a panoramic view of the Bay Area.

The ferry arrives at **Ayala Cove**, where a small snack bar selling hot dogs and cold drinks provides the only sustenance available on the island. Though it is nice to sip expensive beer on the deck while watching the ocean, bring a picnic if you plan to spend the day here. A small stand also rents bikes for $25 per day. The nearby **visitor center** (daily 9am–4pm; ☎435-1915) has displays on the island's history, in an old building that was built as a quarantine facility for soldiers returning from the Philippines after the Spanish–American War. Around the point on the northwest corner of the island the **North Garrison**, built in 1905, was the site of a prisoner-of-war camp during World War II, while the larger **East Garrison**, on the bay a half mile beyond, was the major transfer point for soldiers bound for the South Pacific.

Quarry Beach around the point is the best on the island, a clean sandy shore that's protected from the winds blowing in through the Golden Gate; it's also a popular landing spot for kayakers and canoeists who paddle across the bay from Berkeley. On the weekend, the presence of large groups and families makes the island feel like a venue for school field trips; weekdays are less crowded. If you plan on camping, make reservations for the campsite about two miles from the ferry (☎1-800/444-7275). Camping only costs $9 per night, and it's well worth the view of San Francisco and the East Bay at night.

Sir Francis Drake Boulevard and Central Marin County

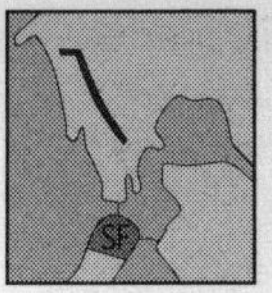

The quickest route to the wilds of the Point Reyes National Seashore, and the only way to get there on public transportation, is by way of **Sir Francis Drake Boulevard**, which cuts across central Marin County through the inland towns of **San Anselmo** and **Fairfax**, reaching the coast thirty miles west at a crescent-shaped bay where, in 1579, Drake landed and claimed all of what he called Nova Albion for England. The route makes an excellent day-long cycling tour, and there are good beaches, a youth hostel and some tasty restaurants at the end of the road.

The *Larkspur Golden Gate Transit* **ferry**, which leaves from the Ferry Building in San Francisco, is the longest and, surprisingly, least expensive of the bay crossings. Primarily a commuter route, it docks at the modern space-frame terminal at Larkspur Landing. The monolithic, red-tile-roofed complex you see on the bayfront a mile east is the maximum-security **San Quentin State Prison**, which houses California's most violent and notorious criminals. If you arrive by car over the Richmond-San Rafael Bridge, follow road signs off Hwy-101 for the San Quentin Prison **Museum** to learn about this penitentiary's history. Building 106, Dolores Way (Mon, Wed, Fri 11am–3pm, Sat 10am–3pm; $3).

San Anselmo, Fairfax and Point Reyes Station

San Anselmo, set in a broad valley two miles north of Mount Tam, calls itself "the antiques capital of Northern California" and sports a tiny centre of specialty shops, furniture stores and cafés that draws out many San Francisco shoppers at weekends. The ivy-covered **San Francisco Theological Seminary**, off Bolinas Avenue, dominates the town from the hill above. It is worth a quick visit for the view and architecture. **Robson-Harrington Park** on Crescent Avenue is a serene park to picnic among well-tended gardens and the very green and leafy **Creek Park** follows the creek that winds through the town centre, but otherwise there's not a lot to do but eat and drink – or browse through fine bookstores such as *Oliver's Books*, at 645 San Anselmo Ave.

This area was the location for Alan Parker's tear-jerking saga of Marin County life, Shoot the Moon, *starring Albert Finney as a philandering writer.*

Center Boulevard follows the tree-lined creek west for a mile to **FAIRFAX**, a much less ostentatiously hedonistic community than the harbourside towns, though in many ways it still typifies Marin lifestyles, with an array of wholefood stores and bookstores geared to a thoughtfully mellow crowd. From Fairfax, the narrow Bolinas Road twists up and over the mountains to the coast at Stinson Beach, while Sir Francis Drake Boulevard winds through a pastoral landscape of ranch houses hidden away up oak-covered valleys.

Ten miles west of Fairfax along Sir Francis Drake Boulevard, **Samuel Taylor State Park** has excellent camping (see above for details); five miles more brings you to the coastal Hwy-1 and the town of Olema, a mile north of which sits the town of **Point Reyes Station**, a good place to stop off for a bite to eat or to pick up picnic supplies before heading off to enjoy the wide open spaces of the Point Reyes National Seashore just beyond. *Trailhead Rentals*, a half-mile from the Point Reyes Visitor Center, Bear Valley Road (☎663-1768), rents mountain bikes – a great way to get around.

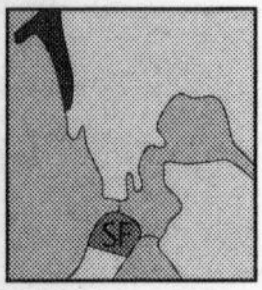

The Point Reyes National Seashore

From Point Reyes Station, Sir Francis Drake Boulevard heads out to the westernmost tip of Marin County at Point Reyes through the **POINT REYES NATIONAL SEASHORE**, a near-island of wilderness surrounded on three sides by more than fifty miles of isolated coastline – pine forests and sunny meadows bordered by rocky cliffs and sandy, windswept beaches. This wing-shaped landmass, something of an aberration along the generally straight coastline north of San Francisco, is in fact a rogue piece of the earth's crust that has been drifting slowly and steadily northwards along the San Andreas Fault, having started some six million years ago as a suburb of Los Angeles. When the great earthquake of 1906 shattered San Francisco, the land here at Point Reyes, the epicentre, shifted over sixteen feet in an instant, though damage was confined to a few skewed cattle fences.

The park's **visitor center** (daily 9am–5pm; ☎663-1092) two miles southwest of Point Reyes Station near Olema, just off Hwy-1 on Bear Valley Road, holds engaging displays on the geology and natural history of the region. Rangers can suggest good hiking and cycling routes, and have up-to-date information on the weather, which can change quickly and be cold and windy along the coast even when it's hot and sunny, three miles inland. They also handle permits and reservations for the various **campgrounds** within the park. Nearby, a replica of a Miwok village has an authentic religious **roundhouse**, and a popular hike follows the Bear Valley Trail along Coast Creek four miles to **Arch Rock**, a large tunnel in the seaside cliffs that you can walk through at low tide.

North of the visitor center, Limantour Road heads west six miles to the Point Reyes **youth hostel**, continuing on another two miles to the coast at **Limantour Beach**, one of the best swimming beaches, and a good place to watch the sea birds in the adjacent estuary. Bear Valley Road rejoins Sir Francis Drake Boulevard just past Limantour Road, leading north along the Tomales Bay through the village of **Inverness**, so-named because the landscape reminded an early settler of his home in the Scottish Highlands. Eight miles west of Inverness, a turn leads down past **Johnson's Oyster Farm** (Tues–Sun 8am–4pm; ☎669-1149) – where you can buy bivalves for around $5 a dozen, less than half the price you'd pay in town – to

Drake's Beach, the presumed landing spot of Sir Francis in 1579. Appropriately, the coastline here resembles the southern coast of England, often cold, wet and windy, with chalk-white cliffs rising above the wide sandy beach. The main road continues west another four miles to the very tip of **Point Reyes**, where a precariously sited **lighthouse** stands firm against the crashing surf. You can't tour the building itself, but you can climb the tiring 300 or so steps down the steep cliffs to reach it. Even without making the trek all the way out, the bluffs along here are excellent places to look out for sea lions and, in winter, migrating grey whales.

For details of the Point Reyes Youth Hostel, see p.220.

The northern tip of the Point Reyes Seashore, **Tomales Point**, is accessible via the Pierce Point Road, which turns off Sir Francis Drake Boulevard two miles north of Inverness. Jutting out into Tomales Bay, it's the least visited section of the park and a refuge for hefty **tule elk**; it's also a great place to admire the lupines, poppies and other wild flowers that appear in the spring. The best swimming (at least the warmest water) is at **Heart's Desire Beach**, a little way before the end of the road; also, down the bluffs from where the road comes to a dead end, there are excellent tidal pools at rocky **McClure's Beach**. North of Point Reyes Station, Hwy-1 continues along the coast, through Bodega Bay up to Mendocino and the northern California coast.

San Rafael and Northern Marin County

You may pass through **SAN RAFAEL** on your way north from San Francisco, but it has little worth stopping for. The county seat and the only big city in Marin County, it has none of the woodsy qualities that make the other towns special, though there are a couple of good restaurants and bars along Fourth Street, the main drag. Its one attraction is an old **Franciscan Mission** (daily 11am–4pm; free), in fact a 1949 replica that was built near the site of the 1817 original, on Fifth Avenue at A Street. The real points of interest are well on the outskirts: the Marin County Civic Center to the north and the little-known China Camp State Park along the bay to the east.

The **Marin County Civic Center** (Mon–Fri 9am–5pm; free; ☎472-3500), spanning the hills just east of US-101 a mile north of central San Rafael, is a strange, otherworldly complex of administrative offices, plus an excellent performance space that looks like a giant viaduct capped by a bright blue-tiled roof. These buildings were architect **Frank Lloyd Wright**'s one and only government project, and although the huge circus tents and amusement park at the core of the designer's conception were never built, it does have some interesting touches, such as the atrium lobbies that open directly to the outdoors.

From the Civic Center, North San Pedro Road loops around the headlands through **China Camp State Park** (☎456-0766), an expansive area of pastures and open spaces that's hard to reach without your own transport. It takes its name from the intact but long-abandoned Chinese shrimp-fishing village at the far eastern tip of the park, the sole survivor of the many small Chinese communities that once dotted the California coast. The ramshackle buildings, small wooden pier and old boats lying on the sand seem straight out of a John Steinbeck tale, the only recent addition being a chain-link fence to protect the site from vandals. At the weekend you can get beer and sandwiches from the old shack at the foot of the pier, but the atmosphere is best during the week, at sunset, when there's often no one around at all. There's a **campground** at the northern end of the park, about two miles from the end of the *Golden Gate Transit* bus #39 route.

Six miles north of San Rafael, the **Lucas Valley Road** turns off west, twisting across Marin to Point Reyes. Although he lives and works here, it was not named after *Star Wars* film-maker George Lucas, whose sprawling **Skywalker Ranch** studios are well hidden off the road. Hwy-37 cuts off east, eight miles north of San Rafael, heading around the top of the bay into the Wine Country of the Sonoma and Napa valleys (see Chapter Eleven).

Chapter 11

The Wine Country

San Francisco during the summer can be a shock – persistent fog and cool temperatures dog the city from May to September – but you only need to travel an hour north to find a warm and sunny climate among the rolling hills of the Napa and Sonoma valleys, known jointly as the **Wine Country**. With its cool, oak-tree-shaded ravines climbing up along creeks and mineral springs to chaparral-covered ridges, it would be a lovely place to visit even without the vineyards, but as it is, the "wine country" tag dominates almost everything here, including many often overlooked points of historical and literary interest. The Wine Country area doesn't actually account for all that much wine – production is something like five percent of the California total, most of which is of the Gallo and Paul Masson jug-wine variety and comes from the Central Valley. But far and away the best wines in the country come from here. The region has been producing wines since the days of the Spanish missions, and though most of the vines withered during Prohibition, the growers have struggled back and these days manage to turn out premium vintages that satisfy wine snobs around the world. Not surprisingly, it's a wealthy region, and rather a smug one, thriving as much on its role as a vacation land for upper-crust San Franciscans as on the wine trade. Designer restaurants (all with massive wine lists) and luxury inns line the narrow roads that, on summer weekends especially, are bumper-to-bumper with wine-tasting tourists.

Wineries are everywhere, and while the town of **Napa** is sprawling and quickly done with, the many small towns further up the valley, particularly **St Helena**, have retained enough of their turn-of-the-century homestead character to be a welcome relief. **Calistoga**, at the top of the valley, offers the best range of non-wine-related distractions – mostly various methods of soaking your bones in tubfuls of hot spring water.

On the western side of the dividing Mayacamas Mountains, the small backroads wineries of the **Sonoma Valley** reflect the more down-to-earth nature of the place, which is both more beautiful and

Cycling in the Wine Country

If you don't want to drive all day, **cycling** is a great way to get around. You can bring your own bike on *Greyhound* (though it costs $10, and the bike must be in a box), or rent one locally for around $25 a day from such outlets as *Bryan's Napa Valley Cyclery*, 4080 Byway East, Napa (☎707/255-3377); *St Helena Cyclery*, 1156 Main St, St Helena (☎707/963-7736); *Getaway Bike Shop*, 1117 Lincoln Ave, Calistoga (☎1-800/859-BIKE); and *Sonoma Wheels*, 523 Broadway, Sonoma (☎707/935-1366).

Both valleys are generally flat, although the peaks in between are steep enough to challenge the hardiest of hill-climbers. If the main roads through the valleys are packed out, as they are most summer weekends, try the smaller parallel routes: the **Silverado Trail** in Napa Valley, and the less evocatively named but nonetheless pretty **Arnold Drive** in Sonoma Valley. For would-be Kings of the Mountains, the **Oakville Grade** between Oakville in the Napa Valley and Glen Ellen in the Sonoma Valley has tested the world's finest riders: you can still make out traces of "Go Hinault!" and "C'mon LeMond!" daubed on the roadway for the *Coors Classic* tours many years ago.

If you feel like some company, or just want to be sure everything goes smoothly, a few local firms organize **tours**, providing bikes, helmets, food and sag wagons in case you get worn out. In Calistoga, *Cruisin' Jules* (☎707/942-0421) specializes in mountain-bike downhill runs, and *Rob Mondavi's Napa Valley Biking Picnics* (☎707/252-1067) sets up more leisurely tours – highlighted by gourmet lunches – all over the Napa area. More ambitious (and quite expensive) overnight tours are run most weekends by *Backroads Bicycle Tours*, 1516 Fifth St, Berkeley (☎510/527-1555).

less crowded than its neighbour, Napa, to the east. The town of **Sonoma** itself is by far the most attractive of the Wine Country communities, retaining a number of fine Mission-era structures around its gracious central plaza. **Santa Rosa**, at the north end of the valley, is the region's sole urban centre, handy for budget accommodation but otherwise unremarkable.

For Wine Country accommodation, see Chapter Twelve; restaurants are on p.245; and cafés and bars on p.255.

As it's only an hour from Union Square to the Wine Country, most people are content to come here for a long day, visiting a few of the wineries and maybe having a picnic or a meal before heading back to the city. This is fine if you have a car and are happy to spend most of the day on the road, but if you really want to absorb properly what the region has to offer, plan to spend at least one night here, pampering yourself in one of the many (generally pricey) **hotels** and **bed and breakfast inns** that provide the bulk of the area's accommodation options. At peak times rooms of all descriptions can seem to be booked up, and if you have a hard time finding a place, avail yourself of one of the many **accommodation services** here: *Bed and Breakfast of Napa* (☎707/255-1280); *Inns of Sonoma Valley* (☎707/996-INNS); *Reservations Unlimited* (☎707/252-1985); or the *Napa Valley Tourist Bureau* (☎707/944-1557).

Arrival and Transport

The Wine Country region spreads north from the top of San Francisco Bay in two parallel, thirty-mile-long valleys, Napa and Sonoma, divided by the oak-covered Mayacamas Mountains. As long

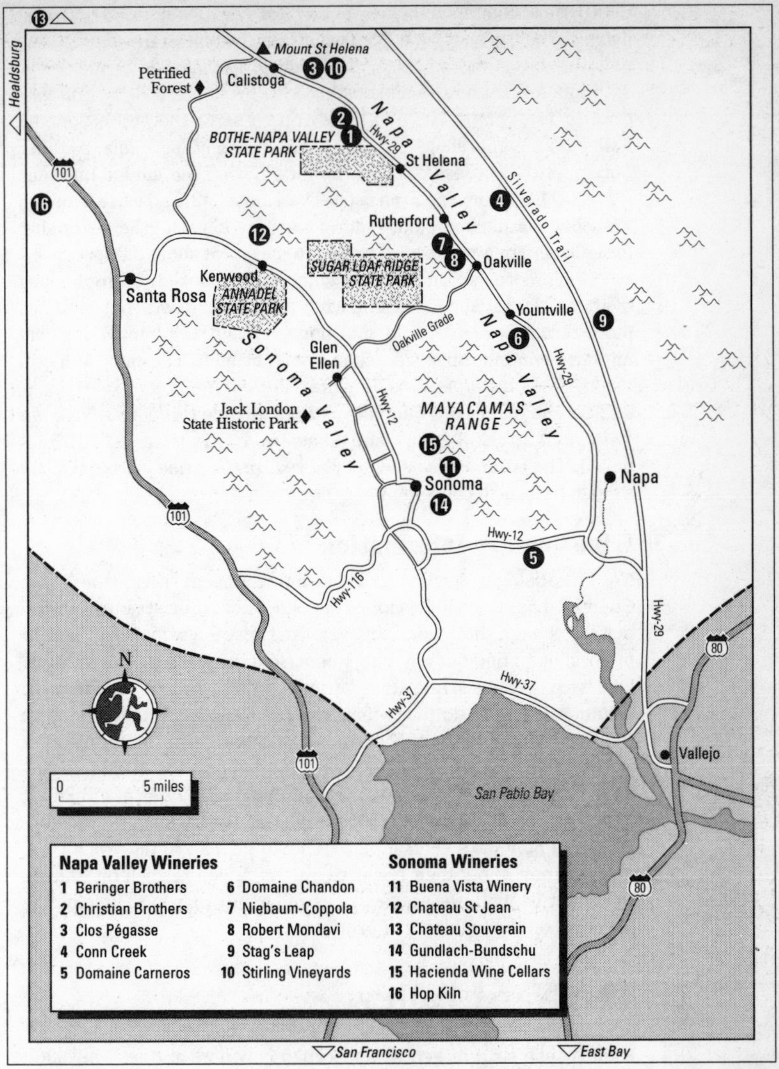

as you avoid the rush-hour traffic, it's about an hour's drive from the city along either of two main routes: take the Golden Gate Bridge to US-101 through Marin County to Hwy-37, or take the Bay Bridge through the East Bay to I-80 to Hwy-37. Hwy-37 intersects Hwy-29 for Napa Valley and Hwy-121 for Sonoma Valley.

As the Wine Country's attractions are spread over a fairly broad area, a car is pretty much essential. *Golden Gate Transit* (☎322-

6600) runs commuter buses all day for the two-hour, $4.50 ride between the city and Santa Rosa which may be of use; *Greyhound* has only one bus a day to the Wine Country, leaving San Francisco at 12.45pm for Santa Rosa and costing $11. From Santa Rosa, *Sonoma County Transit* (☎707/576-RIDE) buses serve the entire Sonoma Valley on a comprehensive, if less than frequent, schedule. Another option for the car-less is to sign up for a *Gray Line* **guided bus tour** (☎558-9400) from San Francisco. These cost $42, and leave from the Transbay Terminal at 9am, visiting a winery in each valley, stopping for lunch in Yountville and returning to the city at about 6.30pm.

Much more exciting are the widely touted **hot-air-balloon rides** over the Napa Valley. These usually lift off at dawn (hot air rises more strongly in the cold morning air) and last ninety magical minutes, winding up with a champagne brunch. The first, and still the best, of the operators is *Napa Valley Balloons* (☎707/253-2224), who fly out of Yountville. Others include *Balloons Above the Valley* (☎707/253-2222) and *Once in a Lifetime* (☎707/942-6541). The crunch comes when you realize the price – around $120 a head, but worth every cent.

Wine Country Information

Not surprisingly for such a tourist-dependent area, the Wine Country has a well-developed network of **tourist information** outlets, though the rivalry between the two valleys makes it next to impossible to find out anything about Sonoma when you're in Napa, and vice versa. While the various small town **Chambers of Commerce** rarely do more than hand out useless brochures, both the **Napa Valley Visitors Bureau**, 1310 Napa Town Center off First Street in downtown Napa (Mon–Fri 10am–5pm, Sat & Sun 11am–3pm; ☎707/226-7459), and the **Sonoma Valley Visitors Bureau**, 453 First St E (Mon–Sat 9am–4pm, Sun 9am–3pm; ☎707/996-1090), in Sonoma's central plaza, should be able to tell you all you need to know about their respective areas. If you're keen on **touring the wineries**, both the above places sell handy **maps** ($1) giving the lowdown on the hundreds of producers.

The Napa Valley

A thirty-mile strip of gently landscaped corridors and lush hillsides, the **Napa Valley** looks more like southern France than a near-neighbour of the Pacific Ocean. In spring the valley floor is covered with brilliant wild flowers which mellow into autumnal shades by grape-harvest time. Local Native Americans named the fish-rich river which flows through the valley "Napa", meaning "plenty"; the name was adopted by Spanish missionaries in the early 1800s, but the Indians themselves were soon wiped out. The few ranchos the Spanish and Mexicans managed to establish were in turn taken over by Yankee traders and, by the 1850s, with California part of the US, the town of Napa had become a thriving river port, sending agricultural goods to San Francisco and serving as a supply point for farmers and ranchers. Before long Napa was bypassed by the railroads and unable to compete with other, deep-water Bay Area ports, but the area's fine climate saved it from oblivion, encouraging a variety of crops including the grape, which spawned the now super-lucrative wine industry.

Lacking both excitement and charm expected for the small, rural entrance to the wine country, **NAPA** can easily be skipped without being missed. At the southern end of the valley, is still the local economic lynchpin, and the highway sprawl that greets travellers is fair warning of what the rest of the town has to offer. But for a proud courthouse, and some intriguingly decrepit old warehouses (ripe for gentrification) along the river, there's not much to see, though it's not bad for food (see p.245), and the **Visitors Bureau** is the most helpful in the whole valley; pick up a detailed winery map. **YOUNTVILLE**, the next town north, has similarly little to see, though it boasts the highest proportion of **places to eat** in the whole region.

If you're looking for an alternative route from Calistoga to Napa, the Silverado Trail offers some breathtaking views of the wine country without the commercialism of Hwy-29.

St Helena

The first town really worth a stop – and it's not much more than a large village really – is pretty **ST HELENA**, 22 miles north of Napa. Its main street, Hwy-29, is lined by some of the Wine Country's finest old buildings, most of which have been restored to – or maintained in – prime condition. The town is also at the heart of the greatest concentration of wineries, as well as boasting some unlikely literary attractions.

The **Silverado Museum** (Tues–Sun noon–4pm; free), housed in St Helena's former Public Library building just off Main Street in the centre of town, has a collection of over 8000 articles relating to Robert Louis Stevenson, who spent just under a year in the area, honeymooning and recovering from an illness. It's claimed to be the second most extensive collection of Stevenson artefacts in the US, though the only thing of interest to any but the most obsessed fan is a scribbled-on manuscript of *Dr Jekyll and Mr Hyde*. The other half of the building is taken up by the **Napa Valley Wine Library** (same hours), a briefly entertaining barrage of photos and clippings relating to the development of local viniculture. Another, more bizarre collection is on display on the north side of town at 1515 Main St, where the **Ambrose Bierce House** bed and breakfast inn is packed with memorabilia of the misanthropic ghost-story writer, who lived here for some fifteen years before heading off to die for Pancho Villa in the Mexican Revolution.

Calistoga

Beyond St Helena, towards the far northern end of the valley, the wineries become prettier and the traffic a little thinner. At the very

Calistoga accommodation options are listed on pp. 213 and 217.

tip of the valley, nestling at the foot of Mount St Helena, **CALISTOGA** is far and away the most enjoyable of the Napa towns, with a few good wineries but really better known for its mud baths and hot springs – and the mineral water which adorns every Californian supermarket shelf. Sam Brannan, the young Mormon entrepreneur who made a mint out of the Gold Rush, established a resort community here in 1860. In his ground-breaking speech he attempted to assert his desire to create the "Saratoga of California", modelled upon the Adirondack gem, but in the event got tongue-tied and coined the town's unique name.

Calistoga's main attraction, then as now, has nothing to do with wines, but rather with another pleasurable activity: soaking in the soothingly hot water that bubbles up here from deep inside the earth. Popular for couples to spend an hour or so of natural-spice relaxing romance and be pampered with body wraps. It's a homey, health-conscious kind of place, which draws jaded city-dwellers each weekend, demanding reservations for accommodation a solid two weeks in advance in summer months. The extravagant might enjoy *Dr. Wilkinson's Hot Springs*, 1507 Lincoln Ave (☎707/942-4102; rooms and treatment from $100 per night) a legendary

Napa Valley Wineries

Almost all of the Napa Valley's **wineries** offer tastings, though comparatively few have tours. Since there are over one hundred wineries in all, producing wines of a very high standard, it's entirely a question of taste which determines the ones you visit. The following selections, **listed from south to north**, are some long-standing favourites, plus a few lesser-known hopefuls. Keep in mind that the intention is for you to get a sense of a winery's product, and perhaps buy some, rather than get drunk on the stuff, so don't expect more than a sip or two of any one sort – though some wineries do sell wines by the glass. If you want to buy a bottle, particularly from the larger producers, you can in fact usually get it cheaper in supermarkets than at the wineries themselves.

Domaine Carneros, 1240 Duhig Rd, Napa ☎707/257-0101. Newly created Austro-Hungarian-style castle surrounded by rolling hills of vineyards in all directions. A pleasant and breathtaking place to taste wine and eat in the sun. Tasting and tours daily 10.30am–6pm.

Domaine Chandon, 1 California Drive, Yountville ☎707/944-2280. Sparkling wines from this progeny of France's Moët & Chandon are known to challenge the authentic champagnes from France. Enormous and modern, this winery and gallery is a standard to be toured by all visiting wine connoisseurs. Decent restaurant. Tours daily 11am–5pm, tasting daily 11am–6pm.

Stag's Leap, 5766 Silverado Trail, east of Yountville ☎707/944-2020. The winery that put Napa Valley on the international map by beating a bottle of Chateau Lafitte-Rothschild at a Paris tasting way back in 1976. Still quite highly rated. Tasting daily 10am–4pm; tours by appointment.

Robert Mondavi, 7801 St Helena Highway, Oakville ☎707/963-9611. Long the standard-bearer for Napa Valley wines ("Bob Red" and "Bob White" are house wines at many California restaurants), they have the most informative and least hard-sell tours. Tours and tasting daily 9am–5pm, book ahead in summer. Free half-day tours are also available.

health spa and hotel whose heated mineral water and volcanic ash tension-relieving treatments have been featured on TV's *Lifestyles of the Rich & Famous*. Or try the elegant but unpretentious *Lavender Hill Spa*, 1015 Foothill Blvd; (☎707/942-4495; $44, reserve one week ahead) special mud baths, which consist of "unthick" mud made from volcanic ash and French sea kelp, known to revitalize and relax. If swaddled luxury is not what you're after, a number of more down-to-earth establishments spread along the mile-long main drag, Lincoln Avenue. *Nance's Hot Springs*, 1614 Lincoln Ave (☎707/942-6211), for example, offers a full mineral rub-down, blanket sweat, steam bath and massage for around $50.

Another sign of Calistoga's lively underground activity is the **Old Faithful Geyser** (daily 9am–5pm; $3), two miles north of town on Tubbs Lane, off Hwy-128, which spurts boiling water sixty feet into the air at fifty-minute intervals. The water source was discovered while drilling for oil here in the 1920s, when search equipment struck a force estimated to be up to a thousand pounds per square foot; the equipment was blown away and, despite heroic efforts to control it, the geyser has continued to go off like clockwork ever

Berringer Brothers, 2000 Main St, St Helena ☎707/963-7115. Napa Valley's most famous piece of architecture, the "Rhine House", modelled on an ancestral German Gothic mansion graces the cover of many a wine magazine. Expansive lawns and a grand tasting room, heavy on dark wood, make for a regal experience. Tours and tasting daily 10am–4pm; closed Aug.

Christian Brothers, 2555 Main St, St Helena ☎707/963-0765. This was the world's largest winery when erected in 1889, but was a bit of a white elephant that kept changing hands until its present owners – oddly enough, a Catholic education order – bought it in 1950, and it now turns out extremely popular sparkling wines. Tours and tasting daily 10am–4pm.

Conn Creek Winery, 8711 Silverado Trail, St Helena ☎707/963-9100. A truly modern organization whose lightweight stone and steel building is worlds away from the cutesy old-stone image that's the norm in the rest of the valley. Tasting 10am–4pm daily; tours by appointment.

Niebaum-Coppola Estate Winery & Vineyards, 1991 St Helena Hwy, Rutherford ☎707/963-9099. Hollywood film director Francis Ford Coppola purchased this Inglenook estate in 1975, which was originally established by Gustav Niebaum in 1879. The wine-tasting room, featuring Rubicon wine, contains a history of Coppola's movie memorabilia. Tasting daily 10am–5pm.

Clos Pégase, 1060 Dunaweal Rd, Calistoga ☎707/942-4981. A flamboyant upstart at the north end of the valley, this high-profile winery emphasizes the links between fine wine and fine art, with a sculpture garden around buildings designed by postmodern architect Michael Graves. No tours; tastings daily 10.30am–4.30pm.

Sterling Vineyards, 1111 Dunweal Lane, Calistoga ☎707/942-3344. Famous for the tram ride from the parking lot bringing visitors for the wine tasting and tour. The extravagant adventure to an otherworldly designed white mansion makes the tasting and touring worth the trip. Tours and tasting 10.30am–4.30pm; $6.

since. Landowners finally realized that they'd never tame it and turned it into a high-yield tourist attraction.

A further local tourist trap is the **Petrified Forest** (daily 10am–5pm; $5), two miles west of Calistoga on the steep road over the hills to Santa Rosa – a forest that was toppled during an eruption of Mount St Helena some three million years ago. The entire redwood grove was petrified by the action of the silica-laden volcanic ash as it gradually seeped into the decomposing fibres of the uprooted trees.

Mount St Helena

The clearest sign of the local volcanic unrest is the massive conical mountain that marks the north end of the Napa Valley, **Mount St Helena**. The 4343-foot summit is worth a climb for its great views – on a very clear day you can see Point Reyes and the Pacific coast to the west, San Francisco to the south, the towering Sierra Nevada to the east and impressive Mount Shasta to the north. It is, however, a long hot climb (five steep miles each way) and you need to set off early in the morning to enjoy it – take plenty of water (and maybe a bottle of wine).

The mountain and most of the surrounding land is protected and preserved as the **Robert Louis Stevenson State Park** (daily 8am–sunset; $2) though the connection with him is fairly weak: Stevenson spent his honeymoon here in 1880 in a bunkhouse with Fanny Osborne, recuperating from tuberculosis and exploring the valley. The bunkhouse remains, but little else about the park's winding roads and dense shrub-growth evokes its days of former notoriety, though it's a pretty enough place to take a break from the wineries and have a picnic. In Stevenson's novel, *Silverado Squatters*, he describes the highlight of the honeymoon as the day he managed to taste eighteen of local wine baron Jacob Schram's champagnes in one sitting. Quite an extravagance, especially when you consider that Schramsberg champagne is held in such high esteem that Richard Nixon took a few bottles when he went to visit Chairman Mao.

The Sonoma Valley

On looks alone the crescent-shaped Sonoma Valley beats Napa hands down. This smaller and altogether more rustic valley curves between oak-covered mountain ranges from Spanish colonial **Sonoma** a few miles north along Hwy-12 to **Glen Ellen**, to end up at the region's main city, **Santa Rosa**. The Sonoma Valley is also known as the "Valley of the Moon", after a Native American legend popularized by long-time resident Jack London that tells how, as you move through the valley, the moon seems to rise several times from behind the various peaks. Far smaller than Napa, most of the

Sonoma Valley's wineries are informal, family-run businesses, many within walking distance of Sonoma itself, and with far fewer visitors – making it very much the stress-free alternative to the busy Napa Valley.

Sonoma

Behind a layer of somewhat touristy stores and restaurants, the small town of **SONOMA** retains a good deal of its Spanish and Mexican architecture. Set around a spacious plaza, the town has a welcoming feel that's refreshing after brash Napa, although as a popular retirement spot, with a median age of about fifty and a matching pace, it's not exactly bubbling with action. The **Visitors' Bureau** (see p.196), in the middle of the leafy central plaza, has walking-tour plans of the town and excellent free maps and guides to the wineries. What there is to see in the town itself will take no

Sonoma Wineries

There is a good concentration of fine wineries in a well-signposted group a mile east of Sonoma Plaza, down East Napa Street. These include: Buena Vista Winery, Hacienda Wine Cellars and Gundlach-Bundschu. Some of the great wineries are along quirky back roads, so take a winery map from the tourist office and follow the signs closely. Those off the beaten path include: Chateau St Jean, Chateau Souverain and Hop Kiln. If you're tired of chasing around, Sonoma also has the handy *Wine Exchange of Sonoma*, 452 First St E (☎707/938-1794), a commercial tasting room where you can sample the best wines from all over California.

Buena Vista Winery, 1800 Old Winery Rd ☎707/938-1266. Oldest and grandest of the wineries, although the wine itself has a reputation for being pretty mediocre, and the century-old stone champagne cellars – the best thing about the place – are being refashioned into yet another pricey restaurant. Tasting daily 10am–5pm, tours daily at 2pm, Sat and Sun also at 11.30am.

Chateau St Jean, 8555 Sonoma Hwy, Kenwood ☎707/833-4134. Attractive estate with an overwhelming aroma of wine throughout the buildings. Quirky tower to climb and admire the view. Tasting daily 10am–4.30pm.

Chateau Souverain, 400 Souverain Rd, Geyserville ☎707/433-8281. A large selection of wines and a café. Tasting daily 10am–6pm.

Gundlach-Bundschu, 3775 Thornsberry Rd ☎707/938-5277. Set back about a mile away from the main cluster, this is more highly regarded for its wine, having stealthily crept up from the lower ranks of the wine league to the point where it now regularly steals from the big names. The plain, functional building is deceptive – this is premium stuff and definitely not to be overlooked. No tours, but tasting daily 10am–5pm.

Hacienda Wine Cellars, 1000 Vineyard Lane ☎707/938-3220. A lavish Spanish colonialist building, with some great topiary in the gardens and extensive vineyards. The wines are relatively inexpensive, middle-of-the-range vintages that appeal to the pocket and palate alike; if you're looking to buy a case, this one's a safe bet. Tastings daily 10am–5pm, tours by appointment.

Hop Kiln, 6050 Westside Rd, Healdsburg ☎707/433-8281. Recently established rustic winery with a traditional atmosphere without a snobbish attitude. Tastings daily 10am–6pm.

more than an hour, Sonoma is a place better known for its history than its sights.

It's hard to believe now that Sonoma was the site of a key event in West Coast history, but the so-called **Bear Flag Revolt** of 1846 was just that – at least as far as the flag-waving Fourth of July crowds who take over the central square are concerned. In this much-romanticized episode, American settlers in the region, who had long lived in uneasy peace under the Spanish and, later, Mexican rulers, were threatened with expulsion from California, along with all other non-Mexican immigrants. In response, a band of thirty armed settlers – some of whom came from as far away as Sacramento – descended upon the disused and unguarded presidio at Sonoma, taking the retired and much-respected commander, Colonel Guadalupe Vallejo, as their prisoner. Ironically, Vallejo had long advocated the American annexation of California and supported the aims of his rebel captors, but he was nonetheless bundled off to Sutter's Fort in Sacramento and held there for the next two months while the militant settlers declared California an independent republic. The Bear Flag, which served as the model for the current state flag, was raised on Sonoma Plaza. A month later, the US declared war on Mexico, and without firing a shot, took possession of the entire Pacific Coast.

In memory of all this, there's a monument to the Bear Flag revolutionaries in the middle of the plaza, and across the street to the north, in **Sonoma State Historic Park**, there are some rusty old cannons and the spooky-looking remains of the old Mexican presidio; the ragged flag is on display inside a small **museum** (daily 8am–5pm; $2). Next door, the restored **Mission San Francisco Solano de Sonoma** (daily 10am–5pm; $1) was the northernmost and last of the California missions, and the only one established while California was under Mexican rule. Half a mile west of the plaza along Spain Street stands the ornate old home of General Vallejo, dominated by decorated filigreed eaves and slender Gothic arched windows. The chalet-style storehouse next door has been turned into a **museum** (daily 9am–5pm; free) of artefacts from the general's reign.

Glen Ellen and Jack London State Park

While the drive up the valley can be soothing, there's really very little to see north of Sonoma apart from a few small villages and the **Jack London State Park** (daily 8am–dusk; $5 per car) – just ten minutes from Sonoma on the London Ranch Road which curves sharply off Hwy-12 close to tiny, charming **GLEN ELLEN** village. Jack London lived here with his wife for the last years of his short, unsettled life, on a 140-acre ranch in the hills above what he described as the "most beautiful, primitive land in California". A series of paths and walking trails leads through densely wooded groves to the remains of the Wolf House, where they lived until an arson attack reduced most of it to a pile of rubble in 1913, leaving only the huge stone chimney and fireplaces. London died three years later and is buried on a hill above the trail to the Wolf House. After his death, London's wife Charmian built the more formal House of Happy Walls, which today serves as a small **museum** (daily 9am–4pm; free). Photographs and artefacts – including the desk where London cranked out his 2000 words a day – enliven the otherwise dry details of the writer's life and work.

Santa Rosa and the North

Sixty miles due north of San Francisco on US-101, and about twenty miles from Sonoma, **SANTA ROSA**, the largest town in Sonoma County, sits at the top end of the Sonoma Valley and is more or less the hub of this part of the Wine Country. It's a very different world from the indulgence of other Wine Country towns, however; much of it is given over to shopping centres and roadside malls, and signs downtown ban teenagers from cruising the rarely packed but confusing system of one-way streets.

Probably the most interesting thing about Santa Rosa is that it was the home town of Raymond Chandler's fictional private eye Philip Marlowe; after that it's all downhill. The **Luther Burbank Home and Gardens** at the junction of Santa Rosa and Sonoma avenues (April–Sept Wed–Sun 10am–3.30pm; $1) may kill an hour or two. California's best-known turn-of-the-century horticulturist is remembered here in the house where he lived and in the splendid gardens where he created some of his most unusual hybrids. If you're not into gardening, nip across the street to the **Ripley Museum**, 492 Sonoma Ave (March–Oct Wed–Sun 11am–4pm; $1.50), where you might expend twenty minutes or so in one of the cartoonist Ripley's mediocre "Believe It or Not" chain of museums – Santa Rosa was Ripley's home town.

Few visitors to the Sonoma region consider the areas beyond Santa Rosa, since there are few, if any, visitor information outlets and the wine-tasting becomes sparse. If time permits, however, continue north on Hwy-101 to the untouched, rural towns of **Healdsburg** and **Geyserville**. Both have little more than pass-by post offices and gas stations, yet the area is so beautiful and offers the opportunity to escape the crowds of the more popular Sonoma and Napa valley areas.

7
ROW K SEAT 15

Part 4

Listings

Chapter 12

Accommodation

Visitors are San Francisco's number one business and the city is fit to bursting with motel, hotel, bed and breakfast and hostel rooms of a consistently high standard. Such standards, however, have their price, and with room rates averaging at around $100 per night, accommodation will almost certainly be the major expense of your stay. Conversely, such an abundance of good options means that failure to phone ahead, even in the peak summer months, needn't result in getting stuck for a place to sleep, though it's always a bit dumb to just turn up in a city with no destination in mind. Even if it's only for the first night, book a room before you travel. Though prices err on the high side, the city does have a good range of options for every budget, and it's well worth shopping around. The price codes at the end of our listings should enable you to find the places within your price range at a glance.

Prices start at around $45 per night for a basic **motel** or **hotel** room – $80 a night is a good deal for something fairly decent and centrally located. The city's stock of **bed and breakfast** inns, starting at around $70 a night, can often be more pleasant and sometimes better value. A **dormitory bed** in a **hostel** will cost in the region of $13 a night, while **camping** is not really an option in San Francisco itself, as there are no sites within an hour's drive of the city.

We've listed our hotel and motel recommendations below, arranged by location; hostels and bed-and-breakfasts are listed separately, as are establishments catering specifically for gay men and lesbians. We've also included a short list of hotels near the airport, in case you're arriving or departing on a late night or early morning flight. Rates are in all cases subject to change and, unless otherwise noted, are for the cheapest double room in peak season. Bear in mind, too, that all quoted room rates are subject to a **room tax** – currently 12 percent on top of your total bill. During the off season, rates can drop considerably and special deals are often available for guests who stay for longer periods.

SAINT BENEDICT SCHOOL
DUFFIELD ROAD
DERBY DE22 1JD

Accommodation Price Codes

All the prices of hotels, motels and bed and breakfasts in this chapter have been graded with the symbols below, according to the cost of the least expensive double room throughout most of the year. Bear in mind that you will have to pay **room tax** – currently twelve percent of the total bill – on top of these rates.

① up to $30	④ $60–80	⑦ $130–175
② $30–45	⑤ $80–100	⑧ $175–250
③ $45–60	⑥ $100–130	⑨ $250+

Accommodation

Finally, if you do have trouble finding a place to stay, try contacting the ultra-efficient and friendly *San Francisco Reservations*, 22 Second St, Fourth Floor (☎1-800/677-1550), who will find you a place somewhere in town without fail, though you should expect to spend upwards of $80 per night. *SF Reservations* also has its own website – http:/www.hotelres.com – which allows you to browse through pictures of hotels and check their locations on a map before you make reservations.

Hotels and Motels

San Francisco hotels and motels have an excellent reputation for comfort and cleanliness and, especially at the lower price ranges, it can be hard to tell the difference between the two. The main distinction is that hotels tend to be more central, and to have better dining facilities, while motels are usually located on main roads and offer free parking – no small consideration in San Francisco, where parking is expensive ($15 a night) and hard to find. Whether you can stand the noise level on a busy road is another matter.

Whichever sort of place you decide to stay at, you can expect a fairly uniform standard of comfort – double rooms with bathroom, colour TV and phone – and on the whole you won't get much more by paying, say, $75 for a night instead of $50. Over $75 and the room simply gets larger and the fittings more luxurious. If you're prepared to pay over $100 per night, that will bring you into the decadent realms of the basement fitness suite and round-the-clock room service.

Hotels in the slightly seedy South of Market and Tenderloin areas start at around $30 per night, $120 per week, though you shouldn't expect a private bath or even a toilet for that amount. In the glitzier areas around Union Square or atop Nob Hill it's hard to find anything at all for under $100 a night.

Wherever you stay, you'll be expected to pay in advance, at least for the first night and perhaps for further nights, too, particularly if it's high season. Some places also request a deposit of a night's room rate when you make your reservation and many will want a credit card number for security, which they will not hesitate to use for the cost of one night's stay should you fail to arrive. Reservations are held until 5 or 6pm unless you've told the hotel you'll be arriving late.

Payment in cash or US dollar traveller's cheques is usually acceptable, though most places prefer to take a swipe of your credit card and have you sign for the full amount when you check out.

Downtown

Campton Place Hotel 340 Stockton St at Sutter ☎781-5555. Smallish Union Square hotel that draws in a quietly moneyed crowd. Luxurious but not showy, with a first-class restaurant. ⑨.

Cartwright Hotel 524 Sutter St at Mason ☎421-2865 or 1-800/227-3844. Distinguishes itself from its rivals with little touches such as fresh flowers, afternoon tea and bend-over-backwards courtesy. Good location one block north of Union Square. ⑥.

Commodore International Hotel 825 Sutter St at Jones ☎923-6800. Classic San Francisco Deco structure a couple of blocks from Union Square with spacious, affordable rooms and a great atmosphere. ④–⑤.

Dakota Hotel 606 Post St at Taylor ☎931-7475. Recently converted 1920s hotel, next door to the *Prescott* near Union Square. Low rates, thanks to the lack of luxury trimmings or fancy service, but all rooms have antique baths. ④.

Fairmont Hotel 950 Mason St at Sacramento ☎772-5000. Most famous of San Francisco's top-notch hotels, the *Fairmont* is an excessively decorated palace with seven restaurants, ten lounges; all in need of a facelift and fantastic views from the rooms. ⑦.

Gates Hotel 140 Ellis St at Powell ☎781-0430. Super-cheap downtown location, with rooms of a predictable standard. ①–②.

Grant Plaza Hotel 465 Grant Ave at Pine ☎434-3883. Newly renovated hotel with clean rooms in the middle of Chinatown. ③.

Accommodation

Harbor Court Hotel 165 Steuart St at Howard ☎882-1300 or 1-800/346-0555. Plush rooms, offering the best bay views of any hotel in the city, and guests have free use of the excellent YMCA health club next door. Next door to the fashionable *Harry Denton's* in the up-and-coming Embarcadero district. ⑦.

Hotel Bedford 761 Post St at Leavenworth ☎673-6040. Allegedly the favourite hotel of Lord Wedgewood, the *Bedford* is excellent value for money and has a high degree of personalized service. When you want to be looked after but don't have a top-dollar budget, alight here. ⑥.

Hotel Griffon 155 Steuart St at Howard ☎495-2100. Hip Embarcadero district hotel with comfortable rooms that have excellent views across the bay and a choice of two wonderful restaurants downstairs depending on how much you want to spend. Recommended. ⑦.

Hotel Monaco 501 Geary St at Taylor ☎292-0100 or 1-800/214-4220. Best of the new wave of San Francisco hotels, offering great style and decor at affordable prices. Next door to the sumptuous but reasonable *Grand Café*. Highly recommended. ⑥.

Hotel Triton 342 Grant Ave at Bush ☎394-0500 or 1-800/433-6611. Very stylish, very comfortable and very central hotel, catering to design professionals and weekend shoppers. Across the street from the Chinatown Gateway, two blocks from Union Square. ⑦.

Huntington Hotel 1075 California St at Taylor ☎474-5400. Understated and quietly elegant compared to its Nob Hill compatriots, this is the hotel for the wealthy who don't need to flash it about. The only large San Francisco hotel that is still family-run, its bars are neither rooftop nor revolving, but instead opt for simple dark-wood furnishing, a piano player and a very intimate atmosphere. Fax machines in all the rooms makes this ideal if you need to do some business, and the limousine service makes it a must if going for the full luxury treatment. ⑧.

Hyde Plaza Hotel 835 Hyde St at Bush ☎885-2987. On the Tenderloin/Nob Hill border, this hotel offers unbelievably cheap accommodation. Small, clean and comfortable rooms with shared bath. ②.

Mandarin Oriental San Francisco 222 Sansome St at California ☎885-0999. You'll need silly amounts of money if you want to stay in what are reputedly San Francisco's most luxurious hotel rooms, but the views from the rooms, which start on the 47th floor of this impressive building, across the Financial District are pretty cool. Amenities include valet, concierge and 24-hour room service. ⑧–⑨.

Mark Hopkins Inter-continental One Nob Hill–999 California St at Mason ☎392-3434. Formerly glorious and elegant residential hotel for writers, movie stars and the very glamorous, *The Mark* caters mostly to business travellers these days but it's a little more affordable and has the wonderfully recherché *Top of the Mark* rooftop bar. ⑧.

Pacific Bay Inn 520 Jones St at Post ☎673-0234. Comfortable renovated hotel in busy downtown location, with a surprisingly high standard of service considering the relatively low rates. Weekly rates only at $299 for walk-ins, discounted to $249 if you call in advance and mention the *Rough Guide*. ②.

Pan Pacific Hotel 500 Post St at Mason ☎771-8600 or 1-800/533-6465. Sleek, modern hotel designed (but no longer owned) by John Portman. If slabs of granite, sparse furnishings and quietly attentive service are what you look for in a luxury hotel, it might just be for you. ⑧.

Prescott Hotel 545 Post St at Mason ☎563-0303 or 1-800/283-7322. The flagship of hotelier Bill Kimpton's San Francisco properties, this small Union Square hotel offers understated luxury, four-star comfort – and preferred seating at the city's most popular restaurant, *Postrio*, with which it shares space. ⑧–⑨.

Raphael Hotel 386 Geary St at Mason ☎986-2000 or 1-800/821-5343. Very popular Union Square hotel with

Price categories:
① up to $30
② $30–45
③ $45–60
④ $60–80
⑤ $80–100
⑥ $100–130
⑦ $130–175
⑧ $175–250
⑨ $250+

Accommodation

See p.224 for a review of the Dining Room *restaurant.*

spacious, good-value rooms and helpful, friendly staff. ⑥.

Ritz-Carlton San Francisco 600 Stockton St at California ☎296-7465 or 1-800/241-3333. The most luxurious hotel in San Francisco perched on the stylish slope of Nob Hill with gorgeously appointed rooms, a swimming pool, multi-million dollar art collection and one of the city's best hotel restaurants, the *Dining Room*. ⑧–⑨.

San Francisco Marriott 777 Market St at New Montgomery ☎777-2799. Most people reckon this 1500-room mirrored monster, looming like a giant jukebox on the skyline, is a much loved blight on San Francisco's cityscape; at least it has a certain surreal quality and ideally placed for the new arts district. ⑦–⑧.

Sheehan Hotel 620 Sutter St at Taylor ☎775-6500 or 1-800/848-1529. Affordable and comfortable Union Square hotel with free use of the gym and pool. ③.

Villa Florence 225 Powell St at Geary ☎397-7700. An elaborate celebration of the Renaissance, this hotel has a colonnaded entrance, *trompe l'oeil* mural and a very good Italian restaurant *Kuleto's*, right on Union Square. ⑥.

See p.57 for more on the St Francis.

Westin St Francis 335 Powell St at Post ☎397-7000 or 1-800/228-3000. Truly grand hotel with a sumptuous lobby, five restaurants, an elegant bar and disappointingly plain rooms. Its reputation far outstrips the reality of a stay here, but, as long as you don't mind the throngs of tourists who pour in to gape at the lobby, you'll be happy. ⑧.

York Hotel 940 Sutter St at Hyde ☎885-6800 or 1-800/808-YORK. Quiet, older hotel on the western edge of downtown. An essential stop for Hitchcock fans, this is where the dramatic stairway scenes in *Vertigo* were filmed. ⑥.

North Beach and the Northern Waterfront

Bel Aire Travelodge 3201 Steiner St at Lombard ☎921-5162. Good-value motel, one block from Lombard Street. ④–⑤.

Days Inn 2358 Lombard St at Divisadero ☎922-2010. Simple, clean, functional accommodation. ④.

Holiday Inn/Fisherman's Wharf 1300 Columbus Ave at North Point ☎771-9000 or 1-800/465-4329. Reliable, if dull, with large clean rooms. ⑦–⑧.

Holiday Lodge 1901 Van Ness Ave at Washington ☎1-800/367-8504. Good family hotel with pool and free parking close to Pacific Heights and Fisherman's Wharf. Landscaped grounds and bungalows give it a resort feel in the middle of town. Comfortable and secure. ⑤.

Howard Johnson's Motor Lodge 580 Beach St at Hyde ☎775-3800. Modern, standard motel. ⑥.

Hyde Park Suites 2655 Hyde St at North Point ☎771-0200 or 1-800/227-3608. Spacious suites, with kitchens, that are ideal family accommodation. Right on the Hyde Street cable-car line, a short walk to Fisherman's Wharf. ⑧.

San Remo Hotel 2237 Mason St at Francisco ☎776-8688 or 1-800/352-7366. Pleasant, old-fashioned rooms (ie you'll have to share a bathroom) in nicely preserved North Beach house. Friendly staff and the best bargain in the area. ②-③.

Sheraton at Fisherman's Wharf 2500 Mason St at North Point ☎362-5500. Reliable business-class accommodation with a pool. ⑦.

Sherman House 2160 Green St at Fillmore ☎563-3600. Rated the best in San Francisco by *Zagat* readers' guide, this small Cow Hollow hotel is one of the city's lesser-known jewels. ⑨.

Tuscan Inn 425 North Point at Taylor ☎561-1100 or 1-800/648-4626. The most upmarket hotel on the waterfront, with afternoon wine-tastings and free limo downtown. ⑥–⑦.

Van Ness Motel 2850 Van Ness Ave at Chestnut ☎776-3220. Large rooms, within walking distance of Fort Mason. ③–④.

Wharf Inn 2601 Mason St at Jefferson ☎673-7411. Comfortable, family-style hotel close to the waterfront with free parking. ⑤–⑥.

Accommodation

Civic Center, South of Market and the Mission

Abigail Hotel 246 McAllister at Larkin ☎861-9728. Comfortable, stylish and affordable, this Civic Center hotel caters mainly to revellers performing at the nearby arts centres, and sports an excellent vegan restaurant (believe it or not) *Millennium*, in its basement. Weekly and monthly rates available. Perfect for the hip but skint. ④.

Bay Bridge Inn 966 Harrison St at Sixth ☎397-0657. Basic and somewhat noisy but perfectly sited for late nights in SoMa's clubland. ④.

Best Western Carriage Inn 140 Seventh St at Howard ☎552-8600. Clean, comfortable rooms in downmarket Civic Center area. Free shuttle service to Union Square and the Civic Center. ④.

Embassy Motor Hotel 610 Polk St at Eddy ☎673-1404. Bland, neat hotel close to the Civic Center. ③.

Friendship Inn 860 Eddy St at Van Ness ☎474-4374. Newly renovated motel in slightly dodgy Tenderloin location. ③–④.

Golden City Inn 1554 Howard St at 12th ☎255-1110. Best of the inexpensive South of Market hotels, smack in the middle of the SoMa nightlife scene. Unbelievably good value. ①–②.

Phoenix Hotel 601 Eddy St at Polk ☎776-1380. Marginal neighbourhood on the edge of the Tenderloin but the hip music-biz crowd who lounge around the pool drinking cocktails don't seem to mind. ⑤.

San Francisco Central Travelodge 1707 Market St at Gough ☎621-6775. Dependable chain motel. Comfortable, but short on glamour. ④–⑤.

Travelodge Downtown 790 Ellis St at Polk ☎775-7612. Same as the above but in a slightly seedier location. ④.

UN Plaza Hotel 45 McAllister Street at Market ☎626-5200. Convenient location, three blocks from the Civic Center and Union Square. Classic Victorian lobby and large, comfy rooms. Great deals to be had in winter; always ask about special offers. ③–⑥.

Victorian Hotel 54 Fourth St at Market ☎986-4400 or 1-800/227-3804. Good SoMa location and, thanks to a recent extensive renovation, clean, comfortable and well-priced rooms from $39 for a single with shared bath to $99 for a suite with its own kitchen. Weekly rates from $139. ②–⑤.

Price categories:
① up to $30
② $30–45
③ $45–60
④ $60–80
⑤ $80–100
⑥ $100–130
⑦ $130–175
⑧ $175–250
⑨ $250+

Airport Hotels

Best Western Grosvenor Hotel 380 South Airport Blvd ☎873-3200. Large comfortable hotel with pool and free shuttle service to the airport. ⑤.

Goose Turets Bed and Breakfast 835 George St, Montara ☎728-5451. Twenty minutes south of the airport, this is a more restful and intimate B&B alternative to the other airport accommodation. Close to the beaches and hiking trails, this is a perfect place to unwind either before or after a long trip. Sadly, no smoking. ⑤.

Hilton at San Francisco Airport San Francisco Airport ☎589-0770. Actually on top of the airport, this is both easy to find and a guarantee that you won't miss your flight. Basic, business-class accommodation. ⑦.

La Quinta Inn 20 Airport Blvd ☎583-2223. Overnight laundry service and a pool make this a comfortable stop-over. Free shuttle service to the airport. ④.

Motel 6 1101 Shoreway Rd, Belmont ☎591-1471. When the money runs out, come to this no-frills motel. Good preparation for a long and uncomfortable journey. ②.

Radisson Hotel San Francisco Airport 1177 Airport Blvd ☎342-9200. Great facilities include restaurant, pool, jacuzzi, live music and a free shuttle to the airport. ⑤.

Super 8 Lodge 111 Mitchell Ave S, San Francisco ☎877-0770. Plain, motel-style accommodation with free airport shuttle between 6am and 11am. ③.

Accommodation

Price categories:
① up to $30
② $30–45
③ $45–60
④ $60–80
⑤ $80–100
⑥ $100–130
⑦ $130–175
⑧ $175–250
⑨ $250+

The Central Neighbourhoods

Beck's Motor Lodge 2222 Market St at Sanchez ☎621-8212. Good Castro location, with large, clean but characterless rooms. See also "Gay accommodation" on p.217 ④.

Best Western Miyako 1800 Sutter St at Buchanan ☎921-4000 or 1-800/528-1234. Immaculate Japan Center hotel, with quiet rooms, some with steam baths. ⑤–⑥.

Casa Loma Hotel 600 Fillmore St ☎552-7100. Mid-sized, friendly hotel with sauna, jacuzzi, sun deck and a lively bar. ③–④.

Jackson Court 2198 Jackson St ☎992-7670. Pacific Heights converted mansion, offering luxury B&B service. Very nice indeed. ⑦.

Metro Hotel 319 Divisadero St at Page ☎861-5364. Homely, clean and comparatively inexpensive Lower Haight hotel. ④.

Stanyan Park Hotel 750 Stanyan St at Waller ☎751-1000. Gorgeous, small Victorian hotel in a great setting across from Golden Gate Park, with friendly staff and free continental breakfast. ⑤.

Twin Peaks Hotel 2160 Market St at Dolores ☎621-9467. Clean, comfortable, inexpensive hotel near the Castro. ②–③.

Golden Gate Park, the beaches and outlying areas

Beach Motel 4211 Judah St ☎681-6618. Very average motel in a good spot by the edge of the park and Ocean Beach. ③.

Mar Oceanview Motel 4340 Judah St ☎661-2300. Good access for the park and zoo and well situated, right on the *MUNI* N–Judah line. ④.

Ocean Park Motel 2690 46th Ave ☎566-7020. A fair way from downtown (25min by *MUNI*) this is nonetheless a great Art Deco motel (San Francisco's first), opposite the zoo and the beach. Outdoor hot tub and jacuzzi and play area for children. ③.

Sunset Motel 821 Taraval St ☎681-3306. One of the finest little motels in San Francisco – clean, friendly and safe. ④.

East Bay

Claremont Hotel 41 Tunnel Rd at Ashby on the Oakland/Berkeley border ☎510/843-3000. At the top end of the scale, this grand Victorian palace has panoramic bay view rooms and all-inclusive "weekend breaks". ⑧.

French Hotel 1538 Shattuck Ave, North Berkeley ☎510/548-9930. Small and comfortable, in the heart of Berkeley's "Gourmet Ghetto". ⑤.

Golden Bear Motel 1620 San Pablo Ave, West Berkeley ☎510/525-6770. The most pleasant of the many motels in the "flatlands" of West Berkeley, though somewhat out of the way. ③.

Holiday Inn Bay Bridge 1800 Powell St, Emeryville ☎510/658-9300. Not outrageously pricey considering the great views to be had from the upper floors. Free parking. ⑤.

Hotel Durant 2600 Durant Ave, Berkeley ☎510/845-8981. Fairly plain but well worn and comfortable, and very handy for the UC Berkeley campus. ⑤.

Marriot Hotel 200 Marina Blvd, Berkeley ☎510/548-7920. Comfortable hotel verging on the upscale. Some rooms have a view of the bay. ⑥.

Ramada Inn 920 University Ave, Berkeley ☎510/849-1121. Bargain rooms with live music nightly, mostly blues. Near Berkeley Marina. ③.

Shattuck Hotel 2086 Allston Way, Berkeley ☎510/845-7300. Very central and recently refurbished, near Berkeley *BART*. ⑤.

Travelodge 423 Seventh St, downtown Oakland ☎510/451-6316. Spacious rooms, some of which have kitchens, make this a good option for families or groups. ④.

Waterfront Plaza Hotel 10 Washington St, Oakland ☎510/836-3800. Newly redecorated hotel moored on the best stretch of the Oakland waterfront. ⑥.

The Peninsula

Best Western Inn 455 S Second St, San Jose ☎408/298-3500. Right in downtown San Jose, with pool and sauna. ④.

Best Western Stanford Park Hotel 100 El Camino Real, Menlo Park ☎322-1234. A very pleasant hotel near Stanford University. ⑧.

Comfort Inn 1350 S First St, San Jose ☎408/280-8700. Basic rooms downtown near the few cafés in the city. ④

Days Inn Palo Alto 4238 El Camino Real, Palo Alto ☎493-4222 or 1-800/325-2525. A mile from anywhere but the rooms are particularly clean and well kept. ④.

Executive Inn 3930 Monterey Rd, San Jose ☎408/281-8700. Basic rooms without frills fifteen minutes outside downtown. ③.

Hotel California 2431 Ash St, Palo Alto ☎322-7666. Small and central, with breakfast included. ③.

Stanford Terrace Inn 531 Stanford Ave, Palo Alto ☎857-0333. Big rooms and a small pool for not much money. ⑥.

Valley Inn 2155 The Alameda, San Jose ☎408/241-8500. Standard motel not far from the Rosicrucian Museum (see p.172). ④.

Marin County

Casa Madrona 801 Bridgeway, Sausalito ☎332-0502. Deluxe hideaway tucked into the hills above the bay. ⑧.

Grand Hotel 15 Brighton Ave, Bolinas ☎868-1757. Budget rooms in comfortable old hotel. ②.

Ocean Court Motel 18 Arenel St, Stinson Beach ☎868-0212. Just a block from the beach, west of Hwy-1. Large rooms with kitchens. ④.

San Rafael Inn 865 E Francisco Blvd, San Rafael ☎454-9470. Large roadside motel, just off US-101. ③.

Stinson Beach Motel 3416 Shoreline Highway, Stinson Beach ☎868-1712. Basic roadside motel right on Hwy-1, five minutes' walk to the beach. ④.

Wine Country

Best Western Hillside Inn 2901 Fourth St, Santa Rosa ☎707/546-9353. Clean, attractive motel with swimming pool. ③.

Calistoga Inn 1250 Lincoln Ave, Calistoga ☎707/942-4101. Comfortable rooms in a landmark building. ③.

Comfort Inn 1865 Lincoln Ave, Calistoga ☎707/942-9400. Quiet, modern motel on the edge of town. ③.

El Bonita Motel 195 Main St, St Helena ☎707/963-3216. Old roadside motel recently done up in Art Deco style. ③.

El Pueblo Motel 896 W Napa St, Sonoma ☎707/996-3651. Standard highway motel. ④.

Indian Hot Springs 1712 Lincoln Ave, Calistoga ☎707/942-4919. Spacious cabins with living areas and kitchenettes. Full spa on premises. ⑥.

Jack London Lodge 13740 Arnold Drive, Glen Ellen ☎707/938-8510. Modern motel near the Jack London State Park (see p.202), with a good restaurant and swimming pool. ④.

Magliulo's Pensione 691 Broadway, Sonoma ☎707/996-1031. Cosy accommodation, despite shared bathroom facility. Also has an excellent Italian restaurant. ⑤.

Mount View Hotel 1457 Lincoln Ave, Calistoga ☎707/942-6877. Lively Art Deco-style hotel with nightly jazz and an excellent restaurant. ④.

Nance's Hot Springs 1614 Lincoln Ave, Calistoga ☎707/942-6211. This modest hotel with full spa among the ritzy Wine Country accommodation is perfect for the budget traveller. Funky rooms with kitchenettes. ③.

Triple-S-Ranch 400 Mount Home Ranch Rd, Calistoga ☎707/942-6730. Just outside Calistoga in the middle of the wilderness, these unpublicized cosy cabins are clean and affordable, and near to a rustic steakhouse/bar. Take Hwy-128 north for one mile, turn left on Petrified Forest Road, follow for two and a half miles until Mount Home Road, turn left and continue one mile. ③.

Vintage Inn 6541 Washington St, Yountville ☎707/944-1112. Huge luxury rooms – all with fireplaces – plus swimming pool and free bike rental. Handy for Yountville's many fine restaurants and great for romantic getaways. ⑦.

Accommodation

Wine Country restaurants are listed on p.245.

Accommodation

Price categories:
① *up to $30*
② *$30–45*
③ *$45–60*
④ *$60–80*
⑤ *$80–100*
⑥ *$100–130*
⑦ *$130–175*
⑧ *$175–250*
⑨ *$250+*

White Sulphur Springs 3100 White Sulphur Springs Rd, west of St Helena ☎707/963-8588. A relaxing retreat from the hyper-tourism of the Napa Valley, unpretentious rooms in a ramshackle old 300-acre hillside resort. ④.

Bed and Breakfast

Bed and breakfast around the Bay Area is good-value luxury, offering a more intimate and often more comfortable alternative to the standard hotel or motel experience. Europeans, accustomed to shabby B&Bs in faded seaside resorts and greasy bacon-and-eggs, may be pleasantly surprised – though the rates, of course, are proportionately higher than in Europe.

Even the largest of establishments tend to have no more than ten rooms, with brass beds, plentiful flowers, stuffed cushions and an almost over-contrived homely atmosphere. Other places, most of which are bookable through the various specialist B&B agencies listed below, may consist merely of a couple of furnished rooms in someone's home, or an entire apartment where you won't even see your host. The latter makes particularly good sense for families or those travelling with small children.

While always including breakfast, the breakfasts themselves vary from granola, fresh fruit and scones, to a full-blown pancakes, eggs and bacon. If you need a big blow-out to start the day, be sure to check. Prices vary greatly, anything from $40 to $200 a night, depending on location and season. Most of the B&Bs listed below fall between $70 and $160 per night for two people sharing. Also bear in mind, that being small, many places are booked up weeks in advance at peak times.

Downtown

Adelaide Inn 5 Isadora Duncan Court between Geary and Post ☎441-2261. Small bed-and-breakfast hotel with shared bathroom facilities. ③.

Alexander Inn 415 O'Farrell St at Taylor ☎928-6800. Bright, well-equipped rooms in a great location, just off Union Square. ④.

Amsterdam Hotel 749 Taylor St at Bush ☎1-800/637-3444. On Nob Hill, but only just. Actually closer to the Tenderloin but good-value, clean, pleasant rooms. ③–④.

Andrews Hotel 624 Post St at Taylor ☎563-6877. "European Style" in hotel trade parlance means small, but this one is also extremely well furnished, comfortable and affordable and has a first-class restaurant in the heart of the city, and for ten dollars more than the cost of a cab they'll either pick you up or drop you off at the airport in a limo. Nice one. ⑤.

Beresford Arms Hotel 701 Post St at Jones ☎673-2600. Luxury B&B in the heart of town, well worth the few extra dollars. ⑥.

Cornell Hotel 715 Bush St at Powell ☎421-3154. Pleasant Nob Hill/Union Square location with basic, clean rooms. ④–⑤.

Nob Hill Lambourne 725 Pine St at Powell ☎433-2287. When you need not just a room, but a room with WordPerfect

B&B Agencies

Bed and Breakfast International PO Box 282910, San Francisco, CA 94128 ☎1-800/872-4500 or 696-1690. Self-catering apartments, home-stays and small inns around the Bay Area and California.

Bed and Breakfast San Francisco PO Box 420009, San Francisco, CA 94142 ☎1-800/452-8249 or 479-1913; e-mail address: bbsf@linex.com. Private rooms and self-catering apartments all over San Francisco and the Bay Area, starting at $55 a night.

Colby International 139 Round Hey, Liverpool L28 1RG, England ☎0151/220 5848 in the UK or 703/551-5005 in the US. Efficient and very reasonable English accommodation agency, dealing in B&B reservations and also self-catering apartments.

software, a fax machine and two telephone lines, this small, comfortable hotel is perfect for the busy and important. ⑧.

Hotel David 480 Geary St ☎771-1600 or 1-800/524-1888. By no means the least expensive place in town, but a great Theater District location above San Francisco's largest and best Jewish delicatessen, where you get an all-you-can-eat breakfast and free transportation to the airport if you stay two nights or more. ④.

Monticello Inn 127 Ellis St at Powell ☎392-8800. Country Colonial style in the thick of things. Lots of reproduction furniture, wine served in the library and other civilized little touches like complimentary entry to a health club make this a good bet for all-round comfort and service. ⑥.

Nob Hill Inn 1000 Pine St ☎673-6080. Decorated by Anglophiles, this is a little bit of antique England for homesick Brits. Upmarket B&B with concierge and whirlpool. ⑥.

Petite Auberge 863 Bush St at Taylor ☎928-6000. One of two opulent downtown B&Bs, next to one another on Bush Street. This one offers complimentary afternoon tea, wine and hors d'oeuvres as well as full breakfast. ⑥–⑦.

White Swan Inn 845 Bush St at Taylor ☎775-1775. The other Bush Street B&B, this one with a convincing English manor-house theme: raging fireplaces, oak-panelled rooms and afternoon tea. ⑨.

North Beach and the Northern Waterfront

Art Center Bed and Breakfast 1902 Filbert St at Laguna ☎567-1526. Quirky little inn that's a real home away from home. ⑤–⑥.

Bed and Breakfast Inn 4 Charlton Court off Union St ☎921-9784. One of the first B&Bs to be established in the city, this lovely, sun-drenched Victorian house, tucked away down a quiet side street, offers some of San Francisco's most pleasant accommodation. ④–⑧ depending on choice of room.

Edward I 3155 Scott St at Francisco ☎922-3000. Large and comfortable inn-style accommodation with free breakfast and afternoon sherry. ④–⑤.

Marina Inn 3110 Octavia St at Chestnut ☎928-1000. Comfortable, homely setup, right off Lombard Street. ④.

Sherman House 2160 Green St at Fillmore ☎563-3600. Rated the best in San Francisco by *Zagat* readers' guide, this is one of the city's lesser-known jewels. ⑨.

Union Street Inn 2229 Union St at Fillmore ☎346-0424. Lovely Edwardian house in the Marina offering six double rooms and full breakfast. ⑥–⑧.

Washington Square Inn 1660 Stockton St at Filbert ☎981-4220. Cosy B&B bang on North Beach's lovely main square. Non-smokers only. ⑥.

Civic Center, South of Market and the Mission

Albion House Inn 135 Gough St at Oak ☎621-0896. Small and comfortable B&B above a fine restaurant. ⑤.

Dolores Park Inn 3641 17th St ☎621-0482. Tiny but elegant boarding house with good access to Lower Haight and Castro districts. Non-smoking. ⑤.

Inn at the Opera 333 Fulton St ☎863-8400. Deluxe B&B with 24-hour room service and morning limo downtown on weekdays. Stay here if you want to bump into visiting divas. ⑥–⑦.

Pensione San Francisco 1668 Market St ☎864-1271. A good base near the Civic Center, within walking distance to SoMa and the Castro. Doesn't offer breakfast but discounts lunch and dinner at the Japanese restaurant in the building. ③.

The Central Neighbourhoods

Alamo Square Inn 719 Scott St at Grove ☎922-2055. A beautifully restored Victorian building. The rates aren't low, but guests get the use of a handsome dwelling, some rooms complete with fireplace and one with jacuzzi. ⑤–⑥.

Archbishops Mansion 1000 Fulton St at Steiner ☎563-7872. Deluxe, grandly camp mansion that has been everything from its namesake to a school for wayward Catholic boys and now a really

Accommodation

Accommodation

quirky bed and breakfast. Attentive personal service and a variety of packages offering everything to getting fit to getting decked out by a professional image consultant. Home to Noel Coward's piano, this place is a riot. ⑦.

Grove Inn 890 Grove St at Fillmore ☎929-0780. Nothing fancy, but good value and a fine location on Alamo Square. ④.

James Court 1353 Bush Street at Polk ☎771-2409. Basic no-frills accommodations with shared bath facilities. Secure, friendly, clean and cheap. ①–②.

The Mansion 2220 Sacramento St at Laguna ☎929-9444. Luxury-swaddled Victorian mansion, perched high up in the fancy reaches of Pacific Heights. ⑦–⑨.

Price categories:
① *up to $30*
② *$30–45*
③ *$45–60*
④ *$60–80*
⑤ *$80–100*
⑥ *$100–130*
⑦ *$130–175*
⑧ *$175–250*
⑨ *$250+*

Red Victorian Bed and Breakfast (aka the Peace Center) 1665 Haight St at Cole ☎864-1978. Bang in the middle of the Haight-Ashbury, a time-warped B&B with hippie art gallery and rooms with New Agey themes, courtesy of owner Sami Sunchild. ④–⑥.

East Bay

Dean's Bed & Breakfast 156 Pedestrian Way, Oakland ☎510/652-5024. A hidden and inexpensive room with pool, hot tub, private entrance and Japanese garden tucked away in Rockridge. The personable owner who stays out of your way needs a reservation in advance. ④.

East Brother Light Station 117 Park Place in San Pablo Bay ☎510/233-2385. A handful of rooms in a converted lighthouse, on an island in the middle of the bay. Not a handy base for seeing the sights, this is a retreat and adventure for an evening. During winter months the foghorns are known to be loud, to some visitors' pleasure, others' displeasure. Prices include highly rated gourmet dinners as well as breakfast. ⑨.

For more on the Green Gulch Zen Center, *see p.184.*

Elmwood House 2609 College Ave, Berkeley ☎510/540-5123. Attractive, turn-of-the-century house with B&B rooms not far from UC Berkeley. ④.

Gramma's 2740 Telegraph Ave, Berkeley ☎510/549-2145. Pleasant, if slightly dull, rooms with fireplaces in a pretty mock-Tudor mansion half a mile south of UC Berkeley. ⑤–⑥.

Hotel Mac 10 Cottage Ave, Point Richmond ☎510/787-0100. A hotel built in 1907, The *Mac* was recently reconverted to its original intention. Luxurious rooms with unbeatable prices give one-nighters more than they pay for. This was supposedly John Rockefeller's favourite place to stay when he would visit his Standard Oil enterprise. ⑤.

Union Hotel and Gardens 401 First Street, Benicia ☎707/746-0100. A bordello from 1882 until 1950; since converted into a comfortable bed and breakfast with twelve rooms. ④.

The Peninsula

Old Thyme Inn 779 Main St, Half Moon Bay ☎726-1616. Half a dozen incredibly quaint rooms, each with private bath, in lovely Victorian house surrounded by luxuriant herb and flower gardens. ⑤.

San Benito House Main St, Half Moon Bay ☎726-3425. Twelve restful rooms in a 100-year-old building, just a mile from the beach. ⑤.

Marin County

Blue Heron Inn 11 Wharf Rd, Bolinas ☎868-1102. Lovely double rooms in an unbeatable locale. Breakfast is served at the owner's cosy restaurant, *The Shop Café* at 46 Wharf Rd, which also serves lunch and dinner. ⑤.

Lindisfarne Guest House *Green Gulch Zen Center*, Muir Beach ☎383-3036. Restful rooms in a meditation retreat set in a secluded valley above Muir Beach. Price includes excellent vegetarian meals. ⑤.

Mountain Home Inn 810 Panoramic Highway, Mill Valley ☎381-9000. Romantically located on Mount Tamalpais' crest, this bed and breakfast offers great views and endless hiking. Some rooms with hot tubs. ⑥.

Pelican Inn 10 Pacific Way, Muir Beach ☎383-6000. Very comfortable rooms in a pseudo-English country inn, with good bar and restaurant downstairs, ten minutes' walk from beautiful Muir Beach. ⑦.

Ten Inverness Way 10 Inverness Way, Inverness ☎669-1648. Quiet and restful, with a hot tub, in small village of good restaurants and bakeries on the fringes of Point Reyes. ⑥.

Wine Country

Calistoga Wine Way Inn 1019 Foothill Blvd, Calistoga ☎707/942-0680 or 1-800/572-0679. Small and friendly B&B with lovely garden and antique-filled rooms, a short walk from the centre of town. ⑤–⑥.

Cinnamon Bear 1407 Kearney St, St Helena ☎707/963-4653. Quirky, sumptuously furnished inn. ⑤–⑥.

Gaige House Inn 13540 Arnold Drive, Glen Ellen ☎707/935-0237. Restored Victorian farmhouse in country setting. No children under twelve. ⑤–⑥.

Hotel St Helena 1309 Main St, St Helena ☎707/963-4388. Opulently redecorated 1881 inn. ④.

Kenwood Inn 10400 Sonoma Hwy, Sonoma ☎707/833-1293. Beautiful, secluded Italian-villa style bed and breakfast spread out like a miniature castle. ⑧.

Madrona Manor 1001 Westside Rd, Healdsburg ☎1-800/258-4003. Luxurious Victorian-style hidden bed and breakfast on a hilltop with gardens. ⑦.

Sonoma Hotel 110 W Spain St, Sonoma ☎707/996-2996. Tasteful bed and breakfast features antique-decorated rooms with brass-legged bathtubs in the heart of downtown Sonoma. ④.

Thistle Dew Inn 171 W Spain St, Sonoma ☎707/938-2909. Newly restored rooms near Sonoma Plaza, plus full breakfast and free bike rental. ⑥.

Gay Accommodation

Not surprisingly, San Francisco has several accommodation options that cater specifically to **gay and lesbian travellers**. Most are geared towards men, although it's unlikely that lesbians would be turned away; see "Women's accommodation" (overleaf) for more suitable alternatives. Information, up-to-date recommendations and referrals are available from a number of sources (see *Basics*, p.39, for details).

In the rest of the Bay Area, gay travellers (including couples) rarely raise eyebrows, and your sexual orientation shouldn't be an issue.

Anna's Three Bears 114 Divisadero at Haight ☎255-3167. Deluxe accommodation including full breakfast, if you want to be near the Castro but not in it. Pricey but worth it. ⑧.

Beck's Motor Lodge 2222 Market St at Church ☎621-8212. Standard motel close to the Castro. ③.

Gough Hayes Hotel 417 Gough St at Hayes ☎431-9131. Bit of a flop house, but popular with a rowdy crowd. ③.

Inn on Castro 321 Castro St at Market ☎861-0321. A long-standing favourite with visiting gays, this luxury bed and breakfast doesn't come cheap, but is worth the price for the large rooms and good breakfasts. About two minutes' walk from the Castro. ⑤–⑥.

Leland Hotel 1315 Polk St at Bush ☎441-5141. Attractively decorated Polk Gulch hotel. Weekly rates available. ③–④.

Queen Anne Hotel 1590 Sutter St at Post ☎262-2663. Very much a gay hotel with overdone decor, full valet service and complimentary afternoon tea and sherry. ⑥–⑦.

24 Henry 24 Henry St ☎864-5686. Intimate guest house in a quiet street just off the heart of the Castro. ④.

Twin Peaks Hotel 2160 Market St at Dolores ☎621-9467. Set in the hills above, this is a quieter and prettier location not far from the Castro, even if the rooms are small and short on luxury. ②–③.

The Willows 710 14th Street at Church ☎431-4770. Attractively decorated and fair-priced accommodation. Eight bath facilities for eleven rooms. Off-street parking for $8 per day. ④–⑥.

Accommodation

Our Wine Country chapter begins on p.193.

The International Gay Travel Association, based in Key West, Florida, has a lot of resources at its fingertips and can book accommodation ahead for you (☎1-800/448-8550).

For more on gay and lesbian San Francisco, see p.38; gay bars are detailed on p.255.

Accommodation

Get Away to Guerneville – Some Weekend Suggestions

Approximately a one-hour car ride out of the city is the popular bed and breakfast getaway town of **Guerneville** on the **Russian River**. Part of Sonoma County, the Russian River is known for its beauty and rustic towns along its edge. Guerneville is a quiet place with a lesbian and gay friendly environment. There are few nightlife activities in Guerneville: people who stay for a weekend are consumed with hiking, mountain biking and taking trips to the wineries in the Sonoma Valley (see p.200). The **Russian River Chamber of Commerce** 16200 First St, Guerneville (☎707/869-9000) is surprisingly conservative and unhelpful for specific lesbian and gay listings. However, it has extensive information on hotels, B&Bs and campgrounds in general. To get there, take route 101 north past Santa Rosa to the River Rd exit. Follow River Rd west for approximately ten miles into town.

Some Bay Area accommodation known to be lesbian- and gay-friendly include:

Faeri Ring Campground 1467 Armstrong Woods Rd ☎707/869-2746. ①.

The Highlands 1400 Woodland Drive ☎707/869-0333. ③.

The Willows 15905 River Rd ☎707/869-2824. ③.

The Woods 16118 Armstrong Woods Rd ☎707/869-0111. ③.

Price categories:
① *up to $30*
② *$30–45*
③ *$45–60*
④ *$60–80*
⑤ *$80–100*
⑥ *$100–130*
⑦ *$130–175*
⑧ *$175–250*
⑨ *$250+*

Women's Accommodation

Campton Place 340 Stockton St at Post ☎781-5555. Not specifically a women's hotel, but favoured by female executives who prefer the discreet profile and safe, quiet floors. ⑦–⑨.

House o' Chicks 2162 15th St at Sanchez ☎861-9849. Catering to "low-maintenance lesbians" who are looking for a communal, homestay-type environment. ③–④.

The Juliana 590 Bush St at Stockton ☎392-2540. Traditional decor and a strong female following. ⑦.

The Langtry 637 Steiner St at Hayes (Alamo Square) ☎863-0538. Each room in this nineteenth-century mansion is dedicated to a famous woman in history. Hot tub, sundeck, views of the city. Fabulous but not cheap. ⑥–⑦.

Mary Elizabeth Inn 1040 Bush St at Jones ☎673-6768. Run by the United Methodist Church, so don't expect a swinging dyke scene. However, you can rely on a safe place to stay. ③–④.

642 Jones 642 Jones St at Post ☎775-1711. Comfortable, secure building that is quite safe despite being situated in the unpleasant Tenderloin district. Weekly rates are among the city's best deals: singles $120 per week, doubles $170. Men are allowed, though outnumbered 40 to 1. ①–②.

Hostels

At the bottom end of the price scale, there are a number of **hostels** in San Francisco and around the Bay Area, some in very beautiful settings. Dormitory beds go for around $13, and many hostels also offer cut-rate single and double rooms.

You can really expect little more from a hostel than a clean, safe bed and somewhere to lock your valuables. Some are livelier and more liberal than others, though those with more regulations (ie nightly curfews and bans on alcohol) also tend to be the safest – for women travelling alone they can often be good places to feel secure and meet other people. The hostels vary between **unofficial** private establishments, where things will in general be more relaxed, and the **official HI hostels**, which tend to be cleaner and better equipped but normally have some kind of curfew.

There are also a couple of **YMCAs**, and a few rooms become available in **university dorms** during the summer vacation – cheap hotels for younger travellers, with single and double rooms ranging from $25 right up to $75, and good facilities including gyms and swimming pools.

If you're planning to stay in a hostel, it's always a good idea to **bring your passport**, even if you're American: many places will insist on seeing it before renting you a bed. This is intended to preserve the hostels for travellers; ie to keep out local homeless people. For similar reasons, many hostels also impose a nominal maximum stay of three to five days, though this is generally enforced only when demand for beds exceeds the available supply.

San Francisco

Grand Central Hostel 1412 Market St at Polk ☎703-9988. Very basic rooms with laundry facilities and gym near Civic Center. ②–③.

A Green Tortoise Guest House 494 Broadway at Kearny ☎834-1000. Funky Chinatown hostel with complimentary breakfast. From $19 per night single, $29 double, dorm $10. ①.

HI-San Francisco at Union Square 312 Mason St at O'Farrell ☎788-5604. Large new downtown hostel with dorm beds for $13 a night. No curfew. HI members only; day memberships cost $3.

HI-San Francisco International Building 240, Fort Mason ☎771-7277. On the waterfront between the Golden Gate Bridge and Fisherman's Wharf. One of the most comfortable and convenient hostels around. No curfew. 150 beds, free parking. $13 per person and no day membership necessary because it's built on federal land. ①.

Interclub/Globe Hostel 10 Hallam Place. Between Seventh & Eighth off Folsom ☎431-0540. Lively, recently redecorated South-of-Market hostel with no curfew. $15 per person, per night; doubles $25.

San Francisco International Guest House 2976 23rd St at Douglass ☎641-1411. Very popular with European travellers. Four-to-a-room dorms in the Mission, plus a few private rooms. $14 per person, five-day minimum stay, after which price goes down to $11. No curfew. ①.

YMCA Central Branch 220 Golden Gate Ave ☎885-0460. Well equipped and centrally located, two blocks from the Civic Center. Singles $28, doubles $38, price includes a free continental breakfast and use of the gym, swimming pool, squash courts and sauna. ①–②.

East Bay

Berkeley YMCA 2001 Allston Way, Berkeley ☎510/848-6800. Ideal East Bay mixed-sex accommodation a block from the Berkeley *BART*, with single rooms for $25, including use of gym and swimming pool. ①.

Haste-Channing Summer Visitor Housing 2424 Channing Ave, Berkeley ☎510/642-5925. Summer-only dorm rooms. ③.

The Peninsula

HI-Hidden Villa 26807 Moody Rd, Los Altos Hills ☎408/941-6407. Located on an 1800-acre ranch in the hills above the Silicon Valley. Closed in summer, and hard to reach without a car. Prices at $13 a night per person. ①

HI-Pigeon Point Lighthouse Hwy-1, just south of Pescadero ☎879-0633. Worth planning a trip around, this beautifully sited hostel, fifty miles south of San Francisco, is ideally placed for exploring the redwood forests in the hills above or for watching the wildlife in nearby Año Nuevo State Reserve. Outdoor hot tub. Office hours 7.30–9.30am and 4.30–9.30pm; doors locked at 11pm. Members $9–11 per night, non-members $12–14; reservations essential in summer. Private rooms $30 a night.

HI-Point Montara Lighthouse 16th St/Hwy-1, Montara ☎728-7177. Dorm rooms in a converted 1875 lighthouse, 25 miles south of San Francisco and accessible by bike or *SamTrans* bus (#1L or #1C; service operates until 5.50pm Mon–Fri, 6.15pm Sat). Outdoor hot tub. Office hours 7.30–9.30am & 4.30–9.30pm; doors locked 11pm. Members $11 per night, non-members $14; reservations essential in summer. ①.

Sanborn Park Hostel 15808 Sanborne Rd, Saratoga ☎741-0166. Comfortable rooms in a wooded area fifteen minutes outside San Jose. $7.50 members, $9.50 non-members. ①.

The Año Nuevo State reserve is described on p.175.

...DICT SCHOOL
DUFFIELD ROAD
DERBY DE22 1JD

Accommodation

Marin County

HI-Marin Headlands Building 941, Fort Barry, Marin Headlands ☎331-2777. Hard to get to without a car – it's near Rodeo Lagoon, five miles west of Sausalito – this cosy old army barracks has dorm beds for $11 a night. Office hours 7.30–9.30am & 4.30–11pm; doors locked at 11pm. ①.

HI-Point Reyes In the Point Reyes National Seashore ☎663-8811. An ideal stop on a cycling tour of Marin, surrounded by meadows and forests and just two miles from the beach. Eight miles from the nearest bus stop. Office hours 7.30–9.30am & 4.30–9.30pm; doors locked 11pm. Dorm beds in an old ranch house cost $16 per night. ①.

Chapter 13

Restaurants

It is no exaggeration to say that in San Francisco you can eat whatever you want, whenever you want. Culinary standards are amongst the highest in the world and not especially expensive. In the city, eating is *the* culture and every budget will buy a wide range of excellent foods. Whether it's for basic daily sustenance or for a special social occasion, people who live in the city spend more per head on dining than the inhabitants of any other US city – an average of $2500 each per year. Swarms of tourists inflate these figures, but it's enough to support a mass of restaurants, sandwich shops and cafés that line every street. Fast food is available everywhere, but somewhat frowned upon; and also a little pointless when you consider the alternatives available.

Matters are further improved by the fact that California is one of the most agriculturally rich – and health-conscious – parts of the country. Locally grown fruits and vegetables, abundant fish and seafood and top-quality meat and dairy produce all find their way into San Francisco kitchens. All you need to do is enjoy it. Lighting up after a fine meal, however, could prove difficult. In 1995, ttate law decreed that there is to be **No Smoking** in any restaurant – a punitive piece of legislation that will soon extend to bars and all public places.

Breakfast

For a good-value and filling breakfast including several eggs, bacon, sausage, pancakes, toast, juice, hash browns, etc – costing around $4–8 – head to a **diner** or, slightly smarter, a **café** or **coffee shop**, all of which serve breakfast until at least 11am (though diners sometimes offer it all day).

Thanks to Californians' love of light food, most restaurants offer the option of **fruit** for breakfast – typically apple, banana, melon, orange, pineapple or strawberry, wonderfully styled and served on their own or with pancakes. The only drawback is that it tends to cost as much as a full-blown fry-up.

Lunch, Fast Food and Soft Drinks

Most San Francisco workers take their **lunch break** between noon and 2.30pm. During those hours, many of the city's restaurants offer low-cost, excellent value **set menus**. Chinese restaurants, for example, frequently have rice and noodles or dim sum for $4–6, and many Japanese restaurants provide an opportunity to eat sushi at much lower prices ($7–10) than usual. Mexican restaurants are exceptionally well priced all the time, and you can get a good-sized lunch in one for $4–5.

One obvious inexpensive option is **pizza**; count on paying $5–7 for a basic two-person pizza, though you can usually buy it by the slice to take out. Most pizza chains and many mid-price restaurants have **salad bars**, where you can help yourself for a couple of dollars.

Restaurants

If you're just looking for a **quick snack**, many **delis** do ready-cooked meals for $3–5, as well as a range of **sandwiches** that can be meals in themselves, filled with a custom-built combination of meat, cheese, seafood, pasta and salad. In addition, San Francisco has its own local chain of burger bars, *Hot n Hunky*, serving up top-quality, tasty burgers that are as substantial as the name implies.

Free Food and Brunch

Downtown bars are listed on p.248.

Some **bars**, particularly in downtown San Francisco, are used as much by diners as drinkers, who turn up in droves to fill up on the free **hors d'oeuvres** laid out between 5 and 7pm Monday to Friday – an attempt to nab the commuting classes before they head off to the suburbs. For the price of a drink, you can stuff yourself silly on nachos, seafood or pasta.

Brunch is another deal to look out for, served between 11am and 2pm, and especially on Sundays. For a set price ($12 and up) you get a light meal and a variety of complimentary cocktails or champagne – perfect for daytime boozing, though rarely great value for money, especially if you don't drink.

Restaurants

Even if it often seems swamped by more fashionable regional and ethnic cuisine, traditional **American cooking** can be found all over the Bay Area.

California Cuisine in particular, geared towards health and aesthetics, is raved about by foodies – and rightly so, especially in Berkeley, its acknowledged birthplace and a not-to-be-missed gourmet ghetto. Basically a development of French *nouvelle cuisine*, utilizing the wide mix of fresh, locally available ingredients, California Cuisine is based on physiological efficiency – eating only what you need to and what your body can process. Vegetables are harvested just before maturity and steamed to preserve a high concentration of vitamins, a strong flavour, and to look better on the plate; seafood comes from oyster farms and the catches of small-time fishermen; and what little meat there is tends to be from animals reared on organic farms. The result is small but beautifully presented portions, and high, high prices – not unusually $50 a head for a full dinner with wine. The minimum you'll need for a sample is $15, which should buy a substantial portion. To whet your appetite, starters include such dishes as mussels in jalapeno and sesame vinaigrette, snails in puff pastry with mushroom puree, and, among main courses, roasted goat's cheese salad with walnuts, swordfish with herb butter, and tuna with cactus ratatouille. San Franciscan chefs being the innovators that they are, the latest craze is for **combining styles** – Chinese/French for example – and it is becoming very difficult to categorize restaurants ethnically. Rather than stay rooted in one tradi-

Mexican Food – A Primer for Foreign Travellers

San Francisco's Mexican food – found all over the city, but especially in the Mission district – is different from that available in Mexico. Here, more use is made of fresh vegetables and fruit, but the essentials are the same. Salsa, a spicy (sometimes very spicy) tomato, onion and cilantro sauce, is the key ingredient, backed by lots of rice and pinto beans, often served refried (boiled, mashed and fried in lard), with a **tortilla** – a thin maize dough pancake that is served in several ways. You can eat it as an accompaniment to your main dish; soft and wrapped around the food – a **burrito**; folded, fried and filled – a **taco**; filled, rolled and baked in a sauce – an **enchilada**; or baked flat and covered with a stack of food, known as a **tostada**. Another, less stodgy, option is the **chile relleno**, a green pepper stuffed with cheese, dipped in egg batter and fried. **El Salvadorian** and **Peruvian** food is often available in Mexican restaurants, with the emphasis on seafood, as in the delicious Peruvian dish *ceviche*, which consists of chunks of fish in a lime juice, onion and coriander marinade.

tion, most chefs utilize the myriad variety of talent and produce available in the Bay Area, creating something peculiarly San Franciscan.

Mexican food is so common it often seems like (and historically is) an indigenous cuisine. Certainly, in the Mission district you can't go more than a couple of doorways without encountering another Mexican restaurant. What's more, day or night, it's the least expensive type of food to eat; even a full dinner with a few drinks rarely costs over $10 anywhere, except in the most upmarket establishment.

Other ethnic cuisines are plentiful, too. **Chinese** food is everywhere, and can often cost as little as Mexican; **Japanese** is more expensive and more trendy, sushi being worshipped by some Californians. **Italian** food is popular everywhere, above all in **North Beach**, but can be expensive once you leave the simple pastas and explore exotic pizza toppings or specialist regional cuisine. **French** food, too, is widely available, though always pricey – the cuisine of social climbers and power-lunchers. **Thai**, **Korean** and **Indonesian** food is similarly in vogue, though usually cheaper. **Indian** restaurants, on the other hand, are thin on the ground and often very expensive – although, as Indian cooking catches on, the situation is gradually changing for the better, with a sprinkling of moderately priced outlets, particularly in West Berkeley.

Not surprisingly, health-conscious San Francisco also has a wide range of **vegetarian** and **wholefood** restaurants, and it's rare to find a menu anywhere that doesn't have at least several meat-free items on the menu.

In addition to great tastes, the Bay Area restaurants outside San Francisco during the week cater more to the locals and less to tourists. Therefore exploring the many eateries will provide an authentic taste of neighbourhood foods, the breakfast/brunch-oriented cafés and diners are full of character, though they rarely take reservations and do command a line of anxiously hungry customers awaiting seats.

Tipping: Guidance for Foreign Travellers

Service in San Francisco's restaurants is always enthusiastic and excellent, mainly due to the system of **tipping**, on which the jovial staff ("Hi! I'm Randy, and I'm your waitperson for this evening") depend for the bulk of their earnings. You should always top up the bill by 15–20 percent; not to tip at all is frowned upon. Many (not all) restaurants accept **payment** in the form of credit/charge cards; if you use one, a space will be left to fill in the appropriate tip.

Finally, remember also that the vineyards of the Napa and Sonoma valleys are on the city's doorstep and produce prize-fighting grapes that are good – and cheap – enough to make European wine growers nervous. Quality **wine** is a high-profile and standard feature of most San Franciscan restaurants.

In the listings that follow, the restaurants are arranged by neighbourhood and thereafter by ethnic type. Use the keys on the district maps for quick reference.

Downtown

American

Aqua 253 California St at Battery ☎956-9662. Gorgeously decorated, mainly seafood restaurant that pulls in a discerning Financial District crowd.

Bentley's Seafood and Grill 185 Sutter St at Kearny ☎989-6895. Classic San Francisco oyster bar and brasserie serving great seafood dishes to the accompaniment of live jazz at weekends.

Biscuit and Blues 401 Mason St at Geary ☎292-2583. Sounds too good to be true, but you can eat great Creole food for around $10 a head and listen to live blues.

Bix 56 Gold St off Montgomery near Jackson Square ☎433-6300. Jackson Square restaurant kitted out like a majestic ocean liner, with torch singer, sax player

Restaurants

and pianist – even if the food was rubbish you'd be enchanted with the place. Actually, the food is great – straightforward, classic dishes. Not surprisingly, a hot spot, where you'd be well advised to reserve in advance. Dinner for two should probably set you back around $80 with drinks, but if you're into elegant dining experiences you should definitely go.

Blondie's 63 Powell St at Ellis ☎282-6168. Union Square hole-in-the-wall, usually packed out; they do well-topped pizzas for $2 a slice.

David's Delicatessen 474 Geary St at Taylor ☎771-1600. Kosher food in giant portions. Eat until you expire for around $10.

The Dining Room *Ritz Carlton Hotel,* 600 Stockton St at California ☎296-7465. The hotel's signature restaurant, run by celebrity chef Gary Danko, this is the perfect place for a special occasion. You'll be lucky to escape for under $80 a head with wine, but sometimes such extravagance is really worth it.

Fog City Diner 1300 Battery St between Greenwich and the Embarcadero ☎982-2000. Expensively done up to look like a top-class diner, this place errs on the pricey side, but provided you don't mind paying for your ambience, the food is pretty good.

Gabiano's One Ferry Plaza, nr Ferry Building, Embarcadero ☎391-8403. If it's

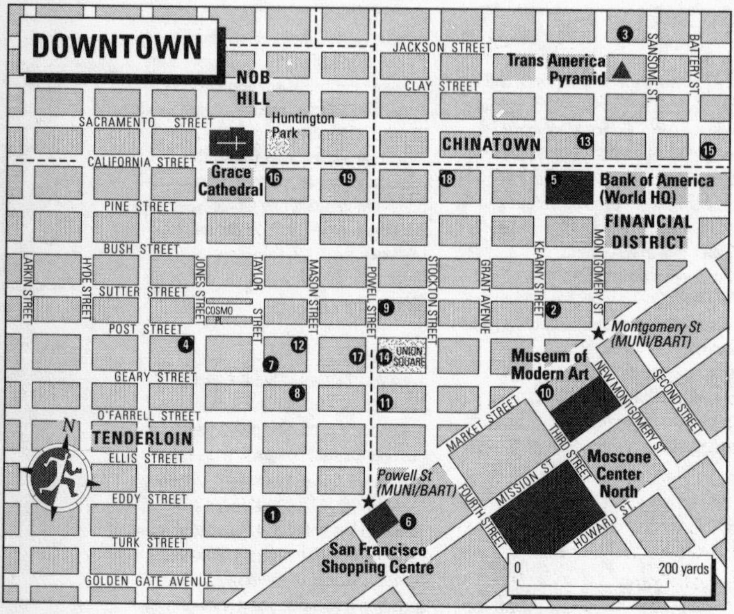

DOWNTOWN RESTAURANTS, BARS AND CAFÉS

1 181 Eddy
2 Bentley's Seafood & Grill
3 Bix
4 Borobudor
5 Carnalian Room
6 Champagne Exchange
7 David's Delicatessen
8 Grand Cafe
9 Harry Denton's Starlight Roof
10 Kinoko
11 Kuleto's
12 Postrio
13 Rubicon
14 Scala's Bistro
15 Tadich's
16 The Big Four
17 The Compass Rose
18 The Dining Room
19 Top of the Mark

a lovely day and you fancy eating outside, it doesn't come much better than this huge, informal, Bayfront restaurant doing excellent standard American items. Classic champagne Sunday brunch.

Gordon Biersch 2 Harrison St at the Embarcadero ☎243-8246. Excellent micro-brewery serving moderately priced, good food in huge Bayfront site. Very popular with the fashionable twenty–thirtysomethings.

Harry Denton's Bar & Grill 161 Steuart St at Howard ☎882-1333. Lively saloon atmosphere with a great bar for cocktails or sit down to hearty brasserie-style cuisine.

John's Grill 63 Ellis St at Powell ☎986-0069. Straight out of the *Maltese Falcon*, the menu at this steak and seafood place hasn't changed since Dashiell Hammett was a regular. The prices have, but it's still reasonable, especially for lunch.

Maye's Original Oyster House 1233 Polk St ☎474-7674. In business since the 1860s, this is one of the city's oldest restaurants, turning out reasonably priced, well-cooked fish dishes. Oysters by the half-dozen with a beer at the bar for the budget-conscious or less hungry.

One Market One Market at Steuart ☎777-5577. New hot spot serving trendy Midwestern cuisine in a huge, well-designed space.

Original Joe's 144 Taylor St at Eddy ☎775-4877. Inexpensive American/Italian restaurant, good for steaks, ribs, salads and the like.

Pine Crest 401 Geary St at Mason ☎885-6407. Every inch the greasy diner, but ideal for getting rid of your spare change and hunger at the same time.

Planet Hollywood 2 Stockton St at Market ☎421-7827. Should standing in a queue for hours to get in and eat burgers on the off chance of seeing a celebrity appeal, go no further than this latest in the Arnie, Bruce and Sly chain emporium.

Sam's Grill 374 Bush St at Kearny ☎421-0594. Moderately pricey seafood place, popular with Financial District types.

Scott's Seafood 3 Embarcadero Center ☎981-0622. Very good, very fresh oysters and other seafood dishes. Adjacent to the *Hyatt Regency*.

Tadich's 240 California St at Battery ☎391-2373. The oldest restaurant in California, wood panelling, and very much a San Francisco institution. Grilled fresh seafood and excellent desserts.

Tina's Restaurant 83 Eddy St at Mason ☎982-3451. Open from 6am weekdays for budget breakfasts.

California Cuisine

Grand Café 501 Geary St at Jones ☎292-0101. European dishes with a Californian twist served in a converted turn-of-the-century ballroom next door to the stylish *Hotel Monaco*. The food is superb but the Art Nouveau decor is even better. Best of all, eating here won't break the bank. Highly recommended.

Postrio 545 Post St at Mason ☎776-7825. Everybody's favourite top-notch San Francisco restaurant – come for breakfast if you can't score a dinner reservation – thanks to the high-style ambience and five-star reputation of chef Wolfgang Puck serving up Californian dishes with Asian and Mediterranean influences.

Rubicon 558 Sacramento St at Montgomery ☎434-4100. Smart new celebrity-owned (Robert de Niro, Robin Williams, Francis Ford Coppola) joint taking advantage of bountiful local produce and serving inventive, whole-some, Northern Californian cuisine.

Scala's Bistro 432 Powell St at Post ☎395-8555. Fresh, seasonal Californian foods served in old-world-style café. Comfortable, informal and good value.

Splendido 4 Embarcadero Center at Battery (third level) ☎986-3222. Brash and lively Euro-Californian restaurant with fine bay views. A huge menu of Mediterranean specialties, plus wood-oven pizzas.

Vertigo 600 Montgomery St at Washington ☎433-7520. The food is Italian/French/Asian (very Californian) and the service is uppity. Built in the base of the Transamerica Pyramid, the interior of

Afternoon Teas

One of the nicest ways to finish an afternoon of intense consuming in the downtown stores is to partake in the latest SF social custom – **afternoon tea** in one of the plush Union Square hotels. In true California style, the food is exquisite and you'll be offered the gamut from cucumber and watercress sandwiches to fresh fruit sorbets and scones with cream.

Four Seasons Clift Hotel 495 Geary St ☎775-4700. A good post-matinee venue in the Theater District. Daily 3–5pm.

Garden Court In the *Sheraton Palace*, 2 New Montgomery St at Market ☎392-8600. The best thing about the recent renovation of this landmark hotel was the restoration of its exquisite lobby, where you can sip fine teas while enjoying the soothing live harp music. Make reservations, it fills up. Tues–Sat 2–4.30pm.

King George Hotel 334 Mason St ☎781-5050. A Laura Ashley nightmare, where customers nibble at finger sandwiches in mock-British cottage surroundings. Only for Anglophiles and homesick Brits. Mon–Sat 3–6.30pm.

Mark Hopkins 999 California St ☎392-3434. Standard high teas served on lovely Wedgwood china. Daily 2.30–5pm.

Neiman Marcus 150 Stockton St ☎362-3900. A personal favourite; tea is served in the glorious *Rotunda* restaurant at the top of the store. Watch the rich, social x-rays nibble fearfully at the calorie-laden food. Daily 2.30–5pm.

Ritz Carlton 600 Stockton St ☎296-7465. The fanciest of them all, this is the place to slurp tea to the accompaniment of a tinkling harp.

the restaurant is more exciting than the expensive grub. Good place to spy smug Financial District types from the safe distance of the bar, where they make excellent drinks.

French

Boulevard 1 Mission St at Steuart ☎543-6084. When you want great French food without the attitude, look no further than this beautifully decorated new brasserie-style restaurant that currently has a waiting list for tables in the happening Embarcadero district. Book in advance. Not cheap, but worth every cent.

Café Claude 7 Claude Lane (between Grant and Kearny) ☎981-5565. More than any of the other imitations in town, this one feels like being in Paris with its great old furnishings. Go in the evening and find a young, loose crowd listening to jazz and getting dinner for around $20 a head.

Ernie's 847 Montgomery St ☎397-5969. Downtown favourite that's far from inexpensive, but has a *haute cuisine* menu and a lovely Victorian interior, made famous by its role in Hitchcock's *Vertigo*. Dinner for two costs around $100, but the $15 prix-fixe, three-course lunches are the city's best budget gourmet treat.

Masa's *Vintage Court Hotel*, 648 Bush St at Powell ☎989-7154. Rated as one of the best French restaurants in the US, *Masa's* serves state-of-the-art French cuisine, for which you will have to pay top-dollar. Worth it if you feel like splashing out.

Splendido 4 Embarcadero Center at Battery (third level) ☎986-3222. A typical San Francisco hybrid, *Splendido* offers French-cum-Italian cuisine with Californian influences (ie a healthy paucity of butter and cream used in the dishes). One for the calorie-counting connoisseur.

Italian

Emporio Armani Express One Grant Ave at O'Farrell ☎677-9010. You can either eat a full-blown meal in the restaurant upstairs or stand at the bar downstairs for *antipasti*, pizza and sandwiches while you consider the clothing that surrounds.

Restaurants

Kuleto's 221 Powell St at O'Farrell ☎397-7720. Very popular with the pre-theatre crowds, this upmarket Italianate bar and restaurant is a feast for the eyes as well as the mouth. Decor focuses on a 100-year-old hardwood bar, originally from the landmark *Palace Hotel*; the food, especially the pastas and fresh bread, is very good.

Chinese and Korean

China Moon Café 639 Post St at Taylor ☎775-4789. Standard Cantonese food, although the restaurant is particularly notable for its excellent budget dim sum lunches.

Harbor Village 4 Embarcadero Center at Battery ☎781-8833. Downtown's best dim sum, especially popular for Sunday lunch, with standard Cantonese dishes for dinner.

Tommy Toy's Cuisine Chinoise 655 Montgomery St at Columbus ☎397-4888. Without rival the most elegant Chinese restaurant in San Francisco. Exotic variations on Cantonese favourites, prepared with a *nouvelle cuisine* emphasis on ultra- fresh ingredients and served in a spacious candlelit room, make for an enchanting dining experience. Power chow mein.

Wu Kong Restaurant 1 Rincon Center, 101 Spear St ☎957-9300. Popular with workers from the Financial District, the excellent Shanghai food here commands some pretty steep prices, but if you just nip in for dim sum you shouldn't be left penniless.

Yank Sing 427 Battery St at Washington ☎362-1640. Join the Financial District workers again as they lunch on dim sum in the fanciest of surroundings.

South East Asian

Borobudor 700 Post St at Jones ☎775-1512. A little pocket of authentic Indonesia just a couple of blocks from Union Square. Eat early if you want to avoid the karaoke.

Thai Stick 698 Post Street at Jones ☎928-7730. Popular downtown Thai hang-out that offers a wide selection of vegetarian dishes and promises that everything is made without MSG.

Japanese

Kinoko San Francisco Marriot, 55 Fourth St at Market ☎896-1600. Fine dining, delicate food and authentic touches like tableside *teppanyaki* cooking. Moderate to pricey.

Vegetarian Restaurants

Amazing Grace 216 Church St at Market ☎626-6411. Rated highly by local vegetarians, with a standard menu starting at around $5 a dish.

Green's Building A, Fort Mason Center, Fort Mason ☎771-6222. A converted army supply warehouse that's now San Francisco's only Zen Buddhist restaurant, serving unusual and delicious macrobiotic and vegetarian food to an eager clientele. Always busy, despite average cost of $40 per head.

Millennium 246 McAllister St at Larkin ☎487-9800. You'd swear it couldn't be done, but this restaurant has managed to make delicious meals for vegans – sugar-, dairy-, cholesterol- and everything else you can think of-free. Stylish un-vegetarian decor. Meat-eaters, go and be amazed.

Milly's 1613 Fourth St, San Rafael ☎459-1601. Healthy, wide-ranging vegetarian dishes such as Thai vegetable curries and jalapeno ravioli. Open evenings only.

Now and Zen 1826 Buchanan St at Sutter ☎922-9696. Cosy vegan restaurant in Japantown that serves excellent food, but steer clear of the organic wine.

Real Good Karma 501 Dolores St at 18th ☎621-4112. Hearty and nutritious portions of vegetarian and wholefood dishes in informal surroundings.

Val 21 995 Valencia St at 21st ☎821-6622. Vegetarian and wholefood finally becomes trendy in this modern Mission hot spot. New York atmosphere with high ceilings and an avant-garde crowd.

Sushi Boat Restaurant 389 Geary Blvd ☎781-5111. Perfect for those who love a gimmick, this place will make your sushi and then float it over to you on a little boat. Hours of fun for the kids if you can find any that eat sushi.

Indian

Maharani 1122 Post St at Van Ness ☎775-1988. Doesn't look like much from the outside, but the interior is fab and the food first-rate.

North Beach and the Northern Waterfront

American

Clown Alley 42 Columbus Ave at Jackson ☎421-2540. Down-at-heel, with a dodgy clientele, but it does serve huge breakfasts and bargain burgers. Open till 3am at weekends.

Hard Rock Café 1699 Van Ness Ave at Clay ☎885-1699. Standard *Hard Rock* clone. Loud music, rock 'n' roll decor and attracting the sort of crowd who don't mind waiting in line for hours for the above-average burgers.

International House of Pancakes 2299 Lombard St at Pierce ☎921-4004. Open 24 hours every day, for famous pancakes smothered with every conceivable topping.

Johnny Love's 1500 Broadway at Polk ☎931-6053. Mainly a singles bar, this raunchy joint also has a large eating area where the food is probably too good to be wasted on the lurching drunks therein. If you like to have your dinner accompanied with booming rock music, look no further.

Johnny Rockets 2201 Chestnut St at Pierce ☎931-6258. Fifties-style diner with juicy burgers and shakes thick enough to constitute a meal in themselves. Open till 3am Fridays and Saturdays.

Liverpool Lil's 2942 Lyon St at Washington ☎921-6664. Modelled on an English pub, except that by serving great cocktails and good food, it lacks the authenticity anyone familiar with real British pubs might expect. Opposite the Presidio gates, and a good place to collapse with a martini after an afternoon's walking.

Lou's Pier 47 300 Jefferson St at Taylor ☎771-0377. Incongruously placed among the pricey seafood joints on the Wharf. Not just one of the best places to hear live r'n'b in the city, it also serves fresh, inexpensive seafood. A must for dinner, a few beers and great music.

Mel's Drive-In 2165 Lombard St at Fillmore ☎921-3039. Straight out of *American Graffiti*, with burgers, fries milkshakes and a lot of rock 'n' roll on the jukebox. No longer a drive-in, but open late – after midnight every night, till 3am at weekends.

Moose's 1652 Stockton St at Filbert ☎989-7800. Run by the former proprietors of the *Washington Square Bar and Grill*, who have taken many of their old clients and become the latest word in power-lunching for the media-politico crowd. Headphone-clad chefs (another gimmick) cook great food from the open kitchen.

Le Petit Café 2164 Larkin St at Vallejo ☎776-5356. Small and friendly Russian Hill neighbourhood bistro famed for its good-value, housemade pastas – and sumptuous Sunday brunch.

Plump Jack 3127 Fillmore St at Filbert ☎563-4755. Good American grill-type food and great drinks, but the main reason to come here is to watch the sleek Pacific Heights matrons eyeing up the wealthy youngsters from the Marina.

24-Hour Eating

Bagdad Café 2295 Market St ☎621-4434

International House of Pancakes 2299 Lombard St ☎921-4004

Lori's Diner 336 Mason St ☎392-8646

Orphan Andy's 3991 17th St ☎864-9795

Pine Crest 401 Geary Blvd at Mason ☎885-6407

Sparky's Diner 242 Church St ☎621-6001

Rendezvous Café 1760 Polk St at Washington ☎441-CAFE. The perfect spot just to sit, eat and read the paper. Classic diner serving breakfast, lunch and dinner. Modern food at old-fashioned prices.

Washington Square Bar and Grill 1707 Powell St at Union ☎982-8123. It may have lost a little of its cachet since the owners sold it and opened *Moose's* across the square (see above), but this is still the place to slip down smart cocktails at the bar and sample the food, cooked to rich and heavy perfection. If you want to catch the corner of San Francisco society that still smokes and drinks, this is your scene.

California Cuisine

Crustacean Top of Chelsea Square, California and Polk streets ☎776-CRAB. Californian seafood with an Asian twist. Very interesting, innovative dishes, even if it's not what you could call a bargain feed.

Cypress Club 500 Jackson St at Columbus ☎296-8555. Jackson Square hot spot famed for its delicately presented, inventive California Cuisine, served up in one of the most stylish dining rooms to be found in San Francisco – a cross between the *Ritz Carlton* and a Bedouin tent.

French

Julius' Castle 1541 Montgomery St at Telegraph Hill ☎392-2222. A San Francisco institution for lovers or just lovers of the romantic, this Telegraph Hill restaurant serves pretty pricey, if delicious food, but hopefully the incredible view of the bay will keep your mind off the bill.

Restaurants

North Beach Restaurants, Bars and Cafés

1 Allegro Ristorante Italiano
2 Bix
3 Bohemian Cigar Store
4 Brandy Ho's
5 Café Trieste
6 Calzone's
7 Capp's Corner
8 Cypress Club
9 Enrico's Sidewalk Café
10 Fior d'Italia
11 Gold Spike
12 Golden Boy
13 Il Pollaio
14 Little Joe's
15 Moose's
16 North Beach Pizza
17 North Beach Restaurant
18 Ristorante Firenze
19 The Saloon
20 San Francisco Brewing Co
21 Savoy Tivoli
22 Sodini's
23 Steps Of Rome Café
24 The Stinking Rose
25 Tosca Café
26 Vesuvio's
27 Washington Square Bar and Grill
28 Yuet Lee

Restaurants

Italian

Allegro Ristorante Italiano 1701 Jones St at Vallejo ☎928-4002. Russian Hill hangout popular with those in the know. If you want to join such enlightened company, perhaps you won't mind paying for it.

Café Pescatore 2455 Mason at North Point ☎561-1111. Trattoria with an open kitchen serving up very good, housemade pastas and wood-fired pizzas.

Calzone's 430 Columbus Ave at Broadway ☎397-3600. Busy bar and restaurant right at the heart of North Beach, serving lush pizzas and calzones.

Capp's Corner 1600 Powell St at Union ☎989-2589. Funky, family-style restaurant, where fashionable clients line up for the big portions.

Fior d'Italia 601 Union St at Powell ☎986-1886. This is the place to go when you're fed up with fancy new-age Italian cooking and posturing and just want the real thing. Great old-timers' scene going on at the bar.

Il Fornaio 1265 Battery St at Filbert ☎986-0100. Very popular Italian restaurant with sunny terrace, just a block from the waterfront on Levi Strauss Plaza.

Frascati 1901 Hyde St at Green ☎928-1406. Attractive Russian Hill venue for delicious pastas and seafood.

Gold Spike 527 Columbus Ave at Vallejo ☎986-9747. More like a museum than a restaurant, with enough photographs, moose heads and war souvenirs to keep you occupied during what can be a long wait for the excellent-value $15 six-course dinner.

Golden Boy 542 Green St at Columbus ☎982-9738. Good venue to sample exotic pizza by the slice. Mix-n-match your flavours.**Little Joe's** 523 Broadway at Montgomery ☎433-4343. "Rain or shine, there's always a line . . .", but the inexpensive, enormous portions of well-cooked food in this North Beach institution are well worth waiting for.

North Beach Pizza 1499 Grant Ave at Union ☎433-2444. Good location in the middle of one of the best bar-hopping areas in the city. Tasty and low priced, it's just the ticket for a drink-induced munchie.

North Beach Restaurant 1512 Stockton St at Green ☎392-1587. Extensive, moderately priced menu, plus great cocktails.

Il Pollaio 555 Columbus Ave at Green ☎362-7727. You'd be hard pushed to spend more than $15 for a blow-out meal in this postage stamp restaurant, where the sheer value for money of the food on offer more than makes up for the lack of elbow room.

Ristorante Firenze 1421 Stockton St ☎421-5813. Modern decor, traditional food, quick service – always an attractive combination.

Sodini's 510 Green St ☎788-9384. Good, hearty meals in a basic but busy place full of locals. Eat till you drop for around $12.

The Stinking Rose 325 Columbus Ave at Broadway ☎781-7673. Subtitled "A Garlic Restaurant", and they're not kidding: everything they serve is steeped in garlic.

Chinese and Korean

Brandy Ho's Original Hunan 217 Columbus Ave at Jackson ☎788-7527. Excellent, long-established Hunan restaurant. There's another, new branch at 450 Broadway.

Celadon 881 Clay St at Stockton ☎982-1168. One of the fancier Cantonese restaurants in town. Not exactly bargain-basement food, but worth shelling out for the beautifully presented, fragrant dishes.

Empress of China 838 Grant Ave at Clay ☎434-1345. Without doubt, the poshest place in town to get to grips with Chinese cooking, with an incredible selection of dishes and amazing views over neighbouring North Beach. You'll be lucky to pay less than $20 for a main course, but if you're in the mood for a blow-out it's quite the place to be decadent.

The Mandarin Ghirardelli Square, Beach St between Polk and Larkin ☎673-8812. Stylish conversion of industrial space stuffed with Oriental antiques. The

Chinese food is excellent but pricey – ideal for a special night out.

New Asia 722 Pacific Ave at Grant ☎391-6666. Considering Chinatown is so pressed for space, it's amazing that a place this big survives. It serves some of the most authentic dim sum in town, with waitresses pushing carts down the aisles, shouting out their wares as they pass.

The Pot Sticker 150 Waverly Place off Clay St between Stockton and Grant ☎397-9985. Extensive menu offering Szechwan and Hunan dishes in this inexpensive and often crowded Chinatown favourite.

Sam Woh's 813 Washington St at Grant ☎982-0596. Your basic late-night (until 3am) restaurant still attracts the North Beach crowds when the bars turn out. You have to climb dodgy old steps through the kitchen to reach the eating area.

Yuet Lee 1300 Stockton St at Broadway ☎982-6020. Cheap and cheerful Chinese restaurant with a good seafood menu and enthusiastic crowds of diners. Beer only, but you can bring your own wine.

South East Asian

The Golden Turtle 2211 Van Ness Ave at Vallejo ☎441-4419. Upscale Vietnamese restaurant selling delicious, well-priced dishes.

Japanese

Osome 1923 Fillmore St at California ☎346-2311. Smart, popular restaurant which is renowned for its highly rated sushi and seafood.

Indian

Gaylord Ghirardelli Square, 900 North Point at Larkin ☎771-8822. One of the very few Indian restaurants in San Francisco and probably the best, though you should expect to pay around $20 for a main course. Still, it's worth it if you're dying for a curry.

Middle Eastern and Greek

Helmand 430 Broadway at Montgomery ☎362-0641. Excellent, inexpensive Afghani food. Exotic, unique and very popular.

Maraketch 419 O'Farrell St at Taylor ☎776-7617. Aromatic Moroccan cuisine and belly dancers to entertain you while you pile it in.

Pasha's 1516 Broadway at Polk ☎885-4477. An extraordinary dining experience. Moroccan and Middle Eastern dishes served while you sit on the floor watching belly dancers gyrate past your table, proffering their cleavage for you to insert dollar bills. Go with a group of rowdy drunks, or not at all.

Civic Center, SoMa and the Mission

American

Brain Wash Laundromat/Café 1122 Folsom St at Seventh ☎861-3663. If you don't mind watching people pile their dirties into the machines, this is a surprisingly good venue for well-prepared, simple sandwiches, pizzas and salad. A boisterous SoMa hangout, providing a good opportunity to check out the locals.

The Connecticut Yankee 100 Connecticut St at 19th ☎552-4440. Pricey Potrero Hill restaurant, serving great weekend brunches accompanied by generous cocktails.

Fringale 570 Fourth St at Brannan ☎543-0573. Trendy but inexpensive bistro, open for lunch and dinner Mon–Fri.

The Grubstake 1525 Pine St at Van Ness ☎673-8268. Converted 1920s railroad dining car, with some of the city's best late-night burgers.

Hamburger Mary's 1582 Folsom St at 12th ☎626-1985. Boisterous South-of-Market burger bar, with funky waiting staff and good range of vegetarian options. Inexpensive, and open late for the club-going crowds.

Ivy's 398 Hayes St at Gough ☎626-3930. Very popular Civic Center restaurant. A great spot for lunch, or for a late dinner after the opera-going crowds – who pack the place in the early evening – have moved on. Stylish but not expensive.

Restaurants

Julie's Supper Club 1123 Folsom St at Seventh ☎861-0707. The cuisine, both at the bar and in the back-room restaurant, defies definition and can only be described as eclectic. The decor, however, is straight out of a B-52s/Jetsons dream. Worth a look, especially if you can get there before 9pm and escape the $5 cover for the live jazz.

Mission Rock Resort 817 China Basin at Mission Rock ☎621-5538. Good bargain breakfasts and lunches, which you can eat on the Wharf when the weather's good. Great location overlooking the old shipyards.

Miss Pearl's Jam House 601 Eddy St at Polk ☎775-5267. The cooking may be Caribbean but the experience is definitely Californian. Run in conjunction with the *Phoenix* motel that shares the site, *Miss Pearl's* is full of muso types who come to look for their peers and enjoy the nightly

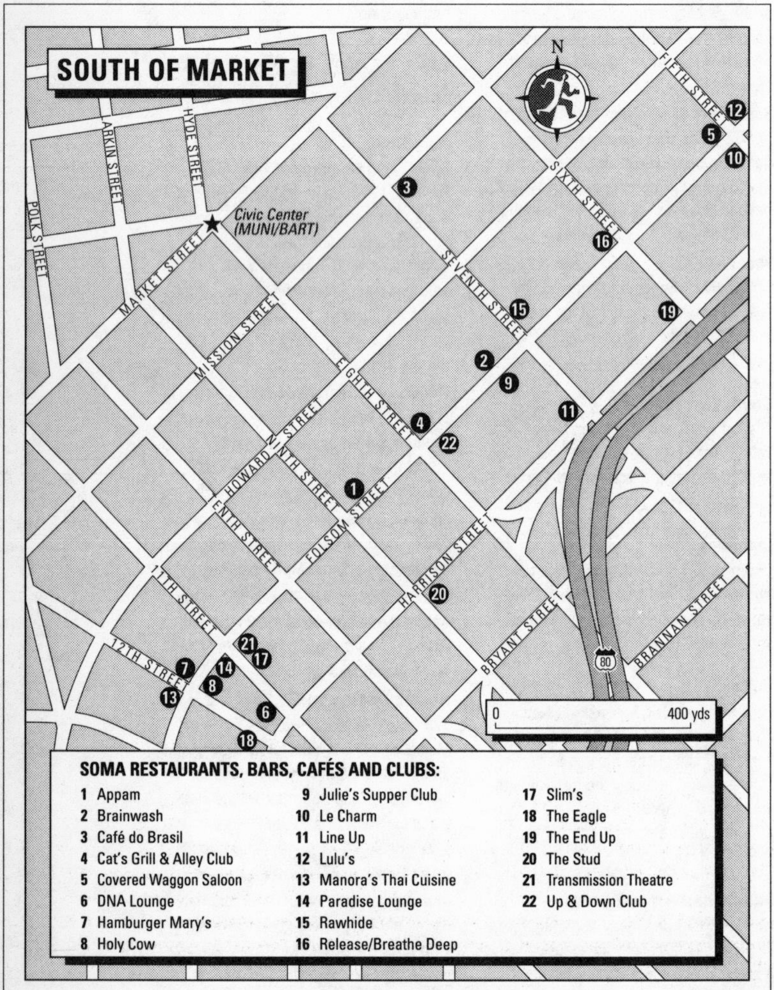

live reggae and down-home atmosphere. Seated at the tables surrounding the pool, you really feel as though you're having a resort holiday in the middle of town. The menu, particularly the fish dishes, is outstanding and not bank-breaking. Highly recommended.

Pauline's Pizza Pie 260 Valencia St at 14th ☎552-2050. Something of a truck stop as far as decor goes, but widely esteemed for serving inventive combinations, in big portions, at good prices.

Slow Club 2501 Mariposa St, Potrero Hill ☎241-9390. Good, reasonably priced imaginative cooking and a very artsy crowd who come to listen to the live jazz at this venerable SoMa hang-out.

Stars 555 Golden Gate Ave at Van Ness ☎861-7827. Trendy, usually well-cooked dishes served to the movers, shakers and socialites of San Francisco. Heavenly people-watching if you can afford the dinner, which errs on the steep side.

Swan's Oyster Depot 1517 Polk St at California ☎673-1101. You wouldn't know it by the simple decor, but this is one of the city's best and oldest seafood places – take a seat at the bar (there are no tables) for half a dozen fresh-shucked West Coast oysters, washed down with a glass of ice-cold *Anchor Steam* beer. Open 8.30am–5.30pm.

Up & Down Club 1151 Folsom St between Seventh and Eighth streets ☎626-2388. Better known for its excellent live jazz, the *Up & Down* also has a perfectly respectable bistro. More a place for light snacking than serious dining.

VAL21 995 Valencia at 21st St ☎821-6622. Trendy new spot, serving eclectic, seasonal dishes with the emphasis on vegetarian, chicken and fish.

Vicolo Pizzeria 201 Ivy St off Franklin ☎863-2382. Popular Civic Center spot with very good, moderately priced designer pizzas and salads.

California Cuisine

Flying Saucer 1000 Guerrero at 22nd ☎641-9955. Exquisitely put together, adventurous cuisine that mixes fruit with meat and every wacky combination you can think of. New Mission hot spot.

42 Degrees 235 16th Street at Third ☎777-5558. At the time of press this was the last word in San Franciscan dining for the fashionable without trust funds. Great location down on the old dockyards with a stark modern interior and well-made simple Californian cuisine. For the time being at least, it's a very cool place.

LuLu's 816 Folsom St at Fourth ☎495-5775. Established chic mastication, *LuLu's* has an international/Californian menu and visible chefs in open kitchens wearing headphones. Such obviously studied catering should not put you off the food, which is excellent.

Lulu Bis As above. Café wing of the restaurant, serving slightly cheaper, quicker food with prix fixe options.

Zuni Café 1658 Market St at Gough ☎552-2522. This has been the chic place to see and be seen for the last five years. Californian *nouvelle cuisine* for around $30 a head with a glass of wine.

French

Le Charm 315 Fifth St at Folsom ☎546-6128. This is more like it. Good unpretentious French food in this SoMa bistro where you can park. Ideally placed for the new museums and arts centres.

Flying Saucer 1000 Guerrero at 23rd ☎641-9955. Tiny Mission restaurant which has only six tables, takes no reservations and has caused a buzz in the culinary community for what is reputedly some of the best French cuisine in North America. How can they tell?

The Rooster 1101 Valencia St at 22nd ☎824-1222. Reasonably priced delicious country cooking, blending various global cuisines, most notably French with an Asian twist. Classic San Franciscan inventiveness.

South Park Café 108 South Park ☎495-7275. Chic SoMa gathering place for aficionados of all things French, especially pastries and good brandy.

Le Trou 1007 Guerrero St at 23rd ☎550-8169. A bit like *Le Charm*, this is another

reasonably priced, unpretentious site for well-cooked French food.

Italian

Mangiafuoco 1001 Guerrero Street at 23rd St ☎206-9881. Exquisite, simple, perfect.

Ristorante Ecco 101 South Park, between Second and Third, Bryant and Brannan ☎495-3291. Robust, imaginative modern cuisine served in this modern trattoria. Good place to look for smart people.

La Traviata 2854 Mission St ☎282-0500. Friendly, noisy and inexpensive Italian Mission restaurant.

Chinese and Korean

Cloisonne 601 Van Ness Ave at Golden Gate ☎441-2232. First-class Cantonese food, moderately priced and served in luxurious surroundings. Draws most of its business from the opera crowd, so it tends to be quite formal. You won't be refused if you turn up in jeans, but you might feel out of place.

Jing Wah 1634 Bush St at Franklin ☎922-5279. Highly rated Cantonese food, served at reasonable prices in very unpretentious surroundings right in the middle of Polk Gulch.

South East Asian

Bangkok 16 3214 16th St ☎431-5838. Moderately priced Thai restaurant down in the Mission, with a great selection for vegetarians. For meat eaters they do a mean lamb satay.

Manora's Thai Cuisine 1600 Folsom St at 12th ☎861-6224. Massively popular and you may have to wait, but it's worth it for the light, spicy and fragrant dishes at around $6–10 each.

Japanese

Moshi Moshi 2092 Third St ☎861-8285. Obscure SoMa restaurant full of people who pride themselves on finding such an out-of-the-way gem. Excellent Japanese, sushi and seafood, moderately priced.

Indian

Appam 1261 Folsom St at Ninth ☎626-2798. Great atmosphere, and the old Indian method of "Dum Pukht" cooking is employed. Dishes are prepared in large clay pots in an open kitchen where you can watch as nan breads and kulchas bake in the tandoori oven.

Scenic India 532 Valencia St at 16th ☎621-7226. Spartan Mission restaurant serving inexpensive food. Part of the new wave of Valencia Corridor restaurants that is doing so much for the area.

Sirtaj India Cuisine 48 Fifth St ☎957-0140. Quiet retreat from the madness of the surrounding SoMa area, this is a lovely place to stop for the bargain thirteen-course buffet lunch for only $6.99.

Zante's 3489 Mission ☎821-3949. This is a weird one, an Indian restaurant that serves pizza – surprisingly tasty.

Middle Eastern and Greek

Asimakopoulos Café 288 Connecticut St at Mariposa ☎552-8789. Upscale Greek cooking, although you get the feeling you're paying for the decor rather than the food.

Steve the Greek 1431 Polk St at California (No phone). Authentic Greek (including plastic tablecloths) and ultra-low-priced spot close to Civic Center.

Central and South American

Alejandro's Sociedad Gastronomica 2937 Mission St at 26th ☎826-8260. Tasty tapas and great South American seafood dishes, including SF's best paella, plus fairly standard Mexican food.

Border Café and Cantina 1198 Folsom St at Eighth ☎626-0414. Authentic Mexican lunches and dinners served in a lively, comfortable atmosphere.

Cadillac Bar 1 Holland Court off Howard St ☎543-8226. By the standards of most Mexican restaurants, this one is fairly upmarket, and offers live guitar music to help your burritos go down.

Café do Brasil 104 Seventh St at Mission ☎626-6432. Great Brazilian tapas and international cuisine.

El Farolito 2777 Mission St at 24th ☎826-4870. Late-night burritos served in a cafeteria atmosphere.

Las Guitarras 3200 24th St ☎285-2684. Noisy Mexican favoured by the locals. Don't expect a fine dining experience, but you can count on a good hearty dinner.

Line-Up 398 Seventh St at Harrison ☎861-2887. Most people come and queue for great takeouts, though if you don't mind overhead neon, you can eat in.

Mission Villa Restaurant 2391 Mission St at 20th ☎826-0454. Enormous burritos and tacos for about $3.

Mom's Cooking 1166 Geneva St ☎586-7000. Small and crowded on the fringes of the Mission district. You may have to wait for a table, but it's worth it for the super-inexpensive fresh Mexican food.

El Nuevo Frutilandia 3077 24th St ☎648-2958. Mission District Cuban/Puerto Rican restaurant.

La Taqueria 2889 Mission St at 25th ☎285-7117. Always busy with locals, which is as good a recommendation as any for its fairly standard Mexican menu. Service is slow, but the food is fresh and delicious.

El Toro 17th and Valencia Sts ☎431-3351. There are always crowds outside waiting for the massive burritos.

Central Neighbourhoods

American

Bagdad Café 2295 Market St at Noe ☎621-4434. Good, hearty breakfasts and burgers served 24 hours per day.

Café du Nord 2170 Market St at Church ☎861-5016. Recently revamped as an inexpensive supper club, this is great for entertainment while you eat the good, inexpensive dishes. On Wednesday evenings, *Ellington Supper Club* features jazz music.

Restaurants

Café Majestic *Majestic Hotel*, 1500 Sutter St at Gough ☎776-6400. Totally out of place in the Japantown neighbourhood, but nonetheless a lovely place for dinner. The full-on classical decor includes high ceiling and columns, and the food is exquisite.

Firefly 4288 24th Street ☎821-7652. Noe Valley restaurant with wide-ranging innovative menu and a knowing crowd. Very much a neighbourhood joint.

Hot n Hunky 4039 18th St at Castro ☎621-6365. As the name suggests, the burgers are on the large side, masses of red meat straining under their buns, in what is generally considered San Francisco's best burger joint. The atmosphere is negligible, but an average serving can feed a family of four.

Liberty Café 410 Cortland Ave ☎695-8777. Excellent food, beautifully prepared in this Bernal Heights favourite. Best of all, dinner for under $20.

Martin Mack's 1568 Haight St at Clayton ☎864-0134. Good, cheap food and excellent beers in this slightly self-conscious Irish "theme" pub.

Noe Valley Pizza 3898 24th St at Sanchez ☎647-1664. If you love garlic, this is your place – every pizza is loaded with it.

Oppenheimer 2050 Divisadero St at California ☎563-0444. Upscale delicatessen serving well-priced basic meals for the budget-conscious.

Orphan Andy's 3991 17th St at Castro ☎864-9795. Favourite Castro hang-out, serving burgers, omelettes and breakfast 24 hours a day.

Patio Café 531 Castro St at 18th ☎621-4640. Casual terrace restaurant, great for wholesome food – mostly grilled meats and pasta dishes as well as good-value weekend brunches where you can sling back inexpensive cocktails.

Spaghetti Western 576 Haight St at Fillmore ☎864-8461. Best breakfasts for miles and a lively Lower Haight crowd to look at while you chow down.

Sparky's Diner 242 Church St at Market ☎621-6001. 24-hour diner cooking up burgers, pastas and pizzas plus breakfasts, including a very good Eggs Florentine. Beer and wine too.

French

Ma Tante Sumi 4243 18th St at Douglass ☎552-6663. Interesting one this. French with a Japanese twist, producing innovative combinations. A popular Castro dining spot.

Italian

Vicolo Pizza 20 Ivy St off Franklin at Market ☎863-2382. You have probably never eaten pizza as good as this and are unlikely to want to have any other kind afterwards. Popular Hayes Valley venue.

Chinese and Korean

Eliza's 205 Oak St ☎621-4819 Not your average Chinese dive, this place is all stained glass and fresh flowers, serving excellent Chinese food to a knowing Hayes Valley crowd.

South East Asian

Thai House 151 Noe St at Henry ☎863-0374. Small neighbourhood restaurant selling a wide selection of fragrant, light Thai dishes.

Thai House Bar & Café 2200 Market St at 15th ☎864-5006. As above but with a larger, more informal space. Often a line, but it moves quickly.

Thep Phanom Restaurant 400 Waller St ☎431-2526. Simple, delicate decor and beautifully prepared Thai dishes make this Lower Haight restaurant seem more expensive than it really is. Expect to pay no more than $8 for main course dishes, but also expect to wait for a table.

Japanese

Isuzu 1581 Webster St at Japan Center ☎922-2290. Fashionable Japan Center restaurant with separate sushi and tempura bars. Rub shoulders with those in the know.

Mifune 1737 Post St at Webster ☎922-0337. Moderately priced Japanese specialities to take away.

Sanppo 1702 Post St at Webster ☎346-3486. Small, busy and unpretentious

Japantown restaurant – the decor might be negligible but the food is low-priced and first-rate.

Sushi Bar 1800 Divisadero at Bush. No phone. Bright, inexpensive and quick.

Yoshida Ya 2909 Webster St at California ☎346-3431. San Francisco has countless sushi bars, but not many where you can actually kick off your shoes and eat at low tables on futoned floors. This is just such a place; expect to pay around $25 per head for a good selection of sushi and a few drinks.

Yoyo Tsunami *Miyako Hotel*, 1625 Post St at Laguna ☎922-7788. Great Japanese food – a kind of Oriental tapas (not to be confused with sushi) – which has created a new challenge for the competition. Great value too. Six Tsunami dishes and beer for $21.

Central and South American

Cha Cha Cha 1805 Haight St at Shrader ☎386-5758. First-rate Caribbean/Cuban cuisine served in loud, brightly painted surroundings. Great place for swilling oversized margaritas. Open late and always packed.

Chabela's 1801 Haight St at Shrader ☎751-6204. Small restaurant with very fast service selling healthy Mexican burritos with tofu and the like.

Tacqueria Balazo 1654 Haight St. No phone. More eco-friendly burritos.

Zona Rosa 1797 Haight St at Shrader ☎668-7717. Much the same as above – additive-free burritos. Inexpensive and cheerful.

Golden Gate Park & Outlying Areas

American

The Boat House 1 Harding Park Ave on Lake Merced ☎681-2727. Great views turn this otherwise uninspiring, if honest sports bar into a great place to stop for lunch of burgers, nachos, potato skins and buffalo wings variety.

Louis' Restaurant 902 Point Lobos Ave ☎387-6330. 1940s-era diner serving great burgers and sandwiches. Overlooking *Sutro Baths*, with a marvellous sunset view. Open for breakfast till 7.30pm.

Mel's Drive-In 3355 Geary Blvd at Stanyan ☎387-2244. Straight out of *American Graffiti*, with burgers (including very good veggie burgers), fries and milkshakes. No longer a drive-in, but open late – after midnight every night, till 3am on weekends.

Owl & Monkey Café 1336 Ninth Ave at Cabrillo ☎665-4840. Huge salads and other healthy foods.

Pig & Whistle Pub 2801 Geary Blvd at Collins ☎885-4779. The only true-to-life English pub in San Francisco – home away from home for INS-dodging British contingent. Massive plates of fish 'n' chips for $7, and 24 beers on draught.

French

Alain Rondelli 126 Clement St at Fourth ☎387-0408. Superb French cuisine, warm and unpretentious service. Naturally, anything this good doesn't come cheap.

Italian

Cafe Riggio 4112 Geary Blvd at Sixth ☎221-2114. Out in the Richmond, this is the original Italian bistro, a genuinely earthy haunt that serves solid if unexceptional food and the lowest-priced Italian wine in town.

Chinese and Korean

Mun's 401 Balboa St at Fifth ☎668-6007. Western Addition venue serving inexpensive, simple Korean dishes.

New Village 4828 Geary Blvd ☎ 668-3678. Richmond restaurant serving good-value set meals with barbecue short ribs, chicken or seafood plus half a dozen Korean specialties from around $12.

South East Asian

Straits Café 3300 Geary Blvd ☎668-1783. Affordable Singapore dishes in authentic surroundings.

Japanese

Ebisu 1283 Ninth Ave at Irving ☎566-1770. Authentic Japanese menu includes seafood, steak and sushi with eighteen-seat sushi bar.

Kabuto Sushi 5116 Geary Blvd ☎752-5652. The Holy Grail for sushi lovers, this one is accepted as probably the best in town.

Middle Eastern and Greek

The Grapeleaf 4031 Balboa St ☎668-1515. Small Lebanese bistro serving unusual and spicy food, and enlivened by belly dancers shimmying around the tables.

Mamounia 441 Balboa St at Fifth ☎752-6566. Eat Moroccan food with your fingers and pay through the nose for the privilege. Tastes good though.

Socca Restaurant 5800 Geary Blvd ☎379-6720. Inspired Mediterranean and Middle Eastern cooking in this smart Richmond restaurant that has comfortable booths and fine bar.

Stoyanof's 1240 Ninth Ave near Irving ☎664-3664. Worth a streetcar ride (*MUNI*'s N–Judah stops a block away), this Sunset District Greek place has some of the best food this side of Golden Gate Park.

Yaya Cuisine 1220 Ninth Ave at Lincoln ☎566-6966. Romantic candlelit Middle Eastern restaurant near the Park, with a Californian twist. Good vegetarian selection.

East Bay

African

The Blue Nile 2525 Telegraph Ave, Berkeley ☎510/540-6777. Come with a group to share the giant platters of Ethiopian stewed meats and veggies, eaten by hand with pancake-like injera bread.

Bay Area bars are listed on p.252.

American

The Baltic 135 Park Place, Point Richmond ☎510/235-2532. Historically a saloon, city hall, residence, funeral parlour, speakeasy and bordello, this oak-wood bar and restaurant hosts casual dining in an elegant atmosphere, weekend music, and a back patio when the weather permits

Barney's 4162 Piedmont Ave, Oakland ☎510/655-7180. Also at 5819 College Ave, Rockridge ☎510/601-0444; 1591 Solano Ave, Berkeley ☎510/526-8185. *Barney's* serves the East Bay's most popular burgers – smothered in dozens of different toppings – plus grilled chicken and fresh salads.

Bay Wolf Café 3853 Piedmont Ave, Oakland ☎510/655-6004. Comfortable restaurant serving grilled meat and fish dishes on an ever-changing, moderately expensive menu.

Bette's Ocean View Diner 1807 Fourth St, Berkeley ☎510/548-9494. Named for the neighbourhood, not for the vista, but serving up some of the Bay Area's best breakfasts and lunches. Very popular on weekends, when you may have to wait an hour for a table, so come during the week if possible.

Blondie's Pizza 2340 Telegraph Ave, Berkeley ☎510/548-1129. Takeout New York-style pizza by the slice ($1.50, plus topping) or by the pie; stays open until late (2am), and always crowded.

Brick Hut Cafe 2510 San Pablo Ave, Berkeley ☎510/486-1124. All appetites satisfied for breakfast and lunch in this welcoming women-owned and operated diner. Large portions with small prices.

Bull Valley Inn 14 Canyon Lake Drive, Port Costa ☎510/787-2244. Upscale, slightly fancy diner complements the town's raw appeal. Large wooden bar among colourful windows.

Cheese Board Pizza 1512 Shattuck Ave, Berkeley ☎510/549-3055. Tiny storefront selling some of the world's best "designer pizza" at very reasonable prices: $1.75 a slice, with a different topping every day. Worth searching out, but be aware of their irregular hours; usually Tues–Sat 11.30am–2pm & 4.30–7pm.

Flint's Barbecue 3314 San Pablo Ave, Oakland ☎510/658-9912. Also at 6609 Shattuck Ave ☎510/653-0593. Open until the early hours of the morning for some of the best ribs and sausage links west of Chicago.

Homemade Cafe 2454 Sacramento St, Berkeley ☎510/845-1940. Non-traditional Californian-style Mexican and Jewish food served for breakfast and lunch at shared tables when crowded.

Hotel Mac 10 Cottage Ave, Point Richmond ☎510/235-0100. Plan to spend money on an elegant dinner in this old red-brick building. Arrive early (Mon-Fri 4–6pm) for free happy hour finger food. Special reservations for dining in the wine cellar. Also, the cheapest prices around for the luxurious bed and breakfast upstairs (see p.216).

Lois the Pie Queen 851 60th St at Adeline, Oakland ☎510/658-5616. Famous around the bay for their Southern-style sweet potato and fresh fruit pies, this cosy diner also serves massive, down-home breakfasts and Sunday dinners to keep you full.

The Nantucket Crockett Marina at the foot of Port St, Crockett ☎510/787-2233. A winding potholed road leads to a gourmet steak and seafood restaurant, among piles of industrial junk, with an ubiquitous view of the Carquinez Bridge.

Pizza Rustica 5422 College Ave, Oakland ☎510/654-1601. Intimate adobe-style, upscale eatery for designer pizza with a pesto and sun-dried tomatoes motif. If it's too expensive, try the tapas bar upstairs.

Ratto's 821 Washington St, Oakland ☎510/832-6503. Old-time establishment has remained in refurbished "Old Oakland", providing an excellent selection of gourmet fine foods. The attached restaurant hosts weekend opera for about $20, including dinner.

Rick & Ann's 2922 Domingo Ave, Berkeley ☎510/649-8538. Across the street from the *Claremont Hotel*, this homey diner pulls in the crowds for its moderately priced "comfort food" – meat loaf and mashed potatoes, pork chops, pastas and fresh fish.

Rockridge Café 5492 College Ave, Rockridge ☎510/653-1567. Chrome-and-lino breakfast and burger bar with good desserts. Opens at 7am every day.

Saul's Deli 1475 Shattuck Ave, Berkeley ☎510/848-DELI. For pastrami, corned beef, kreplach or knishes, this is the place. Great sandwiches and picnic fixings to take away, plus a full range of sit-down evening meals.

Spenger's 1919 Fourth St, Berkeley ☎510/845-7771. About as far as you can get from the subtle charms of Berkeley's high-style restaurants, this is nonetheless a local institution. As the largest restaurant in the whole Bay Area, *Spenger's* serve up literally tons of seafood to thousands of clients every day.

Spettro 3355 Lakeshore Ave, Oakland ☎465-8320. A subtle graveyard motif surrounds as you enjoy excellent and affordable California-ized Italian-meets-Caribbean-meets-Thai food. With the friendliest staff in the area, if you stay past closing, they may ask you to join them for dessert.

Time to Eat 325 Franklin St, in Oakland's Produce Market ☎510/835-4455. A Chinese bar and café that serves breakfasts from 5am. Cheap beer, plus a pool table at 25¢ per game.

Top Dog 2534 Durant Ave, Berkeley ☎510/843-7250. Not just a hot-dog stand, it stays open late for such assorted goodies as bockwurst, bratwurst, kielbasas, Louisiana Hot Sausages and veggie dogs.

Tropix 3814 Piedmont Ave, Oakland ☎510/653-2444. Large portions of fruity Jamaican delicacies at reasonable prices with plenty of authentic jerk sauce and thirst-quenching mango juice.

Zachary's Pizza 5801 College Ave, Rockridge ☎510/655-6385. Also at 1853 Solano Ave, North Berkeley ☎510/525-5950. Good salads, and arguably the best pizzas in the East Bay.

California Cuisine

Chez Panisse 1517 Shattuck Ave, North Berkeley ☎510/548-5525. The first and still the best of the California Cuisineries - although at $45, $55 and $65 a head

Restaurants

A walking tour of Berkeley is described on p.152 onwards.

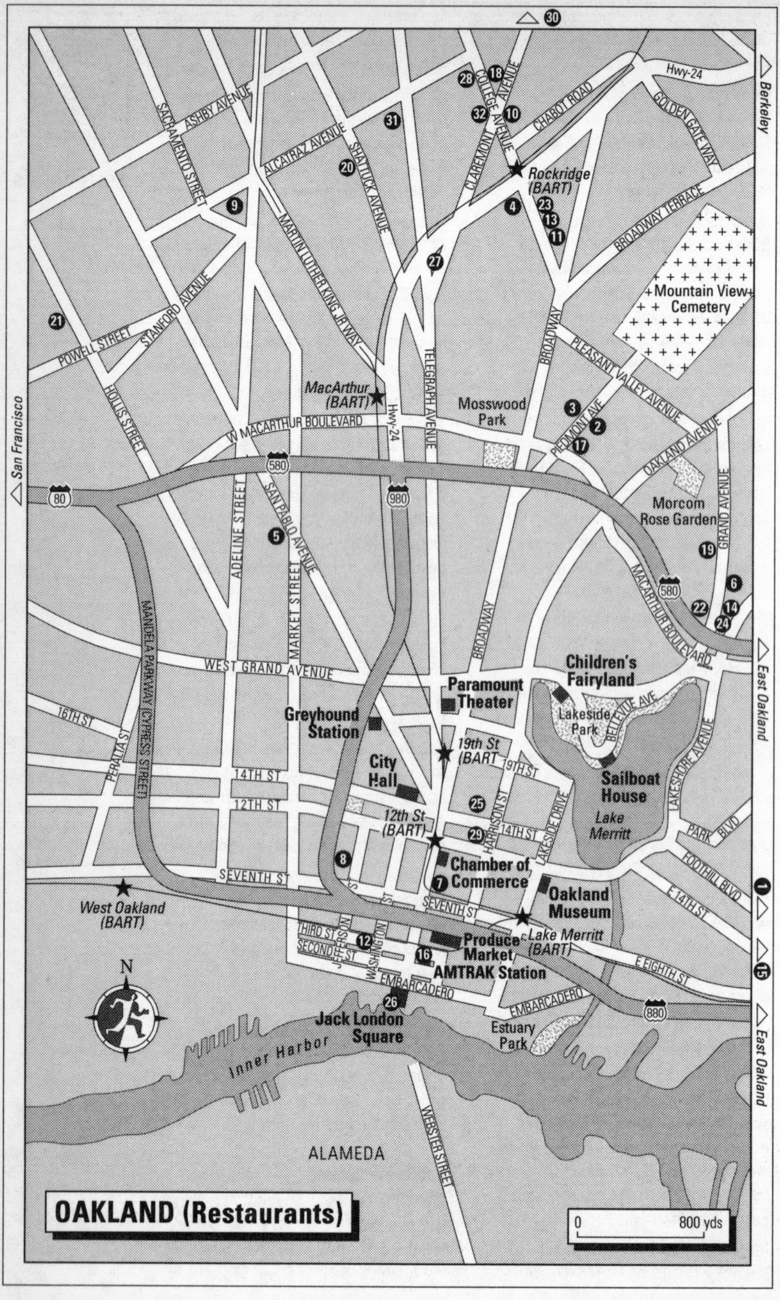
OAKLAND (Restaurants)
Berkeley
San Francisco
East Oakland
East Oakland
Hwy-24
ASHBY AVENUE
SACRAMENTO STREET
ALCATRAZ AVENUE
SHATTUCK AVENUE
COLLEGE AVENUE
CLAREMONT AVENUE
CHABOT ROAD
GOLDEN GATE WAY
Rockridge (BART)
BROADWAY TERRACE
MARTIN LUTHER KING JR WAY
Mountain View Cemetery
STANFORD AVENUE
POWELL STREET
HOLLIS STREET
BROADWAY
PLEASANT VALLEY AVENUE
MacArthur (BART)
TELEGRAPH AVENUE
Mosswood Park
PIEDMONT AVE
W MACARTHUR BOULEVARD
OAKLAND AVENUE
GRAND AVENUE
Morcom Rose Garden
ADELINE STREET
SAN PABLO AVENUE
MARKET STREET
MANDELA PARKWAY (CYPRESS STREET)
MACARTHUR BOULEVARD
WEST GRAND AVENUE
Children's Fairyland
Paramount Theater
Greyhound Station
Lakeside Park
BELLEVUE AVE
16TH ST
PERALTA ST
19th St (BART)
19TH ST
City Hall
14TH ST
12TH ST
Sailboat House
LAKESHORE AVENUE
12th St (BART)
HARRISON ST
14TH ST
LAKESIDE DRIVE
Lake Merritt
PARK BLVD
FOOTHILL BLVD
Chamber of Commerce
SEVENTH ST
E 14TH ST
West Oakland (BART)
Oakland Museum
SEVENTH ST
THIRD ST
JEFFERSON ST
WASHINGTON ST
Produce Market
Lake Merritt (BART)
SECOND ST
AMTRAK Station
E EIGHTH ST
EMBARCADERO
EMBARCADERO
Jack London Square
Estuary Park
Inner Harbor
WEBSTER STREET
ALAMEDA
N
0
800 yds
80
580
980
580
880
1 2 3 4 5 6 7 8 9 10 11 12 13 14 15 16 17 18 19 20 21 22 23 24 25 26 27 28 29 30 31 32

Oakland Restaurants, Bars and Cafés

Restaurants

1 Alvita's Restaurant 3522 Foothill Blvd, East Oakland

2 Barney's 4162 Piedmont Ave, Oakland

3 Bay Wolf Café 3853 Piedmont Ave, Oakland

4 Café Oliveto 5655 College Ave, Rockridge

5 Flint's Barbecue 3314 San Pablo Ave, Oakland

6 Holy Land Kosher Food 677 Rand Ave, Oakland

7 Jade Villa 800 Broadway, downtown Oakland

8 Le Cheval 1414 Jefferson St, Oakland

9 Lois the Pie Queen 851 60th St at Adeline, Oakland

10 Nan Yang 6048 College Ave, Oakland

11 Pizza Rustica 5422 College Ave, Oakland

12 Ratto's 821 Washington St, Oakland

13 Rockridge Café 5492 College Ave, Rockridge

14 Spettro 3355 Lakeshore Ave, Oakland

15 Taqueria Morelia 4481 E 14th St, East Oakland

16 Time to Eat 325 Franklin St, in Oakland's Produce Market

17 Tropix 3814 Piedmont Ave, Oakland

18 Zachary's Pizza 5801 College Ave, Rockridge

Bars and Cafés

19 The Alley 3325 Grand Ave, Oakland

20 Bosn's Locker 5817 Shattuck Ave, Oakland

21 Chalkers Billiard Club 5900 Hollis St, Emeryville

22 Coffee Mill 3393 Grand Ave, Oakland

23 Eline Ale House 5612 College Ave, Oakland

24 The Fifth Amendment 3255 Lakeshore Ave, Oakland

25 Geoffrey's Inner Circle 410 14th St, Oakland

26 Heinhold's First and Last Chance Saloon 56 Jack London Square, Oakland

27 The Kingfish 5227 Claremont Ave, Oakland

28 Royal Coffee 307 63rd St, Oakland

29 Stork Club 380 12th St, Oakland

30 Terrace Lounge *Claremont Hotel*, corner of Ashby and Domingo St, Oakland

31 The White Horse 6560 Telegraph Ave at 66th St, Oakland

32 Yoshi's Restaurant and Nitespot 6030 Claremont, Oakland

Restaurants

prix fixe (plus wine) on Mon, Tues-Thurs and Fri respectively, you may prefer to try the comparatively inexpensive cafe upstairs, especially if you don't have the obligatory three-months-in-advance reservation.

Soleil 1555 Bonanza St, Walnut Creek ☎520/939-6310. Serving delicious and pricey California Cuisine that combines Asian, French and Italian influences, sometimes on the same plate. Perfect after a day's hiking on Mount Diablo; put on some nice clothes.

Italian

Café Oliveto 5655 College Ave, Rockridge ☎510/547-5356. Popular sidewalk tapas bar, where good-sized portions cost around $4 per plate. Upstairs is a pricey Italian restaurant where you can watch the chef and the cooking team in action.

Gio's Trattoria 2220 First St, Livermore ☎510/606-6644. Offers outstanding Italian food in an elegant atmosphere.

Chinese and Korean

Jade Villa 800 Broadway, downtown Oakland ☎510/839-1688. For endless dim sum lunches or traditional Cantonese meals, this is one of the best places in Oakland's thriving Chinatown.

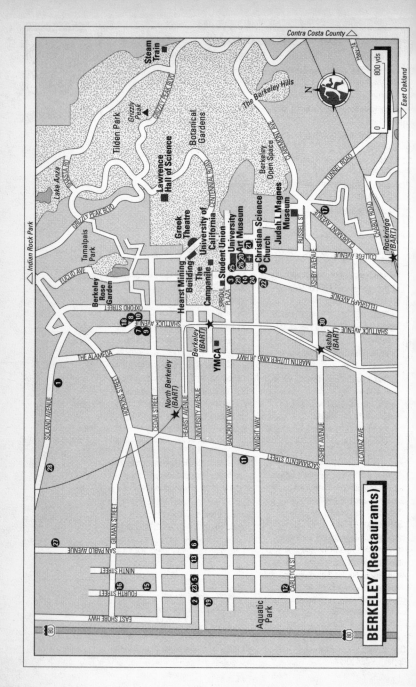

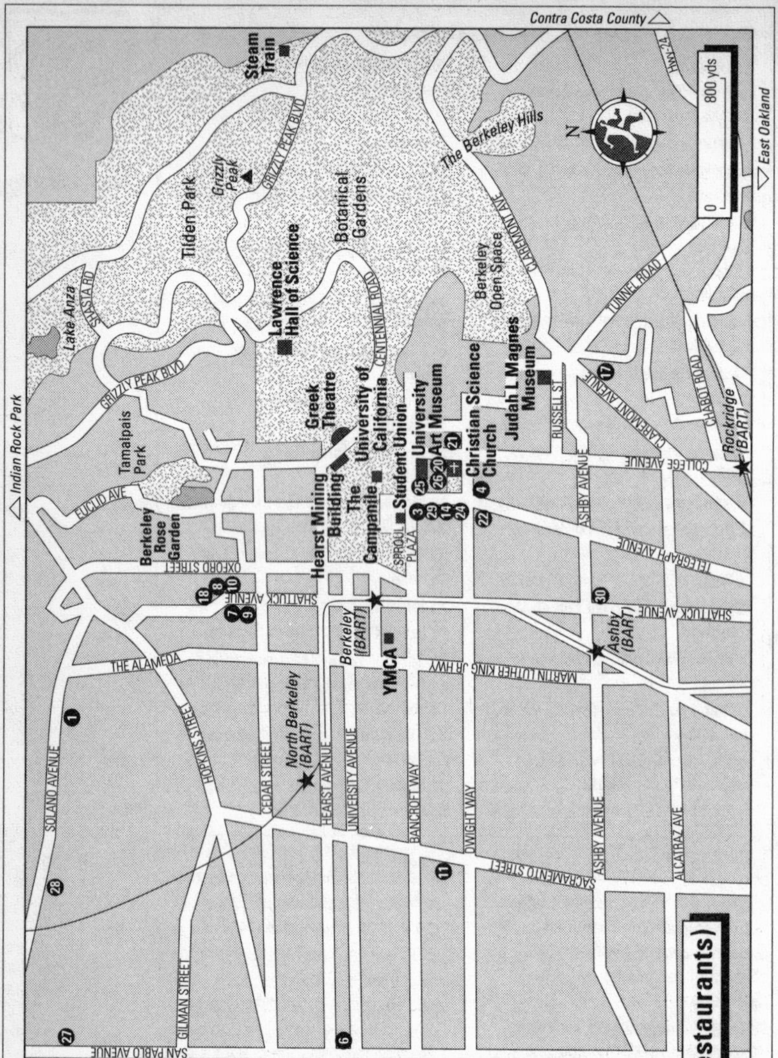
BERKELEY (Restaurants)
Indian Rock Park
Contra Costa County
East Oakland
Steam Train
Tilden Park
Grizzly Peak
GRIZZLY PEAK BLVD
Lake Anza
SHASTA RD
Lawrence Hall of Science
Botanical Gardens
The Berkeley Hills
Berkeley Open Space
CLAREMONT AVE
Hwy-24
N
0
800 yds
Tamalpais Park
EUCLID AVE
Berkeley Rose Garden
Greek Theatre
University of California
CENTENNIAL ROAD
Hearst Mining Building
The Campanile
Student Union
SPROUL PLAZA
University Art Museum
Christian Science Church
Judah L Magnes Museum
RUSSELL ST
OXFORD STREET
SHATTUCK AVENUE
TELEGRAPH AVENUE
COLLEGE AVENUE
ASHBY AVENUE
CLAREMONT AVENUE
TUNNEL ROAD
CHABOT ROAD
Rockridge (BART)
THE ALAMEDA
Berkeley (BART)
YMCA
MARTIN LUTHER KING JR HWY
Ashby (BART)
SOLANO AVENUE
HOPKINS STREET
North Berkeley (BART)
CEDAR STREET
HEARST AVENUE
UNIVERSITY AVENUE
BANCROFT WAY
DWIGHT WAY
SACRAMENTO STREET
ALCATRAZ AVE
GILMAN STREET
SAN PABLO AVENUE
NINTH STREET
FOURTH STREET
CARLETON ST
EAST SHORE HWY
Aquatic Park
80

Restaurants

Berkeley Restaurants, Bars and Cafés

Restaurants

1 Ajanta 1888 Solano Ave, Berkeley

2 Bette's Ocean View Diner 1807 Fourth St, Berkeley

3 Blondie's Pizza 2340 Telegraph Ave, Berkeley

4 The Blue Nile 2525 Telegraph Ave, Berkeley

5 Bombay Cuisine 2006 Ninth St at University Ave, Berkeley

6 Brick Hut Cafe 2510 San Pablo Ave, Berkeley

7 Café de la Paz 1600 Shattuck Ave, Berkeley

8 Cha-Am 1543 Shattuck Ave, Berkeley

9 Cheese Board Pizza 1512 Shattuck Ave, Berkeley

10 Chez Panisse 1517 Shattuck Ave, North Berkeley

11 Homemade Cafe 2454 Sacramento St, Berkeley

12 Juan's Place 941 Carleton St, West Berkeley

13 Maharani 1025 University Ave, West Berkeley

14 Mario's La Fiesta 2444 Telegraph Ave at Haste St, Berkeley

15 O Chame 1830 Fourth St, West Berkeley

16 Picante 1328 Sixth St at Gilman St, West Berkeley

17 Rick & Ann's 2922 Domingo Ave, Berkeley

18 Saul's Deli 1475 Shattuck Ave, Berkeley

19 Spenger's 1919 Fourth St, Berkeley

20 Steve's Barbeque In the Durant Center, 2521 Durant Ave, Berkeley

21 Top Dog 2534 Durant Ave, Berkeley

Bars and Cafés

22 Bison Brewing Company 2598 Telegraph Ave, Berkeley

23 Brennan's Fourth St and University, Berkeley

24 Café Mediterraneum 2475 Telegraph Ave, Berkeley

25 Café Milano 2522 Bancroft Way, Berkeley

26 Café Strada 2300 College Ave, Berkeley

27 The Ivy Room 858 San Pablo Ave, Albany

28 The Pub 1492 Solano Ave, Albany

29 Raleigh's 2438 Telegraph Ave, Berkeley

30 Starry Plough 3103 Shattuck Ave, Berkeley

Steve's Barbeque In the Durant Center, 2521 Durant Ave, Berkeley ☎510/848-6166. Excellent, low priced Korean food (kim chee to die for); not to mention bargain pitchers of beer.

South East Asian

Cha-Am 1543 Shattuck Ave, Berkeley ☎510/848-9664. Climb up the stairs to this unlikely-looking, always crowded, small restaurant, for deliciously spicy Thai food at bargain prices.

Le Cheval 1414 Jefferson St, Oakland ☎510/763-8495. Also at 1007 Clay St, Oakland ☎763-8495. Huge quantities of top-quality Vietnamese food at an affordable price. Full lunches cost under $5.

Nan Yang 6048 College Ave, Oakland ☎510/655-3298. Burmese food served in colourful, large, palate-exciting portions. The political refugee owner/chef is willing to discuss all of his esoteric delicacies. Do not miss the ginger salad.

Sala Thai 807 First Street, Benicia ☎707/745-4331. Tasty, aromatic and affordable Thai food in Benicia. Check out the enormous fish tank as you await your meal.

Japanese

O Chame 1830 Fourth St, West Berkeley ☎510/841-8783. One of the very best Japanese restaurants in the US, with beautifully prepared sashimi and sushi as well as a full range of authentic Japanese specialties. A treat.

Indian

Ajanta 1888 Solano Ave, Berkeley ☎510/526-4373. Lots of delicious Indian food in an elegant room among large colourful murals.

Bombay Cuisine 2006 Ninth St at University Ave, Berkeley ☎510/843-9601. Great Indian food at reasonable prices, tucked away in the back room of a spice shop.

Maharani 1025 University Ave, West Berkeley ☎510/848-7777. One of the best of the handful of restaurants that have sprung up here in Little India, and certainly the least expensive, with $6 lunchtime buffets on weekdays.

Middle Eastern and Greek

Berkeley bars and cafés are reviewed on p.252.

Holy Land Kosher Food 677 Rand Ave, Oakland ☎510/272-0535. Casual diner-style restaurant near the lake serving Israeli food, including excellent falafel, to those who can find it.

Central and South American

Alvita's Restaurant 3522 Foothill Blvd, East Oakland ☎510/536-7880. Arguably the best Mexican restaurant in the Bay Area, with great *chiles rellenos,* carnitas, and a range of seafood dishes.

Café de la Paz 1600 Shattuck Ave, Berkeley ☎510/843-0662. Located upstairs inside a complex of boutiques, Latin American entrées and tapas are served fresh and sometimes spicy. Don't miss the Brazilian seafood stew.

Juan's Place 941 Carleton St, West Berkeley ☎510/845-6904. The original Berkeley Mexican restaurant, with great food (tons of it) and an interesting mix of people.

Mario's La Fiesta 2444 Telegraph Ave at Haste St, Berkeley ☎510/540-9123. Always crowded with students and other budget-minded souls who flock here for the heaped portions of good, inexpensive Mexican food.

Picante 1328 Sixth St at Gilman, West Berkeley ☎510/525-3121. Good, inexpensive tacos with fresh salsa, plus live jazz at weekends.

Taqueria Morelia 4481 E 14th St, East Oakland ☎510/535-6030. Excellent burritos and the more unusual but authentic tortas.

The Peninsula

American

Duarte's 202 Stage Rd, Pescadero ☎879-0464. Platefuls of traditional American food, especially fish, for around $10 are served in this down-home find connected to a bar full of locals in cowboy hats.

Fresco 3398 El Camino Real, Palo Alto ☎493-3470. Wide selection of pastas, pizzas, and a menu of salads with palpably fresh ingredients in unusual combinations. Opens early.

Original Joe's 301 S First St, San Jose ☎408/292-7030. Grab a stool at the counter or settle into one of the comfy booths and enjoy a burger and fries or a plate of pasta at this San Jose institution, where $10 goes a long way.

The Peninsula Creamery 566 Emerson St, Palo Alto ☎323-3175. Nearly authentic 1950s American diner serving notable ice cream, milkshakes and hearty burgers.

Pudley's Burger Saloon 255 University Ave, Palo Alto ☎328-2021. Burgers and beers in retro-American 1940s setting.

California Cuisine

Eulipia 374 S First St, San Jose ☎408/280-6161. Upscale and stylish spot featuring well-prepared versions of California Cuisine staples like grilled fish and fresh pastas. Dinner and drinks will set you back $15–25.

French

Chateau de Flores 532 Church St, Half Moon Bay ☎712-8837. The exquisite flower garden in front welcomes you to a small, pricey French restaurant.

South East Asian

Barrio Fiesta 909 Antoinette Lane, South San Francisco ☎871-8703. Hard to find amid the shopping malls of South City, but worth hunting out for the huge portions of beautifully presented, delicious

Filipino dishes, especially seafood. Full meals cost around $15; bring your own wine or beer.

Krung Thai Cuisine 1699 W San Carlos St, San Jose ☎408/295-5508. Excellent range of satays and delicious, unusual seafood dishes. Start off with a *po-tak* soup of clams and crab legs in citrus broth.

Little Garden 4127 El Camino Real, Palo Alto ☎494-1230. Simple, spicy, well-prepared Vietnamese food – fried chicken on a bed of cabbage, shrimp and hot peppers in peanut sauce – in unpretentious surroundings.

Marin County

American

Dipsea Café 1 El Paseo, Mill Valley ☎381-0298. Hearty diner food, especially good for breakfast before a day out hiking on Mount Tamalpais.

Greater Gatsby's 39 Caledonia St, Sausalito ☎332-4500. Handy, inexpensive pizza parlour a block from the waterfront on the north side of town.

Hilda's 639 San Anselmo Ave, San Anselmo ☎457-9266. Great breakfasts and lunches in this down-home, cosy café.

Mountain Home Inn 810 Panoramic Highway, above Mill Valley ☎381-9000. A place that's as good for the atmosphere as for the food, with broiled meat and fish dishes served up in a rustic lodge on the slopes of Mount Tamalpais.

New Morning Café 1696 Tiburon Blvd, Tiburon ☎435-4315. Lots of healthy wholegrain sandwiches, plus salads and omelettes.

Pelican Inn Hwy-1, Muir Beach ☎383-6000. Traditional roast beef and fine ale in a coach-house atmosphere complete with stone fireplace.

Sam's Anchor Café 27 Main St, Tiburon ☎435-4527. This rough-hewn, amiable waterfront café and bar has been around for more than 75 years. Good burgers, soups and sandwiches, plus very popular Sunday brunches.

Station House Café 11180 Hwy-1 (Main St), Point Reyes Station ☎663-1515. Open daily for lunch and dinner, this friendly local favourite entices diners from miles around to sample their grilled seafood and great steaks.

California Cuisine

Casa Madrona 801 Bridgeway, Sausalito ☎381-5888. Mediterranean staples meet California Cuisine in this expensive, but highly rated hotel-restaurant. Great view of the harbour and excellent seafood.

Stinson Beach Grill Stinson Beach ☎868-2002. Somewhat pricey California Cuisine in a beachfront setting – look out for the bright-blue building right in the heart of town.

Italian

Da Angelo 22 Miller Ave, Mill Valley ☎388-2000. Good salads and tasty pasta and pizzas, served up in a lively but comfortable room right off the downtown plaza.

South East Asian

Rice Table 1617 Fourth St, San Rafael ☎456-1808. From the shrimp chips through the crab pancakes and noodles onto the fried plantain desserts, these fragrant and spicy Indonesian dishes are worth planning a day around. Dinners only, but excellent value at around $15 a head for a very filling meal.

Central and South American

The Cantina 651 E Blithedale Rd at Camino Alto, Mill Valley ☎381-1070. Usually packed, some of the best Mexican food in Marin, spiced by what's certainly the hottest salsa for miles.

Wine Country

American

Amedeo 14301 Arnold Drive, Jack London Village, Glen Ellen ☎707/996-3077. Creekside dining in a converted spacious mill. One of the few affordable eateries with a range of food to satisfy carnivore and vegetarian palates. Closed Mondays.

La Boucane 1778 Second St, Napa ☎707/253-1177. Mouthwatering chunks

Restaurants

Wine Country accommodation is listed in Chapter Twelve.

Wine Country wineries are listed on p.198 and p.201.

of tender meat prepared in traditional but imaginative sauces, plus perfect fish (especially shellfish) and vegetables. Very expensive, dinner only.

Café Sarafornia 1413 Lincoln Ave, Calistoga ☎707/942-0555. Though new, already famous for delicious and enormous breakfasts and lunches which command a waiting line around the block on weekends. Let the owner talk your ear off.

Calistoga Inn 1250 Lincoln Ave, Calistoga ☎707/942-4101. Very good seafood – spicy Cajun prawns, or crispy crab cakes – plus wide range of wines, microbrewed beers and excellent desserts.

Checkers Pizza 1414 Lincoln Ave, Calistoga ☎707/942-9300. Soups, salads and sandwiches, plus adventurous pizzas and good pasta dishes.

Feed Store Café & Bakery 529 First St West, Sonoma ☎707/938-2122. Big breakfasts and lunches representing many various regions and cultures. Slightly off Sonoma's main drag.

Ford's Café 22900 Broadway, Sonoma ☎707/938-9811. Hearty, working-class American diner food served to locals in this hidden diner.

Glen Ellen Inn 13670 Arnold Drive, Glen Ellen ☎707/996-6409. Husband-and-wife team cook and manage a romantic, slightly pricey dining experience with half a dozen tables. Tues–Fri 11.30am–2.30pm; Tues–Sun 5.30–9.30pm.

Greystone Restaurant at the Culinary Institute of America 2555 Main St, St Helena ☎707/967-0600. Mediterranean cuisine served in an elegant ivy-walled mansion outside of town. Reasonable for the delicious large portions.

Mustards 7399 St Helena Highway (Hwy-29), Yountville ☎707/944-2424. Credited with starting the late-1980s trend toward "grazing" food, emphasizing tapas-like titbits rather than main meals. Reckon on spending $15–20 a head, and waiting for a table if you come on a weekend.

PJ's Café 1001 Second St, Napa ☎707/224-0607. A Napa institution, open 11am to 10pm every day for pasta, pizzas and sandwiches.

Regina's 110 W Spain St in the *Sonoma Hotel*, Sonoma ☎707/938-0254. Very good Italian-American food, right off Sonoma Plaza.

The Spot One mile south of St Helena on Hwy-29 ☎707/963-2844. This 1950s-retro roadside diner is conveniently located for lunchtime on the cheap.

Sunnyside Coffee Club 140 East Napa St, Sonoma ☎707/935-0366. Southwestern- style breakfasts and lunches. Closed Wed.

California Cuisine

All Seasons 1400 Lincoln Ave, Calistoga ☎707/942-9111. This friendly bistro, serving up good-sized portions of California Cuisine, is probably best known locally for its massive wine list, many of which are available by the glass.

Italian

Bosko's Ristorante 1403 Lincoln Ave, Calistoga ☎707/942-9088. Standard Italian restaurant preparing good-value, fresh pasta dishes. Cheap and cheerful, and popular with families.

Tra Vigne 1050 Charter Oak Ave, St Helena ☎707/963-4444. Just north of town, but it feels as if you've been transported to Tuscany. Excellent food and fine wines, served up in a lovely vine-covered courtyard. They also have a small deli, where you can pick up picnic goodies.

Central and South American

The Diner 6476 Washington St, Yountville ☎707/944-2626. Start the day's wine-touring off right, with good strong coffee and brilliant breakfasts where locals and day-trippers mix. Open until 3pm Tues–Fri, until 10pm at weekends for flavoursome Mexican dinners.

La Casa 121 E Spain St, Sonoma ☎707/996-3406. Friendly, festive and inexpensive Mexican restaurant just across from Sonoma Mission. Excellent salsa – buy some to take away.

Chapter 14

Bars and Cafés

San Francisco for many years possessed a reputation as a consummate drinking town. Though still blessed with a huge range of bars and cafés where you can imbibe endlessly, socially the scene has gone the way of much of the rest of California and abandoned boozing in favour of Coffee House culture – the Nineties' equivalent of singles bars.

The faint whiff of sanctimony notwithstanding, San Francisco's **cafés** are on the whole superb, serving first-rate coffees, teas and soft drinks, in addition to beer and wine. More social than utilitarian, people hang out in these lively venues to pass time, cruise or just read the paper as much as refresh themselves. If you need to while away a couple of hours on no money, they are an excellent bet. Furthermore, many non-drinkers looking for social alternatives to bars are opting instead for the relatively new pastime, the old English tradition of **afternoon tea**. So far it has only taken off in the big hotels, but it is beginning to spread to the neighbourhood cafés who should be able to price it more reasonably.

There are around two thousand bars in the city, varying from seedy late-night dives to rooftop piano lounges with glittering views. Though spread fairly evenly throughout the city, they are particularly numerous in North Beach, the Haight, SoMa and Mission. As with most cities, the more central the bar, the slicker, with neighbourhood joints tending to be more rough-hewn, informal and affordable affairs.

To **buy and consume alcohol** on the West Coast, you have to be at least 21 years old, and you could well be asked for ID even if you look much older. **Licensing laws** are, however, among the most liberal in the country (though laws on drinking and driving are not): alcohol can be bought and drunk any time between 6 and 2am, seven days a week; this is surplus to the requirements of

Java Jive

Knowing a caffè latte from a café au lait is easy once you get to grips with the espresso lingo. Here's a quick list to assist your coffee choice.

café au lait coffee with frothy steamed milk

caffè mocha, or espresso-choc hot chocolate with a shot of espresso

caffè latte steamed milk with a shot of espresso

cappuccino espresso topped with hot, frothy milk

espresso con panna espresso topped with whipped cream

espresso macchiato espresso with a small amount of milk froth

espresso small, but highly charged – made from filtering steam through finely ground coffee under pressure

Bars and Cafés

most, but handy for travellers who keep strange hours. Rules about **smoking** are less generous, with state law now stipulating that where there is food, there is no smoke.

Most bars open mid-morning and close around 2am. In addition to the personal favourites that follow, you should also look at the listings in Chapter Fifteen, which include many good cocktail spots for a drink before things hot up later in the evening.

Downtown

For a map of Downtown bars, cafés and restaurants see p.224.

The Big Four *Huntington Hotel*, 1075 California St at Taylor. Classy hotel bar, aimed squarely at the sedate set who want a well-made drink in civilized surroundings.

Carnelian Room 555 California St at Kearny. The best of the rooftop cocktail lounges, 52 floors up in the Bank of America Building. A truly elegant spot for some smart cocktails; bring smart money.

Champagne Exchange In *Nordstrom's*, Fourth Floor, San Francisco Center, Fifth and Market Sts. Take a break from your shopping to quaff a bottle of bubbly, looking out over the Powell Street cable-car turnaround. Besides the champers (five types by the glass, plus another thirty by the bottle) they've got an assortment of ice-cold vodkas from around the world at $3.50 a shot.

Good spots to enjoy afternoon tea downtown are listed on p.226.

Equinox *Hyatt Regency*, the Embarcadero. Good for the novelty value only, this rooftop cocktail lounge attracts crowds of tourists who ascend its dizzy spires just to look at the views. The whole thing revolves, so you get a 360° view of the city without ever leaving your seat. Serious drinkers wouldn't be caught dead in here, however: have a drink, revolve and leave.

Gordon Biersch Brewery 2 Harrison St at Embarcadero. Bayfront microbrewery housed in converted Hills Brothers coffee warehouse. Good bar food and some of the best beers in San Francisco bring out downtown's overpaid twentysomethings.

Harry Denton's 161 Steuart St at Howard. For the after-work Financial District crowd, this is San Francisco's prime place to cruise and be cruised. Fortunately, the fully stocked bar has enough rare bourbons and West Coast microbrews to make whiling away an evening very pleasant indeed, even if you're not on the prowl. Great interior.

Harry Denton's Starlight Roof Top floor of the *Sir Francis Drake Hotel*, 450 Powell St at Sutter. Dress up and drink martinis. This is a sophisticated grown-up scene with a moneyed crowd who come for the live jazz.

Johnny Love's 1500 Broadway at Polk. Straight pick-up scene on an industrial scale. Hormone-driven Young Republicans line up around the block nightly to get a piece of the action.

Li Po's Bar 916 Grant Ave at Jackson. Named after the Chinese poet, *Li Po's* is something of a literary hang-out among the Chinatown regulars. Enter through the false cavern front and sit at the very dimly lit bar where Wayne Wang filmed *Chang is Missing*.

San Francisco Beer

Much American **beer** may be fizzy and tasteless, but the brews concocted by the San Francisco-based *Anchor Brewery* are well worth sampling. The tasty, medium-bodied *Anchor Steam* beer and the richer-flavoured, creamy *Liberty Ale* are both available by the bottle in most bars and cafés, and on draught at better establishments. The widely available *Sierra Nevada Ale* is also tasty, as are the products of the dozens of small microbreweries popping up all over the West Coast; any good bar or liquor store should stock a range. Another recent development are the so-called **brewpubs**, serving a range of generally good beers brewed on the premises.

Expect to pay $2 for a small glass (just over half a pint) or around $3.50 a pint for draught beer, $2–3 for a bottle of imported beer.

The London Wine Bar 415 Sansome St at Sacramento. Dubiously tagged as "America's first wine bar", this place is a suitably pretentious and expensive locale for the Financial District clones that flock here after work. Open Mon-Fri until 9pm.

The Occidental Grill 453 Pine St at Kearny. Barbary Coast style-drinking den, claims to be the home of the first martini (disputed) and certainly makes a mean one.

The Redwood Room *Clift Hotel*, 495 Geary St at Taylor. Gorgeous redwood-panelled Art Deco lounge, dulled only slightly by the wealthy geriatric hotel guests who frequent it.

Royal Exchange 301 Sacramento St ☎956-1710. The consummate Financial District after-work hang-out for the pretty people.

Tonga Room *Fairmont Hotel*, Powell and Mason streets. Outrageously lavish Polynesian theme bar with waitresses in grass skirts, a native-laden raft floating around the room, and expensive cocktails. Fun if you like the joke and are in the mood for camp hilarity.

Top of the Mark *Mark Hopkins Hotel*, California St at Mason. The most famous of the rooftop bars, its reputation surpasses the actual experience of drinking up here, and generally it only attracts tourists and hotel guests who can't be bothered to find anywhere else.

North Beach and the Northern Waterfront

Art Institute Café 800 Chestnut St at Jones. Perched above North Beach, this is part of the art college and hang-out for art students as well as regular punters. Good, unpretentious atmosphere and great view.

Balboa Café 3199 Fillmore St at Greenwich. A favourite with the young, upmarket singles of the Marina. Very good food, too.

Bohemian Cigar Store 566 Columbus Ave at Union. Small, informal North Beach hang-out for sipping coffee or slinging beers.

Buena Vista Café 2765 Hyde St, at Beach, Fisherman's Wharf. If you like your coffee with a kick, this is the place for you. Claims to be the home of the world's first Irish coffee, which is hard to believe, but who cares – it's certainly the best in town and the crowds who pack the place are testimony to the generously laced coffee. Good, inexpensive food too, making it a decent stopoff for a sightseeing lunch.

Café Francisco 2161 Powell St at Francisco. North Beach home of the ponderous coffee-drinker.

Café Roma 414 Columbus Ave at Green. Not big on atmosphere, but a quiet spot to read the paper over a coffee, while checking out the classical, cherub-adorned murals and ornate decor.

Café Trieste 601 Vallejo St at Grant. Noisy North Beach Italian café, popular with a serious literary crowd who hang out and listen to the opera classics which boom from the jukebox. Saturday lunchtimes are a treat – the family who run it get up and sing. Get there by noon if you want a seat.

Chestnut Street Grill 2231 Chestnut St at Scott. A neighbourhood bar and grill that is a fine place for a well-made cocktail before dinner.

Eagle Café Pier 39, Fisherman's Wharf. Cheap diner by day and venue for drinks and free live music at night, this place survives remarkably untarnished amid all the waterfront tat at the Wharf.

Enrico's Sidewalk Café 504 Broadway at Kearny. Busy little place for listening to jazz and having your milkshake spiked with the liquor of your choice.

Moose's 1652 Stockton St at Filbert. Upscale, beautifully designed hang-out for the glamorous. Although it's ostensibly a restaurant, save yourself money and just check out the bar scene which features nightly jazz. See and be seen.

Pacific Heights Bar and Grill Fillmore and Pine. Overstuffed chairs make this the city's most comfortable bar, and it also has a good range of bar food, including fresh-shucked oysters.

Bars and Cafés

The map on p.229 shows the locations of many of the North Beach bars and cafés listed here.

Bars and Cafés

Paragon 3251 Scott St at Francisco. Slick Marina supper club that's more about the music and drinking than eating, though that too is tasty and inexpensive. Nightly jazz and a smooth crowd. To be recommended.

Perry's 1944 Union St at Buchanan. Sophisticated meat market, featured in Armistead Maupin's *Tales of the City* as the quintessential breeder bar.

The Saloon 1232 Grant Ave at Vallejo. This bar has stood for over a hundred years and has seen use as a whore-house and Prohibition speakeasy. Today the old structure creaks nightly as blues bands and crowds of enthusiastic dancers do their thing.

San Francisco Brewing Co 155 Columbus Ave at Pacific. A must for beer fans who tire quickly of the insipid American variety, this North Beach hang-out makes its own full-flavoured brews on the premises.

Savoy Tivoli 1434 Grant Ave at Green. Without a doubt, this place is North Beach's most attractively decorated and populated bar, also serving good, reasonably priced food – although the emphasis is definitely on liquid enjoyment.

Steps of Rome Café 348 Columbus Ave at Vallejo. By day, just another moderately cool café, by night the noisy favourite hang-out of North Beach taxi-drivers and midnight prowlers looking for a sobering double espresso. Open late.

Tosca Café 242 Columbus Ave at Broadway. The theme here is opera, in time-worn but still stylish surroundings. Mingle with media people at the bar or slump into a comfy, red leather booth and try to talk above the sound-level of the arias.

Vesuvio's 255 Columbus Ave at Broadway. Legendary North Beach Beat haunt in the 1950s and still catering to an arty but friendly crowd who prop up the bar into the small hours. Situated next to *City Lights Bookstore*, it's a good place to peruse your new purchases over a drink.

Washington Square Bar and Grill 1707 Powell St at Union. Primarily a restaurant, but worth checking out for the great bar and the chance to spy on the media and literary crowd who have made this their second home. Some of the thunder has been stolen by *Moose's* across the square, but regulars still flock.

Civic Center, SoMa and the Mission

Above Paradise (formerly *Paradise Lounge)* 1501 Folsom St at 11th. Cleverly constructed on two floors, you can suit your mood with a game of pool and a drink upstairs or dance to live music downstairs.

Bouncer's Bar 2496 Third St, one block from the Waterfront. Good down-home joint, there is live music on a Sunday when the house band sets up a r'n'b jam session.

Brainwash 1122 Folsom St at Seventh. Great idea – a café/bar and laundromat where you can have breakfast or a beer while you do your washing. Needless to say it's popular with the young and novelty-conscious.

Bull's Texas Café 25 Van Ness Ave at Market. Cheesy Tex-Mex bar-cum-restaurant, but a great place to wolf down the free food at happy hour with your bucket of cheap frozen Margarita. First stop for those seeking oblivion on a budget.

Café Babar 994 Guerrero St at 22nd. Hip hang-out in the Mission with pool tables and a young, alternative crowd.

Café La Boheme 3318 24th St at Mission. A diverse crowd and a staggering range of coffees keeps the Mission's caffeine addicts coming from sunup until late at night.

Café Picaro 3120 16th St at Mission. Chic Spanish tapas bar with live flamenco on Thurs & Sun 8pm.

The Dovre Club 3541 18th St at Guerrero. Solid Irish bar, full of Gaelic charmers.

El Rio 3158 Mission St at Army. When it isn't staging one of its specials (salsa on Sun, funk on Wed and world music on Fri), this is a great place for a quiet drink and a game on one of San Francisco's most handsome pool tables.

Hayes and Vine 337 Hayes St at Gough. A wine bar with a mission to "make more good wine accessible to more people and at reasonably prices". Cosy, well-designed spot in trendy Hayes Valley with a truly excellent selection of local and international wines.

Julie's Supper Club 1123 Folsom St at Seventh. A popular restaurant, but best for sitting at the bar munching good-value Cajun snacks and listening to the free live jazz – if you get in before 9pm; after that it's $5.

Max's Opera Café Opera Plaza, Van Ness Ave. Slightly sterile atmosphere, but very interesting people-watching when the dinner-suited opera, ballet and symphony fans pop in for a quick one before and after performances at the Civic Center venues.

Mission Rock Resort 817 China Basin at Mission Rock. Scruffy, blue-collar bar down the old dockyards, great for a cheap beer and views of the bay.

Muddy Waters 3913 24th Street at Valencia and 521 Valencia at 16th. The Mission's young and funky come here to wake up or waste an afternoon. Fashionably scruffy and festooned with newsprint.

The Ramp 855 China Basin at Mission Rock. Way out on the old docks, this is well worth the half-mile trek from downtown (you'll need a car unless you're a seasoned walker) to sit out on the patio and sip beers and eat burgers overlooking the abandoned piers and new boatyards.

Slow Club 2501 Mariposa, Potrero Hill. Cool bar and jazz club with an informal neighbourhood feel. Perfect for low-key socializing.

South Park Café 108 South Park. Between Second and Third, Bryant and Brannan. Chic SoMa rendezvous, where architects and other creative professionals meet their peers to drink in tasteful surroundings.

The Up & Down Club 1151 Folsom St at Eighth. One of the city's best jazz venues, this small club split across two floors serves great drinks and attracts a lively attractive crowd out for a good time.

The Uptown 200 Capp St at 17th and Mission. Best of the Mission's neighbourhood bars, embracing an eclectic clientele who shoot pool, drink like fiends and fall all over the scruffy leatherette upholstery. Some simply go to watch the ball game on TV. A more bizarre collection of characters would be hard to find. Don't miss it.

Zeitgeist 199 Valencia St at Duboce. A favourite in the Mission for bikers and those who like to dress in black. Comfortably scruffy.

Central Neighbourhoods

Achilles Heel 1601 Haight St at Clayton. Attractive, Victorian-style English pub in the Haight. Respectable, clean and quiet despite the neighbourhood.

Café du Nord 2170 Market St at Church. A quiet neighbourhood restaurant for years, this has recently become hyper-hip since it started its programme of live nightly music reviving the old tradition of supper clubs. Quite the place for dinner and drinks, though it's OK just to have a beer at the bar.

Café Flore 2298 Market St at Noe. Lively, mostly gay café near the Castro serving great breakfasts and lunch and dinner till 10pm. A popular cruising spot for the locals who come to string a coffee out for hours and be seen reading the latest in hip gay literature. Drown in a sea of newspapers and pretty faces.

Community Blend Café 233 Fillmore St at Haight. Enjoy an excellent breakfast (served all day) or glass of wine in the contrived shabbiness of this Lower Haight gallery-cum-café, where groovy people come to write in their journals.

Courtyard Café 3913 24th Street at Church. Doubles up as a deli and newsstand, making it perfect for browsing magazines with a coffee and, if you're peckish, great food.

Don's Different Ducks 668 Haight St at Steiner ☎ 431-4727. Formerly the splendid *Jimmy's West Point* of local legend,

Bars and Cafés

For a map of SoMa bars, and cafés, see p.232.

Bars and cafés in the Mission and Castro districts are shown on the map on p.235.

Bars and Cafés

Clubs in the Castro are listed on p.264.

now pretty unchanged and sleazed to perfection in red leatherette with a great soul jukebox and just a hint of danger. Not for the nervous.

Harry's On Fillmore 2020 Fillmore St at Clay. This elegantly decorated hang-out serves a mixed, unpretentious crowd and makes for a great night's drinking. Nightly jazz and blues in this laid-back locals bar where the Western Addition becomes Pacific Heights.

Hayes & Vine 377 Hayes St. Well-decorated, affordable wine bar in the up and coming Hayes Valley district.

Jack's Bailey Bar 26th St at Church. Comfy neighbourhood bar with proper armchairs, where you can really recline into a pint.

Jumping Java Coffee House 701 Cole at Waller. Relative peace on a leafy side-street one block from the Haight serving excellent coffee to a slightly serious crowd who are treated to the odd poetry reading.

The Mad Dog in the Fog 530 Haight St at Steiner. Aptly named by the two lads from Birmingham, England who own the joint, this is one of the Lower Haight's most loyally patronized bars with darts, English beer, copies of the *Sun* and a typical pub menu that includes bangers and mash, hearty ploughman's and the like. Amazingly, it is not the English but the trend-conscious young blades of the Lower Haight who find it so groovy.

Martin Mack's 1568 Haight St at Clayton. The Irish theme is a little bit overdone, but the beer is excellent and the bar packed.

Nickies 460 Haight St at Fillmore. High energy Lower Haight hang-out where the music styles change nightly and the crowd is always dancing.

Noc Noc 557 Haight St at Steiner. Decorated like an Egyptian tomb. Draws a fashionable but informal young crowd in for new wave music and flasks of hot sake.

Noe's 1199 Church St. Blue-collar sports bar; come here to catch a game on the giant video screen and have a jeer and cheer with the locals who can't take their eyes off it.

Orbit Room Cafe 1900 Market St at Laguna. The interior design is straight out of *Bladerunner*, and cyberpunk crowds flock here for the good coffees, great beers and ice-cold *Blackthorn* cider.

The Rat and the Raven 4054 24th St. Friendly, hard-drinking neighbourhood bar with pool, darts, and if you're into country music, a superb jukebox.

Toronado 547 Haight St at Steiner. With 44 varieties on tap, this is definitely a beer-drinker's haven. Mixed crowd, lots of leather.

Golden Gate Park, the Beaches and Outlying Areas

Blue Danube Coffee House 306 Clement St at Third. Café society alive and well in the suburbs? Not quite, but about as alternative as you'll get in the Richmond.

Boathouse 1 Harding Park Ave (on Lake Merced). Popular sports bar, with a superb view of Lake Merced and occasional live music.

Last Day Saloon 406 Clement St at Fourth. Very lively bar in the Richmond with regular live music including rock, surfer rock, blues and soul. $5 cover.

Pig & Whistle Pub 2801 Geary Blvd at Collins. Good range of English and California microbrews, and the cheapest happy hour in SF – $2 pints of beer 4–7pm daily. Pool table and dartboards, plus very good pub food.

The Plough and Stars 116 Clement St at First. Irish expat bar with live music on alternate evenings.

East Bay

The Alley 3325 Grand Ave, Oakland ☎510/444-8505. Sing along with the drunken locals at this cosy piano bar. Suggestions welcome from a songbook of favourites over inexpensive cocktails.

Bison Brewing Company 2598 Telegraph Ave, Berkeley ☎510/841-7734. Eat and drink on the terrace, at great prices, where some of the best Bay Area beers are brewed. Honey Basil ale is highly recommended. Noisy bands on the weekend.

Bosn's Locker 5817 Shattuck Ave, Oakland ☎510/652-1520. West Coast blues greats play in this intimate bar with an armed guard at the door protecting a notorious reputation.

Brennan's Fourth St and University, Berkeley ☎510/841-0960. Solidly blue-collar hangout that's a great place for drinking inexpensive beers, watching a game on TV.

Café Mediterraneum 2475 Telegraph Ave, Berkeley ☎510/841-5634. Berkeley's oldest café, straight out of the Beat archives: beards and berets optional, battered paperbacks *de rigueur*.

Café Milano 2522 Bancroft Way, Berkeley ☎510/644-3100. Airy, arty café across from UC Berkeley.

Café Strada 2300 College Ave, Berkeley ☎510/843-5282. Upmarket, open-air café where art and architecture students cross paths with would-be lawyers and chess wizards.

Chalkers Billiard Club 5900 Hollis St, Emeryville ☎658-5821. The antithesis of a pool-hall dive, this posh hall has the best tables and equipment around. Pay by the hour, which is not cheap. Drinks served to tables.

Coffee Mill 3393 Grand Ave, Oakland ☎510/465-4224. Spacious room that doubles as an art gallery, and often hosts poetry readings.

Eline Ale House 5612 College Ave, Oakland ☎510/547-8786. Large selection of microbrewed beer from around the US and excellent food of mixed orgins.

The Fifth Amendment 3255 Lakeshore Ave, Oakland ☎510/832-3242. Looks like a dive from the outside, but local blues greats play at this small, slightly elegant club. No cover, but a two-drink minimum.

Geoffrey's Inner Circle 410 14th St, Oakland ☎510/839-4644. Dress up for a glamorous evening in downtown Oakland with local jazz, blues and soul. $10 cover charge.

Heinhold's First and Last Chance Saloon 56 Jack London Square, Oakland ☎510/839-6761. Authentic waterfront bar that's hardly changed since the turn of the century, when Jack London was a regular.

Hidden City Cafe 109 Park Place, Point Richmond ☎510/232-9738. Breakfasts and lunches in a cosy out-of-the-way cafe. Great cornmeal pancakes.

In the Company of Wolves 737 First Street, Benicia ☎707/746-0572. Progressive coffee house featuring sketch pads on the tables for collecting doodles by customers.

The Ivy Room 858 San Pablo Ave, Albany ☎524-9220. Friendly bar with pool table; rock, jazz, blues and soul bands play for a boisterous crowd.

The Kingfish 5227 Claremont Ave, Oakland ☎510/655-7373. More like a tumbledown shed than a bar, selling low-priced pitchers of cold beer to UC Berkeley rugby players and other headbangers.

Peet's Coffee and Tea throughout the Bay Area. Originating in Berkeley, *Peet's* has grown from a dedicated cult following to an established range of charming cafés. Considered by most caffeine addicts as the standard of extra-strong coffee. Some locations include: 2124 Vine St, Berkeley ☎510/841-0564; 2916 Domingo Ave, Berkeley ☎510/843-1434; 3258 Lakeshore Ave, Oakland ☎510/832-6761; 4050 Piedmont Ave, Oakland ☎510/655-3228.

The Pub 1492 Solano Ave, Albany ☎510/525-1900. Cornucopia of pipe tobacco and cigar brands sold with beer, coffee and wine from this funky, converted house.

Raleigh's 2438 Telegraph Ave, Berkeley ☎510/848-8652. Very popular studenty pub with wide range of West Coast microbrewed beers.

Royal Coffee 307 63rd St, Oakland ☎510/653-5458. Shoe box-sized café with only outside seating serving strong java.

Starry Plough 3103 Shattuck Ave, Berkeley ☎510/841-2082. Very comfortable, politically charged Irish bar with

Bars and Cafés

East Bay restaurants are reviewed on p.238.

Guinness on draft, Powers Whiskey on call and sporadic collections for the IRA. Very near Ashby *BART*, with live music most nights.

Stork Club 380 12th St, Oakland ☎510/444-6147. Local alternative bands and experimental musicians play at one of the few lively, yet divey, downtown Oakland bars with pool table. Doubles as a country and western bar during the day.

Terrace Lounge *Claremont Hotel*, corner of Ashby and Domingo St, Oakland ☎510/843-3000. Drink here for the night-view of the entire Bay Area, if not for the music. Occasionally, good jazz bands play at the top the Oakland hills in a "lounge act" atmosphere.

Warehouse Cafe 5 Canyon Lake Drive, Port Costa ☎510/787-1287. Large turn-of- the-century warehouse converted into a friendly working-class bar. Features a stuffed bear watching patrons, who eat in the adjoining steak and seafood restaurant offering one-price all-you-can-eat food. Antique knick-knack shop in back.

The White Horse 6560 Telegraph Ave at 66th St, Oakland ☎510/652-3820. Oakland's oldest gay bar – a smallish, friendly place, with mixed nightly dancing for men and women.

Yoshi's Restaurant and Nitespot 6030 Claremont, Oakland ☎510/652-9200. Tap a toe to contemporary jazz and blues greats over sushi. Cover $15–20.

The Peninsula

Abigail's Pub 265 N First St, San Jose ☎408/294-4111. Ersatz English pub catering to beer-drinking computer wizards.

Café Matisse 371 First St, San Jose ☎408/298-7788. Mostly nude art grace the walls of this funky artist studio-esque space, with fresh coffee and pastries.

Douglas Beach House Miramar Beach, two and a half miles north of Half Moon Bay on Hwy-1, go west down Medio Ave ☎726-4143. Two-storey country beach-house with fireplace and outside deck hosts West Coast jazz performers.

Five Spot Coffee Shop 869 S First St, San Jose ☎408/293-0653. An inexpensive, traditional diner with American flag and optional drive-up service if you don't want to get out of your car.

Gordon Biersch Brewery 640 Emerson St, Palo Alto ☎323-7723. Also in SF (see p.248) and in downtown San Jose at 33 E San Fernando St ☎294-6785. Among the first and still the best of the Bay Area's microbrewery-cum-restaurants.

Lytton Street Roasting Company 401 Lytton St, Palo Alto ☎324-4320. Sit among large cloth bags of coffee beans in this small café a few blocks off the hustle of University Avenue serving all coffee types.

M Coffee 522 Main St, Half Moon Bay ☎726-6241. Coffees, teas, sandwiches and ice cream in a small, homely eatery.

Pudley's Saloon 255 University Ave, Palo Alto ☎328-2021. A 1940s-style retro-American beer-and-burger bar.

St Mike's Alley 806 Emerson St, Palo Alto ☎326-2530. Small, cosy café for students and locals, serving light breakfasts and lunches. Art exhibits on the walls and live music at night.

Vicolo Pizzeria 473 University Ave, Palo Alto ☎324-4877. Café serving a variety of tasty, affordable gourmet pizza.

Marin County

Book Depot and Café 87 Throckmorton Ave, Mill Valley ☎383-2665. Lively café in an old train station, sharing space with a bookstore and newsstand.

Café Trieste 1000 Bridgeway, Sausalito ☎332-7770. This distant relative of the North Beach institution (see p.249) serves good coffee, a wide menu of pastas and salads, and great gelati.

Caffe Nuvo 556 San Anselmo Ave, San Anselmo ☎454-4530. Great coffee and pastries, with a large balcony overhanging a creek, plus poetry readings and live music most nights

Fairfix Cafe 33 Broadway, Fairfax ☎459-6404. Excellent Mediterranean food with occasional evening poetry readings.

Marin Brewing Company 1809 Larkspur Landing, Larkspur ☎461-4677. Lively pub opposite the Larkspur ferry terminal, with half a dozen tasty ales – try the malty Albion Amber or the creamy St Brendan's Irish Red – all brewed on site.

Mill Valley Coffee Roasters 2 Miller Ave, Mill Valley ☎383-2912. Boisterous, crowded coffee house right in the centre of town.

No Name Bar 757 Bridgeway, Sausalito ☎332-1392. A thriving ex-haunt of the Beats which still hosts poetry readings and evening jam sessions.

Patrick's Bookshop and Café 9 Bolinas Rd, Fairfax ☎454-2428. Coffees, teas, tasty soups and sandwiches, in this low-key hippie hold-out; good selection of books and magazines, too.

Pelican Inn Hwy-1, Muir Beach ☎383-6000. Fair selection of traditional English and modern Californian ales, plus fish'n'chips (and rooms if you overdo it).

Sam's Anchor Café 27 Main St, Tiburon ☎435-2676. Slightly posey hang-out for Marin's yacht-club brigades. Right on the water, you can get a drink or two (or brunch; see p.245) while waiting for the ferry back to SF.

Sunnyside Cafe 31 Sunnyvale Ave, Mill Valley ☎388-5260. Unpretentious diner whose motto is "the customers are rarely right". Affordable breakfasts and lunches are eaten in this unpretentious diner.

Sweetwater 153 Throckmorton Ave, Mill Valley ☎388-3820. Large open room full of beer-drinking locals that after dark evolves into Marin's prime live music venue (see p.260).

Wine Country

Ana's Cantina 1205 Main St, St Helena ☎963-4921. Long-standing unpretentious saloon and Mexican restaurant.

The Coffee Garden 421 First St W, Sonoma ☎707/996-6645. 150-year-old adobe converted into a café with small gift shop. Fresh sandwiches served on the back patio.

Joe Frogger's 527 Fourth Ave, Santa Rosa ☎526-0539. Lively bar with free live music most nights.

Pancha's 5764 Washington St, Yountville ☎707/944-2125. If wine-tasting becomes boring, a dive bar actually exists in Napa Valley in the form of a western saloon.

Sonoma Saloon 110 W Spain St, Sonoma ☎707/996-2996. Funky old saloon that's a hundred years old and still going strong; the adjoining dining room focuses on local cheeses and baked goods.

Wine Exchange of Sonoma 452 E First St, Sonoma ☎707/938-1794. Right on Sonoma's main plaza, with an extensive range of California wines by the glass and by the bottle, this handy shop saves you having to tramp around dozens of far-flung wineries.

Gay and Lesbian Bars

San Francisco's gay bars are many and varied, though in the last few years almost every single lesbian bar (never more than a couple anyway) has disappeared. If you want exclusively female company you'll have to check the *Nightlife* chapter for lists of clubs that have lesbian nights, or venture over to the East Bay, which has traditionally catered rather better to gay women. Bear in mind, however, that the increasingly integrated nature of the gay scene means that formerly exclusively male bars now have a sizable lesbian contingent.

Options for the boys are as lively as ever, and though the scene is not quite as wild as it was at its zenith in the 1970s, you can still find establishments that range from the cosy cocktail bar to full no-holds-barred leather and chain affairs. It's hard to imagine a city that could rival San Francisco for gay entertainment.

The Castro, traditional home of the gay bar, has mellowed in recent years and you'll need to visit **SoMa** or **Polk Street** – or to a lesser extent the **Mission** – for anything outside the mainstream. Take note that places we've listed as bars may switch on some music later on and transform into a club;

Bars and Cafés

Castro bars are shown on the map on p.235.

we've listed the better ones that do this in Chapter Fifteen.

Finally, remember that the vast majority of places welcome straight customers too, especially in the Castro, and if you can't decide where to head for just ask: gays in San Francisco are on the whole a friendly and communicative lot and will normally be glad to point you to the kind of thing you're looking for. There's no shortage of printed matter to give you ideas either: check out the *Sentinel*, *Bay Times* and *Bay Area Reporter*. Alternatively, if you don't mind forking out the $11 for a copy, a must-have for every visiting gay with a sense of humour is *Betty & Pansy's Severe Queer Review*, listing everything from the best place to eat upscale food to the best cruising alleys.

Alta Plaza 2301 Fillmore at Clay. Catering to the Pacific Heights junior executive crowd. Boys in suits looking for similar.

Badlands 4121 18th St at Noe. Not quite as cruisy as the *Midnight Sun* (below), but the lively thirtysomething crowd are not exactly here to read the papers either.

The Café 2367 Market St near Castro. One of the few gay places in town that is not the exclusive domain of men, *The Café* gets a good mixed crowd who come to drink, dance and play pool at this hot, dark, and – be warned – young, hi-energy bar-cum-club.

Café Flore 2298 Market St at Noe. Very much the in-spot before dark. Attractive café, with matching clientele and leafy outdoor area, and no shortage of people eyeing each other up. Very mixed, lots of women.

The Castro Station 456 Castro St at 18th. Noisy disco bar that manages to pack 'em in even in the middle of the day. Very much the die-hard scene of the 1970s, with a fair number in their leather trousers.

The Cinch 1723 Polk St at Washington. Lively neighbourhood bar that pulls a mixed crowd and has a nice patio area for when you tire of playing pool.

Daddy's 440 Castro St at 18th. Dimly lit, lots of leather and lots of smoke. A butch scene.

DeLuxe 1511 Haight St at Ashbury. 1940s Swing retro-style bar for a mixed crowd.

Detour 2348 Market St between Noe and Castro. Arguably the most popular bar in the Castro, the crowd is young and horny. Loud, sexy atmosphere.

The Edge 4149 18th St at Castro. Leather bar with a cosy neighbourhood feel to it. Lots of black paint and red lights and great house music.

La India Bonita 3089 16th St at Valencia. Family-run, lighthearted drag-queen bar. Mostly for Hispanics; there were no English speakers at the last visit. Highly recommended.

Empress Lily 4 Valencia at Market. Formerly an old, little-frequented drive known as the *Travel Lounge*, this bar has had a big revival of its fortunes since the gay community got hold of it and turned it into one of the liveliest venues for drag shows for miles. Draws a good, mixed crowd.

Mary's Backside Bar 269 12th St at Folsom. Where gay meets straight in perfect harmony, *Mary's* is relaxed, sociable and attracts a lot of women.

Midnight Sun 4067 18th St at Castro. Young, white boys dressed to the nines and cruising like maniacs in this noisy Castro video bar.

The Mint 1942 Market St at Guerrero. Relaxed karaoke bar bringing out the star in us all. Mixed, middle-aged, well-dressed and well-behaved scene.

Moby Dick 4049 18th St at Noe. Civilized-looking neighbourhood bar by day, gets rowdier by night. Pool tables and TV screens for the shy.

The Phoenix 482 Castro St at 18th. Being only one of Castro's two dance bars, it not surprisingly draws a large, exuberant crowd.

Rawhide 280 Seventh St at Folsom. If men in chaps are your scene, go no further than this dimly lit SoMa landmark that plays country and western and blue-

grass music to a jovial mixed crowd. Definitely recommended. $5 cover at weekend includes two drinks.

El Rio 3158 Mission St at Army (Cesar Chavez). Mixed crowds gather for changing nightly entertainment. All music styles and some great giveaways, like oysters on the half-shell on a Friday. Most popular though, live salsa on a Sunday afternoon that draws a predominantly female crowd.

SF Eagle 398 12th St at Harrison. Easily the best-known leather bar in San Francisco. Large outdoor area with stage. Best time for a visit is for the $8 Sunday brunch when they have a "beer bust" 3 to 6pm to raise money for AIDS.

The Stud 399 Ninth St at Harrison. A favourite dancing spot with a mixed but mostly gay crowd. Variable cover charge depending on the night and some raucous times and shameless freaking out on the dance floor. A San Francisco institution, highly recommended. Check local listings for details or call ☎252-STUD.

The Swallow 1750 Polk Street at Clay. This sophisticated piano bar pulls in a well-behaved middle-aged crowd who just want a good drink and some conversation. Not for randy party animals.

Twin Peaks 17th and Castro St. The Castro's first blatantly gay bar, with large see-through windows to make the point. Draws a low-key older crowd who gather for quiet drinks and conversation.

Uncle Bert's Place 4086 18th St at Castro. Lives up to its name – a cosy neighbourhood bar.

Chapter 15

Nightlife

Compared to New York or Los Angeles, where you need money and attitude in equal amounts, San Francisco's nightlife demands little of either.

Though replete with its fair share of all-night raves, this is not, on the whole, a 24-hour city. The approach to socializing is often surprisingly low-key, manifest in its smooth supper clubs where you can listen to excellent music *and* eat your dinner. San Franciscans love their grub and do not see why they should forsake it in order to have a good night out. Though obviously subject to fads and fashions, and usually very on top of the music scene, the city has a style peculiar to itself – it is done without addiction to hip credentials and yet has a kind of cool-camp. The casualness is contagious, and manifest in a **club scene** that – far as it is from the cutting edge – is encouragingly inexpensive compared to other cities. Thirty dollars can buy you a decent night out, including cover charge, a few drinks and maybe even a taxi home.

The **live music** scene is similarly economical – and, frankly, what the city does best. San Franciscans may be relatively unconcerned with being up-to-the-minute, but there are some excellent rock, jazz and folk venues all over town, many entertaining you for no more than the price of a drink.

San Francisco has a somewhat better reputation for **opera** and **classical music**. Its orchestra and opera association are among the most highly regarded in the country. **Theatre** is more accessible and much less costly, with discount tickets available, but most of the mainstream downtown venues – barring a couple of exceptions – are mediocre, forever staging Broadway reruns. You'd do better to take some time to explore the infinitely more interesting fringe circuit.

Cabaret and comedy are also lively: some excellent clubs host an increasingly healthy and varied diet of good comedians. **Film**, too, is almost as big an obsession as eating in San Francisco. The range of film is first-class, and you may well be

Listings and Ticket Information

Apart from the flyers posted up around town, the *Sunday Chronicle*'s "Pink Pages" supplement is about the best source of **listings** and **what's on** information; you might also check the free weekly *Bay Guardian*, the *San Francisco Weekly*, and a host of other more specific publications listed below under the relevant sections.

For **tickets**, *BASS* (☎ 776-1999 or 510/762-2277), the *Bay Area Seating Service*, is the major Bay Area booking agency. You can either reserve with a credit card on these numbers, or in person at one of their many branches in record stores such as *Tower Records* or *Wherehouse*. **Theatre tickets** are also on sale at the *Tix* ticket booth on Union Square; see "Theatre" on p.266 for details.

surprised by the sheer number of movie theatres – repertory and current-release – that flourish. The **Pacific Film Archive**, one of the world's finest film libraries, fills its screens with obscure, but brilliant art flicks. The Hong Kong Film Festival, Jewish Film Festival and San Rafael Film Festival are also successful Bay Area screenings.

Live Music: Rock, Jazz and Folk

San Francisco's **music scene** reflects the character of the city as a whole: laid-back, eclectic and a little nostalgic. The options for catching **live music** are wide and the scene is consistently progressive, characterized by the frequent emergence of good young bands.

However, San Francisco has yet to recapture its crucial 1960s role, and these days is principally renowned as a venue for good r'n'b, psychedelia, folk and rock standards, as well as c'n'w and Latin American bands. **Jazz** is also very good and not just confined to the city proper: the East Bay in particular is very strong on jazz/funk/blues bands.

Live bands are extremely easy to catch. As well as the big names, for whom the Bay Area is an essential stop on nationwide tours, many restaurants offer live music, so you can eat, drink and dance all at once and often with no cover charge. Ordinary neighbourhood bars regularly host groups, often for free; and there are any number of good and inexpensive small venues.

Although clubs tend to be concentrated in the South of Market area, live music venues are spread out across the city. Few fall into any particular camp, with most varying their bill throughout the week, and it can be hard to specify which of them cater to a certain music style. Many also double as clubs, hosting some kind of disco after the live music has stopped.

What follows is a pretty comprehensive list of established venues, but be sure to check the music press, the best of which is the free *BAM* (*Bay Area Music*). Available in most record stores in the city, it carries exhaustive listings of events in the city and Bay Area.

The Large Performance Venues

The easiest way to book seats for the following venues is through *BASS*, either with a major credit card several weeks in advance, or at one of their record store branches; either way you'll have to pay a service charge of around $3. Bear in mind that some of the Bay Area's best large-scale venues, where the big names tend to play, are actually across the bay in Oakland and Berkeley.

Berkeley Community Theater 1930 Allston Way, Berkeley ☎510/845-2308. Jimi Hendrix played here, and the 3500-seat theatre still hosts major rock concerts and community events.

Center for Contemporary Music Mills College, 5000 Mac Arthur Blvd, Oakland ☎510/430-2191. One of the prime centres in the world for experimental music. Mozart is only a shadow compared to John Cage, Lou Harrison, John Zorn or Pauline Oliveras. See concerts where the musicians use the insides of the pianos rather than the keys.

Great American Music Hall 859 O'Farrell St at Polk ☎885-0750. Civic Center venue, too small for major names but too large for local yokels, and hosting a range of musical styles from balladeers to thrash bands. The lovely interior – it used to be a burlesque house and upscale bordello – makes for a great night out.

Oakland Coliseum Complex Coliseum *BART*, near Oakland Airport ☎510/639-7700. Stadium rock – inside the 17,000 seat *Arena*, or outside in the 60,000 seat *Coliseum*.

Paramount Theater 2025 Broadway, downtown Oakland ☎510/465-6400. Beautifully restored Art Deco masterpiece, hosting classical concerts, big-name crooners, ballets and operas. Classic Hollywood films are shown on Friday nights.

The Warfield 982 Market St at Sixth ☎775-7722. *The Warfield* can usually be relied upon to stage major rock crowd-

Nightlife

pullers. Chart bands, big-name indie groups and popular old-timers keep the place packed.

Zellerbach Hall UC Berkeley ☎510/642-9988. Together with the outdoor Greek Theatre, two of the prime spots for catching touring big names in the Bay Area.

Rock, Folk and Country

Albion 3139 16th St at Valencia ☎552-8558. Primarily just a Mission neighbourhood bar, which occasionally hosts local bands on its tiny stage. Small, inexpensive and intimate, it's ideal for a night out on the cheap. No cover.

Babylon 2260 Van Ness at Vallejo ☎567-1222. Although this attractive Russian Hill, tomb-like venue is ostensibly for eating, most of the lusty young singles are there to down cocktails and attract attention by dancing vigorously.

Club Boomerang 1840 Haight St at Stanyan ☎387-2996. Modern Rock, Haight-style, with a good nightly line-up of lesser-known bands.

Hotel Utah 500 Fourth St at Bryant ☎421-8308. Good selection of mainly country bands which you can usually see for free or a very small cover.

Last Day Saloon 406 Clement St at Fifth ☎387-6343. A bit out of the way, but if you find yourself in the Richmond and you're wondering where to find some action, this is the best the area has to offer. Great range of rock, surfer rock, soul, blues and r'n'b. Bands play nightly. Cover $3–6.

Lost and Found Saloon 1353 Grant Ave at Columbus ☎397-3751. Informal North Beach hang-out with a catch-all selection of music styles.

Lou's 300 Jefferson St at Taylor ☎771-0377. Country/rock and blues bar down on Fisherman's Wharf that hosts some good local bands. Weekend lunchtimes are a good time to check out the lesser-known in relative peace. Come nightfall it's madness. No cover before 9pm.

Nightbreak 1821 Haight St at Shrader ☎221-9008. Slightly shabby, small Haight venue where new wave and Goth bands play to a matching crowd. Very dark, very loud, and very crowded.

Paradise Lounge 1501 Folsom St at 11th ☎861-6906. Good SoMa venue to see up-and-coming rock bands (usually three per night), or take a break for a game of pool upstairs in *Above Paradise*.

The Plough and Stars 116 Clement St at Second ☎751-1122. Quite a way from downtown but worth the trip if you're into Irish folk music. Very much the haunt of the Irish expat community.

Purple Onion 140 Columbus Ave at Broadway ☎398-8415. Established North Beach venue for hearing a good selection of rock and country.

Saloon 1232 Grant Ave at Columbus ☎989-7666. Always packed to the gills, this is undeniably North Beach's best spot for some rowdy r'n'b.

BAY AREA

Freight and Salvage 1111 Addison St, West Berkeley ☎510/548-1761. Singer-songwriters in a coffee-house setting. Cover $6–12.

Gilman Street Project 924 Gilman St, West Berkeley ☎510/525-9926. On the outer edge of the hardcore punk scene.

La Peña Cultural Center 3105 Shattuck Ave, Berkeley nr Ashby *BART* ☎510/849-2568. More folk than rock, often politically charged. Cover $3–6.

Stork Club 380 12th St, Oakland ☎510/444-6147. Local alternative bands and experimental musicians play at this downtown Oakland bar with pool table. Doubles as a country and western bar during the day.

Sweetwater 153 Throckmorton Ave, Mill Valley ☎388-2820. Well worth a trip north of Marin, this comfortable saloon brings in some of the biggest names in music, from jazz and blues all-stars to Jefferson Airplane survivors.

Jazz, Latin American and World Music

Bahia Cabana 1600 Market St at Franklin ☎626-3306. High-energy hang-out and supper club with good Brazilian and samba bands – attracts a skilled dancing crowd who can shake it with a vengeance. Live music and DJ dancing seven nights a week.

Bimbo's 365 Club 1025 Columbus Ave at Chestnut ☎474-0365. Varied menu of music styles from jazz to ska, always something worth seeing on the weekly bill.

Blondie's Bar & No Grill 540 Valencia St at 16th ☎864-2419. One of the reasons the Mission is such an up-and-coming nightlife area. The varied menu of music and entertainment pulls a fashionable, good-time crowd.

Café du Nord 2170 Market St at Church ☎861-5016. Excellent, friendly and affordable venue to catch nightly live music while you sample the food on offer or just drink at the bar. Nightly changing music styles. Recommended.

The Compass Rose Lobby of the *St Francis Hotel*, Union Square ☎774-0167. With a jazz trio on Wed & Thurs evenings and piano tunes on Mon & Tues, this is quite the place to sit in deluxe surroundings and sip expensive drinks.

Elbo Room 647 Valencia at 16th ☎552-7788. Beautiful wood-panelled bar with pool tables downstairs and live music for a small cover upstairs. Usually acid-jazz or variations thereof.

Gold Dust Lounge 247 Powell St ☎397-1695. So close to Union Square it's a bit of a tourist hang-out, but good for a sing-song and old-time Dixieland jazz. No cover.

Jacks Bar 1601 Fillmore St at Geary ☎567-3227. Small, intimate bar with jazz and blues three nights a week. Open-mike comedy night Tues.

Kimball's 300 Grove St at Polk ☎861-5585. Slick establishment jazz-club-cum-restaurant with a clientele bordering on middle age. Luckily, you don't have to eat, which is handy as the cover tends to be high. Open daily until 3am.

Miss Pearl's Jam House 601 Eddy St at Polk ☎775-JAMS. Attached to the super-hip *Phoenix* motel – see p.211 – this Caribbean restaurant features some great reggae bands or just lounging round the pool with a cocktail.

181 Eddy 181 Eddy St at Taylor ☎673-8181. If you're not afraid of the slightly dodgy neighbourhood, make the effort to get down to this trendy venue with great dance music and excellent soul and funk bands. Something of a hot spot for the cognoscenti.

Paragon 3251 Scott St at Francisco ☎922-2456. Smart, cool new Marina venue for a fashion-conscious crowd who come to enjoy the nightly jazz, jazz fusion, funk and soul. Recommended.

Pasand Lounge 1875 Union St at Laguna ☎922-4498. Unusual club where you can come to eat Indian food and listen to very mellow jazz in the comfortable lounge.

Pearl's 256 Columbus Ave at Broadway ☎291-8255. Cosy North Beach supper club, where you enjoy jazz while sitting down with a good meal. No cover, but you must eat or drink.

The Plush Room *York Hotel*, 940 Sutter St at Hyde ☎885-2800. Newly revived San Francisco institution, which has successfully recreated its former glory and on a good night attracts a very glamorous crowd. Tickets around $20; 21 and over only.

The Rite Spot Café 2099 Folsom St at 17th ☎552-6066. Informal, café-style club with jazz and r'n'b bands. Open Mon–Sat, and serving snacks, drinks and coffee until 1am. Small cover at weekends.

Slim's 333 11th St at Folsom ☎621-3330. Slick but reliable showcase for internationally known bands. Not cheap, but a better class of jazz act and a grown-up crowd.

Slow Club 2501 Mariposa, Potrero Hill ☎241-9390. Smooth, low-key supper club with a fairly stylish clientele.

Sol y Luna 475 Sacramento St at Sansome ☎296 8191. Spanish supper club with live Flamenco shows every Wed & Sat with rumba & salsa dancing afterwards. $10 cover, but free parking in Embarcadero One.

Many of the clubs listed here are shown on the district maps in Restaurants, *Chapter Thirteen.*

Nightlife

330 Ritch St Ritch Alley between Third and Fourth, Townsend and Brannan ☎522-9558. Trendy SoMa nightspot with dancing to salsa, soul, dance hall, deep house. Small cover after 9pm.

The Tonga Room Basement of the *Fairmont Hotel*, 950 Mason St at Powell ☎772-5000. An absolute must for fans of the ludicrous or just the very drunk. The whole place is decked out as a Polynesian village, complete with pond, simulated rainstorms, and a grass-skirted band that play terrible jazz and pop covers on a raft in the middle of the water.

The Up & Down Club 1151 Folsom St at Eighth ☎626-2388. One of the best additions to the live music circuit in years, The *Up & Down* is a small, comfortably styled bar full of grown-up people enjoying top-notch jazz and knocking back well-made drinks. If you want something quieter, you can eat downstairs and listen to something mellower. With the benefit of recent patronage by local girl Christy Turlington, who bought the place, it has an element of fame, too.

Check out the East Bay Express *for current music, film, readings and lecture listings in the Bay Area.*

BAY AREA

Ashkenaz 1317 San Pablo Ave, Berkeley ☎510/525-5054. World music and dance café. Acts range from modern Afro-beat to the best of the Balkans. Kids and under-21s welcome. Cover $5–8.

Caribee Dance Center 1408 Webster St, Oakland ☎510/835-4006. For reggae, rockers, calypso, soca, dub, salsa or lambada, this place is hard to beat. Cover $3–8.

Eli's Mile High Club 3629 Martin Luther King Jr Way, North Oakland ☎510/655-6661. The best of the Bay Area blues clubs. Waitresses balance pitchers of beer on their heads to facilitate safer passage through the rocking crowds. Cover $5–8.

Kimball's East 4800 Shellmound St, Emeryville ☎510/658-2555. Very comfortable, intimate room hosting some of the world's best jazz and blues performers. Energetic dancing downstairs to live salsa and merengue. Cover $10–25.

Koncepts Cultural Gallery 247 Fourth St no. 110, Oakland ☎510/763-0682. Excellent, ground-breaking jazz organization, hosting a wide variety of different acts at venues around Oakland. Cover $8–25.

Yoshi's Restaurant and Nitespot 6030 Claremont, Oakland ☎510/652-9200. Tap a toe to contemporary jazz and blues greats over sushi. Cover $15–20.

Clubbing

As mentioned earlier, San Francisco **nightclubs**, whilst not of the ultra-hip, cavernous variety found in other American cities, have manifold compensations – no waiting for hours, or high cover charges, ridiculously priced drinks and feverish posing. Instead you'll find a diverse range of small- to medium-sized affordable clubs in which San Francisco's miscellaneous assortment of clubbers rub shoulders with each other to a dizzying variety of sounds. The key to San Francisco's nightclubs is not to be seen so much as to HAVE A GOOD TIME.

The greatest concentration of clubs is in **SoMa**, especially the area around 11th Street and Folsom, though the **Mission** is similarly well provided with bars and small live music venues – not to mention a couple of outrageous drag bars – of almost exclusively Latin origin.

Unlike most other cities, where the action never gets going until after midnight, many San Francisco **clubs** have to close at 2am during the week, so you can usually be sure of finding things well under way by 11.00pm. At weekends, most places stay open until 3 or 4am. San Francisco isn't really big or club-oriented enough to sport a serious attitude towards weekend out-of-towners; often are more exciting at the weekend.

Few venues operate any kind of restrictive admission policy, and only on very busy nights are you likely to have to wait. It's usually entirely acceptable to wander in and out of clubs, so long as you have the regulation hand-stamp.

Note that many **gay clubs**, particularly those listed under "Mixed", are by no means no-go areas for straight people – and frankly they're often the best.

Several places charge no **cover** at all and only the most chi-chi of clubs will charge a fortune for drinks. The entry age to all bars is 21, and it's a good idea to carry **ID** with you at all times: as a general rule, if you look under thirty you'll definitely need it.

The Clubs

Casanova 527 Valencia St at 16th ☎863-9328. Laid-back neighbourhood bar until the sun goes down and the music gets turned up, drawing a fashion-conscious body-pierced Mission crowd. Get in early for Happy Hour, make a night of it and avoid the cover charge.

Cat's Grill and Alley Club 1190 Folsom St at Eighth ☎431-3332. Perfect for the mature clubber, the *Cat's Grill* puts on a bit of entertainment – anything from belly-dancing snake-charmers to women's open mike – to get everybody warmed up, serves a few tapas and then turns the music up for a right good dance. Perfect.

Club Oz *Westin St Francis Hotel*, 335 Powell St ☎956-7777. Skyline dance room on the 32nd floor of the hotel draws a young dance-crazy crowd. Worth going just for the view.

Covered Wagon Saloon 917 Folsom St at Fifth ☎974-1585. Definitely one of the better SoMa places, they serve up a varied menu of one-nighters offering everything from hip-hop to Sixties pop.

DNA Lounge 375 11th St at Harrison ☎626-1409. Club which changes its music style nightly but draws the same young hipsters. Large dance floor downstairs and when the dancing gets too much you can lounge around in comfy sofas on the mezzanine. Cover $3 and up. Tues–Sun 9pm–4am.

DV8 55 Natoma St between First and Second, Mission & Howard ☎777-1419. Huge, ornate and fashionable, this is the closest San Francisco comes to rivalling the big clubs of New York and Los Angeles, decorated by Keith Haring pop art and playing high-energy funk and house music. It also has a nice members-only bar that's worth bluffing your way into if you can. About the only club in town worth dressing up for. Cover $10. Wed–Sat.

El Rio 3158 Mission St at Army ☎ 282-3325. Latin, jazz and samba are the specialty here, with live salsa bands on Sunday, dancing to modern funk on Friday, in a friendly, anything-goes atmosphere. Open 3pm–2am during the week, and 3pm–6am at weekends.

The End Up Harrison and Sixth streets ☎495-9550. A mostly gay crowd, but recently discovered by the weekend clubbers, and a good place for the hard-core party animal. Open continuously from 6am on Sat morning until 2am Mon. Small cover.

Holy Cow 1531 Folsom St at 12th ☎621-6087. Young club fiends trying hard to be cool, but a good rave once it warms up. A huge plastic cow hangs outside, you can't miss it. Usually no cover. Tues–Sun.

Leopard Lounge 2125 Lombard St at Fillmore ☎771-2583. Seventies funk and acid jazz DJs help the Marina professionals remember the importance of going out and having a good time.

Nickies 460 Haight St ☎621-6058. Varied menu of music styles keeps this small Lower Haight joint rocking.

Nightbreak 1821 Haight St at Shrader ☎221-9008. Small Haight club that tags itself with the slogan "All the funk that's fit to pump". House, hip-hop and funk most nights.

The Palladium 1031 Kearny St at Columbus ☎434-1308. Cavernous night-

One excellent way to get the flavour of San Francisco's clubs when you first arrive is to experience the *Three Babes and a Bus* tour (☎552-2582) of various hot spots around town. For $30 the three women who organize the tours will drag you around on their bus for an evening visiting clubs and throwing in the odd drink. In between visits there is much carousing and game-playing on board; your companions are likely to be other gawky tourists, but you can always ditch them between rides.

club with three dance floors, flashing lights and modern rock for 18 and over crowd. Open till 6am Fri & Sat.

Pierce Street Annex 3138 Fillmore St at Filbert ☎ 567-1400. The archetypal singles hang-out, known as the "Bermuda Triangle" for its uncanny ability to make people disappear overnight with one another. DJs nightly, no or small cover. Live jazz Fridays.

Release 1015 Folsom St at Sixth ☎337-7475. Another dance club pumping out 1970s nostalgia which seems to have a limitless supply of punters – nice barbecue on the outside patio for when the dancing gets too much.

TEN15 1015 Folsom St at Sixth ☎431-1200. Three dance floors playing Seventies disco, funk and deep house. Dancing till 6am at weekends.

Townsend 177 Townsend St at Third ☎ 974-6020. A must for house fans, this place really cranks up the bass and keeps it blaring. Thurs–Sat. Cover $5.

Gay and Lesbian Clubs

Many **gay and lesbian clubs** are bars that host various club nights at least once a week. Pleasingly unpretentious, the city's gay clubs rank among the city's best, and although a number are purely male affairs, with women-only discos dotted here and there, the majority welcome gay people of both sexes.

Bear in mind that there's a fine line between gay bars and **gay clubs**, and many gay bars convert to discos in the evening. Because all the lesbian bars seem to have disappeared, the women now usually share space with boy bars and host one-night affairs from selected venues; check for details in the local press – *Oblivion Magazine, Odyssey Magazine, Bay Times and Bay Area Reporter* offer the most comprehensive listings.

For gay men there is no better companion to exploring the penthouses and pavements of queer SF than *Betty & Pansy's Severe Queer Review*, ($11) which gives unashamedly explicit advice on getting the most out of your visit.

Mixed

Baby Judy's Discotheque 527 Valencia St. Goodness, what a group gathers here on a Wednesday. Most of the crowd are body-pierced, tattooed, arty and flamboyant.

The Box 715 Harrison St at Third. Very popular dance club that plays a good selection of funk and house music. Currently the hot favourite for dance-serious men and women. Thurs.

Breathe Deep 1015 Folsom St at Sixth ☎998-9515. Set in a small room of a large SoMa nightspot on Tuesdays, this is the club for people who want to get stoned and talk. Not just for dancing.

Club Universe 177 Townsend St at Third ☎985-5241. San Francisco's hottest Saturday night club, this large, cavernous space draws people of all ages, orientation and gender for dancing to progressive house music until 7am. One for the tireless or very high. $10.

El Rio 3158 Mission St at Army ☎282-3325. Mixed crowds gather for dancing to live salsa on Sundays in the open-air courtyard, with a varying menu of music styles the rest of the week. For a good night out, you can't go wrong.

The End Up Sixth St at Harrison ☎495-9550. Changes its bill weekly, but most nights are gay or mixed, with girls-only dancing on Saturdays and Sundays (see opposite).

Rawhide 280 Seventh St at Folsom ☎621-1197. Country and western dance hall. Hysterical good fun if you're into square-dancing and the like. A San Francisco gem.

Mainly for men

Asia at the King St Garage 174 King St at Third behind club *Townsend* ☎665-6715. Every other Friday the site of the Pacific Rim's largest gay Asian dance spot.

Esta Noche 3079 16th St at Valencia ☎861-5757. Discomania Latin-style. Young men and their pursuers dance to a high-energy disco beat reminiscent of the 1970s.

Futura 174 King St at Third behind club *Townsend* ☎974-6020. On Thursday

nights, San Francisco's gay Latin contingent gathers to dance to high-energy Spanish house music. Quite a scene.

La India Bonita 3089 16th at Valencia ☎621-9294. Family-run drag queen bar. Latin high-jinx and revelry.

My Place 1225 Folsom St at Eighth ☎863-2329. Back with a vengeance after a fire that put it out of action for a while, *My Place* is a 1970s-style joint, with heavy cruising, heavy drinking and heavy petting. Cheap drinks help the entertainment right along.

Pleasuredome 177 Townsend St at Third ☎985-5256. As the name suggests, this club draws a bare-chested, good-time crowd. One of the city's favourite men-spots.

The Stud 399 Ninth St at Harrison ☎863-6623. An oldie but a goodie. Has been popular for years for its energetic, uninhibited dancing and good times.

Mainly for Women

Avalon At the *Transmission Theater*, 314 11th St at Folsom. All-women dance night on last Saturday of every month.

Club Q At the *Kennel Club*, 628 Divisadero St ☎931-9858. Friday disco patronized by a young, ethnically mixed group of women. Always packed.

Comme Nous At the *Coco Club*, 139 Eighth St at Mission ☎553-8719. Slightly precious lesbian gathering happens every Saturday night. If you take your sexuality very seriously and want others to do the same, join the navel-gazers here.

Diva At the *Transmission Theater*, 314 11th St at Folsom ☎487-6305. All-women dance night on the third Friday of every month.

The End Up Sixth St at Harrison ☎487-6277. Sunday evenings kick off with a tea dance at 6pm, moving onto harder grooves as the night progresses.

Faster Pussycat 911 Folsom St at Fifth ☎561-9771. Wednesday night dance club for twenty–thirtysomething lipstick lesbian crowd.

Girl Spot (at The Stud) 399 Ninth St at Harrison ☎337-4962. The City's most friendly women-only evening where everyone from the toughest dyke to the most fey femme just wants to have a good time. No politics, no posturing, just fun on a Saturday night.

Junk (at The Stud) 399 Ninth St at Harrison. Leather and flannel night for wimmin on Thurs.

Muff Dive – a dive for dykes 911 Folsom St at Fifth ☎974-1585. Sunday-evening club night for a mixed bag of women of all ages and styles.

Classical Music, Opera and Dance

Though the San Francisco arts scene has to fight against a reputation for provincialism, this is the only city on the West Coast to boast its own professional **symphony**, **ballet** and **opera** companies, each of which has a thriving upper-crust social support scene, wining and dining its way through fund-raisers and the like. The *War Memorial Opera House* will be closed until 1997 for essential engineering work, and the ballet and opera will be performing at temporary venues around the city, including Center for the Arts in Yerba Buena Gardens (☎978-ARTS) and the Palace of Fine Arts (Bay and Lyon streets ☎567-6642). Call for details and check the local listings.

Louise M Davies Symphony Hall 201 Van Ness Ave at Hayes ☎431-5400. The permanent home of the San Francisco Symphony, which offers a year-round season of classical music and sometimes performances by other, often offbeat musical and touring groups. Established in 1909 as a small musical group, the Symphony rose to international prominence in the 1950s when it started touring and recording. Without exactly being world-beaters, they've scooped up several awards on the international circuit. Non-stop recording work has included at least sixteen symphonies and the soundtracks for *Amadeus* and *The Unbearable Lightness of Being*. Their status was given a further boost in 1995, by the appointment of world-renowned conductor Michael Tilson Thomas. Prices obviously

depend on the performance, but are marginally lower than either the opera or ballet, with the least expensive seats going for around $20. If you're willing to chance it, standby tickets are available two hours before a performance with terrace seats behind stage going for $9–12 and remaining second-tier balcony seats for $15.

War Memorial Opera House ☎864-3330. Ticket and schedule information ☎864-3330. A night at the opera in San Francisco is no small-time affair. The Opera House, designed by architect Arthur Brown Jr, the creator of City Hall and Coit Tower, makes a very opulent venue for both the San Francisco Opera Association – which has been performing here since the building opened in 1932 – and the ballet.

By far the strongest of San Francisco's cultural trio, the Opera Association has won critical acclaim for its performances of the classics as well as obscure Russian productions that other companies prefer not to tackle. The SF Opera carries considerable international weight and pulls in big names on a regular basis. Its main season runs from the end of September for thirteen weeks, and its opening night is one of the principal social events on the West Coast. Sporadically, they also have a summer season during June and July. Tickets cost upwards of $40 – for which you do at least get supertitles with the foreign-language operas. **Standing room** costs a bargain $8, and 300 tickets are available (one per person) at 10.30am on the day of performance.

The San Francisco Ballet Performances usually held at the Opera House, so check local listings for venue details until the Opera House reopens (☎861-5600). The city's ballet company, the oldest and third-largest in the US, has a four-month season (Feb–May) with a programme of both classical and contemporary dance. Founded in 1933, the Ballet was the first American company to stage full-length productions of *Swan Lake* and *The Nutcracker*. They've won Emmys, broadcast, toured and generally earned themselves a reputation for ambition: overreach drove them toward bankruptcy in the 1970s and they seemed to be sliding until 1985, when the Icelandic Helgi Tomasson, "premier danseur" of the New York City Ballet, stepped in as artistic director. Since his appointment, the company can seem to do no wrong and some proud San Franciscans consider it "America's premier ballet company". Critical opinion hasn't quite concurred as yet, but the tickets (which cost upwards of $30) are by no means overpriced. Student rush tickets at fifty percent off, are on sale afternoon of performance, bring some ID.

> During the summer months, look out for the **free concerts in Stern Grove** (at 19th Avenue and Sloat Boulevard) where the symphony, opera and ballet give open-air performances for ten successive Sundays (starting in June).

Theatre

The majority of San Francisco's **theatres** congregate downtown around the Theater District. Most aren't especially innovative (although a handful of more inventive fringe places are scattered in other parts of town, notably SoMa), but tickets are reasonably inexpensive – up to $30 a seat – and there's usually good availability.

Tickets can be bought direct from the theatre box offices, or, using a credit card, through ***BASS*** (☎776-1999 or 510/762-2277). The *Tix Bay Area* ticket booth on the Stockton Street side of Union Square regularly has last-minute tickets for as much as half off the marked price (Tues–Thurs 11am–6pm; Fri–Sat 11am–7pm, closed Sun and Mon. ☎433-7827).

Downtown

American Conservatory Theater (ACT) *Geary Theater*, 450 Geary St at Taylor ☎749-2228. The Bay Area's leading resident theatre group. Despite suffering the wholesale destruction of its theatre in the 1989 earthquake, it has managed to bounce back and today continues to stage San Francisco's most impressive plays from its newly restored auditorium.

Curran Theatre 445 Geary St at Taylor ☎474-3800. Tackles bigger productions and musicals of the Andrew Lloyd-Webber genre.

Golden Gate Theatre 1 Taylor St at Market ☎474-3800. Originally constructed during the 1920s and recently restored to its former splendour, the *Golden Gate* is San Francisco's most elegant theatre, with marble flooring, rococo ceilings and gilt trimmings. It's a pity that the programmes don't live up to the surroundings – generally a mainstream diet of Broadway musicals on their latest rerun, although they occasionally manage to pull a big name out of the bag for a one-man Vegas-type show.

Lorraine Hansberry Theatre 620 Sutter St at Mason ☎474-8800. Radical young group of black performers whose work covers traditional theatre as well as more contemporary political pieces and jazz/blues musical reviews. Impressive.

Orpheum Theatre 1192 Market St at Eighth ☎474-3800. Showtime, song and dance performances and "light" cabaret-style theatre.

Stage Door Theatre 420 Mason St at Post ☎749-2228. Attractive, medium-sized turn-of-the-century theatre, run by the *American Conservatory Theater* group.

Theater for the Arts Yerba Buena Gardens, 701 Mission St at Third ☎978-ARTS. San Francisco's newest theatrical venue offering a diverse range of productions. Check listings for details.

Theatre On The Square 450 Post St at Mason ☎433-9500. Converted Gothic theatre with drama, musicals, comedy and mainstream theatre pieces.

Elsewhere in the City

Beach Blanket Babylon Series *Club Fugazi Cabaret*, 678 Green St at Powell ☎421-4222. One of the few musts for theatre-goers in the city, its formality smacks of a Royal Command Performance, but the shows themselves are zany and fast-paced cabarets of jazz singers, dance routines and comedy very slickly put together.

Climate Theater 252 Ninth St at Folsom ☎978-2345. Small, reputable SoMa theatre, specializing in fringe/alternative productions. Cheaper and probably a lot more stimulating than some of the downtown efforts.

Intersection for the Arts 446 Valencia St at 16th ☎626-3311. Well-meaning, community-based group that tackle interesting productions in inadequate facilities. Dance, comedy and straight theatre alternating with art exhibitions and lectures.

The Lab 2948 16th St at Mission ☎864-8855. Experimental, interdisciplinary gallery and performance space. Interesting.

The Magic Theatre Fort Mason Center, Building D ☎441-8822. The busiest and largest company after the *ACT*, and probably the most exciting, *The Magic Theater* specializes in the works of contemporary playwrights and emerging new talent; Sam Shepard traditionally premieres his work here. They have been described as the "most adventuresome company in the West".

Mission Cultural Center 2868 Mission St at 24th ☎821-1155. An organization dedicated to preserving and developing Latin culture, staging small, but worthy, productions using the wealth of talented but underrated performers in San Francisco's Latin community.

Phoenix Theatre 301 Eighth St ☎621-4423. Small SoMa playhouse that specializes in readings, one-act plays and sketches.

Theater Artaud 450 Florida St ☎621-7797. Very modern theatre in a converted warehouse that tackles the obscure and abstract: visiting performers, both dance and theatrical. Always something interesting.

Theatre Rhinoceros 2926 16th St ☎861-5079. San Francisco's only uniquely gay theatre group, this company, not surprisingly, tackles productions that confront gay issues, as well as lighter, humorous productions.

Bay Area

Berkeley Repertory Theater 2025 Addison St, Berkeley ☎510/845-4700.

The Theater District is described on p.57.

One of the West Coast's most highly respected theatre companies, presenting updated classics and contemporary plays in an intimate, modern theatre. Tickets $6–25.

Black Repertory Group 3201 Adeline St, Berkeley nr Ashby *BART* ☎510/652-2120. After years of struggling, this politically conscious company moved into its own specially built home in 1987, since when it has encouraged new talent with great success. Tickets $5–15.

Julia Morgan Theater 2640 College Ave, Berkeley ☎510/845-8542. A variety of touring shows stop off in this cunningly converted old church. Tickets $8–20.

Comedy

Comedians have always found a welcoming audience in San Francisco, but recently the alternative **comedy and cabaret scene** has been reborn. Some new, excellent venues have opened up and, while many may be smartening up beyond the tastes of some, they will undoubtedly be able to draw bigger names to the city.

Few of the comedians are likely to be familiar: as with any cabaret you take your chances, and whether you consider a particular club to be good will depend on who happens to be playing the week you go. You can expect to pay roughly the same kind of cover in most of the clubs ($7–15), and two-drink minimums are common. There are usually two shows per night, the first kicking off around 8pm and a late show starting at around 11pm. For bargains, check the press for "Open Mike" nights when unknowns and members of the audience get up and have a go; there's rarely a cover charge for these evenings and, even if the acts are diabolical, it can be a fun night out.

Comedy Clubs

Cobb's Comedy Club *The Cannery*, 2801 Leavenworth St at Beach ☎928-4320. Small venue, popular on the cabaret circuit, where new performers often get the chance of their first live appearance.

Coconut Grove 1415 Van Ness Ave at Bush ☎776-1616. The cover is a little higher than usual at this venue, but worth it for the plush, spacious interior, grown-up vibe and excellent acts that this classy joint manages to pull in. A well-needed antidote to the often well-worn "alternative comedy" circuit.

Finocchio's 506 Broadway at Kearny ☎982-9388. A San Francisco institution, *Finocchio's* presents a small cast of female impersonators who run through textbook routines, heavy on the sauciness. At one time it was considered outrageous; these days it's more than a little tame, good for cheap laughs and expensive drinks.

Josie's Cabaret and Juice Joint 3583 16th St at Noe ☎ 861-7933. A good all-rounder offering a mixed menu of cabaret, comedy, live music and dancing.

The Punch Line 444 Battery St at Washington ☎ 397-7573. Frontrunner of the city's "polished" cabaret venues, this place has an intimate, smoky feel that's ideal for downing expensive cocktails and laughing your head off. The club usually hosts the bigger names in the world of stand-up and is always packed.

Film

After eating, watching **films** is the favourite San Francisco pastime. For one thing it's inexpensive (rarely more than $8, sometimes as little as $4) and, secondly, there's a staggering assortment of current-release and repertory film houses, with programmes ranging from the latest general-release films to Hollywood classics, iconoclastic 1960s pieces, and a selection of foreign and art films that are usually as good as (if not better than) most European centres. Film-going in San Francisco is a pleasure: there are rarely queues, and the cinemas are often beautiful Spanish-revival and Art Deco buildings that are in themselves a delight to behold.

The Alhambra Polk St and Union ☎775-2137. One of the city's grandest movie theatres; a gorgeous, plush, Moorish interior. Shows a mix of current releases and reruns.

ATA-Artists Television Access 992 Valencia St at 21st ☎824-3890. Non-profit media centre that puts on the city's most challenging barrage of film and TV productions, often with a political or psychosexual bent.

The Castro Theater 429 Castro St at Market ☎621-6120. Perhaps San Francisco's most beautiful movie house, offering a steady stream of reruns, Hollywood classics and (best of all) a Wurlitzer organ played between films by a man who rises up from the stage. A fond favourite with the gay community, it hosts the annual Gay and Lesbian Film Festival each June.

Cinematheque At *San Francisco Art Institute*, 800 Chestnut St ☎558-8129. Adventurous international programme of vaguely alternative movies shown on Sundays at 7.30pm. On Thursdays, *Cinematheque* moves to the Center for the Arts, 701 Mission St at Third ☎978-ARTS.

The Clay 2261 Fillmore St at Clay ☎346-1123. Small, elegant, art-house cinema.

Kabuki Cinemas Post St and Fillmore ☎931-9800. Attractive, modern building in the Japan Center complex, where eight screens show mainly current-release movies.

The Lumiere 1572 California St at Polk ☎885-3200. Another opulent Spanish-revival art house, a bit run down but often with an interesting programme of obscure art films as well as a select choice of current-release films.

Opera Plaza 601 Van Ness Ave at Golden Gate ☎771-0102. Modern Civic Center complex where four theatres screen the better pick of current-release films.

The Red Vic 1727 Haight St at Cole ☎668-3994. Friendly collective, formerly housed in a room full of ancient couches where you could put your feet up, and now moved to smarter premises up the street. Same idea, though, showing popular reruns and cult films.

The Roxie 3117 16th St at Valencia ☎863-1087. San Francisco's trendiest, independent rep house in the heart of the Mission, showing a steady diet of punk, new wave and political movies.

The Royal 1529 Polk St at Sacramento ☎474-0353. Once elegant, now a decaying old theatre looking about a week away from demolition. Current releases with the odd interesting late-night showing of an old favourite.

The Strand 1127 Market St ☎621-2227. Dark, appropriately scruffy surroundings for cult films and B-movies.

Bay Area

Act One and Act Two 2128 Center St, Berkeley ☎510/548-7200. Screening both foreign films and non-mainstream American features.

Grand Lake Theater 3200 Grand Ave ☎510/452-3556. The grand dame of East Bay picture palaces, right on Lake Merritt, showing the best of the current major releases.

Pacific Film Archive 2621 Durant Ave, Berkeley, in the University Art Museum ☎510/642-1124. For the serious film fan, this is perhaps the best movie theatre in all California, with seasons of contemporary works from around the world, plus revivals of otherwise forgotten favourites. Two films a night: tickets $5.50 each, $7 for both.

UC Theater 2036 University Ave, Berkeley, just below Shattuck Ave ☎510/843-6267. Popular revival house, with a huge auditorium and a daily double feature.

The San Francisco Film Festival is held at various cinemas around the city, but usually centring on the *Kabuki* eight-screen theatre (see above), in the first couple of weeks in May. It specializes in political and short films you wouldn't normally see. Tickets sell extremely fast and you'll need to book around four days in advance for all but the most obscure movies.

Just as popular is the **Gay and Lesbian Film Festival**, held in June at *The Castro Theater*. If you know you're going to be in town for either, call ahead for programmes by contacting the theatres.

Chapter 16

Shops and Galleries

Though San Francisco may not have all the big prestige department stores of cities like New York or London, or even Los Angeles, it is an American centre nonetheless and has an abundant range of items for you to consume. Where it excels is in its range of smaller-scale outlets, great for picking up odd and unusual things you wouldn't find at home. One thing is for sure – it is not hard to spend a lot of money here.

Though all the international names are displayed in downtown storefronts, the great majority of places are low-key and unpretentious. Not only does this mean slightly lower prices, but it also makes shopping a more pleasant, stress-free activity all round.

If you want to run the gauntlet of designer labels, or just watch the style brigades in all their consumer fury, **Union Square** is the place you should aim for. Despite losing the beautiful *I Magnin* department store, it remains the classy heart of the city's shopping territory, it has a good selection of big-name and chic stores – unashamedly expensive, but very good for browsing, especially in the district's many art galleries.

For things that you can actually afford to buy, you'll have a less disheartening and more interesting time in neighbourhoods like **Haight-Ashbury, Noe Valley** and the **Mission**. These are home to a profusion of the second-hand, quirky and plain bizarre, fascinating to pick through if you're at a loose end or on the lookout for some kitsch and unique souvenirs; the Mission, especially, has some marvellous second-hand clothing stores. The **Civic Center** is also good: stores specializing in Art Deco and retro-Americana abound around Market and Gough streets, while the stretch of Hayes Street between Franklin and Laguna holds San Francisco's most unusual array of galleries and one-off stores.

The city, and the Bay Area in general, is home to a number of excellent **bookstores**, and its many independent **music stores** are unbeatable for rare birds to add to your collection. Berkeley's college crowd is a ripe market for the **second-hand apparel** stores and other used-item boutiques in the East Bay. Most clothes are reasonably marked so that you can get treasure-trove finds at trash-level deals. Alternatively, cruise the **flea markets** in the region for desirable schlock of all shapes and sizes.

Most places are open Monday to Saturday, from 9am until 6pm, with quite a number open on Sunday, too, particularly for basic things like food and drink. Many **supermarkets** are open 24 hours a day, so you'll never have to go without.

Credit cards are accepted in most stores for purchases above a minimum of $10; **traveller's cheques** are as good as cash, provided they're in US dollar denominations and that you have your passport or other photo ID.

Shops and Galleries

Department Stores and Shopping Malls

If you want to pick up a variety of things in a hurry, without having to roam all over town, it's hard to beat the one-stop convenience of **department stores** or, increasingly, **shopping malls**. Though even San Francisco's most opulent stores aren't in the same league as *Harrods* or *Bloomingdales*, and the few urban shopping malls still feel as though they'd be happier in the suburbs, they are useful and can even be quite lively.

Department Stores

Emporium 835 Market St, near Powell St ☎764-2222. San Francisco's largest general department store, with a very average range of merchandise – everything the suburban home could possibly need.

Macy's Stockton St and O'Farrell ☎397-3333. Probably the city's best-stocked store, and as such a good place for general shopping, even if it's not a patch on its New York counterpart. Nonetheless, brimming with trinkets of the consumer society, and a dangerous place to go with a wallet full of money. Beautifully presented merchandise is hawked noisily from all sides.

Neiman Marcus 150 Stockton St at O'Farrell ☎362-3900. The sheer cheek of the pricing department has earned this store the nickname "Needless Mark-up". Undoubtedly Union Square's most beautiful department store, however, with its classic rotunda, and good for enjoyable browsing. Good bar and restaurant on the top floor from where you can gaze down on the shoppers.

Nordstrom 865 Market St at Powell ☎243-8500. Shoppers flock here for the high-quality fashions, as well as a chance to ride on the spiral escalators that climb the four-storey atrium.

Sak's Fifth Avenue 384 Post St at Powell ☎986-4300. A scaled-down version of its New York sister store. High-end fashion geared largely to the middle-aged shopaholic, but the beauty hall on the ground floor makes for heavenly browsing.

Shopping Malls

Crocker Galleria 50 Post St at Kearny ☎393-1505. The most recent in the new wave of shopping malls, this has been built to as modern and attractive a design as possible, and features some very pricey showcase boutiques. It's all very nice for a wander, but don't plan on spending money unless your reserves are bottomless.

Embarcadero Center At Embarcadero *BART/MUNI* station at the foot of California St ☎772-0500. Ugly, six-block shopping complex with almost 200 stores, distinguished from other anaesthetic shopping malls only by the occasional work of art.

Ghirardelli Square 900 North Point at Larkin ☎775-5500. This attractive turn-of-the-century building used to be a chocolate factory, but is now home to seventy stores and some great restaurants. The nicest way to drop dollars near the Wharf.

Japan Center Post St and Buchanan ☎922-6776. Surprisingly banal and characterless five-acre complex of stores, movie theatres and restaurants with a Japanese theme.

Rincon Center Bounded by Mission and Howard, Steuart and Spear streets ☎543-8600. Formerly the Rincon Annexe Post Office, this attractive 1930s Deco landmark, adorned with murals and skylit atrium, make this a very pleasant place to shop. Over thirty shops and restaurants.

San Francisco Shopping Centre Fifth and Market ☎495-5656. A good-looking mall this one: glass, Italian marble, polished green granite and spiral escalators up and down its nine storeys all add to the seductive appeal of spending money with California-style panache.

Drugstores, Beauty Products and Toiletries

Standard **drugstores** can be found in every San Francisco neighbourhood. A few are open 24 hours a day, selling essentials like film, batteries for your Walkman, aspirin, tampons, condoms, etc, and all have a pharmacy that can dispense medications and fill prescriptions.

24-Hour Pharmacies

The following branches of **Walgreen** are **open 24 hours:**

498 Castro St	☎861-6276
3201 Divisadero St	☎931-6415

Walgreens is the largest chain pharmacy with numerous branches throughout the city, selling prescription drugs and general medical supplies, as well as cosmetics and toiletries. Most are open long hours (Mon–Sat 8am–10pm, Sun 9am–8pm); the most central is at 135 Powell St ☎391-4433.

Outlets for such indulgences as body oils and bubble bath tend to congregate in the pricier neighbourhoods.

Drugstores

Embarcadero Center Pharmacy 1 Embarcadero Center ☎788-4511. Prescription drugs and general medical and toiletry supplies.

Fairmont Pharmacy 801 Powell St ☎362-3000. Huge pharmacy, perfumery and toiletry supply store that also has a good selection of maps and books on San Francisco.

Mandarin Pharmacy 895 Washington St ☎989-9292. This amiable, well-stocked drugstore is a sanctuary in the bustle of Chinatown.

Walgreen Drug Store 135 Powell St at Ellis ☎391-4433. Good place to shop for discounted merchandise, multiple offers, etc. For stockpilers of cosmetics and toiletries.

Toiletries and Beauty Supplies

The Beauty Store Upper Market 3600 16th St at Market ☎861-2019. Also at 1560 Haight St. Make-up, hair dye and massage oils.

Body Time 2072 Union St ☎922-4076. Though they sold the original name to the UK-based *Body Shop*, they still put out a full range of aromatic natural bath oils, shampoos and skin creams.

Common Scents 3920 24th St ☎826-1019. Natural oils, cures, remedies and bath salts as well as great hair and skin-care products.

Crabtree and Evelyn Embarcadero Center ☎781-7926; Ghiradelli Square ☎474-5547. Anglophile toiletries store that is full of scented body-care products and potpourri. Cheesy but cute.

Isa's Hair Studio 3836 24th St at Church ☎641-8948. Great hairdressing salon upstairs and a wide selection of hair and skin-care products in the shop below. Good place for stocking up on quality essentials.

Merle Norman Cosmetics Studio 150 Powell St at O'Farrell ☎362-2387. Make-up lessons available as well as an exhaustive rang of cosmetics. Girlie heaven.

Skin Zone 575 Castro at 19th ☎626-7933. Well-priced toiletries, cosmetics and hair care. Everything for the body beautiful.

Bay Area

Body Time 2911 College Ave ☎510/845-2101, with outlets in Berkeley and Oakland. Natural scents, lotions and soap and hair product collection.

Whole Foods Market 3000 Telegraph Ave, Berkeley ☎510/649-1333. For the alternative-remedy addict, an excellent selection of homeopathic herbs and medicinal products in an upscale natural-foods supermarket.

Clothes and Accessories

Perhaps, more than anywhere else in the US, San Francisco's power-dressing **designer clothes** stores are distinct from the bulk of the city's clothing outfitters.

Though Ralph Lauren chic definitely rules the Financial District, style elsewhere in the city is a much more open concept. Dozens of stores – *Esprit* and *The Gap* are two of the bigger names – sell very Californian **casual wear**, mainly jeans and polo-type shirts in pastel, but if you're feeling adventurous, check out the countless **second-hand clothes** stores specializing in period costume, from 1920s gear to leftover hippie garb. Better still, explore the myriad charitable thrift stores, where you can pick up high-quality castoffs for virtually next to nothing.

Designer Clothes

Backseat Betty 1584 Haight St at Clayton ☎431-8393. Small range of exquisite, affordable dresses and very feminine separates by lesser-known designers. Recommended.

Betsey Johnson 2031 Fillmore St at California ☎567-2726. One of the few American designers who doesn't see women in business suits. Her clothes are stylish and have flair without being silly – and, by designer standards, they are also affordable.

Brooks Brothers 201 Post St at Grant ☎397-4500. The original preppy clothes store: traditional men's clothing, well tailored and conservative. This is where the Financial District clones go to get their clobber.

Bullock and Jones 340 Post St at Stockton ☎392-4243. Much the same as *Brooks*, but if you have to buy suits and look the part this is the better choice and even has its own barber's shop.

Emporio Armani 1 Grant Ave at Market ☎677-9400. European chic comes to SF big time. This large store with its own cafeteria is the perfect place to deck yourself out in simple style.

MAC (Modern Appealing Clothing) 1543 Grant Ave at Union ☎775-2515. Showcase for contemporary designers such as Vivienne Westwood, Yamamoto, Comme des Garcons, etc.

Rolo 2351 Market St at Church ☎626-7171. Moderately priced and well-made menswear in simple, easy-to-wear styles.

Under Cover 535 Castro St at 19th ☎864-0505. Tiny store, crammed with unusual and body-conscious club-wear by lesser-known designers and tons of shoes. Mostly gay clientele.

Wilkes Bashford 375 Sutter St at Stockton ☎986-4380. Five floors of fabulous designer finery for men. A fashion victim's fantasy.

Designer Accessories: Bags, Shoes, Hats, Jewellery

China Gem Co 500 Grant Ave at Pine ☎397-5070. Good place for jade, opals and gold.

The Coach Store 190 Post St at Grant ☎392-1772. Well-made, simple and expensive handbags and luggage. Definitely worth the investment if you've got the money, *Coach* bags are timeless in their style and come with a lifetime guarantee.

Gucci 200 Stockton St at Geary ☎392-2808. Classic Italian shoes, bags and apparel that you need a trust fund to indulge in. Snoop around the store and be fascinated by the rich ladies who come in and say "I'll have one of those, two of those, one of those", etc.

Hats on Post 210 Post St at Grant ☎392-3737. Interesting, odd designs, very contemporary, but only worth shelling out for if you're *really* into hats.

Hermes 212 Stockton St at Geary ☎391-7200. Classy French luggage and accessories for the super-rich. Again, good only for spying on those who can afford it.

Kenneth Cole 2078 Union St at Webster ☎346-2121; also at 865 Market at Powell ☎227-4536. State-of-the-art boutique selling the well-designed shoes of this New York designer. His men's shoes are imaginative and funky, but the women's stuff is more wearable.

Pearl of the Orient 900 North Point, Ghirardelli Square ☎441-2288. Reputedly the largest stock of pearls in the Bay Area; and very nice, too.

Shapur 245 Post St at Grant ☎392-1200. Unusual fittings for uniquely cut diamonds and various other gems; each piece is created individually.

Shreve & Co 200 Post St at Grant ☎421-2600. The oldest jewellers in town and quite possibly the best. Known for their fine silverware and flawless diamonds.

Tiffany 350 Post St at Powell ☎781-7000. Luxurious new site on several floors, where the extraordinarily courteous staff are happy to let you try the stuff on even if it's obvious that you can't afford it. One of the friendlier branches.

BAY AREA

Nordstrom Rack 1285 Marina Blvd, San Leandro ☎510/614-1742. After merchandise has been in the San Francisco store for three months, it's sold at a fifty percent discount here.

Vivacity 6251 College Ave, Oakland ☎510/658-7105. Small, friendly women's clothing boutique selling formal urban styles which border on high fashion. Moderate to expensive.

Casual Wear

Banana Republic 256 Grant Ave at Sutter ☎788-3087. Stylish clothes for the travelling yuppie, in this main branch of the San Francisco-based nationwide chain.

Daljeets 541 Valencia St at 16th ☎626-9000; 1744 Haight St at Cole ☎752-5610. Amazing selection of shoes from the sensible to the bizarre and a nice little sideline in rubberwear (ahem).

Esprit 499 Illinois Ave at 16th ☎957-2550. Warehouse-sized store in SoMa that is the flagship of the wildly successful international chain selling sporty "California-style" casual wear in California colours. For basics, T-shirts, etc, it's pretty good.

The Gap 890 Market St at Powell ☎788-5909. Also at 1975 Market St at Dolores ☎861-8442, and all over the city and Bay Area. Hugely successful chain store selling jeans, T-shirts and casual wear.

Groger's Western Wear 1445 Valencia St at 25th ☎647-0700. Mission store selling cowboy boots, Stetson hats, boot tips and traditional brand-name Western clothes. Fun shopping.

North Beach Leather 190 Geary St at Stockton ☎362-8300. Leather everything, and in some pretty sickly colours, but for basic black jackets and simple pieces there are some well-made styles. Actually in the Union Square district, despite the name.

Patagonia 770 North Point, near Fisherman's Wharf ☎771-2050. Functional, outdoor clothing that has a cult, semi-yuppie following.

Ragwood 1764 Haight St at Shrader ☎221-9760. Smart and distinctive designs that won't break the bank in this unusual store that also sells old furniture

Villains 1672 and 1682 Haight St at Belvedere ☎626-5939. Cheap, distinctive, youthful, fun clothing. For when you want to dress up in club gear, but don't want to splash out.

Second-hand Clothes

Aardvark's Odd Ark 1501 Haight St ☎621-3141. Large second-hand clothing store in Haight-Ashbury. Some junk, but also some priceless pieces and an infinite supply of perfectly faded Levis.

American Rag Co 1305 Van Ness Ave at Bush ☎474-5214. As second-hand clothing stores go, this one is expensive, but it's probably also superior to most others in San Francisco. Also a good selection of stylish new clothing.

Buffalo Exchange 1800 Polk St at Washington ☎346-5726. Also at 1555 Haight St ☎431-7733. Cheap and occasionally tatty store, but if you've got the patience to search through the piles of clothing, you may turn up some gems.

Third Hand Store 1839 Divisadero St at Bush ☎567-7332. As other stores cash in on the craze for vintage clothing, this Western Addition store keeps its prices reasonable and has some interesting pieces.

Wasteland 1660 Haight St at Belvedere ☎863-3150. Massive selection of well-priced second-hand clothing. It's a day's work getting through it all. Lots of 1950s and 1960s offcasts.

Worn Out West 582 Castro St at 19th ☎431-6020. Gay second-hand cowboy gear store – a trip for browsing, but if you're serious about getting some Wild West kit, this is the least expensive place in town to pick out a good pair of boots, stylish Western shirts and chaps.

BAY AREA

Buffalo Exchange 3333 Lakeshore Ave, Oakland ☎510/452-4464; also at 2512 Telegraph, Berkeley ☎510/644-9202. Part of the second-hand clothing chain, this branch is the dumping ground for residents of the upscale Piedmont community. High-class treasures aplenty.

Crossroads Trading Company 5636 College Ave, Oakland ☎510/420-1952. Second-hand clothing of high-quality, vintage styles for men and women.

Jeremy's 2967 College Ave, Berkeley ☎510/849-0701. Specializing in designer clothing for men and women previously used in fashion shows.

Sharks 2505 Telegraph Ave, Berkeley ☎510/841-8736. Great prices on retro-Americana. Dress up as the young Frank Sinatra or his date.

Slash Clothing 2840 College Ave, Berkeley ☎510/841-7803. Barely room to walk in this tiny non-trendy basement with second-hand Levis piled from floor to ceiling.

Thrift Stores

Bargain Mart 1823 Divisadero St at Bush ☎921-7380. Downscale second-hand clothes that look as though they're about to fall apart, but are ideal if you need to get decked out on the cheap.

Community Thrift 625 Valencia St at 18th ☎861-4910. Gay thrift store in the Mission with clothing, furniture and general junk. All proceeds are ploughed back into gay groups in the community.

Goodwill 241 10th St at Howard ☎252-1677; also 822 Geary St at Hyde ☎922-0405 and 2279 Mission St at 19th ☎826-5759. There are *Goodwill* outlets all over the city, stocking everything from lampshades to handbags to three-piece suites. Exhaustive selection of junk and gems.

San Francisco Symphony Thrift Store 2223 Fillmore St ☎563-3123. Top-rate vintage clothing store in Pacific Heights, selling at top dollar. All proceeds go to the Symphony.

St Vincent de Paul 1519 Haight St ☎863-3615. Also at 425 Fourth St at Harrison. Queen of the junk stores, *St Vinnies* will keep you amused for hours. You could spend money all day and still have change from $50.

Thrift Town 2101 Mission St at 17th ☎861-1132. Huge and well-displayed selection, with some of San Francisco's better quality trash as well as pretty stylish second-hand clothing bargains.

BAY AREA

Ashby Flea Market Ashby *BART* Station, corner of Ashby Ave and Martin Luther King Jr Way, Berkeley. Parking lot is open on weekends for independent vendors to sell second-hand clothes, furniture and myriad bits. Perfect for booty-hunting.

Marin Flea Market 147 Donahue Rd at Drake ☎332-1441. Get up early to join the weekend scavengers in their quest for that special something.

Soweto Thrift 4365 Adeline, Emeryville ☎510/655-1360. Among industrial warehouses near West Oakland sits this small, secret used-everything store. Great buys on old clothes and oddities.

Food and Drink

Food faddists will have a field day in San Francisco's many **gourmet stores**, which are on a par with the city's restaurants for culinary quality and diversity. The simplest neighbourhood deli will get your taste buds jumping, while the most sophisticated places are enough to make you swoon.

Be sure to try such **local specialties** as *Boudin*'s sourdough bread, *Gallo* salami and *Anchor Steam* beer. Bear in mind, too, that however overwhelming the food on offer in San Francisco itself may seem, some of the very best places are to be found across the bay in Berkeley. For more basic stocking up there are, of course, **supermarkets** all over the city (*Safeway* is probably the most widespread name), some of them open 24 hours per day.

Any of the above will sell you an array of beers, wines and spirits – provided you're over 21, and have a photo ID to prove it – but for the best selection head to a specialist retailer.

Delis and Groceries

Auntie Pasta 3101 Fillmore St at Filbert ☎921-7576. Fresh pasta and sauces to

Shops and Galleries

> **24-Hour Stores**
>
> If you're caught short by hunger in the middle of the night, the following are just a few of the many stores open **24 hours**: *Safeway* at 15 Marina Blvd in the Marina, 1355 Webster St in the Western Addition, 2020 Market St and 2300 16th St in the Mission; and *Cala Foods* at 4201 18th St in the Castro, on California at Hyde St, and another at the end of Haight St opposite Golden Gate Park.

heat and eat. Great if you don't want to dine out or cook.

Casa Lucas 2934 24th St at Guerrero ☎826-4334. Mission store with an astonishing array of exotic fruits and vegetables that includes a dozen varieties of banana.

The Cheesery 427 Castro St at 17th ☎552-6676. Reasonably priced coffees (from $3/lb) and cheeses from around the world.

David's 474 Geary St at Taylor ☎771-1600. The consummate Jewish deli, open until 12am. A downtown haven for the after-theatre crowd and night owls.

Lo-Cost Market 498 Haight St at Fillmore ☎621-4338. Asian market selling a wonderful selection of dirt-cheap meats and seafood for cash only.

Lucca Ravioli 1100 Valencia St at 22nd ☎647-5581. Pasta factory that you can spy on through the big picture windows before you go into the store.

Molinari's 373 Columbus Ave ☎421-2337. Bustling North Beach Italian deli, jammed to the rafters with goodies.

Rainbow Grocery 1899 Mission St at 15th ☎863-0620. Progressive politics and organic food in this Mission wholefood store. A classic California shopping experience.

San Francisco Farmer's Market 100 Alemany Blvd at Crescent Ave ☎647-9423. Covered market, established since the 1940s, offering customers the chance to purchase food fresh from the farms at fresh-from-the-farm prices. Invaluable if you're cooking for crowds or just love a bargain.

San Francisco Health Foods 333 Sutter St at Grant ☎392-8477. Dried fruits, juices and wholefood.

San Francisco Herb Company 250 14th St at Mission ☎861-3018. SoMa-based store with large quantities of fresh herbs at wholesale prices.

Sunrise Deli and Café 2115 Irving St at 25th Ave ☎664-8210. Specialty Middle Eastern foodstuffs – stuffed vine leaves, aubergine and hummus.

Williams Sonoma 150 Post St at Kearny ☎362-6904. A few gourmet foods amid an incredible selection of cookware.

BAY AREA

Auntie Pasta 6311 College Ave, Oakland ☎510/655-4094. Suburban version of the San Francisco store.

Berkeley Bowl 2777 Shattuck Ave, Berkeley ☎510/841-6346. Converted bowling alley is now an enormous produce, bulk and health-food market. Least expensive grocery in town with the largest selection of fresh produce.

Cheese Board 1504 Shattuck Ave, Berkeley ☎510/549-3183. Collectively owned and operated since 1967, this was one of the first outposts in Berkeley's Gourmet Ghetto and is still going strong, offering over 200 varieties of cheese and freshly baked bread.

Genova Delicatessen and Ravioli Factory corner of 50th St and Telegraph Ave, Oakland ☎510/652-7401. Tiny traditional deli complete with myriads of hanging sausages. Enormous and cheap sandwich creations.

Market Hall 5655 College Ave, Oakland ☎510/601-8208. Conveniently located next to Rockridge *BART*. Offers all possible gourmet eats to local yuppies and students. Comprises a variety of small, fine food shops serving to eat there or take out.

Ratto's 821 Washington St, Oakland ☎510/832-6503. Old-time establishment has remained in refurbished "Old Oakland", providing an excellent selection of gourmet fine foods.

Bread, Pastries and Sweets

Bakers of Paris 3989 24th St at Sanchez ☎863-8725. Noe Valley bakery that serves up mountains of baguettes and croissants.

Boudin 156 Jefferson St at Taylor, Fisherman's Wharf ☎928-1849. They only make one thing – sourdough bread – but it's the best around.

Godiva Chocolates 865 Market St at Fifth ☎543-8910. Rich Belgian chocolates at around a dollar a nibble. Heaven for the chocaholic.

Italian French Baking Co 1501 Grant Ave at Union ☎421-3796. In the heart of North Beach, selling mouthwatering breads, rolls, muffins and home-made biscotti.

Liguria Bakery 1700 Stockton St at Filbert ☎421-3786. Marvellous old-world Italian bakery in North Beach with deliciously fresh *focaccia.*

Tea, Coffee and Spices

Freed, Teller & Freed 1326 Polk St at Bush ☎673-0922. Polk Gulch coffee and tea emporium. Every conceivable legal addiction and all the paraphernalia to go with it.

Graffeo Coffee 735 Columbus Ave at Filbert ☎986-2420. Huge sacks of coffee are piled up all around this North Beach store – you can smell the place from half a block away. Great coffees, reasonably priced.

Haig's Delicacies 642 Clement St at Seventh Ave ☎752-6283. Way out in the Richmond, but for Indian and Middle Eastern spices and delicacies this is the place.

New Bombay Bazar 548 Valencia St at 17th ☎621-1717. Exotic spices and tons of pulses, grains and other staples.

Peet's Coffee 2156 Chestnut St at Pierce ☎931-8302. Also at 2257 Market (Upper Castro) and 2139 Polk at Vallejo. Marina-based San Francisco flagship of this venerable Berkeley coffee-roaster, offering some thirty different blends.

Wines and Spirits

California Wine Merchant 3237 Pierce St ☎567-0646. Before you set off for the Wine Country, pick up a sample selection at this Marina wine emporium so you know what to look out for.

Cannery Wine Cellars The Cannery, Fisherman's Wharf ☎673-0400. An astounding selection of wines and imported beers, as well as Armagnac and Scotch, lines the walls.

Coit Liquor 585 Columbus Ave at Union ☎986-4036. North Beach specialty wine store, with the accent on rare Italian vintages. Good stock of regular booze.

D & M Wine & Liquor Co 2200 Fillmore at Sacramento ☎346-1325. Great selection of Californian wines, but located as they are in Pacific Heights, their specialty is champagne – bargains abound.

The Jug Shop 1567 Pacific Ave at Polk ☎885-2922. *The Jug Shop* is famous for its cheap Californian wines, but, it also has over 200 varieties of beer which are similarly well priced. One of the city's best places for booze.

Urban Cellars 3821 24th St at Church ☎824-2300. The dipsomaniac's dream – hundreds of wines and over 300 beers take booze shopping to its zenith.

The Wine Club 953 Harrison St at Sixth ☎ 512-9086. Huge warehouse lacking in comfort, but filled with wine on which the mark-up is sometimes as low as 5 percent. Makes you realise how much you're being ripped off in other places.

BAY AREA

Takahara Sake USA 708 Addison, Berkeley ☎510/540-8250. Producers of *ShoChiku Bai* sake give free tastings in an intimate bar. The distillery on the premises can be viewed through glass. Tastings daily from noon to 5pm.

Books

Although San Francisco does boast some truly excellent **bookstores**, the range of reading material on offer is surprisingly small for a city with such a literary reputation.

The established focus for literature has long been in North Beach, in the area around the legendary *City Lights* bookstore, but increasingly the best spots, particularly for contemporary creative writing, are to be found in the lower-rent Mission district, which is home to some of the city's more energized – and politicized – bookstores.

There are a few **second-hand booksellers** in the city itself (the best bargains are found in thrift stores; see above), but these can't compare with the diverse bunch across the bay in Oakland and Berkeley. Most bookstores tend to open every day, roughly 10am–8pm, though *City Lights* is open daily until midnight.

See p.155 for a full list of Berkeley bookstores.

General Bookstores

The Booksmith 1644 Haight St at Belvedere ☎863-8688. Good general Haight-Ashbury bookstore with an excellent stock of counter-cultural titles. Very Haight-Ashbury.

Borders 400 Post St at Powell ☎399-1633. Massive emporium-style bookstore stocking over 160,000 book titles as well as a music department with over 60,000 choices. It's a day's work getting through this lot, but they've thoughtfully built a café within the store to refresh yourself. Union Square's finest addition in years.

City Lights Bookstore 261 Columbus Ave at Broadway ☎362-8193. America's first paperback bookstore, and still San Francisco's best, with a range of titles including *City Lights*' own publications (see p.76).

A Clean, Well Lighted Place for Books Opera Plaza, 601 Van Ness Ave at Golden Gate ☎441-6670. Good selection of rather high-minded titles and a truly interesting calendar of readings from authors. One to check out.

B Dalton Bookstore 200 Kearny St at Sutter ☎956-2850. Main San Francisco branch of the Doubleday nationwide chain selling general titles over two floors. Very good service and help on hand.

Philosopher's Stone Bookshop 3814 24th St at Sanchez. General bookstore with a decent range of titles, though rather heavy on the New Age stuff.

Tillman Place Bookstore 8 Tillman Place, off Grant Ave, near Union Square ☎392-4668. Downtown's premier general bookstore and certainly one of the oldest, with a beautifully elegant feel.

Discount and Second-hand Bookstores

Around the World 1346 Polk St at Pine ☎474-5568. Musty, dusty and a bit of a mess, this is a great place to spend hours of poring over first editions, rare books and records.

Austen Books 1687 Haight St at Cole ☎552-4122. Proper scruffy, chaotic used-book store. Heavenly browsing.

Books Etc 538 Castro St at 18th ☎621-8631. Crammed with books of every category including a good selection of gay and lesbian at knock-down prices. Well worth a look.

Columbus Books 540 Broadway at Union ☎986-3872. North Beach store with a good selection of new and used books, and a large guide and travel books section.

Crown Books 1245 Sutter St at Polk ☎441-7479 and 518 Castro St at 18th ☎552-5213. San Francisco branches of the nationwide chain, selling new general books at discounted prices.

Phoenix Books and Records 3850 24th St at Sanchez ☎821-3477. Wide selection of new and used books at knock-down prices. Come out with armloads for $20.

Russian Hill Bookstore 2234 Polk St at Vallejo ☎929-0997. Used books in very good condition. A better class of bargain.

BAY AREA

Walden Pond Books 3316 Grand Ave, Oakland ☎510/832-4438. Large used and new bookstore carries the best selection of international fiction around at reasonable prices.

Specialist Bookstores

Bound Together Anarchist Collective Bookstore 1369 Haight St at Masonic ☎431-8355. Haight-Ashbury store specializing in radical and progressive publications.

China Books 2929 24th St ☎282-2994. Mission bookstore dealing in books and periodicals from China, although they also stock a good number of publications on the history and politics of the Third World.

Fanning's Bookstore Second floor, Ghirardelli Square. Specialty bookstore that only offers works of Northern Californian writers – including Hammett, London, Twain and Steinbeck.

Fields Bookstore 1419 Polk St at Pine ☎673-2027. Metaphysical and New Age books.

Good Vibrations 1210 Valencia St at 23rd ☎974-8980. A comfortable, decidedly un-sleazy place to buy sex books, specializing in women's sexuality. so keen are this outfit to promote women's sexuality they even publish their own titles under the Down There Press imprint. Also sells a bewildering diversity of sex toys, condoms and intimate apparel.

Great Expectations 1512 Haight St at Ashbury ☎863-5515. Radical liberal bookstore with hundreds of T-shirts bearing political slogans, some funnier than others.

Kinokuniya Second floor, Japan Center, 1581 Webster St. ☎567-7625. Large stock of Japanese and English-language books, but they really excel in art books.

Lodestar Books 313 Noe at 16th ☎864-3746. Specailizes in religion, healing arts, metaphysical and psychology books. One of *those* places.

The Maritime Store San Francisco Maritime National Historic Park, Hyde Street Pier, Fisherman's Wharf ☎775-2665. All seafaring enthusiasts stop here for maritime history, navigation, boat-building and sailing books.

Modern Times 888 Valencia St at 20th ☎282-9246. Alternative community bookstore in the Mission. Good selection of Spanish literature and hard-to-find contemporary cultural studies.

Rand McNally 595 Market St at Second ☎777-3131. Large store selling travel guides, maps and paraphernalia for the person on the move.

Sierra Club Bookstore 730 Polk St at Eddy ☎923-5600. Everything for the walker, camper and general outdoor enthusiast. Good stock of maps and trail guides for within California.

William Stout Architectural Books 804 Montgomery St at Jackson ☎391-6757. One of San Francisco's world-class booksellers, with an excellent range of books on architecture, building and urban studies.

Gay and Lesbian Bookstores

Books Etc 538 Castro St at 18th ☎621-8631. Stocks the gamut of gay publishing, from psychology to soft-core porn with a few general titles thrown in for good measure.

A Different Light 489 Castro St at 18th ☎431-0891. Well stocked, diverse and usually crammed with people.

Good Vibrations 1210 Valencia St at 23rd ☎974-8980. Sex shop and bookstore with a comprehensive stock of gay and lesbian erotica.

BAY AREA

Mama Bear's 6536 Telegraph Ave, Oakland ☎510/428-9684. Cosy women-owned bookstore and café with an enormous selection of lesbian and feminist literature.

Good Vibrations 2504 San Pablo Ave, Berkeley ☎510/841-8987. The Bay Area sister store of SF's safe sex emporium.

Music

San Francisco's **music stores** are of two types: massive, anodyne warehouses pushing all the latest releases, and impossibly small specialist stores crammed to the rafters with obscure discs.

The big places like *Tower Records* are more or less identical to those throughout the world, though foreign visitors tend to find the prices marginally cheaper than back home. More exciting is the large number of **independent** retailers and **second-hand and collectors' stores**, where you can track down anything you've ever wanted, especially in West Coast jazz or psychedelic rock.

New and Used

Aquarius Music 3961 24th St at Noe ☎647-2272. Small neighbourhood store with friendly, knowledgeable staff and a good selection of indie rock, jazz and anything experimental and obscure.

Shops and Galleries

Butch Wax Records 4077 18th St at Castro ☎431-0904. A hangover from 1970s gay discomania, this Castro shop is the best place in town for hard-to-find 12" singles, rare grooves and Euro-beat.

CD & Record Rack 3987 18th St at Castro ☎552-4990. Castro emporium with a brilliant selection of dance music including old 1970s twelve-inch singles. The accent is definitely on stuff you can get down to.

Discolandia 2964 24th St at Mission ☎826-9446. Join the snake-hipped groovers looking for the latest in salsa and Central American sounds in this Mission outlet.

Discoteca Habana 24th and Harrison St. No phone. Caribbean and samba recordings.

Embarcadero Discs and Tapes 2 Embarcadero Center, the Embarcadero ☎956-2204. Up-to-the-minute CDs and tapes.

Musica Latina/American Music Store 2388 Mission St at 19th ☎647-2098. Mission store selling music from all over the continent, but especially South America.

Reckless Records 1401 Haight St at Masonic ☎431-3434. Specializes in independent music, buys and sells new and used.

Record Finder 258 Noe St at Market ☎431-4443. One of the best independents, with a range as broad as it's absorbing. Take a wad and keep spending.

Rough Trade 695 Third St at Townsend ☎543-7091. Because of its London connections, this is the first place in town to get British imports. Good reggae department in particular and indie rock in general.

Streetlight Records 3979 24th St ☎282-3550. Also at 2350 Market St. A great selection of used records, tapes and CDs. The perfect opportunity to beef up your collection on the cheap.

Tower Records Columbus Ave and Bay St, nr Fisherman's Wharf ☎885-0500. Main San Francisco location of the multinational empire.

Virgin Megastore Corner of Market and Stockton sts ☎387-4525. As the name implies, it is a big shop. "The largest music, media and book store in America" actually.

Wherehouse Records 2083 Union St at Webster ☎346-0944. Large, general store, with a wide range of new releases and used stock.

Second-hand and Specialty Music

Bay Area Records and Tapes 1409 Polk St at Pine ☎441-9093. Well-rounded assortment of new and used recordings.

Groove Merchant Records 776 Haight St ☎252-5766. Very groovy Lower Haight soul and jazz shop.

Jack's Record Cellar 254 Scott St ☎431-3047. The city's best source for American music – r'n'b, jazz, country and rock'n' roll. They'll track down rare discs and offer the chance to listen before you buy.

The Jazz Quarter 1267 20th Ave near Irving ☎661-2331. A bit of a trek to get to, out in the Sunset District near Golden Gate Park, but if you're a jazz fiend on the lookout for rarities, it's worth the effort.

Let It Be Records 2434 Judah St ☎681-2113. Out in the Sunset, and selling Beatles memorabilia and rock rarities.

Recycled Records 1377 Haight St at Masonic ☎626-4075. Good all-round store, that also stocks a good selection of used music magazines.

Rooky Ricardo's 448 Haight St at Fillmore ☎864-7526. Albums and singles specialising in soul, funk and jazz from 1950s to 1970s. Brilliant.

Star Alley 322 Linden Alley between Fell St and Hayes ☎552-3017. Underground house, club rap, soul, jazz, gospel and reggae specialist in Hayes Valley selling to DJs. Any track ever cut by a black artist, you'll find here.

BAY AREA

Amoeba Music 2455 Telegraph Ave, Berkeley ☎510/549-1125. The biggest and best selection of used records and CDs in the Bay Area, with an admirably liberal trade-in policy. Aural satisfaction for cravings of every persuasion.

Down Home Music 10341 San Pablo Ave, El Cerrito ☎510/525-2129. As you might guess from the name, the excellent selection of folk, blues and bluegrass music makes it well worth the trek across to the East Bay. One of the best record stores in the US.

Mod Lang 2136 University Ave, Berkeley ☎510/486-1850. Mail order ☎510/486-1880. Knowledgeable staff will inform and sell you a whole range of indie and progressive CDs and vinyl.

Art Galleries

At first glance the low-profile San Francisco **art scene** seems provincial compared to the glamorous internationalism of New York and Los Angeles. And in many respects it is. But there is a scene of sorts, and it could be argued that artists here have the freedom to be more concerned with the quality of their own work than with the stylistic vagaries of the world art market.

Out-of-towners tend to find it difficult to get a sense of what's going on, as most younger artists shun **commercial galleries**, especially the mainstream ones around Union Square, and prefer to show their work in their favourite cafés and bars. That said, there is a core of relatively innovative galleries around the South of Market area – though even here the asking prices can be pretty steep.

Union Square and Around

The Allrich Gallery 251 Post St at Stockton ☎398-8896. Contemporary painting and sculpture as well as textiles.

American Indian Contemporary Arts 685 Market St at Kearny ☎495-7600. Non-profit gallery run by and for contemporary Native American artists.

Atelier Dore 771 Bush St at Mason ☎391-2423. Salon-style gallery hung floor-to-ceiling with top-quality paintings. Historical genre paintings from California, including WPA works, and about the only place that carries the work of nineteenth- and twentieth-century black American painters.

Caldwell Snyder Gallery 357 Geary St at Mason ☎296-7896. Expensive contemporary coveted stuff.

Circle Gallery 140 Maiden Lane off Union Square at Stockton ☎989-2100. Dull and overpriced contemporary art, ceramics and glassware; worth a look for the Frank Lloyd Wright building.

Contemporary Realist Gallery 250 Sutter St at Grant ☎362-7152. One of the more interesting galleries; the first in California to be dedicated to promoting current realist drawing. Also features painting and sculpture.

James Willis Gallery 77 Geary St at Grant ☎989-4485. Tribal artefacts from India, Africa and Indonesia. Unusual carvings and fabrics.

Japonesque 824 Montgomery St at Jackson ☎391-8860. Museum-quality Japanese art, including pottery, sculpture and prints.

John Berggruen Gallery 228 Grant Ave at Post ☎781-4629. Ultra-trendy gallery on three floors, showing big-name American and international artists.

John Pence Gallery 750 Post St at Jones ☎441-1138. Realist painting and sculpture. Some beautiful pieces.

Modernism 685 Market St at Third ☎541-0461. Futurism, Expressionism, Pop Art, Minimalism and American modern art.

Smile, A Gallery with Tongue in Chic 500 Sutter St at Powell ☎362-3436. From the whimsical to the very serious, this gallery is one of very few into it just for the fun of it. They'll exhibit anything.

Vorpal Gallery 393 Grove St at Franklin ☎397-9200. Contemporary Californian and local work.

SoMa and Elsewhere

Art Warehouse 3654 Sacramento St at Spruce ☎474-9999. Claims to be the city's only art gallery collective and shows work from different galleries all over the Bay Area.

Crown Point Press 20 Hawthorne, SoMa ☎974-6273. Showcase; limited editions of etchings changing every six weeks.

Joanne Chappel Gallery 625 Second St at Bryant ☎777-5711. Works by nationally known and West Coast artists.

Joseph Chowning Art Gallery 1717 17th St at De Haro ☎626-7496. Massive forum for modern and contemporary painting and sculpture.

Shops and Galleries

Erickson & Elins Fine Art 345 Sutter at Grant ☎ 981-1080. Nineteenth- and twentieth-century fine art.

Folk Art International and Xanadu 900 North Point, Ghirardelli Square, Fisherman's Wharf ☎928 3340 (Xanadu ☎441-5211). Latin American Art at *Folk Art International*; African, Indian, Chinese and folk art at *Xanadu*.

New Langton Arts 1246 Folsom St at Ninth ☎626-5416. Non-commercial gallery space showing cutting-edge works in all media, and hosting lectures, readings and performances.

San Francisco Art Institute 800 Chestnut St at Jones ☎771-7020. Local avant-garde contemporary art and student work.

SF MOMA Rental Gallery Building A, Fort Mason ☎441-4777. Large space where over 500 artists try to break into the commercial art world. Sales as well as rentals.

Vision Gallery Mission St at Seventh ☎621-2107. Photography by the well known and the unknown.

Specialty Stores

In among the designer clothes stores and art galleries of the Union Square area, a handful of stores sell **antiques and other treasurable objects**; though prohibitively expensive, many repay a look-in at least. We've also pulled together in this section some of the city's odd shops specializing in things you often need desperately but never know where to find – stationery, birthday cards, nuts and bolts, flowers, camping gear, children's toys, etc.

Antiques and Collectibles

Antonio's Antiques 701 Bryant St ☎781-1737. Three floors of antiques from around the world. Good porcelain and sculpture.

Asakichi Japanese Antiques and Art Japan Center, 1730 Geary Blvd at Webster ☎921-2147. Lovely pieces, but definitely geared towards the tourist dollar.

Biordi 412 Columbus Ave at Vallejo ☎392-8096. North Beach store selling lovely hand-painted Italian dinnerware and ornaments. It's unlikely that you'd ever buy this kind of stuff while travelling, but it makes for very enjoyable browsing.

Genji Antiques 22 Peace Plaza, Japantown ☎931-1616. Expensive oddments and beautiful wooden chests.

Gump's 135 Post St at Kearny ☎982-1616. Famous for its jade, Oriental rugs and objects cast in crystal, silver and china. More fuel for fantasies than genuine consumption.

Miscellaneous

Brooks Cameras 125 Kearny St at Post ☎362-4708. High-quality camera store with full repair department.

Cliff's Variety 479 Castro St at 18th ☎431-5365. Hardware store selling everything useful from toilet paper to rawlplugs to kettles and more. A brilliant browsing store if you're into home improvements.

FAO Schwarz 48 Stockton St at Market ☎394-8700. Mega-toy store on three floors designed to turn children into monsters.

Figoni Hardware 1351 Grant Ave at Green ☎392-4765. Ancient-looking but incredibly well-stocked North Beach hardware store.

Good Vibrations 1210 Valencia St at 23rd ☎974-8980. This atypical adult book and accessory store is owned and operated by women who have created a safe and friendly atmosphere for women, men, and giddy couples to explore erotica books and other safe-sex items for the lady seeking priapic alternatives.

Headlines 838 Market St ☎989-8240 and 557 Castro St ☎626-8061. Good, cheap clothes and huge range of novelty gift items. Fun to browse, even if you don't want to spend any money.

Star Magic 4026 24th St at Castro ☎641-8626. Situated down in Noe Valley, this is the ultimate New Age store, full of crystals to cleanse your chakras and the like.

Union Street Papery 2162 Union St at Fillmore ☎563-0200. Excellent, pricey stationers selling fine writing paper and a range of cards and pens.

Chapter 17

Sports and Outdoor Activities

With such a mild climate and wide range of landscapes to choose from, it's not surprising that so many San Franciscans spend so much time outdoors. The fitness exuded by many locals is not the cosmetic "body-beautiful" kind that California, especially LA, is renowned for. Rather, people here just seem to lead more healthy lives. However, for all the windsurfers and hikers in the great outdoors, there are equal numbers of armchair sports fans who watch avidly but would collapse if forced to take part.

Spectator Sports

Although they're still reeling from the 1993 departure of 49ers quarterback Joe Montana, the dedication of San Franciscans to their professional sports teams can verge on the obsessive. Tickets for the big events sometimes sell out well in advance, though it's generally possible to take in a game if you show up on the day, and it needn't cost all that much: a seat in the sun-drenched "bleachers" (the outfield grandstand) to watch a baseball game goes for around $7, with seats closer in topping the scale at around $15.

Advance tickets for all Bay Area sports events are available through the ***BASS*** charge-by-phone ticket service (☎ 510/762-BASS), as well as from the teams themselves.

Baseball's **Oakland A's** play at the usually sunny Oakland Coliseum (☎ 510/638-0500), the San Francisco Giants at often cold and foggy **3Com Park** (formerly known as Candlestick Park until the Silicon Valley computer technology company paid $500,000 for the rights to rename the classic park for the year's football season with an option of $3m annual renewal) south of the city (☎ 467-8000).

Football's fabulous **San Francisco 49ers,** many-time Super Bowl champions, also appear at 3Com Park (☎ 468-2249). The 49ers' use of intelligence, speed and grace rather than brute strength give them a rather bourgeois, fine-tuned reputation. It really can be hard to get hold of a ticket for their games; you may be lucky and get in for around $25, but you have to be prepared to fork out as much as $100 for a good seat. Even more expensive is a ticket to see blue-collar heroes the **Oakland *Raiders*** play a football game at the Oakland Coliseum (☎ 510/639-7700). Tickets are at least $60 since they moved back to Oakland in 1995 after abandoning the city for Los Angeles thirteen years previously and then abandoning LA when the fan base wasn't proving as profitable as expected. Oakland Coliseum colluded with the Raiders' demands that more luxury VIP boxes be fitted in the stadium. Very blue-collar.

In brief, the baseball season runs from April to October, basketball is from November to June and football from September to January.

Sports and Outdoor Activities

The **Golden State Warriors** play basketball at Oakland Arena (☎510/638-6000). The Bay Area's newest sports team is ice hockey's **San Jose Sharks** (☎408/287-4275), based at their own brand-new arena in the South Bay.

Participant Sports

Cycling is quickly becoming San Francisco's favourite sporting pastime; almost every evening or weekend, bikes tend to outnumber motorists on the most popular routes. As well as enjoyable circuits in the East Bay and Marin County, a fine tour follows the crest of the coastal mountains from the city south down the Peninsula, looking out over the bay and the Pacific. For more ambitious, overnight tours, the Wine Country is hard to beat; see "Cycling in the Wine Country" on p.194 for further information and bike rental locations.

To the dismay of hikers and environmentalists, the biggest boom has been the rise of **mountain biking**, which is said to have been invented on the steep slopes of Mount Tamalpais in Marin County, across the Golden Gate.

Local shops rent touring bikes with costs starting at about $25 per day, or mountain bikes starting from $25, and can usually suggest good routes. Outlets in San Francisco include *Waller Sports*, 1749 Waller St (☎752-8383) and *Presidio Bicycles*, 5335 Geary Blvd (☎752-2453). In the East Bay, try *Start to Finish*, 2200 Bancroft Way at Fulton (☎510/704-1000); another Berkeley outfit, *Missing Link Mountain Bikes*, 1988 Shattuck St, Berkeley (☎510/843-7471) will rent bikes from $20–35 per day. In Tiburon, where you can cycle along the bayfront, *Planeaway Bicycles* is at 1 Blackfield Drive in the Cove Shopping Center (☎415/383-2123). Half a mile east of the Point Reyes Visitor Center is *Trailhead Rentals* on Bear Valley Road (☎415/663-1958).

Golden Gate Park and the Marina Green have become popular localities for **roller-blading**; if you want to have a go, rent skates from *Nuvo Colors*, 3108 Fillmore St (☎771-6886). To some extent, cycling and roller-blading have supplanted the Bay Area's former obsession, **jogging**, though you'll still see people running in the parks, and late May's **Bay-to-Breakers Race**, a distinctly San Franciscan institution, continues to thrive. Throngs of costumed joggers – waiters carrying wine glasses, giant centipedes and the like – follow a dozen world-class runners from the Embarcadero, seven and a half miles across the city to Ocean Beach. If you're tempted to join in, call ☎777-2424 for details. In Marin County's much more serious **Dipsea Race**, which takes place on the second Sunday in June, several hundred runners race across the mountains from Mill Valley to Stinson Beach. If you want to participate, contact, Dipsea Race, PO Box 30, Mill Valley, CA 94942.

The water off the San Francisco coast tends to be pretty chilly, so **surfing** remains more of a Southern California phenomenon. However, wet-suited enthusiasts do get radical off most Bay Area beaches, particularly Stinson Beach in northern Marin County and along the Peninsula south of San Francisco – Gray Whale Cove and San Gregorio to name just two.

For simple **suntanning** or sandcastle-building, there are only two good beaches within the city itself: Baker Beach, just west of the Golden Gate Bridge, and China Beach near Lincoln Park.

Windsurfing is especially visible around Crissy Field and the Presidio, from where sailors race out and around the Golden Gate. At the Berkeley Marina, another centre for windsurfers, you can also rent sailboats from the *Cal Sailing Club* (☎510/287-5905) and cruise around the bay.

For those of you who don't care about the temperature of the water, **kayaking** is popular in the East Bay and Marin for about $25–50 per day. Kayaks can be rented in Oakland's Jack London Square at *California Canoe and Kayak* (☎510/893-7833); *Cal Adventures* in the Berkeley Marina (☎510/642-4000) or *Stinson Beach Health Club* (☎868-2739)

on Hwy-1. Without experience, you may be required to take a two-to-four hour lesson.

Those who wish to put the connection between mind and body through a rigorous test may go **rock-climbing**. There are many climbing walls for beginners as well as advanced climbers with ropes. Some outdoor walls include Mickey's Beach off of Tiburon and Berkeley's famous Indian Rock, off Indian Rock Road. Climbing enthusiasm has led to indoor climbing walls, too – *City Rock* in Emeryville (☎510/644-2510) and UC Berkeley's *Cal Adventure's Wall* (☎510/642-4000). But the truly daring will go **hang-gliding** at Fort Funston on the southernmost portion of Ocean Beach. Mostly, this life-threatening endeavour is best enjoyed from a distance on the beach below.

Other Outdoor Activities

Besides the above, there's a whole range of considerably less athletic things to do in the great outdoors. If you're into gambling or just a great day out and a few drinks, you might fancy one of the two Bay Area **horse-racing** tracks: *Golden Gate Fields* in Albany in the East Bay (☎510/526-3020), or *Bay Meadows*, south of San Francisco down the Peninsula (☎574-7223). If you prefer to ride horses yourself, *Chabot Riding Stables*, above East Oakland (☎510/638-0610), do guided rides for $20 per hour or $35 for two hours, and *Miwok Livery* (☎383-8048) in Marin County charge $50 for two hours' trail-riding in fine locations.

Perhaps the most exceptional outdoor adventure available in the Bay Area is **whale-watching**, following pods of mighty California Gray Whales on their annual migration – generally between December and April – from Alaska to the Sea of Cortez. You can usually spot them from headlands (Point Reyes is one of the best), but to get a real sense of their size and might, you have to join them on the seas. The best local operator of boat trips is the non-profit *Oceanic Society*, Building E, Fort Mason Center (☎441-1106), who offer all-day trips out to the Farrallon Islands, where, even if it's not the right time of year for gray whales, you'll see thousands of seabirds, including pelicans, cormorants and rarer creatures, and may possibly spy the world's largest mammal, the glorious blue whale.

Another possibility for wildlife-watchers (especially good for those prone to seasickness) happens around the same time as the whale migration – the mating season of the massive and grotesquely beautiful Northern Elephant Seals. These two-ton creatures spend most of January and February at Año Nuevo State Reserve, down the coast thirty miles south of San Francisco. If you fancy watching the trunk-nosed males as they battle it out for the right to make babies, see p.175 for details.

Part 5

The Contexts

A history of San Francisco

Though its recorded history may not stretch back very far by European standards, in its 150 years of existence San Francisco has more than made up for time. The city first came to life during the California Gold Rush of 1849, an adventure which set a tone for the place that it sustains to this day, both in its valuing of individual effort above corporate enterprise and in the often non-conformist policies that have given it perhaps the most liberal image of any US city. The following account is intended to give an overall view of the city's development; for a rundown of the figures – both past and present – who have helped to shape the city, see the "San Francisco people" glossary on p.313.

Native Peoples

For thousands of years prior to the arrival of Europeans, the **aboriginal peoples** of the Bay Area lived healthily and apparently fairly peacefully on the naturally abundant land. Numbering around 15,000, and grouped in small, tribal villages of a few hundred people, they supported themselves mainly by hunting and fishing rather than agriculture. Most belonged to the coastal **Miwok** tribe, who inhabited most of what is now Marin County, as well as the Sonoma and Napa valleys; the rest were **Ohlone**, who lived in smaller villages sprinkled around the bay and down the south coast of the peninsula.

Very few artefacts from the period survive, and most of what anthropologists have deduced is based on the observations of the early explorers, who were by and large impressed by the Indian way of life – if not their "heathen" religion. One of the first colonists characterized them as "constant in their good friendship, and gentle in their manners". Indian boats, fashioned from lengths of tule reed, were remarkably agile and seaworthy. Of the buildings, few of which were ever intended to last beyond the change of seasons, the most distinctive was the *temescal* or sweat lodge. Kule Loklo, a replica Miwok village in the Point Reyes National Seashore, provides a good sense of what their settlements might have looked like.

Since there was no political or social organization beyond the immediate tribal level, it did not take long for the colonizing Spaniards effectively to wipe them out, if more through epidemics than through outright genocide. Nowadays no Bay Area Native Americans survive on their aboriginal homelands.

Exploration and Conquest

Looking at the Golden Gate from almost any vantage point, it's hard to imagine that anyone might fail to notice such a remarkable opening to the Pacific. Nevertheless, dozens of **European explorers**, including some of the most legendary names of the New World conquest – Juan Cabrillo, Sir Francis Drake, Sebastian Vizcaino – managed to sail past for centuries, oblivious of the great harbour it protected. Admittedly, the passage is often obscured by fogs, and even on a clear day the Bay's islands, and the East Bay hills which rise up behind, do disguise the entrance to the point of invisibility.

The Englishman **Sir Francis Drake** came close to finding the Bay when he arrived in the *Golden Hind* in **1579**, taking a break from plundering Spanish vessels in order to make repairs. The "white bancks and cliffes" of his supposed landing spot – now called Drake's Bay, off Point Reyes north of San Francisco – reminded him of Dover. Upon going ashore, he was met by a band of Miwok, who greeted him with food and drink and placed a feathered crown upon his head; in return, he claimed all of their lands, which he called Nova Albion (New England), for Queen Elizabeth. Supposedly, he left behind a brass plaque; although this has been proved to be a fake, a copy remains on display in the Bancroft Library at the University of California in Berkeley.

Fifteen years later the Spanish galleon **San Augustín** – loaded to the gunwales with treasure from the Philippines – moored in the same spot, but met with tragically different results. After renaming Drake's Bay to honour their patron saint, San Francisco de Asis (Francis of Assisi), disaster struck: the ship was dashed against the rocks of Point Reyes and wrecked. The crew were able to salvage some of the cargo and enough of the ship to build a small lifeboat, on which they travelled south all the way to Acapulco, the Spanish base of operations in the Pacific, hugging the coast for the entire voyage and still sailing right past the Golden Gate. Indeed it was not until the end of 1769 that Western eyes set sight on the great body of water now called San Francisco Bay.

Colonization: The Mission Era

The **Spanish occupation** of the West Coast, which they called "Alta California", began in earnest in the late 1760s, following the Seven Years' War, partly due to military expediency (to prevent another power from gaining a foothold), and partly to Catholic missionary zeal to convert the heathen Indians. Early in **1769**, a company of three hundred soldiers and clergy set off from Mexico to establish an outpost at Monterey, half of them by ship, the other half overland. A number stopped to set up the first California mission at San Diego, while an advance party – made up of some sixty soldiers, mule skinners, priests and Indians, and led by Gaspàr de Portola – continued up the coast, blazing an overland route. It was hard-going, especially with their inadequate maps, and not surprisingly they overshot their mark, ending up somewhere around Half Moon Bay.

Trying to regain their bearings, Portola sent out two scouting parties, one north along the coast and one east into the mountains. Both groups returned with extraordinary descriptions of the Golden Gate and the great bay, which they thought must be the same "Bahia de San Francisco" where the *San Agustín* had come to grief almost two centuries earlier. On November 4, 1769, the entire party gathered together on the ridgetop, overwhelmed by the incredible sight: Father Crespi, their priest, wrote that the bay "could hold not only all the armadas of our Catholic Monarch, but also all those of Europe". Portola's band barely stayed long enough to gather up supplies before turning around and heading back to Monterey; that mission was to become the capital and commercial centre of Spanish California.

It took the Spanish another six years to send an expedition 85 miles north to the bay Portola had discovered. In May **1775**, when he piloted the *San Carlos* through the Golden Gate, Juan Manuel de Ayala became the first European to sail into San Francisco Bay. The next year Captain **Juan Bautista de Anza** returned with some 200 soldiers and settlers to establish the **Presidio of San Francisco** overlooking the Golden Gate, as well as a mission three miles to the southeast, along a creek he named *Nuestra Señora de Dolores* – "Our Lady of Sorrows". From this came the mission's popular – and still current – name, **Mission Dolores**.

Over the coming years four other Bay Area **missions** were established. Santa Clara de Asis, forty miles south of Mission Dolores, was founded in 1777; San José de Guadalupe, set up in 1797 near today's Fremont, grew into the most successful of the lot. In 1817, the *asistencia*, or auxiliary mission, San Rafael Arcangel was built in sunny Marin County as a convalescent hospital for priests and Indians who had been taken ill at Mission Dolores. The last, San Francisco Solano, built at Sonoma in 1823, was the only mission established under Mexican rule.

Each of the mission complexes was broadly similar, with a church and cloistered residence structure surrounded by irrigated fields, vineyards and more distant ranchlands, the whole protected by a small contingent of soldiers. Indian catechumens were put to work making soap and candles, but were treated as retarded children, often beaten and never educated. Objective facts about the missionaries' treatment of the Indians are hard to come by, though mission registries record twice as many deaths as they do births, and their cemeteries are packed with Indian dead. Many of the missions suffered from Indian raids; the now ubiquitous red-tiled roofs replaced the earlier thatch to resist fire.

To grow food for the missions and the forts or presidios, **towns** – called *pueblos* – were established, part of the ongoing effort to attract settlers to this distant and as yet undesirable territory. The first was laid out in 1777 at San José in a broad fertile valley south of the Mission Santa Clara. Though it was quite successful at growing crops, it had no more than a hundred inhabitants until well into the 1800s. Meanwhile, a small village – not sanctioned by the Spanish authorities – was beginning to emerge between Mission Dolores and the presidio, around the one deepwater landing spot, southeast of today's Telegraph Hill. Called **Yerba Buena**, "good grass", after the sweet-smelling minty herb that grew wild over the windswept hills, it was little more than a collection of shacks and ramshackle jetties. Although the name "San Francisco" was not applied to it until the late 1840s, this tiny outpost formed the basis of today's metropolis.

The Mexican Revolutions and The Coming of the Americans

The emergence of an independent **Mexican state** in 1821 spelt the end of the mission era. Within a few years the new republic had secularized the missions and handed over their lands to the few powerful families of the "Californios" – mostly ex-soldiers who had settled here after completing their military service. The Mexican government exerted hardly any control over distant Yerba Buena, and was generally much more willing than the Spanish had been to allow foreigners to remain as they were, so long as they behaved themselves. A few trappers and adventurers had passed by in the early 1800s and, beginning in the early 1820s, a number of British and Americans started arriving in the Bay Area, most of them sailors who jumped ship, but also including a few men of property. The most notable of these immigrants was **William Richardson**, an Englishman who arrived on a whaling ship in 1822 and stayed for the rest of his life, marrying the daughter of the Presidio commander and eventually coming to own most of southern Marin County, from where he started a profitable shipping company and ran the sole ferry service across the tricky bay waters. In Richardson's wake, dozens followed – almost without exception males who, like him, tended to fit in with the existing Mexican culture, often marrying into established families and converting to the Catholic faith.

As late as the mid-1840s, Monterey was still the only town of any size on the entire West Coast, and tiny Yerba Buena (population 200 or so) made its livelihood from supplying passing ships, mainly Boston-based whaling vessels and the fur-traders of the English-owned **Hudson's Bay Company**. Though locals lived well, the Bay Area was not obviously rich in resources, and so was not by any means a major issue in international relations. However, from the 1830s onwards, the **US government** decided that it wanted to buy all of Mexico's lands north of the Rio Grande, California included, in order to fulfil the "Manifest Destiny" of the United States to cover the continent from coast to coast. Any negotiations were rendered unnecessary when, in June 1846, the Mexican–American War broke out in Texas, and US naval forces quickly took over the entire West Coast, capturing San Francisco's presidio on **July 9, 1846**.

A revealing – although historically insignificant – episode, which set the tone for the anarchic growth of the Bay Area over the next fifty years, took place around this time. An ambitious US Army captain, John C Fremont, had been working to encourage unhappy settlers to declare independence from Mexico, and to set himself up as their leader. By assembling an unofficial force of some sixty sharpshooting ex-soldiers, and by spreading rumours that war with Mexico was imminent and unstoppable, he managed to persuade settlers to take action: the **Bear Flag Revolt**. On June 14, some thirty farmers and trappers descended upon the abandoned presidio in Sonoma and took the retired commandant, Colonel Guadupe Vallejo, captive, raising a makeshift flag over the plaza and declaring California independent. The flag – which featured a roughly drawn grizzly bear above the words "California Republic" – was eventually adopted as the California state flag, but this "Republic" was short-lived. Three weeks after the disgruntled settlers hoisted their flag in Sonoma, it was replaced by the Stars and Stripes, and California was thereafter **US territory**. Ironically, just nine days before the Americans took formal control, **gold** was discovered on January 24, 1848, in the Sierra Nevada foothills a hundred miles east of the city – something that was to change the face of San Francisco for ever.

The Gold Rush

At the time gold was discovered, the Bay Area had a total (non-native) population of around two thousand, about a quarter of whom lived in tiny **San Francisco**, which had only changed its name from Yerba Buena the year before. By the summer of 1848, rumours of the find attracted a trickle of gold seekers, and when news of their subsequent success filtered back to the coast (relayed by a local shopkeeper **Sam Brannan**, in Portsmouth Square), soldiers deserted and sailors jumped ship, and most towns were abandoned. Would-be settlers dropped everything to head for the gold fields. The first prospectors on the scene made fantastic fortunes – those working the richest "diggings" could extract more than an ounce every hour – but the real money was being made by merchants charging equally outrageous prices for essentials. Even the most basic supplies were hard to come by, and what little was available cost exorbitant amounts: a dozen eggs for $50, a shovel or pickaxe twice that. Exuberant miners willingly traded glasses of gold dust for an equal amount of whisky – something like $1000 a shot. Though it took some time for news of the riches to travel, soon men were flooding into California from all over the globe to share the wealth, in the most madcap migration in world history. Within a year some 100,000 men – known collectively as the **Forty-Niners** – had arrived in California. About half of them came overland, after a three-month slog across the continent, and headed straight for the mines. The rest arrived by ship and landed at San Francisco, expecting to find a city where they could recuperate before continuing on the arduous journey. They must have been disappointed with what they found: hulks of abandoned ships formed the only solidly constructed buildings, rats overran the filthy streets, and drinking water was sparse and often contaminated.

Few of the new arrivals stayed very long in San Francisco, but, if anything, life in the mining camps proved even less hospitable. As thousands of moderately successful but worn-out miners returned to San Francisco, especially during the torrential rains of the **winter of 1849–50**, the shanty-town settlement began to grow into a proper city. Ex-miners set up foundries and sawmills to provide those starting out with the tools of their trade, and traders arrived to profit from the miners' success, selling them clothing, food, drink and entertainment. The city where the successful miners came to blow their hard-earned cash was a place of luxury hotels and burlesque theatres, which featured the likes of Lola Montez, whose semi-clad "spider dance" enthralled legions of fans. Throughout the early 1850s immigrants continued to pour through the Golden Gate, and although the great majority hurried on to the mines, enough stayed around to bring the city's population up to around 35,000 by the end of 1853. Of these, more than half were from foreign parts – a wide-ranging mix of Mexicans, Germans, Chinese, Italians and others.

Within five years of the discovery of gold the easy pickings were all but gone, and as the free-wheeling mining camps evolved into increasingly large-scale, corporate operations, San Francisco swelled from frontier outpost into a substantial city, with a growing industrial base, a few newspapers, and even its own branch of the US Mint. When revenues from the gold fields ceased to expand in the late 1850s, the speculative base that had made so many fortunes quickly vanished. Lots that had been selling at a premium couldn't be given away, banks went bust, and San Francisco had to declare itself **bankrupt** as a result of years of corrupt dealings. The already volatile city descended into near-anarchy, with vigilante mobs roaming the streets enforcing their particular brand of justice. By the summer of 1856 the "Committee of Vigilance", led by William Coleman and the ever-present Sam Brannan and composed of the city's most successful businessmen, was the **de facto government** of the city, having taken over the state militia and installed themselves inside their "Fort Gunnybags" headquarters, outside which they regularly hanged petty criminals (admittedly after giving them a fair trial), to the amusement of gathered throngs. A few of the most radically minded vigilantes proposed secession from the US, but calmer heads prevailed, and the city was soon restored to more legitimate governance. The rest of the 1850s were comparatively uneventful, as San Francisco prepared for what was to become the biggest boom in the city's boom-and-bust cycle.

The Boom Years (1860–1900)

In the 1860s San Francisco enjoyed a bigger boom than that of the Gold Rush, following the discovery of an even more lucrative band of precious **silver ore** in the Great Basin mountains of western Nevada. Discovered just east of Reno in late 1859 and soon known as the **Comstock Lode**, it was one of the most fantastic deposits ever encountered: a single, solid vein of silver, mixed with gold, that ranged from ten to over a hundred feet wide and stretched a little over two miles long, most of it buried hundreds of feet underground. Mining here was in complete contrast to the freelance prospecting of the California gold fields, and required a scale of operations unimagined in the California mines. Many of San Francisco's great engineers, including George Hearst, Andrew Hallidie and Adolph Sutro, put their minds to the task.

As the mines had to go increasingly deeper to get at the valuable ore, the mining companies needed larger and larger amounts of capital, which they attracted by issuing shares dealt on the burgeoning San Francisco **Stock Exchange**. Speculation was rampant, and the value of shares could rise or fall by a factor of ten, depending on the day's rumours and forecasts; Mark Twain got his literary start publicizing, for a fee, various new "discoveries" in his employers' mines. Hundreds of thousands of dollars were made and lost in a day's trading, and the cagier players, like James Flood and James Fair, made millions.

While the Comstock silver enabled many San Franciscans to enjoy an unsurpassed prosperity throughout the 1860s, few people gave much thought to the decade's other major development, the building of the **transcontinental railroad**, completed in 1869 using imported Chinese labourers. Originally set up in Sacramento to build the western link, the **Central Pacific** and later **Southern Pacific** railroad soon expanded to cover most of the West, ensnaring San Francisco in its web. Wholly owned by the so-called **Big Four** – Charles Crocker, Collis P Huntington, Mark Hopkins and Leland Stanford – the Southern Pacific "octopus", as it was caricatured in the popular press, exercised an essential monopoly over transportation in the Bay Area. Besides controlling the long-distance railroads, they also owned San Francisco's streetcar system, the network of ferry boats that criss-crossed the bay, and even the cable-car line that lifted them up California Street to their Nob Hill palaces (see p.69).

However, not everyone reaped the good fortune of the Nob Hill elite. The coming of the railroad usurped San Francisco's primacy as the West Coast's supply point, and products from the East began flooding in at prices well under anything local industry could manage. At the same time the Comstock mines ceased to produce such enormous fortunes, and depression began to set in. The lowering of economic confidence was compounded by a series of droughts which wiped out agricultural harvests, and by the arrival in San Francisco of thousands of now unwanted **Chinese workers**. As unemployment rose throughout the late 1870s frustrated workers took out their aggression in racist assaults on the city's substantial Chinese population. While there were many instances of violent acts against individual Chinese people, most of the workers' displeasure was channelled into political activity. At mass demonstrations all over the city, thousands rallied behind the slogan "The Chinese Must Go!"

Though San Francisco was popularly seen as being powered by ignoble motives and full of self-serving money-grabbers, there were a few exceptions, even among its wealthiest elite. **Adolph Sutro**, for example, was a German-born engineer who made one fortune in the Comstock mines and another buying up land in the city – in 1890 he was said to own ten percent of San Francisco, even more than the Big Four. But Sutro was an unlikely millionaire, as compassionate and public-spirited as the Big Four were ruthlessly single-minded; in fact, when the Southern Pacific tripled fares to a quarter on the trolley line out to Golden Gate Park, Sutro built a parallel line that charged a nickel. He also built the Sutro Baths and the Cliff House and in 1894 was elected mayor of San Francisco on the Populist Party ticket, campaigning on an anti-Southern Pacific manifesto which promised to rid San Francisco of "this horrible monster which is devouring our substance and debauching our people, and by its devilish instincts and criminal methods is every day more firmly grasping us in its tentacles". Sutro died in 1898, with the city still firmly in the grasp of the "octopus".

The Great Earthquake and After

San Francisco experienced another period of economic expansion in the **early years of the 1900s**, due in equal part to the Spanish–American War and the Klondike Gold Rush in Alaska. Both of these events increased ship traffic through the port, where dockworkers were beginning to organize themselves into **unions** on an unprecedented scale. The mighty longshoremen's association they formed was to become a political force to be reckoned with. The fight to win recognition and better wages was long and hard; unrest was virtually constant, and police were brought in to scare off strikers and prevent picket lines from shutting down the waterfront. But this economic instability was nothing compared to the one truly earth-shattering event of the time: the **Great Earthquake of 1906.**

The quake that hit San Francisco on the morning of April 18, 1906 was, at 8.1 on the Richter Scale, the most powerful ever to hit anywhere in the US, before or since (over ten times the force of the 1989 earthquake). It destroyed hundreds of buildings, but by far the worst destruction was wrought by the **post-earthquake conflagration** that followed, as ruptured gas mains exploded and chimneys toppled, starting fires that spread right across the city. It all but levelled the entire area from the waterfront, north and south of Market Street, west to Van Ness Avenue, whose grand mansions were dynamited to form a firebreak. Comparatively few people, around 500 in total, were killed, but about half of the population – some 100,000 people – were left homeless and fled the city. Many of those who stayed set up camp in the barren reaches of what's now Golden Gate Park, where soldiers from the Presidio undertook the mammoth task of establishing and maintaining a tent city for about 20,000 displaced San Franciscans.

During the ensuing ten years, San Francisco was rebuilt with a vengeance, reconstructing the city as it was and largely ignoring the grand plan drawn up by designer Daniel Burnham just a year before the disaster. The city council had given its approval to this plan, which would have replaced the rigid grid of streets with an eminently more sensible system of axial main boulevards filled in with curving avenues skirting the hills and smaller, residential streets climbing their heights. However, such was the power and influence of the city's vested interests that the status quo was quickly reinstated, despite the clear opportunity afforded by the earthquake.

To celebrate its recovery, and the opening of the Panama Canal – a project which had definite implications for San Francisco's trade-based economy – the city fathers set out to create the magnificent **1915 Panama Pacific International Exhibition**. Land was reclaimed from the bay for the exhibition and on it an elaborate complex of exotic buildings was constructed, including Bernard Maybeck's exquisite Palace of Fine Arts and centring on the 100-yard-high, gem-encrusted Tower of Jewels. Hundreds of thousands visited the fair, which lasted throughout the year, but when it ended all the buildings, save the Palace of Fine Arts, were torn down, and the land sold off for the houses that now make up the Marina district.

The great success of the exhibition proved to the world that San Francisco had recovered from the earthquake. But the newly recovered civic pride was tested the next year by one of the city's more disgraceful episodes. On the eve of America's involvement in **World War I**, a pro-war parade organized by San Francisco's business community was devastated by a **bomb attack** that killed ten marchers and severely wounded another forty. In their haste to find the culprit, the San Francisco police arrested half a dozen radical union agitators. With no evidence other than perjured testimony, activist **Tom Mooney** was convicted and sentenced to death, along with his alleged co-conspirator Warren Billings. Neither, fortunately, was executed, but both spent most of the rest of their lives in prison; Billings wasn't pardoned until 1961, 45 years after his fraudulent conviction.

The Roaring Twenties

The war years had little effect on San Francisco, but the period thereafter, the **Roaring Twenties**, was in many ways the city's finest era. Despite Prohibition, the jazz clubs and speakeasies of the Barbary Coast district were in full swing. San Francisco was still the premier artistic and cultural centre of the West Coast, a role it would relinquish to Los Angeles by the next decade, and its status as an international financial hub (both major international credit card companies – today's *Visa* and *Access* – had their start here) was as yet unchallenged by the upstart southern megalopolis. The strength of San Francisco as a banking power was highlighted by the rise of the Bank of America – founded as the Bank of Italy in 1904 by A P Giannini in North Beach – into the largest bank in the world.

The buoyant 1920s gave way to the Depression of the 1930s, but, despite the sharp increases in unemployment, there was only one major battle on the industrial relations front. On **"Bloody Thursday"** – July 5, 1934 – police protecting strike-breakers from angry picketers fired into the crowd, wounding thirty and killing two longshoremen. The Army was sent in to restore order, and in retaliation the unions called a **General Strike** that saw some 125,000 workers down-tools, bringing the Bay Area economy to a halt for four days. Otherwise there was little unrest, and, thanks in part to **WPA sponsorship**, some of the city's finest monuments – Coit Tower for example and, most importantly, the two great bridges – were built during this time. Before the **Bay and Golden Gate bridges** went up, in 1936 and 1937 respectively, links between the city and the surrounding towns of the Bay Area were provided by an impressive network of **ferry boats**, some of which were among the world's largest. In 1935, the ferries' peak year, some 100,000 commuters per day crossed the bay by boat; just five years later the last of the boats was withdrawn from service, unable to compete with the increasingly popular automobile.

World War II

The Japanese attack on Pearl Harbor and US involvement in **World War II** transformed the Bay Area into a massive war machine, its industry mobilizing quickly to provide weaponry and ships for the war effort. **Shipyards** opened all around the bay – the largest, the Kaiser Shipyards in Richmond, was employing over 100,000 workers on round-the-clock shifts just six months after its inception – and men and women flooded into the region from all over the country to work in the lucrative concerns. Entire cities were constructed to house them, many of which survive – not least Hunter's Point, on the southern edge of the San Francisco waterfront, which was never intended to last beyond the end of hostilities but still houses some 15,000 of the city's poorest people. A more successful example is Marin City, a workers' housing community just north of Sausalito, which – surprisingly, considering its present-day air of leisured affluence – was one of the most successful wartime shipyards, able to crank out a ship a day.

The Fifties

After the war, thousands of GIs returning from the South Pacific came home through San Francisco, and many decided to stay. The city spilled out into new districts, and, especially in suburbs like the Sunset, massive tracts of identical dwellings, subsidized by federal loans and grants, were thrown up to house the returning heroes – many of whom still live here. The accompanying economic prosperity continued unabated well into the 1950s, and in order to accommodate increasing numbers of cars on the roads, huge **freeways** were constructed, cutting through the city. The Embarcadero Freeway in particular formed an imposing barrier, perhaps appropriately dividing the increasingly office-orientated Financial District from the declining docks and warehouses of the waterfront, which for so long had been the heart of San Francisco's economy.

As the increasingly mobile and prosperous middle classes moved out from the inner city, new bands of literate but disenchanted middle-class youth began to move into the areas left behind, starting, in the middle part of the decade, in the bars and cafés of North Beach, which swiftly changed from a staunch Italian neighbourhood into the Greenwich Village of the West Coast. The **Beat Generation**, as they became known, reacted against what they saw as the empty materialism of 1950s America by losing themselves in a bohemian orgy of jazz, drugs and Buddhism, expressing their disillusionment with the status quo through a new, highly personal and expressive brand of fiction and poetry. The writer **Jack Kerouac**, whose *On the Road* became widely accepted as the handbook of the Beats, both for the style of writing (fast, passionate, unpunctuated) and the lifestyle it described, was in some ways the movement's main spokesman, and is credited with coining the term "Beat" – meaning "beatific" – to describe the group. Later, columnist Herb Caen somewhat derisively turned "beat" into "beatnik", after Sputnik. San Francisco, and particularly the **City Lights Bookstore**, at the centre of North Beach, became the main meeting point and focus of this diffuse group, though whatever impetus the movement had was gone by the early 1960s.

The Sixties

Though the long-term value of their writing is still debatable, there's no doubt that the Beats opened people's minds. However, it was an offshoot of the group, the **hippies**, that really took this task to heart. The term was originally a Beat put-down of the inexperienced but enthusiastic young people who followed in their hedonistic footsteps. The first hippies appeared in the early 1960s, in cafés and folk music clubs around the fringes of Bay Area university campuses. They, too, eschewed the materialism and the nine-to-five consumer world, but preferred an escapist fantasy of music and marijuana that became adapted as a half-baked political indictment of society and where it was going wrong.

The main difference between the Beats and the early hippies, besides the five years that elapsed, was that the hippies had discovered – and regularly experimented with – a new hallucinogenic drug called LSD, better known as **acid**. Since its synthesis, LSD had been legally and readily available, mainly through psychologists who were interested in studying its possible therapeutic benefits. Other, less scientific research was also being done by a variety of people, many of whom, from around 1965 onwards, began to settle in the Haight-Ashbury district west of the city centre, living communally in huge low-rent Victorian houses, in which they could take acid and "trip" in safe, controlled circumstances. **Music** was an integral part of the acid experience, and a number of bands – the Charlatans, Jefferson Airplane and the Grateful Dead – came together in San Francisco during the summer of 1966, playing open-ended dance music at such places as the Fillmore Auditorium and the Avalon Ballroom.

Things remained on a fairly small scale until the spring of **1967**, when a free concert in Golden Gate Park drew a crowd of 20,000 and, for the first time, media attention. Articles describing the hippies, most of which focused on their prolific appetites for sex and drugs, attracted a stream of newcomers to the Haight from all over the country, and within a few months the **"Summer of Love"** was well under way, with some 100,000 young people descending upon the district.

In contrast to the hippie indulgence of the Haight-Ashbury scene, across the bay in Berkeley and Oakland **revolutionary politics**, rather than drugs, were at the top of the agenda. While many of the hippies opted out of politics, the student radicals threw themselves into political activism, beginning with the Free Speech Movement at the University of California in 1964. The FSM, originally a reaction against the university's banning of on-campus political activity, laid the groundwork for the more passionate, **anti-Vietnam War** protests that rocked the entire country for the rest of the decade. The first of what turned out to be dozens of **riots** occurred in June 1968, when students marching down Telegraph Avenue in support of the Paris student uprising were met by a wall of police, leading to rioting that continued for the next few days. Probably the most famous event in Berkeley's radical history took place in **People's Park**, a plot of university-owned land that was taken over as a community open space by local people. Four days later an army of police, under the command of Edwin Meese – who later headed the US Department of Justice in the Reagan years – tear-gassed and stormed the park, accidentally killing a bystander and seriously injuring over 100 others.

Probably the most extreme element of late 1960s San Francisco emerged out of the impoverished flatlands of Oakland – the **Black Panthers**, established by Bobby Seale, Huey Newton and Eldridge Cleaver in 1966. The Panthers were a heavily armed but numerically small band of militant black activists with an announced goal of securing self-determination for America's blacks. From their Oakland base they set up a nationwide organization, but the threat they posed, and the chances they were willing to take in pursuit of their cause, were too great. Thirty of their members died in gun battles with the police, and the surviving Panthers lost track of their aims: Eldridge Cleaver later became a right-wing Republican, while Huey Newton was killed over a drugs deal in West Oakland in 1989.

Contemporary San Francisco

The unrest of the 1960s continued into the **early 1970s**, if not at such a fever pitch. One last headline-grabber was the kidnapping in 1974 of heiress Patty Hearst from her Berkeley apartment by the *Symbionese Liberation Army*, or **SLA**, a hard-core bunch of revolutionaries who used their wealthy hostage to demand free food for Oakland's poor. Hearst later helped the gang to rob a San Francisco bank, wielding a sub-machine gun. Otherwise, certainly compared to the previous decade, the 1970s were quiet times, which saw the opening of the long-delayed ***BART*** high-speed transportation system, as well as the establishment of the **Golden Gate National Recreation Area** to protect and preserve 75,000 acres of open space on both sides of the Golden Gate Bridge.

Throughout the 1970s, it wasn't so much that San Francisco's rebellious thread had been broken, but rather that the battle-lines were being drawn elsewhere. The most distinctive political voices were those of the city's large **gay and lesbian communities**. Inspired by the so-called Stonewall Riots in New York City in 1969, San Francisco's homosexuals began to organize themselves politically, demanding equal status with heterosexuals. Most importantly, gays and lesbians stepped out into the open and refused to hide their sexuality behind closed doors, giving rise to the gay liberation movement that has prospered worldwide. One of the leaders of the gay community in San Francisco, **Harvey Milk**, won a seat on the Board of Supervisors, becoming the first openly gay man to take public office. When Milk was **assassinated** in City Hall, along with Mayor George Moscone, by former Supervisor Dan White in 1978 – see p.117 – the whole city was shaken. The fact that White was found guilty of manslaughter, not murder, caused the gay community to erupt in riotous frustration, burning police cars and laying siege to City Hall.

The **1980s** saw the city's gay community in retreat to some extent, with the advent of AIDS in the early part of the decade devastating the confidence of activists and toning down what was a very promiscuous scene. The community – in conjunction with City Hall – fought, and continues to fight, an impressive and dignified rearguard battle to deal with the disease.

Mayor **Diane Feinstein**, who took over after the death of Moscone, oversaw the construction of millions of square feet of office towers in downtown's Financial District, despite angry protests against the **Manhattanization** of the city. Although she dumped a tangled mess of financial worries in the lap of her successor, **Art Agnos**, Feinstein remains one of the most prominent female politicians in America.

Many of the problems that face San Francisco – urban poverty, drug abuse, homelessness and of course the AIDS crisis – are much the same as those encountered by any major Western city. On top of this, the city was shaken by a major earthquake in October 1989, 7.1 on the Richter Scale – an event watched by 100 million people on nationwide TV, since it hit during a World Series game between Bay Area rivals, the *San Francisco Giants* and the *Oakland A's*. That disaster was followed two years later by a horrific fire in the Oakland hills, which killed 26 people and destroyed three thousand homes.

In the latter half of the 1990s, San Francisco finds itself grappling with fundamental questions. Frank Jordan, the city's unpopular mayor until 1995, established the Matrix programme – a scheme whereby the city's homeless were dealt with simply by moving them on. San Francisco's latest incumbent – known affectionately as "da Mayor" – is flamboyant ex Senate-Head Willie Brown, who has raised hopes that the arrival of a truly big fish can guarantee federal funding for the city. Upon entering office he immediately scrapped the Matrix programme – a move backed by fellow high-ranking Liberals, but one that has raised fears for a new wave of homelessness in the city. Style-freak Brown also had the courage to tackle the California-casual dress ethic by telling City Hall employees to smarten up or get out. Nice one, Willie. Meanwhile, the effects of the ongoing economic downturn in California have been amplified in the Bay Area by post-Cold War military cut-backs which have caused the closure of a number of military bases and cost 35,000 civilian jobs. Hard times or not, however, few San Franciscans would forsake their city for anywhere else.

Writers on San Francisco

Writers seem to pull out all the stops trying to capture San Francisco's great beauty and unique energy. Some of the city's best writing has been in the form of journalism; the pieces below are essentially dispatches from various key points in its history.

Herb Caen

The irascible, indefatigable **Herb Caen** *has been giving the inside story of San Francisco people and places in his daily column for the* San Francisco Chronicle *since 1938. Although a fine satirist and good reporter of political happenings, he is best loved for daily dishing the dirt on San Francisco "society", and his 56 years of unstinting praise for the town he chose as home. The city's sole surviving upholder of politically incorrect journalism – we'll not see his like again. The two columns reproduced below are taken from* The Best of Herb Caen, *published by Chronicle Books.*

The Terrific Triangle

The clean old man was lounging against a wall at Taylor and Ellis, watching the new Hilton rise in all its sterile glory. "Well, that's it, kid," he said with a resigned smile. "That's the end of the Tenderloin."

As he spoke he was rhythmically flipping a $20 gold piece, that talisman of the old crowd. "Of course," he went on, "the Tenderloin has been dying for years. But that thing there" – he jabbed a finger at the monumental blockhouse – "that's the gravestone," he chuckled without amusement. "Sort of looks like one, too."

I glanced around. There were more parking lots and fewer places to go. Nearby, a new jewellery shop was being installed. A streamlined branch of the world's biggest bank was already in business. A small hotel once noted for all-night revels has become a "residence" for "senior citizens", that irritating euphemism.

His purple-veined face shadowed under the pearl-gray fedora. The Clean Old man squinted into the late afternoon sun. Two hard-looking blondes in linty black slacks and high heels gave him a brief "Hi, baby" as they walked past. His eyes followed their rears down Ellis. "Won't see much of that any more," he said. "The old Tenderloin is about to get as square as that hotel. Now tell me about the conventions Mr Hilton is gonna bring to town, and I'll ask you – where they gonna go for laughs when they get here?"

* * *

The old Tenderloin – the "Terrific Triangle" bounded by Jones, O'Farrell and Market. Tenderloin: a peculiarly American term, born in New York. The lexicographers aren't too sure about its origin; the most educated guess surmises that the cops on a certain beat in Manhattan were able to afford tenderloin steaks. In San Francisco, the juice was rich enough for filet mignons, sparkling burgundy, apartment houses and places in the country.

* * *

In the few blocks of the "Terrific Triangle," for a comparatively few years as a city's time is reckoned, there was more action than anywhere else in the country. There were fine restaurants: the Techau Tavern at 1 Powell, Newman's College Inn, the Bay City Grill, Herbert's Bachelor Grill. There were the "French" places – Blanco's, the St. Germain – with utter respectability on the ground floor, shady booths on the second, "riding academies" (as they were known) on the third.

You could drink till dawn in Dutch White's at 110 Eddy, and at Chad Milligan's Sport Club on Ellis. Franchon & Marco danced at Tait's Pavo Real on O'Farrell, where a kid named Rudolph Valentino was a busboy. Frank Shaw and Les Poe reigned at Coffee Dan's. It was unthinkable to miss a Sunday night at the old Orpheum, and if the bill there was a little weak (Jack Benny and Sophie Tucker), there was always the Tivoli, the Warfield, the Capitol, the Alcazar or Will King's Casino, with Will singing "I've got a girl who paints her cheeks, another with a voice that squeaks, they both ran away with a pair of Greeks – I wish I owned a restaurant!"

Girls, girls, girls. Every theatre had a line, with Stage Door Johns to match. Every other small hotel was a house (the old Drexel alone had thirty girls). A doll with the marvelously San Francisco name of Dodie Valencia was a legend.

Even the manicurists at Joe Ruben's barbershop were "as beautiful as Follies girls," the supreme accolade of the era.

* * *

But the lifeblood of the Old Tenderloin was gambling. The cars shuffled and the dice rattled through the smoky nights at the Menlo Club and the Kingston and at Chad Milligan's. The high rollers – Nick the Greek, Titanic Thompson, Joe "Silver Fox" Bernstein, Eddie Sahati – faded in and out with the foggy dawns. At Tom Kyne's in Opal Place, the cul-de-sac alongside the Warfield, you could bet on anything from the Mayor's race to the St Mary's–Santa Clara football game to how many passengers the ferries would carry the next day.

The gamblers were the kings of the Tenderloin, and their names rang true, straight out of Runyon and Lardner. Carnation Willie and Benny the Gent, Bones Remmer and Siggie Rosener, Freddy the Glut, and Jelly and Marty Breslauer. At 10am – the end of the day that started at midnight – the bookies gathered at John's Grill on Ellis. Over the corned beef hash and the eggs sunnyside up they counted the cash and paid off the winners. Enough long green was scattered over the tables to carpet Ireland. Marty Breslauer alone packed $100,000, and one night a kid he'd befriended gunned him down for his roll.

But violence was rare. It was an underworld with class, a closed corporation. The cops, who were getting their share, kept it-that way, and the hoods of the Organization never had a chance to move in. When they arrived at Third and Townsend they were met by the two toughest Inspectors on the force, who put them right back on the train.

The cops knew a good thing, and they had it: The mother of a Captain on the Force was the biggest madam in the area. One day at Bay Meadows a rookie cop who didn't know the score told her: "One of these nights I'm gonna come into your place and close you down." "And when you do," she replied coolly, "you'll find your boss in the kitchen drinking coffee."

* * *

It was a world we'll never see again. Godliness and purity now reign – don't they? – and the final long shadow is being cast over the Tenderloin by the Rising Hilton. The section is about to become infinitely more respectable. And infinitely duller.

June 2, 1963

The view from the Heights

A reader writes: "As a newcomer to San Francisco, I am confused by the constant newspaper references to a district known as Pacific Heights, which I cannot find on any map of the city. Where – and what – is it?"

* * *

One is tempted to reply that Pacific Heights is a mythical faubourg that exists only in the minds of society editors, columnists and real estate agents, but that wouldn't be entirely accurate. For there really is a Pacific Heights, with its own peculiar view of San Francisco – perhaps the only view in town that looks inward rather than out.

Literally, Pacific Heights is a bit of a misnomer. Since it lies on the Northern flank of the city, it overlooks the Bay, not the Pacific. Physically, its boundaries are as loose as its restrictions are tight – let us say, from around Fillmore to Presidio, and from Clay to Union (westward from Presidio to about Arguello the section becomes Presidio Heights, with no marked difference in income or outlook).

However, as you may infer from these loose delineations, there is more to Pacific Heights than location, for many poor or socially unacceptable people live in the areas sketched above, and to be Really Pacific Heights you may not be either. But as long as you are neither, you may even live on Russian, Nob or Telegraph hills, and, in rare instances, Sea Cliff or even Jordan Park (VERY rare). Potrero Hill may make it yet, but never St Francis Wood.

A further salient of Pacific Heights juts down the Peninsula into parts of Burlingame, Hillsborough and Woodside, somehow avoiding Atherton almost completely. The late Mr Atherton would be astounded.

* * *

In sum, Pacific Heights is a point of view that points at itself with pride. Ideally, it is Old Money, which, as anybody knows, is much better than new, inflated stuff. It is Pucci pants, little Chanel suits, English bootmakers and an accent compounded of Ivy League schools, the proper upbringing and Old Forester.

Pacific Heights is "let's hop in the Jag and buzz down to Pebble for the weekend." It's knowing Paris much better than Los Angeles, New York better than Oakland, and the Right People in both. It's "couldn't be nicer, couldn't be more attractive, couldn't be more fun" and "couldn't have been duller," with or without the quotes. It's saying on long weekends, "Let's go away – EVERYBODY will be out of town anyway."

Pacific Heights is houseboys in white jackets walking poodles in clipped jackets, polished windows with shades drawn by polished butlers, indifferent dinners cooked by indifferent cooks ("good ones are SO hard to get"), surprisingly strong martinis and surprisingly bad wines. The houses are pleasant, whether done in Early Michael Taylor or Late Anthony Hail, and the mirrors are generally superior to, and looked at more often than, the pictures. As the finger bowls come, the ladies go to powder their noses.

Pacific Heights is an eternal cocktail party at which everybody knows everybody else, an endless bridge game involving the identical foursome, musical chairs to the same old tune, packages from Gump's, I Magnin, Podesta and Laykin, Tuesday and Friday nights at the opera and a third-base box at Candlestick. If you're not With It, where are you?

Through all the changes it changes not. It is the city's power and sometimes glory, the Northern Lights and the Southern Cross, the day-and-night repository of all that is gilded and glamorous about San Francisco. It is Big Business and Big Pleasure, and it keeps a lot of money in circulation, occasionally its own. And if it sometimes appears to be out of touch with reality, weep not. Reality could very well be out of touch with Pacific Heights.

* * *

Without Pacific Heights – and let me stress again that I use the term loosely – San Francisco would not be what it is today, for better or worse. To the world of stylish travellers and slick magazine editors, it IS San Francisco – or at least the part of it that is thought of (and written about) as '"sophisticated, gay and sparkling." When any distinguished visitor says, "I just adore San Francisco," you may be sure he isn't referring to picnics in Golden Gate Park or the English muffins at Foster's. He has been taken in by The Group, he has been given the Pacific Heights whirl, and this, forevermore, is San Francisco to him.

He is one of the fortunate few, for The Group is as clannish as its counterparts anywhere (visitors who say San Francisco is "cold" and "hard to get to know" didn't make it through the pearly gates). The cable cars, the bridges and Twin Peaks are fine to see, but if you haven't been invited into the hushed drawing rooms, where the minions of Thomas the Butler pass the canapes, you haven't been inside the San Francisco where names are dropped and unlisted phone numbers picked up.

So I say hail to Pacific Heights, wherever it may be. As the city grows away from itself, it grows more deeply into itself, perhaps in self-protection. It is the last of the constants, where children still curtsy, manners are excellent, the ladies are lovely, and drinking a bit too much is not only acceptable but almost mandatory. Life may be equally pleasant in the Deep Mission or the Far Sunset, but Pacific Heights has the panache and the postiche, not to mention the Beluga and the Malassol, and the Aubusson underfoot.

Whatever high style still accrues to San Francisco lives on in this glorious Never-Never Land of three cars for every two-car garage and Chicken à la Kiev in every pot. Long may it be preserved, sous cloche or on the rocks.

October 18, 1964

Hunter S Thompson

One of America's most exciting and controversial essayists, **Hunter S Thompson** *is a trouble-maker and muck-raker of the first order. Equally wild away from his typewriter, his experiences have included a spell with the Hell's Angels in San Francisco, about whom he wrote his first book. His later fascination with Richard Nixon reached its culmination in his long and consistently unforgiving book* The Great Shark Hunt, *from which the extract below is taken. After lying relatively low for a while at his Colorado ranch, he resurfaced in the 1980s to write a column for the* San Francisco Examiner, *pieces of which have been brought together in his latest collection of essays,* Generation of Swine.

The "Hashbury" Is the Capital of the Hippies

In 1965 Berkeley was the axis of what was just beginning to be called the "new left". Its leaders were radical, but they were also deeply committed to the society they wanted to change. A prestigious faculty committee said the Berkeley activists were the vanguard of "a moral revolution among the young," and many professors approved.

Now in 1967 there is not much doubt that Berkeley has gone through a revolution of some kind, but the end result is not exactly what the original leaders had in mind. Many one-time activists have forsaken politics entirely and turned to drugs. Others have even forsaken Berkeley. During 1966, the hot center of revolutionary action on the coast began moving across the bay to San Francisco's Haight-Ashbury district, a run-down Victorian neighborhood of about forty square blocks between the Negro/Fillmore district and Golden Gate Park.

The "Hashbury" is the new capital of what is rapidly becoming a drug culture. Its denizens are not called radicals or beatniks, but "hippies" and perhaps as many as half are refugees from Berkeley and the old North Beach scene, the cradle and the casket of the so-called beat generation.

The other half of the hippy population is too young to identify with Jack Kerouac, or even with Mario Savio. Their average age is about twenty, and most are native Californians. The North Beach types of the late nineteen-fifties were not nearly as provincial as the Haight-Ashbury types are today. The majority of beatniks who flocked into San Francisco ten years ago were transients of the East and Midwest. The literary artistic nucleus – Kerouac, Ginsberg, et al – was a package deal from New York. San Francisco was only a stop on the big circuit: Tangier, Paris, Greenwich Village, Tokyo and India. The senior Beats had a pretty good idea what was going on in the world; they read newspapers, travelled constantly and had friends all over the globe.

The word "hip" translates roughly as "wise" or "tuned-in". A hippy is somebody who "knows" what's really happening, and who adjusts or grooves with it. Hippies despise phoniness; they want to be open, honest, loving, free. They reject the plastic pretence of twentieth-century America, preferring to go back to the "natural life", like Adam and Eve. They reject any kinship with the Beat Generation on the ground that "those cats were negative but our thing is positive". They also reject politics, which is "just another game". They don't like money, either, or any kind of aggressiveness.

A serious problem in writing about the Haight-Ashbury is that most of the people you have to talk to are involved, one way or another, in the drug traffic. They have good reason to be leery of strangers who ask questions. A twenty-two-year-old student was recently sentenced to two years in prison for telling an undercover narcotics agent where to buy some marijuana. "Love" is the password in the Haight-Ashbury, but paranoia is the style. Nobody wants to go to jail.

At the same time, marijuana is everywhere. People smoke it on the sidewalks, in doughnut shops, sitting in parked cars or lounging on the grass in Golden Gate Park. Nearly everyone on the streets between twenty and thirty is a "head", a user of either marijuana, LSD, or both. To refuse the proferred joint is to risk being labelled a "nark" – a narcotics agent – a threat and a menace to almost everybody.

With a few loud exceptions, it is only the younger hippies who see themselves as a new breed. "A completely new thing in this world, man." The ex-beatniks among them, many of whom are now making money off the new scene, incline to the view that hippies are, in fact, second generation beatniks and that everything genuine in the Haight-Ashbury is about to be swallowed – like North Beach and the Village – in a wave of publicity and commercialism.

Haight Street, the great white way of what the local papers call "hippieland", is already dotted with stores catering mainly to the tourist trade. Few hippies can afford a pair of $20 sandals or a "Mod outfit" for $67.50. Nor can they afford the $3.50 door charge at the Fillmore Auditorium and the Avalon Ballroom, the twin wombs of the "psychedelic, San Francisco, acid-rock sound". Both the Fillmore and the Avalon are jammed every weekend with borderline hippies who don't mind paying for the music and the light shows. There is always a sprinkling of genuine, bare-foot, freaked-out types on the dance floor, but few of them pay to get in. They arrive with the musicians or have other good connections.

Neither of the dance palaces is within walking distance of the Hashbury, especially if you're stoned, and since only a few of the hippies have contacts in the psychedelic power structure, most of them spend their weekend nights either drifting around on Haight Street or loading up on acid – LSD – in somebody's pad. Some of the rock bands play free concerts in Golden Gate Park for the benefit of those brethren who can't afford the dances. But beyond an occasional Happening in the park, the Haight-Ashbury scene is almost devoid of anything "to do" – at least by conventional standards. An at-home entertainment is nude parties at which celebrants paint designs on each other.

There are no hippy bars, for instance, and only one restaurant above the level of a diner or a lunch counter. This is a reflection of the drug culture which has no use for booze and regards food as a necessity to be acquired at the least possible expense. A "family" of hippies will work for hours over an exotic stew or curry in a communal kitchen, but the idea of paying $3 for a meal in a restaurant is out of the question.

Some hippies work, others live on money from home and many are full-time beggars. The post office is a major source of hippy income. Jobs like sorting mail don't require much thought or effort. A hippy named Admiral Love of the Psychedelic Rangers delivers special-delivery letters at night. The Admiral is in his mid-twenties and makes enough money to support an apartmentful of younger hippies who depend on him for their daily bread.

There is also a hippy-run employment agency on Haight Street and anyone needing part-time labor or some kind of specialized work can call and order as many freaks as he needs; they might look a bit weird, but many are far more capable than most "temporary help", and vastly more interesting to have around.

Those hippies who don't work can easily pick up a few dollars a day panhandling along Haight Street. The fresh influx of curiosity-seekers has proved a great boon to the legion of psychedelic beggars. During several days of roaming around the area, I was touched so often that I began to keep a supply of quarters in my pocket so I wouldn't have to haggle over change. The panhandlers are usually barefoot, always young and never apologetic. They'll share what they collect anyway, so it seems entirely reasonable that strangers should share with them.

The best show on Haight Street is usually on the sidewalk in front of the Drog Store, a new coffee bar at the corner of Masonic Street. The Drog Store features an all-hippy revue that runs day and night. The acts change sporadically, but nobody cares. There will always be at least one man with long hair and sunglasses playing a wooden pipe of some kind. He will be wearing either a Dracula cape, a long Buddhist robe, or a Sioux Indian costume. There will also be a hairy blond fellow wearing a Black Bart cowboy hat and a spangled jacket that originally belonged to a drum major in the 1949 Rose Bowl parade. He will be playing the bongo drums. Next to the drummer will be a dazed-looking girl wearing a blouse (but no bra) and a plastic mini-skirt, slapping her thighs to the rhythm of it all.

These three will be the nucleus of the show. Backing them up will be an all-star cast of freaks, every one of them stoned. They will be stretched out on the sidewalk, twitching and babbling in time to the music. Now and then somebody will fall out of the audience and join the revue; perhaps a Hell's Angel or some grubby, chain-draped impostor who never owned a motorcycle in his life. Or maybe a girl wrapped in gauze or a thin man with wild eyes who took an overdose of acid nine days ago and changed himself into a raven. For those on a quick tour of the Hashbury, the Drog Store revue is a must.

Most of the local action is beyond the reach of anyone without access to drugs. There are four or five bars a nervous square might relax in, but one is a Lesbian place, another is a hangout for brutal-looking leather fetishists and the others are old neighborhood taverns full of brooding middle-aged drunks. Prior to the hippy era there were three good Negro-run jazz bars on Haight Street, but they soon went out of style. Who needs jazz, or even beer, when you can sit down on a public kerbstone, drop a pill on your mouth and hear fantastic music for hours at a time in your own head? A cap of good acid costs $5, and for that you can hear the Universal Symphony, with God singing solo and the Holy Ghost on drums.

Drugs have made formal entertainment obsolete in the Hashbury, but only until somebody comes up with something appropriate to the new style of the neighborhood. This summer will see the opening of the new Straight Theater, formerly the Haight Theater, featuring homosexual movies for the trade, meetings, concerts, dances. "It's going to be a kind of hippy community center", said Brent Dangerfield, a young radio engineer from Salt Lake City who stopped off in San Francisco on his way to a job in Hawaii and is now a partner in the Straight. When I asked him how old he was he had to think for a minute. "I'm twenty-two," he said finally, "but I used to be much older."

Another new divertissement, maybe, will be a hippy bus line running up and down Haight Street, housed in a 1930 Fagol bus – a huge, lumbering vehicle that might have been the world's first house trailer. I rode in it one afternoon with the driver, a young hippy named Tim

Thibeau who proudly displayed a bathtub under one of the rear seats. The bus was a spectacle even on Haight Street: people stopped, stared and cheered as we rumbled by, going nowhere at all. Thibeau honked the horn and waved. He was from Chicago, he said, but when he got out of the Army he stopped in San Francisco and decided to stay. He was living, for the moment, on unemployment insurance, and his plans for the future were hazy. "I'm in no hurry", he said. "Right now I'm just taking it easy, just floating along." He smiled and reached for a beer can in the Fagol's icebox.

Dangerfield and Thibeau reflect the blind optimism of the younger hippy element. They see themselves as the vanguard of a new way of life in America – the psychedelic way – where love abounds and work is fun and people help each other. The young hippies are confident that things are going their way.

The older hippies are not so sure. They've been waiting a long time for the world to go their way, and those most involved in the hip scene are hedging their bets this time. "That back to nature scene is okay when you're twenty," said one. "But when you're looking at thirty-five you want to know something's happening to you."

Ed Denson, at twenty-seven, is an ex-beatnik, ex-Goldwaterite, ex-Berkeley radical and currently the manager of a successful rock band called Country Joe and the Fish. His home and headquarters is a complex of rooms above a liquor store in Berkeley. One room is an art studio, another is an office: there is also a kitchen, a bedroom and several sparsely furnished areas without definition.

Denson is deeply involved in the hippy music scene, but insists he's not a hippy. "I'm very pessimistic about where this thing is going," he said. "Right now it's good for a lot of people. It's still very open. But I have to look back at the Berkeley scene. There was a tremendous optimism there, too, but look where all that went. The beat generation? Where are they now? What about hula-hoops? Maybe this hippy thing is more than a fad; maybe the whole world is turning on but I'm not optimistic. Most of the hippies I know don't really understand what kind of a world they're living in. I get tired of hearing about what beautiful people we all are. If the hippies were more realistic they'd stand a better chance of surviving."

Lewis Lapham

Lewis Lapham *comes from a firmly establishment San Francisco family: his grandfather was mayor of the city. Despite these top-notch connections, he grew completely disenchanted with the town and California as a whole, and headed East to become the editor of the highly respected* Harpers Magazine. *The following account describes what irks him about a city that so many people love so unquestioningly.*

Lost Horizon

For the past six or seven weeks I have been answering angry questions about San Francisco. People who know that I was born in that city assume that I have access to confidential information, presumably at the highest levels of psychic consciousness. Their questions sound like accusations, as if they were demanding a statement about the poisoning of the reservoirs. Who were those people that the Reverend Jim Jones murdered in Guyana, and how did they get there? Why would anybody follow such a madman into the wilderness, and how did the Reverend Jones come by those letters from Vice-President Mondale and Mrs Rosalynn Carter? Why did the fireman kill the mayor of San Francisco and the homosexual city official? What has gone wrong in California, and who brought evil into paradise? Fortunately I don't know the answers to these questions; if I knew them, I would be bound to proclaim myself a god and return to San Francisco in search of followers, a mandala, and a storefront shrine. Anybody who would understand the enigma of San Francisco must first know something about the dreaming narcissism of the city, and rather than try to explain this in so many words, I offer into evidence the story of my last assignment for the *San Francisco Examiner.*

I had been employed on the paper for two years when, on a Saturday morning in December of 1959 reported for work to find the editors talking to one another in the hushed and self-important way that usually means that at least fifty people have been killed. I assumed that a ship had sunk or that a building had collapsed. The editors were not in the habit of taking me into their confidence, and I didn't expect to learn the terms of the calamity until I had a chance to read the AP wire. Much to my surprise, the city editor motioned impatiently in my direction, indicating that I should join the circle of people standing around his desk and turning slowing through the pages of the pictorial supplement that the paper was obliged to publish the next day. Aghast at what they saw, unable to stifle small cries of anguished disbelief, they were examining twelve pages of text and photographs arranged under the heading LOS ANGELES – THE ATHENS OF THE WEST. To readers unfamiliar with the ethos of San Francisco, I'm not sure that I can convey the full and terrible effect of this headline. Not only was it wrong, it was monstrous heresy. The residents of San Francisco dote on a romantic image of the city, and they imagine themselves living at a height of civilization accessible only to Erasmus or a nineteenth-century British peer. They flatter themselves on their sophistication, their exquisite sensibility, their devotion to the arts. Los Angeles represents the antithesis of these graces; it is the land of the Philistines, lying somewhere to the south in the midst of housing developments that stand as the embodiment of ugliness, vulgarity, and corruptions of the spirit.

Pity, then, the poor editors in San Francisco. In those days there was also a *Los Angeles Examiner*, and the same printing plant supplied supplements to both papers. The text and photographs intended for a Los Angeles audience had been printed in the Sunday pictorial bearing the imprimatur of the *San Francisco Examiner*. It was impossible to correct the mistake, and so the editors in San Francisco had no choice but to publish and give credence to despised anathema.

This so distressed them that they resolved to print a denial. The city editor, knowing that my grandfather had been mayor of San Francisco and that I had been raised in the city, assumed that he could count on my dedication to the parochial truth. He also knew that I had studied at Yale and Cambridge universities, and although on most days he made jokes about the future of a literary education, on this particular occasion he saw a use for it. What was the point of reading all those books if they didn't impart the skills of a sophist? He handed me the damnable pages and said that I had until five o'clock in the afternoon to refute them as false doctrine. The story was marked for page 1 and an eight-column headline. I was to spare no expense of adjectives.

The task was hopeless. Los Angeles at the time could claim the residence of Igor Stravinsky, Aldous Huxley, and Christopher Isherwood. Admittedly they had done their best work before coming west to ripen in the sun, but their names and photographs, together with those of a few well-known painters and a number of established authors temporarily engaged in the writing of screenplays, make for an impressive display in a newspaper. Even before I put through my first telephone call, to a poet in North Beach experimenting with random verse, I knew that cultural enterprise in San Francisco could not sustain the pretension of a comparison to New York or Chicago, much less to Periclean Athens.

Ernest Bloch had died, and Darius Milhaud taught at Mills College only during the odd years; Henry Miller lived 140 miles to the south at Big Sur, which placed him outside the city's penumbra of light. The Beat Generation had disbanded. Allen Ginsberg still could be seen brooding in the cellar of the City Lights Bookshop, but Kerouac had left town, and the tourists were occupying the best tables at Cassandra's, asking the waiters about psychedelic drugs and for connections to the Buddhist underground. Although I admired the work of Evan Connell and Lawrence Ferlinghetti, I doubted that they would say the kinds of things that the city editor wanted to hear. The San Francisco school of painting consisted of watercolor views of Sausalito and Fisherman's Wharf; there was no theater, and the opera was a means of setting wealth to music. The lack of art or energy in the city reflected the lassitude of a citizenry content to believe its own press notices. The circumference of the local interest extended no more than 150 miles in three directions – as far as Sonoma County and Bolinas in the north, to Woodside and Monterey in the south, and to Yosemite and Tahoe in the east. In a westerly direction the civic imagination didn't reach beyond the Golden Gate Bridge. Within this narrow arc the inhabitants of San Francisco entertained themselves with a passionate exchange of gossip.

At about three o'clock in the afternoon I gave up hope of writing a believable story. Queasy with embarrassment and apology, I informed the city editor that the thing couldn't be done, that if there was such a place as an Athens of the West – which was doubtful – then it probably was to be found on the back lot of a movie studio in Los Angeles. San Francisco might compare to a Greek colony on the coast of Asia Minor in the fourth century B.C., but that was the extent of it.

The city editor heard me out, and then after an awful and incredulous silence, he rose from behind his desk and denounced me as a fool and an apostate. I had betrayed the city of my birth and the imperatives of the first edition. Never could I hope to succeed in the newspaper business. Perhaps I might find work in a drug-store chain, preferably somewhere east of St Louis, but even then he would find himself hard-pressed to recommend me as anything but a liar and an assassin. He assigned the story to an older and wiser reporter, who relied on the local authorities (Herb Caen, Barnaby Conrad, the presidents of department stores, the director of the film festival), and who found it easy enough to persuade them to say that San Francisco should be more appropriately compared to Mount Olympus.

I left San Francisco within a matter of weeks, depressed by the dreamlike torpor of the city. Although in the past eighteen years I often have thought of the city with feelings of sadness, as if in mourning for the beauty of the hills and the clarity of the light in September when the wind blows from the north, I have no wish to return. The atmosphere of unreality seems to me more palpable and oppressive in San Francisco than it does in New York. Apparently this has always been so. Few of the writers associated with the city stayed longer than a few seasons. Twain broke camp and moved on; so did Bierce and Brett Harte. In his novel *The Octopus*, Frank Norris describes the way in which the Southern Pacific Railroad in the 1890s forced the farmers of the San Joaquin Valley to become its serfs. The protagonist of the novel, hoping to stir the farmers to revolt and to an idea of liberty, looks for political allies among the high-minded citizens of San Francisco. He might as well have been looking for the civic conscience in a bordello. A character modelled after Collis Huntington, the most epicurean of the local robber barons, explains to him that San Francisco cannot conceive of such a thing as social justice. The conversation takes place in the bar at the Bohemian Club, and the financier gently says to Norris's hero that "San Francisco is not a city . . . it is a midway plaisance".

The same thing can be said for San Francisco almost a hundred years later, except that in the modern idiom people talk about the city as "carnival." The somnambulism of the past has been joined with the androgynous frenzy of the present, and in the ensuing confusion who knows what's true and not true, or who's doing what to whom and for what reason? The wandering bedouin of the American desert traditionally migrate to California in hope of satisfying their hearts' desire under the palm tree of the national oasis. They seek to set themselves free, to rid themselves of all restraint, to find the Eden or the fountain of eternal youth withheld or concealed from them by the authorities (nurses, teachers, parents, caliphs) in the walled towns of the East. They desire simply to be, and they think of freedom as a banquet. Thus their unhappiness and despair when their journey proves to have been in vain. The miracle fails to take place, and things remain pretty much as they were in Buffalo or Indianapolis. Perhaps this explains the high rate of divorce, alcoholism, and suicide. The *San Francisco Examiner* kept a record of the people who jumped off the Golden Gate Bridge, and the headline always specified the number of the most recent victim as if adding up the expense of the sacrifice to the stone-faced gods of happiness.

© 1979 *Harpers Magazine*. All rights reserved. Reprinted from the February issue by special permission.

Books

Where the books we recommend below are in print, the publisher's name is given in parentheses after the title: the US publishers first, separated, where applicable, from the UK publisher by an oblique slash. Where books are published in only one of these countries, we have specified which one; when the same company publishes the book in both, it appears just once. The titles listed as being out of print (o/p) in both countries should be easy enough to find in second-hand bookstores.

Travel/Impressions

Martin Amis *The Moronic Inferno and Other Visits to America* (Penguin). An assortment of essays that pull no punches in their dealings with American life and culture, including the moral majority, militarism and high-energy consumerism.

John Miller (ed) *San Francisco Stories* (o/p). Patchy collection of writings on the city with contributions from Lewis Lapham, Tom Wolfe, Dylan Thomas and Hunter S Thompson to name a few.

Czeslaw Milosz *Visions from San Francisco Bay* (US Farrar, Straus & Giroux). Written in Berkeley during the unrest of 1968, these dense and somewhat ponderous essays show a European mind trying to come to grips with California's nascent Aquarian Age.

Mark Twain *Roughing It* (Penguin). Vivid tales of frontier California, particularly evocative of life in the silver mines of the 1860s Comstock Lode, where Twain got his start as a journalist and storyteller. His descriptions of San Francisco include a moment-by-moment description of an earthquake.

Tom Wolfe *The Electric Kool-Aid Acid Test* (Bantam/Black Swan). Tom Wolfe at his most expansive, riding with the Grateful Dead and Hell's Angels on the magic bus of Ken Kesey and the Merry Pranksters as they travel through the early 1960s, turning California onto LSD.

History, Politics and Society

Walton Bean *California: An Interpretive History* (UK McGraw-Hill). Blow-by-blow account of the history of California, including all the shady deals and back-room politicking, presented in accessible, anecdotal form.

Joan Didion *Slouching Towards Bethlehem* (Farrar, Straus & Giroux/Flamingo). Selected essays from one of California's most renowned journalists, taking a critical look at the West Coast of the Sixties, including San Francisco's acid-culture and a profile of American hero John Wayne. In a similar style, *The White Album* (Penguin) traces the West Coast characters and events that shaped the Sixties and Seventies, including The Doors, Charles Manson and the Black Panthers.

Edmund Fawcett and Tony Thomas *America and the Americans* (o/p). A wide-ranging, up-to-the-minute and engagingly written rundown on the USA in all its aspects from politics to sport and religion. An essential beginner's guide to the nation.

Frances Fitzgerald *Cities on a Hill* (US Simon & Schuster). Intelligent, thorough and sympathetic exploration of four of the odder corners of American culture, including San Francisco's Castro district, the Rajneeshi community of Oregon, and TV evangelism.

Jamie Jensen *Built to Last – 25 Years of the Grateful Dead* (US NAL-Dutton). Photo-filled history of San Francisco's psychedelic heroes from their early days in the Haight to their present near-divine stature, by one of the authors of this guide.

Charles Perry *The Haight-Ashbury* (US Random House). Curiously distant but detailed account of the Haight during the Flower Power years, written by an editor of *Rolling Stone*, a magazine that got its start there.

Mel Scott *The San Francisco Bay Area: A Metropolis in Perspective* (o/p). Though somewhat dry and academic, this enormous tome will tell you all you ever wanted to know about the evolution of San Francisco and the Bay Area.

Jay Stevens *Storming Heaven: LSD and the American Dream* (HarperCollins/Grafton). An engaging account of psychedelic drugs and their effect on American society through the Sixties, with an epilogue covering "designer drugs" – Venus, Ecstasy, Vitamin K and others – and the inner space they help some modern Californians to find.

Hunter S Thompson *The Great Shark Hunt* (Ballantine/Picador). Collection of often barbed and cynical essays on 1960s American life and politics – thought-provoking and hilarious. *Generation of Swine* (Random/Picador) is a more recent collection of caustic musings on the state of America and those who control it, assembled from his regular column in the *San Francisco Examiner.*

Tom Wolfe *Radical Chic & Mau Mauing the Flak Catchers* (US Farrar, Straus & Giroux). Wolfe's waspish account of Leonard Bernstein's fund-raising party for the Black Panthers – a protracted exercise in character assassination – is coupled with an equally sharp analysis of white guilt and radical politics in City Hall, San Francisco. Often ideologically unsound, always very funny.

Specific Guides

Adab Bakalinsky *Stairway Walks in San Francisco* (US Wilderness Press). Small, nicely illustrated guide detailing pretty back streets and stairways through San Francisco's hills. Excellent for turning up lesser-known spots on a walking tour.

California Coastal Commission *California Coastal Access Guide* (UC Press). The most useful and comprehensive plant and wildlife guide to the California coast, packed with maps and background information.

Don Herron *The Literary World of San Francisco* (City Lights). A walk through the San Francisco neighbourhoods associated with authors who have lived in and written about the city. Detailed and well presented, it's an essential handbook for anyone interested in San Francisco's literary heritage.

Judith Kahn *Indulge Yourself* (US Kahn Publishing). The ideal companion for the café animal, this book covers San Francisco's most famous and beautiful coffee spots, giving hints on when to go, what sort of people you'll see and what's on offer.

Karen Liberatore *The Complete Guide to the Golden Gate National Recreation Area* (o/p). Easy-to-read book covering San Francisco's extensive waterfront areas and large green spaces, with historical perspective. Lots of photos.

Don and Betty Martin *The Best of San Francisco* (Chronicle Books). A lighthearted series of top-ten listings of the best that San Francisco has to offer. Categories range from the "Top Ten Seafood Restaurants" to the "Ten Naughtiest Things to do in San Francisco". More amusing than helpful, but some interesting pointers.

Grant Peterson *Roads to Ride* (US Heyday Books). As its subtitle says, this is a bicyclist's topographic guide to the whole Bay Area, and is particularly good on the back roads of Marin County.

Don Pitcher *Berkeley Inside/Out* (US Heyday Books). This is an extremely well-written, fully illustrated and encyclopedic guidebook to the most dynamic small town in the Bay Area.

Peggy Wayburn *Adventuring in the San Francisco Bay Area* (US Sierra Club). If you are planning to spend any time hiking in the Bay Area's many fine wilderness regions, pick up this fact-filled guide, which also details a number of historic walks through the city's urban areas.

Fiction and Poetry

Ambrose Bierce *The Enlarged Devil's Dictionary* (Dover/Penguin). Spiteful but hilarious compilation of definitions (ie "Bore: a person who talks when you wish him to listen") by turn-of-the-century journalist. Bierce also wrote some great horror stories, including the stream-of-consciousness "An Occurrence at Owl Creek Bridge", collected in *Can Such Things Be* (Citadel, US) and his *Collected Works* (Citadel/Picador).

Richard Brautigan *The Hawkline Monster* (US Houghton-Mifflin). Whimsical, surreal tales by noted Bay Area hippy writer.

Philip K Dick *The Man in the High Castle* (Random House/Penguin). Long-time Berkeley- and Marin County-based science fiction author imagines an alternative San Francisco, following a Japanese victory in World War II. Of his dozens of other brilliant novels and short stories, *Bladerunner* (Balantine/Panther) and *The Transmigration of Timothy Archer* (Random House/ Gollancz o/p) make good use of Bay Area locales.

John Dos Passos USA (NAL-Dutton/Penguin). Massive, groundbreaking trilogy, combining fiction, poetry and reportage to tap the various strands of the American Experience. Much of the first part, *The 42nd Parallel*, takes place around Sutro Baths and Golden Gate Park.

Allen Ginsberg *Howl and Other Poems* (US Friendship Press). The attempted banning of the title poem assured its fame; *Howl* itself is an angry rant that will often make you wince, but a Whitmanesque voice shines through in places.

Dashiell Hammett *The Four Great Novels* (Random House/Picador). Seminal detective stories including *The Maltese Falcon* and starring Sam Spade, the private investigator working out of San Francisco. See also Diane Johnson's absorbing *The Life of Dashiell Hammet* (Fawcett/ Picador).

Jack Kerouac *On the Road* (Penguin). The book that launched a generation with its "spontaneous bop prosody", it chronicles Beat life in a series of road adventures, featuring some of San Francisco and a lot of the rest of the US. His other books include *Lonesome Traveller* (Grove-Atlantic/ Paladin), *The Dharma Bums* (Penguin/Paladin) and *Desolation Angels* (Riverhead Books/Paladin).

David Lodge *Changing Places* (Penguin). Thinly disguised autobiographical tale of an English academic who spends a year teaching at UC Berkeley (renamed in the book) and finds himself bang in the middle of the late-1960s student upheaval.

Jack London *Martin Eden* (Penguin). Jack Kerouac's favourite book; a semi-autobiographical account tracking the early years of this San Francisco-born, Oakland-bred adventure writer. The lengthy opus tells of his rise from waterfront hoodlum to high brow intellectual, and of his subsequent disenchantment with the trappings of success.

Armistead Maupin *Tales of the City* (HarperCollins/Black Swan); *Further Tales of the City* (HarperCollins/Corgi); *More Tales of the City* (HarperCollins/Corgi); *Babycakes* (HarperCollins/ Corgi); *Significant Others* (HarperCollins/Black Swan); *Sure of You* (HarperCollins/Black Swan). Six lively consecutive soap operas, wittily detailing the sexual and emotional antics of a select group of archetypal San Francisco characters, taking them from the late 1970s to the end of the 1980s.

Seth Morgan *Homeboy* (Random House/ Vintage). Novel charting the sleazy San Francisco experiences of the former junkie boyfriend of Janis Joplin.

Frank Norris *McTeague: A Story of San Francisco* (Norton/Penguin). Dramatic, extremely violent but engrossing saga of love and revenge in turn-of-the-century San Francisco; later filmed by Erich von Stroheim as *Greed*. Norris's *Octopus* (Penguin) tells the bitter tale of the Southern Pacific Railroad's stranglehold over the California economy.

Thomas Pynchon *The Crying of Lot 49* (HarperCollins/Vintage). Follows the labyrinthine adventures of techno-freaks and potheads in 1960s California, revealing the sexy side of stamp collecting.

Vikram Seth *The Golden Gate* (Random House/ Faber). Slick novel in verse, tracing the complex social lives of a group of San Francisco yuppies, by the subsequent author of the spellbinding blockbuster *A Suitable Boy*.

Gary Snyder *Left Out in the Rain* (US Farrar, Straus & Giroux). One of the original Beat writers, and the only one whose work ever matured, Snyder's poetry is direct and spare, yet manages to conjure up a deep animistic spirituality underlying everyday life.

Amy Tan *The Joy Luck Club* (Putnam/Minerva). Four Chinese-American women and their daughters gather together to look back over their lives. Moving story of immigrant struggle in the sweatshops of Chinatown.

William T Vollman *The Rainbow Stories* (Penguin/Deutsch). Gut-level portraits of San Francisco street life: Tenderloin whores, Haight Street skinheads, beggars, junkies and homeless Vietnam vets. Visceral and involving stuff.

San Francisco on film

San Francisco is a favourite with Californian film-makers, the city's staggering range of settings and chameleon-like geography making an often economical choice for the director who needs sunny beaches, swirling fogs, urban decay and pastoral elegance all at once. Thrillers, in particular, seem to get good mileage out of the city; Hitchcock loved it, while the ridiculous gradients are almost ideally suited to the car chases that Hollywood loves so much. Below is a list of the obvious and not-so-obvious films made about or in California's most beautiful city.

An Eye for an Eye (Steve Carver 1981). Chuck Norris plays an undercover San Francisco narcotics officer who quits the force when his partner is set up and killed. Typical lone-wolf action flick, with Norris flexing his bulk through a series of violent acts on an Oriental drug ring until he nails the bad guy.

Barbary Coast (Howard Hawks 1935). Set in misty, fog-bound turn-of-the-century San Francisco, Edward G Robinson finds he has competition when he tries to seduce the exotic dancer played by Miriam Hopkins. A brawling adventure film that captures the spirit of a lawless San Francisco.

Basic Instinct (Paul Verhoeven 1992). Surprisingly conventional sex murder mystery that makes good use of San Francisco locales.

Birdman of Alcatraz (John Frankenheimer 1962). Earnest but overlong study of real-life convicted killer Robert Stroud (Burt Lancaster) who becomes an authority on birds while kept in America's highest security prison.

The Birds (Alfred Hitchcock 1963). Some brilliant set-pieces in this allegory about our hostile feathered friends, set on the rugged coast just north of San Francisco.

Bullitt (Peter Yates 1968). Steve McQueen gives an assured central performance in this overpraised but entertaining cop thriller, which contains the definitive San Francisco car chase.

Chan is Missing (Wayne Wang 1982). Low-budget sleeper hangs a thoroughly unpredictable study of San Francisco's Chinatown and the Chinese-American experience on a mystery-suspense peg. Often satirical, it shows a Chinatown the tourists don't usually see.

Common Threads: Stories from the Quilt (Robert Epstein 1989). The maker of *The Times of Harvey Milk* again focuses on gay San Francisco in his sensitive feature-length documentary about the Names Project Memorial Quilt. Talking to six bereaved partners of AIDS victims, it tackles the political and social impact of the disease as well as concentrating on the sacrifice of those involved.

The Conversation (Francis Ford Coppola 1974). This chilling character study of San Francisco surveillance expert Harry Caul (Gene Hackman at his finest) is one of the best films of the Watergate era. The key titular sequence is set in San Francisco's Union Square.

The Counsellor (Alberto De Martino 1973). Italian Mafia movie, dubbed into English and shot in San Francisco. Little more than a takeoff of *Bullitt* and *The Godfather*.

Crackers (Louis Malle 1983). Donald Sutherland rescues what is otherwise a limp art film about struggling on the back streets of San Francisco. One of a million films to romanticize being poor.

Dark Passage (Delmer Davies 1947). Classic thriller set in fog-bound San Francisco, where Humphrey Bogart, with Lauren Bacall's help, tries to clear his name of a murder of which he is wrongly accused. Beautifully shot, if unconvincing.

Days of Wine and Roses (Martin Manulis 1962). Jack Lemmon plays a likeable drunk who drags his wife into alcoholism, too, only to leave her there once he's on the road to recovery. Smart satirical comedy that occasionally slips into melodrama.

The Dead Pool (Buddy Van Horn 1988). Clint Eastwood maintains his unflinching facial expression through this *Dirty Harry Part Five* as he stalks the streets of San Francisco's Chinatown looking for trouble. Repetitive rubbish.

Dim Sum (Wayne Wang 1985). Appealing little film about a more-or-less Westernized Chinese family in San Francisco. A treat.

Dirty Harry (Don Siegel 1971). Sleek and exciting sequel-spawning thriller casts Clint Eastwood in definitive role as neofascist San Francisco cop. Morally debatable, technically dynamic.

D.O.A. (Rudolph Mate 1949). Surprisingly involving suspense movie in which Edmond O'Brien tries to discover who poisoned him before he dies. Excellent use of LA and San Francisco locales.

The Enforcer (James Fargo 1976). *Dirty Harry Part Three* finds Clint Eastwood in typically aggressive mood, at odds with the liberal supervisors who want to stop him from killing every teenage delinquent on the streets of San Francisco. The predictability is relieved only slightly by the appearance of Tyne Daly, who plays a female police officer against ridiculous odds.

Escape From Alcatraz (Don Siegel 1979). Tense, well-crafted picture, based on a true story about an attempted escape from the infamous prison.

Experiment in Terror (Blake Edwards 1962). The inspiration for David Lynch's *Twin Peaks*, this entertaining Cold War period piece has dozens of FBI agents tying to track down an obscene phone caller in SF's Twin Peaks neighbourhood.

Eye of the Cat (David Lowell Rich 1969). *Psycho*-esque thriller in which a man with a cat phobia goes to stay with an ageing aunt who has an army of them.

Family Plot (Alfred Hitchcock 1976). The master's last film is a lark about stolen jewels, kidnapping and psychic sleuthing in and around San Francisco.

Fillmore (Richard T Heffron 1972). Bad rock movie about San Francisco's famous music venue in the last week of its existence. Good footage of the Grateful Dead, Jefferson Airplane and Boz Scaggs, but Bill Graham's egomaniacal ranting between the acts soon becomes wearying.

Flower Drum Song (Ross Hunter 1961). Patronizing, remorselessly cute Rodgers and Hammerstein musical about love dilemmas in San Francisco's Chinatown.

Fog over Frisco (William Dieterle 1934). A very young Bette Davis plays a wayward heiress who is kidnapped in this terse thriller.

48 Hours (Walter Hill 1982). Eddie Murphy puts in a slick comic performance as the criminal sidekick to Nick Nolte's tough-talking cop, who has 48 hours to wrap up a homicide case. Fantastic shots of San Francisco and quick-witted dialogue make this fast-paced comedy-thriller immensely entertaining.

Foul Play (Colin Higgins 1978). Entertaining comedy thriller in which Goldie Hawn plays against type as a dizzy blonde next to a similarly petite Dudley Moore. Chevy Chase is a great pothead.

Freebie and the Bean (Richard Rush 1974). Another San Francisco cop movie that tries to be at once achingly funny and disturbingly violent. James Caan does a credible job of playing one half of a wise-cracking duo, but overall it's a cheap, manipulative piece of tat.

The Frisco Kid (Samuel Bischoff 1935). James Cagney stars in this rough-and-tumble tale of a shanghaied sailor who rises to power amid the riffraff of the 1860s Barbary Coast.

The Frisco Kid (Howard Koch Jr 1979). Implausible but amusing comedy about a rabbi who befriends an outlaw on his way to San Francisco. Silly and sentimental, it nonetheless has good comic performances from Gene Wilder and Harrison Ford.

Gentleman Jim (Raoul Walsh 1942). Rich evocation of 1880s San Francisco with Errol Flynn playing the charming, social-climbing boxer, Gentleman Jim Corbett.

Gimme Shelter (David & Albert Maysles/Charlotte Zwerin 1970). Legendary film about the Rolling Stones' Altamont concert (see p.166). Lots of shots of Mick Jagger looking bemused during and after the notorious murder.

Greed (Erich von Stroheim 1924). Legendary, lengthy silent masterpiece based on Frank Norris's *McTeague* – see p.308 – detailing the squalid, ultimately tragic marriage between a blunt ex-miner with a dental practice on San Francisco's Polk Street, and a simple girl from nearby Oakland. Dated but nonetheless unforgettable, including the classic finale in Death Valley.

Guess Who's Coming to Dinner (Stanley Kramer 1967). Well-meaning but slightly flat interracial comedy in which Spencer Tracy and Katharine Hepburn playing the supposedly liberal but bewildered parents of a woman who brings home the black man (Sidney Poitier) she intends to marry.

Hammett (Wim Wenders 1982). The film that broke Coppola's *Zoetrope* production company, this is a rich tribute to Dashiell Hammett's search for fiction material in the back streets of San Francisco's Chinatown.

Harold and Maude (Hal Ashby 1971). Very funny black comedy about a death-obsessed teenager and the eighty-year-old woman he befriends at various funerals. A bizarre love story with kooky twists, it clarifies very little but manages to entertain thoroughly.

High Anxiety (Mel Brooks 1977). Juvenile but amusing spoof of Hitchcock's San Francisco-based thrillers – *Vertigo, The Birds* and *Spellbound*. Silly story based around a psychologist who works at the Institute for the Very Very Nervous.

I Remember Mama (George Stevens 1948). Sentimental, nostalgic tribute to family life circa 1910 for a group of Norwegian immigrants in San Francisco. Told through the memories of a now successful authoress, who dwells on her tough past and credits it with making her the woman she is. Enjoyable, if shamelessly romanticized, vision of poverty.

Invasion of the Body Snatchers (Phillip Kaufman 1978). Thanks largely to Donald Sutherland, a good remake of the 1956 classic tale of extraterrestrial pod people erupting into and replacing humans.

It Came from Beneath the Sea (Charles Schneer 1955). A giant octopus destroys San Francisco. Feeble monster movie with laughable special effects.

Jimi Plays Berkeley (Peter Pilafian 1971). The historic Memorial Day Jimi Hendrix concert in Berkeley, interspersed with lots of shots of rampaging students waving their peace signs. Hendrix ignores the peripheral action and just plays.

Joy Luck Club (Wayne Wang 1993). Amy Tan's bestselling novel, which chronicled the lives of four Chinatown women, faithfully translated to the screen with mixed results. Excellent performances in all roles.

The Killer Elite (Sam Peckinpah 1975). Familiar themes of betrayal and trust in this mostly straightforward action flick, built around the internal politics of an underground San Francisco company and a wounded agent (James Caan) who seeks revenge. Excellent set-pieces include a Chinatown shoot-out and siege.

The Lady from Shanghai (Orson Welles 1948). Orson Welles and Rita Hayworth star in this twisted and impossible plot about murder, mystery and sexual unease on board a cruise ship. Compelling, if rambling account of the relationship between a clever young man and beautiful older woman.

The Laughing Policeman (Stuart Rosenberg 1973). Walter Matthau and Bruce Dern pair up in yet another brutal San Francisco cop thriller, triggered by the gunning down of a busload of people in the Mission district. Queasy use of gay characters.

The Lenny Bruce Performance Film (John Magnuson 1967). A historical document of Lenny Bruce's penultimate performance at San Francisco's *Basin Street West* club, one of the few places he was still allowed to perform, during his lengthy obscenity trial. The film catches Bruce at his maniacal and scalding best, though the excerpts from his trial, which he reads obsessively, get to be exhausting.

The Lineup (Frank Cooper 1958). Film adaptation of the TV series *San Francisco Beat*, about the SFPD capturing a junkie gunman. An unconvincing plot, but polished acting and fantastic shots of San Francisco.

Magnum Force (Ted Post 1973). Sequel to *Dirty Harry*, with more shots of Clint Eastwood looking tough and San Francisco looking spectacular. The storyline, detailing Harry's rejection of vigilante policing methods, is pathetically unbelievable.

The Maltese Falcon (John Huston 1941). Diamond-hard candidate for the best-ever detective movie, with Humphrey Bogart as San Francisco private dick Sam Spade.

Out of the Past (Jacques Tourneur 1947). Definitive flashback *film noir* starring Robert Mitchum who has a rendezvous with death and his own past in the shape of Jane Greer. Beautiful and bewildering.

Pal Joey (Fred Kohlmar 1957). Frank Sinatra, Rita Hayworth and Kim Novak star in this slick musical about a lovable cad and rising nightclub entertainer. Begins well, but slides alarmingly into cheap sentiment.

Petulia (Richard Lester 1968). San Francisco surgeon George C Scott takes up with unhappily married kook Julie Christie in richly detailed, deliberately fragmentary comedy drama set in druggy, decadent society.

Play it Again Sam (Herbert Ross 1972). Woody Allen as (what else?) neurotic San Francisco film critic who has an affair with his best friend's wife, Diane Keaton.

Point Blank (John Boorman 1967). Lee Marvin plays a double-crossed gangster out for revenge on his cheating partner. Stands up well as a violent gang thriller, with good location shots of LA and San Francisco, but occasionally overreaches itself. Angie Dickinson plays a convincingly faithless wife.

The Presidio (Peter Hyams 1988). Crime thriller about a couple of ill-matched cops investigating the murder of a military policewoman. Sean Connery plays a by-the-book army man with conviction, but the story falls embarrassingly apart with inept handling of romance and father/daughter conflicts.

Psych Out (Richard Rush 1968). Pumped out quickly to capitalize on the "Summer of Love". Good performances from Jack Nicholson and Bruce Dern can't save what is basically a compendium of every hippie cliché in the book. That didn't stop it from quickly becoming a cult movie, though.

San Francisco (W S Van Dyke 1936). Elaborate, entertaining hokum about a Barbary Coast love triangle circa 1906. The script is upstaged by the climactic earthquake sequence.

Shoot the Moon (Alan Parker 1981). Albert Finney and Diane Keaton star in this strained tale of self-obsessed Marin County trauma and heartbreak. About as affecting as an episode of *Dallas*.

Skidoo (Otto Preminger 1968). By far the strangest of all the Flower Power-era films, this has an all-star cast – Carole Channing, Jackie Gleason, Slim Pickens et al – dropping acid on Alcatraz and generally tripping out. Worth watching to see Groucho Marx, playing God, smoke a joint, and for the Harry Nilsson soundtrack.

Star Trek IV – The Voyage Home (Leonard Nimoy 1986). Morality crusaders Kirk and Co return through time to San Francisco, to save the whales in the best of the *Star Trek* movies.

They Call Me Mister Tibbs! (Gordon Douglas 1970). Sidney Poitier plays Virgil Tibbs, the black San Francisco cop who sleuths his way to unravelling a murder mystery. Benign thriller.

Time After Time (Nicholas Meyer 1979). Courtesy of the Time Machine, Malcolm McDowell chases Jack the Ripper into twentieth-century San Francisco accompanied by a lot of cheap jokes and violence.

The Times of Harvey Milk (Robert Epstein 1984). Exemplary feature-length documentary about America's first openly gay politician, chronicling his career in San Francisco and the aftermath of his 1978 assassination.

The Towering Inferno (John Guillermin/Irwin Allen 1974). Disaster film that opened the door for a whole decade of banal catastrophes, this one telling the tale of how the world's tallest building is destroyed by fire on the night of its inauguration. Verging on the ridiculous but saved by great special effects and a cast of stars that includes Steve McQueen, Paul Newman, Faye Dunaway and Fred Astaire.

Vertigo (Alfred Hitchcock 1958). A tragedy of obsession, stunningly set in San Francisco, in which detective (and lonely voyeur) James Stewart tracks down the long-dead Madeleine played by Kim Novak. Perhaps Hitchcock's most personal and psychologically revealing work.

What's Up, Doc? (Peter Bogdanovich 1972). Wildly likeable screwball comedy pastiche, set in San Francisco and starring Barbra Streisand and Ryan O'Neal as a cook and a naive professor.

Glossaries

American cities have a jargon all their own, and none more so than San Francisco. Some of the listings here would be of use anywhere; others are specifically San Franciscan (or at least Californian), not least the gay slang section, very much a product of the city's Castro district. We've also included a rundown of San Franciscan personalities, past and present, which may both aid your reading of the main part of the Guide, and help to decipher the city at ground level.

San Francisco People

AGNOS Art Former mayor of San Francisco, elected on a liberal platform in 1987 when Diane Feinstein stepped down to pursue her career in state politics.

BIERCE Ambrose Came to San Francisco on an army assignment, where he began his literary career as a journalist and went on to become the *San Francisco Examiner*'s most satirical and witty staff writer. Spent his old age writing ghost and detective stories, gathered together in his *Collected Works*.

BRANNAN Sam Founded a Mormon colony in the early years of the city and started San Francisco's first newspaper, the *California Star*. Most famous, however, as the man who brought the news of the discovery of gold in the Sierras, Brannan made a fortune in real estate before drinking his way into poverty and spending his last years alone and forgotten in Escondido, San Diego.

BRIDGES Harry Inspired by Jack London's fiction to leave his native Australia and come to San Francisco to work on sailing vessels, Bridges went on to become the militant leader of the International Longshoremen's Association, a career which brought him disciples and enemies in equal numbers as he led his union through major battles with the Pacific Coast shipowners in 1934, and again in 1971, when he came out of retirement on behalf of his longshoremen. A genuine working-class hero.

BROWER David California-born conservationist, Brower was long-time director of the Sierra Club (1952–69) and went on to help found Friends of the Earth.

BROWN Arthur (1874–1957). Oakland-born architect who built San Francisco's City Hall and Coit Tower.

BROWN Willie San Francisco's flamboyant and outspoken black Democrat politician, who has climbed the political ladder very quickly and was Jesse Jackson's campaign manager in the 1988 Presidential race.

BRUBECK Dave Oakland-born pianist and jazz composer (notably of *Take Five*), Brubeck brought attention to so-called West Coast Jazz, achieving international celebrity status for himself as a jazz musician along the way.

BRUNDAGE Avery Michigan-born engineer, Brundage went on to become the president of the International Olympic Committee, but he is most famous for his enormous collection of Oriental art, donated to San Francisco's de Young Museum and now known as the Asian Art Museum.

BURNHAM Daniel Chicago architect who was invited by San Francisco's mayor, James D Phelan, to plan the city's development in the early twentieth century, giving rise to the Beaux Arts complex of Civic Center – though this was in fact only a small part of his ambitious scheme.

CAEN Herb San Francisco's most prominent columnist, Caen has been writing for the *San Francisco Chronicle* since the year dot. Though a touch overrated, he occasionally digs up good dirt on San Francisco's more prominent society figures. Worth reading for the indiscreet gossip. See p.298.

COIT Lillie Renowned for her unusual behaviour, Lillie Coit came to San Francisco as a child and was reared in the best social circles. Married briefly to Howard Coit, on her death she left $100,000 to the city in order to build Coit Tower, Telegraph Hill's principal landmark, as a memorial to San Francisco's volunteer firefighters.

COOLBRITH Ina San Francisco poet who introduced Jack London to literature when working for the Oakland Public Library. Her poems are collected in the books *Singer of the Sea, A Perfect Day* and *Songs of the Golden Gate*. In recognition for her organization of the World Congress of Authors, for the Panama Pacific Exhibition in 1915, the legislature made her the state's first Poet Laureate.

COPPOLA Francis Ford San Francisco-based filmmaker, whose works include *Apocalypse Now, The Conversation* and *One from the Heart*. He still lives in the city and is the owner of the Columbus Tower in North Beach.

DI MAGGIO Joe Began his baseball career in 1932 with the San Francisco Seals and went on to stardom as centrefielder with the New York Yankees. Married Marilyn Monroe in the 1950s.

FEINSTEIN Diane Ex-San Francisco mayor who stepped in when George Moscone and Harvey Milk were assassinated and is now a US Senator. Very much the career politician, rumours abound about her dealings with the big business corporations in the late 1970s that led to massive development in San Francisco's Financial District.

FERLINGHETTI Lawrence Founder and still owner of the *City Lights Bookstore*, America's first paperback bookshop, Ferlinghetti became a prominent figure during the Beat movement of the 1950s and had close links with its major figures.

GARCIA Jerry Lead guitarist and vocalist for psychedelic rock gods, the Grateful Dead.

GINSBERG Allen Though born in New Jersey, Ginsberg is associated with San Francisco because of the controversial Beat poem *Howl*, which he wrote in North Beach.

GRAHAM Bill Rock music impresario Graham, who died in a helicopter accident in 1992, can in part be credited with the success of psychedelic music, which he promoted through the concerts he staged at the famous Fillmore Auditorium.

HALLIDIE Andrew English-born engineer who emigrated to California in the nineteenth century to work in the Comstock mines, in 1873 he invented the universally loved cable car, and thereby made travel over San Francisco's ridiculous gradients possible.

HAMMETT Dashiell Hammett, who travelled to San Francisco as a young man and worked for the Pinkerton Detective Agency, drawing on his experiences to write the hard-boiled detective stories that inspired Raymond Chandler and others. His most famous works include *The Maltese Falcon* and *The Thin Man*. In his later years, Hammett was involved in the Hollywood Ten McCarthy witch hunts concerning allegedly un-American activities, and was sent to prison for refusing to testify.

HEARST William Randolph Publishing magnate who as a young man worked on the *San Francisco Examiner* and went on to acquire a string of successful daily newspapers, motion picture companies and radio stations; he later served briefly as a congressman in New York. Famous for his lavish lifestyle and the incredible Hearst Castle at San Simeon, south of the city. Orson Welles' classic *Citizen Kane* was loosely based on his life.

HOBART Lewis P Missouri-born architect, who came to study at the University of California and went on to design the Bohemian Club, Grace Cathedral and the Steinhart Aquarium.

JOPLIN Janis Texas-born Joplin came to San Francisco at the age of eighteen, where she began her singing career with Big Brother and the Holding Company. A central figure in the psychedelic scene, her problem was not LSD but booze and heroin, an overdose of which finally killed her in 1970.

KEROUAC Jack A leading figure of the Beat movement in New York, Kerouac came out to San Francisco in the 1950s, where he drew on his experiences to write the Beats' bible *On the Road*. Spent much of his life returning to stay with his mother in Massachusetts and eventually drank himself into an early grave at the age of 46.

KESEY Ken Oregon-reared Kesey enrolled in a creative writing programme at Stanford University, during which time he became involved with psychiatric experiments with LSD – experiences which inspired him to write *One Flew over the Cuckoo's Nest*. Important, too, for his involvement in San Francisco's psychedelic scene, Kesey toured the country with his busload of Merry Pranksters in the Sixties, a time richly chronicled in Tom Wolfe's *The Electric Kool-Aid Acid Test*.

LONDON Jack London was an illegitimate child who grew up with little formal education but read books compulsively, a habit that was later to serve him well when he began his prolific writing career that produced *The Call of the Wild*.

MAYBECK Bernard Early modern architect responsible for some of the most beautiful buildings in the Bay Area, including the magnificent Palace of Fine Arts for the Panama Pacific Exhibition in 1915.

MIEGGS Henry Mieggs came to San Francisco at the beginning of the Gold Rush, and made a small fortune carrying lumber from upstate New York. He went on to become a civic leader and built Mieggs Wharf – today's Fisherman's Wharf. Later in life he was involved in a scandal concerning forged city treasury warrants and fled to South America.

MILK Harvey San Francisco's (and perhaps the world's) first openly gay politician, Milk played a key role in the gay emancipation of the 1970s, only to be assassinated at the height of his career and popularity by political rival, Dan White (see p.117).

MONTGOMERY John B Nineteenth-century naval captain in command of the *Portsmouth* during the Mexican War, who occupied San Francisco in 1846 and raised the American flag on the plaza that was the one-time waterfront.

MOONEY Tom Radical Socialist labour leader, charged with planting the bomb that killed ten people during a Preparedness Day Parade on San Francisco's Market Street in 1916. He was sentenced to hang for the killings, but the injustice of his conviction became a cause célèbre for years and in 1939 he was pardoned.

MOSCONE George San Francisco's liberal mayor who was assassinated along with Harvey Milk in 1978.

NORRIS Frank (1870–1902). Highly respected writer, who studied at the University of California and went on to produce acclaimed works such as *McTeague*, *The Octopus* and *The Pit*.

NORTON Joshua Abraham "Emperor" London-born Norton came to be known as Emperor Norton after declaring himself "Norton I, Emperor of the United States" – a claim that was no doubt symptomatic of the insanity provoked by his bankruptcy in the rice market. He comported himself regally around San Francisco wearing a military suit and sword, usually accompanied by his two dogs, Bummer and Lazarus. His "loyal subjects" received him sympathetically and were tolerant of his various proclamations and commands, the most famous of which was a plan to build a bridge across the bay. Upon his death, the city conducted a formal civic funeral in honour of his services to the city.

POLK Willis (1865–1924). An architect, he came to San Francisco as a young man and became involved with a bohemian group known as Les Jeunes. He also headed Daniel Burnham's San Francisco office and worked on his city plan. Known for his elegant brown shingle designs.

SANTANA Carlos San Francisco-based guitar virtuoso renowned for his blending of Latin rhythms into pop music.

STANFORD Leland Made his fortune as one of the Big Four who constructed the Central Pacific Railroad. During a two-year term as governor he was a staunch union supporter, although he is perhaps best known now for the creation of the university in Palo Alto that bears his name.

SUTRO Adolph Prussian-born philanthropist who came to San Francisco and made his fortune in the Comstock silver bonanza. Heavy investment in San Francisco real estate led to his ownership of almost a twelfth of the entire city, to which he donated many developments, including the Cliff House, Sutro Baths and the Sutro Library.

TWAIN Mark (Samuel Langhorne Clemens) Spent his early years in Missouri before embarking on a journalistic career that brought him to San Francisco in 1864. A regular contributor to such publications as *The Golden Era*, *Californian* and *Territorial Enterprise*, he gained his biggest popularity after writing *Roughing It*, telling exaggerated tales of adventures in the Comstock mining era.

WHITE Dan The murderer of Harvey Milk and George Moscone, White was a disgruntled ex-policeman and city supervisor whose trial came to be known as the "Twinkie Defence" after his lawyer claimed that White was suffering from temporary insanity caused by harmful additives in fast food. After serving a controversially brief five-year sentence, White was released and committed suicide several months later.

Terms and Acronyms

Art Deco Style of decoration popular in the 1930s, characterized by elegant geometrical shapes and patterns.

Art Nouveau Art, architecture and design of the 1890s typified by stylized organic forms.

Atrium Enclosed, covered pedestrian space often forming the lobby of a corporate building.

The Avenues Catch-all term for the Richmond and Sunset neighbourhoods.

BART (Bay Area Rapid Transit). The Bay Area's underground train system, linking San Francisco with Oakland, Berkeley and other parts of the East Bay.

Beaux Arts Style of Neoclassical architecture taught at the Ecole de Beaux Arts in Paris at the end of the last century, the best example of which in the Bay Area is Civic Center.

The Big Four Collis P Huntington, Mark Hopkins, Charles Crocker and Leland Stanford – the four railroad barons who made their fortune building the Central Pacific Railroad in the late 1800s.

Cal Nickname for University of California, Berkeley.

City Hall Not just the building, but also used to describe the local government as a whole.

Clapboard House covered with overlapping timber boards, in evidence throughout the city.

Colonial Dames of America Patriotic organization of women descended from worthy ancestors who became American residents before 1750.

Condo Short for "condominium", an individually owned apartment within a building.

Co-op Not very common, but a form of apartment ownership in the city. A co-op differs from a condo in that you buy shares in the building in which the apartment is sited, rather than the apartment itself.

Federal National government, and as such not subject to state government – ie a federal housing programme would be one funded by Congress and not the state.

Loft Large open space usually at the top of an old warehouse, popular with artists because of the direct lighting.

MUNI (San Francisco Municipal Railway). Not just a railway, but a system of buses, trolley buses, cable cars and streetcars that serves the city.

Plaza Wide open space that acts as a pedestrian forecourt to a skyscraper or set of buildings.

Project Council estate or blocks of public housing.

Skyscraper The word comes from the highest sail on a sailing ship, and hence refers to any high building.

WPA (Works Project Administration). Work-relief agency begun by Roosevelt in 1935 (then known as the Works Progress Administration). The WPA's Public Works of Art Project produced many murals in public buildings and a renowned set of guidebooks to the entire country.

Index

NORTH SOUTH TRAVEL

DISCOUNT FARES

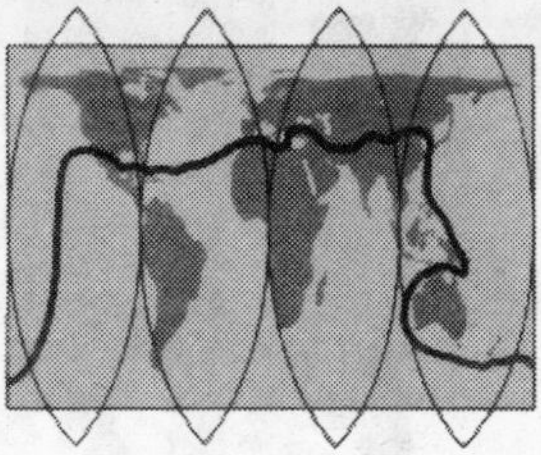

PROFITS TO CHARITIES

- North South Travel is a friendly, competitive travel agency, offering discount fares world-wide.
- North South Travel's profits contribute to community projects in the developing world.
- We have special experience of booking destinations in Africa, Asia and Latin America.
- Clients who book through North South Travel include exchange groups, students and independent travellers, as well as charities, church organisations and small businesses.

To discuss your booking requirements: contact Brenda Skinner between 9am and 5pm, Monday to Friday, on (01245) 492 882: Fax (01245) 356 612, any time. Or write to:
North South Travel Limited, Moulsham Mill Centre, Parkway,
Chelmsford, Essex CM2 7PX, UK

Help us to help others – Your travel can make a difference

Our Holidays Their Homes

Exploring New Destinations?
Ever wondered what that means to the locals?
Ever seen things you're uncomfortable with?
Ever thought of joining Tourism Concern?

Tourism Concern is the only independent British organisation seeking ways to make tourism just, participatory and sustainable - world-wide.

For a membership fee of only £15 (£8 unwaged) UK, £25 overseas, you will support us in our work, receive our quarterly magazine, and learn about what is happening in tourism around the world.

We'll help find answers to the questions.

Tourism Concern, Southlands College, Wimbledon Parkside, London SW19 5NN UK Tel: 0181-944 0464 Fax: 0181-944 6583.

SLEEP EASY
BOOK AHEAD
AUSTRALIA
02 261 1111
CANADA
FREEPHONE 0800 663 5777
DUBLIN
01 301766
LONDON
0171 836 1036
BELFAST
01232 324733
GLASGOW
0141 332 3004
WASHINGTON
0202 783 6161
NEW ZEALAND
09 379 4224
IBN INTERNATIONAL BOOKING NETWORK
Call any of these numbers and your credit card secures a good nights sleep …
in more than 26 countries
up to six months ahead
with immediate confirmation
HOSTELLING INTERNATIONAL
Budget accommodation you can Trust

AS SEEN ON TV ★ AS HEARD ON RADIO

Bed & Breakfast accommodation
and self-catering apartments in the USA,
at reasonable rates.

COLBY
INTERNATIONAL

139 Round Hey, Liverpool L28 1RG
Telephone: 0151 220 5848
Fax: 0151 228 5453
US Telephone: 404 - 8185877

'A traveller without knowledge is like a bird without wings.'

Mushariff-Ud-Din (1184-1291)

STANFORDS

The World's Largest Map and Travel Book Shop

AT 12-14 LONG ACRE LONDON WC2E 9LP
MAIL ORDER SERVICE TEL 0171 836 1321 FAX 0171 836 0189

AND STANFORDS AT BRITISH AIRWAYS
156 REGENT STREET LONDON W1R 5TA

THE LOWEST PRE-BOOKED CAR RENTAL OR YOUR MONEY BACK.

Holiday Autos is the only company to actually guarantee the lowest prices or your money back at over 4000 worldwide rental locations in Europe, USA, Canada, and Australasia.
All our rates are truly fully inclusive and FREE of any nasty hidden extras. Also available in the USA and Canada are our range of luxury motorhomes and campervans. Don't waste money - book with Holiday Autos - guaranteed always to be the lowest on the market.

Holiday Autos.
NOBODY BEATS OUR PRICES.
0171 - 491 1111

SAINT BENEDICT SCHOOL
FIELD ROAD
1JD